Multisystemic Therapy for Antisocial Behavior in Children and Adolescents

Multisystemic Therapy for Antisocial Behavior in Children and Adolescents

SECOND EDITION

Scott W. Henggeler
Sonja K. Schoenwald
Charles M. Borduin
Melisa D. Rowland
Phillippe B. Cunningham

THE GUILFORD PRESS
New York   London

© 2009 The Guilford Press
A Division of Guilford Publications, Inc.
72 Spring Street, New York, NY 10012
www.guilford.com

Printed in the United States of America

This book is printed on acid-free paper.

Last digit is print number: 9   8   7   6   5   4   3   2

Library of Congress Cataloging-in-Publication Data
Multisystemic therapy for antisocial behavior in children and adolescents / Scott
W. Henggeler ... [et al.]. — 2nd ed.
     p. ; cm.
   Rev. ed. of: Multisystemic treatment of antisocial behavior in children and
adolescents / Scott W. Henggeler ... [et al.]. c1998.
   Includes bibliographical references and index.
   ISBN 978-1-60623-071-8 (hardcover : alk. paper)
   1. Conduct disorders in children—Treatment.   2. Conduct disorders in
adolescence—Treatment.   3. Antisocial personality disorders—Treatment.
4. Combined modality therapy.   5. Family psychotherapy.   I. Henggeler,
Scott W., 1950–   II. Multisystemic treatment of antisocial behavior in children
and adolescents.
   [DNLM: 1. Social Behavior Disorders—therapy.   2. Adolescent.   3. Child.
4. Combined Modality Therapy—methods.   5. Psychotherapy—methods.
6. Social Support. WS 350.8.S6 M961 2009]
   RJ506.C65M84 2009
   618.92′858206—dc22

                                                                    2008050425

About the Authors

Scott W. Henggeler, PhD, is Professor of Psychiatry and Behavioral Sciences at the Medical University of South Carolina. He is also Director of the University's Family Services Research Center, which recently received the Annie E. Casey Foundation Families Count Award, as well as the Points of Light Foundation President's Award in recognition of excellence in community service directed at solving community problems. Dr. Henggeler has published more than 250 journal articles, book chapters, and books, and is on the editorial boards of nine journals. His research and social policy interests include the development and validation of innovative methods of mental health and substance abuse services for disadvantaged children and their families; efforts for redistributing mental health and substance abuse treatment resources to services that are clinically effective and cost-effective, and preserve family integrity; and investigating the transport of evidence-based treatments to community settings.

Sonja K. Schoenwald, PhD, is Professor of Psychiatry and Behavioral Sciences at the Medical University of South Carolina. She served as Associate Director of the Family Services Research Center from 1994 to 2004. Dr. Schoenwald pioneered the development, refinement, and empirical testing of the training and quality assurance protocols used to transport multisystemic therapy to usual care settings. Her research focuses on the transportability, implementation, and dissemination of effective community-based treatments for youth and families. She has published numerous peer-reviewed papers and book chapters, and has coauthored three books and several treatment manuals and monographs.

Charles M. Borduin, PhD, is Professor of Psychology at the University of Missouri–Columbia and Director of the Missouri Delinquency Project. He has published more than 100 journal articles, book chapters, and books on the development and validation of effective mental health services for youth with complex clinical problems, and has served as a national and international consultant to government and private agencies on the reform of children's mental health services.

Melisa D. Rowland, MD, is Associate Professor of Psychiatry and Behavioral Sciences in the Family Services Research Center of the Medical University of South Carolina. Her research interests focus on developing, implementing, and evaluating clinically effective family-based interventions for youth presenting with serious emotional and behavioral problems. Dr. Rowland is the coinvestigator in charge of clinical and project implementation on a National Institute on Drug Abuse–funded study designed to evaluate the relative effectiveness of three training protocols with increasing intensity in supporting the implementation of contingency management by practitioners treating adolescent substance abusers in the South Carolina mental health and substance abuse sectors. She is also the coinvestigator in charge of clinical implementation for an Annie E. Casey Foundation–funded project designed to develop an evidence-based continuum of services for youth with antisocial behaviors at risk of out-of-home placement in New York City.

Phillippe B. Cunningham, PhD, is Professor of Psychiatry and Behavioral Sciences in the Family Services Research Center of the Medical University of South Carolina. He has had a long-standing commitment to addressing the psychosocial needs of children and adolescents, especially those who are disadvantaged and underserved. Dr. Cunningham is a recipient of the 2000 Theodore H. Blau Early Career Award from the American Psychological Association's Society of Clinical Psychology. In 2006, he participated in the First Lady's Conference on Helping America's Youth.

Preface

In 1998 we published *Multisystemic Treatment of Antisocial Behavior in Children and Adolescents*, which has provided the most extensive description of multisystemic therapy (MST) clinical processes until the publication of this volume. At the time of that publication, MST was being implemented in several sites scattered across the United States and Canada. Today, in excess of 400 MST programs are operating in more than 30 states and 10 nations, serving approximately 17,500 youth and their families annually.

The proliferation of MST programs during the past decade is likely due to several interrelated factors:

- Practitioners, families, and stakeholders appreciate the inherent logic linking the MST theory of change, clinical procedures, and youth outcomes.
- Many government entities and community stakeholders recognized the limitations of traditional, restrictive services for juvenile offenders and advocated for more effective services in their communities.
- MST outcome-related research conducted by many investigators has typically continued to support the clinical and cost-effectiveness of the model. And we have endeavored to improve the model by incorporating "lessons learned" in those few cases when results were suboptimal.
- MST implementation-related research has been in the forefront of the emerging field of implementation science, and findings have been used to reinforce a quality assurance system that effectively supports treatment fidelity and youth outcomes across MST programs worldwide.
- MST Services and its Network Partner organizations have been committed to disseminating the MST model with full integrity and fidelity.

This second edition reflects our continuing efforts to communicate the clinical foundations and practicalities of the MST model to practitioners. During the past decade, we have continued to be directly involved in the operations of many MST programs and the training and supervision of many MST therapists and supervisors. These experiences prompted several changes in this edition:

- A new section on procedures to promote the safety of youth, families, and practitioners was added to Chapter 2, on clinical foundations.
- We made the text of the clinical chapters (Chapters 3–7), on family, peer, school, individual, and social support interventions, more consumer friendly and less academic. More attention was devoted to clinical description and less to theoretical and research rationale. New case examples, figures, and tables were added for ease of communication.
- A section on enhancing vocational outcomes was added to Chapter 5, on school-related interventions, as educational options have become limited for many youth in MST programs.
- Chapter 8, on treating substance abuse, a common problem among juvenile offenders, was added; this topic was not addressed substantively in the first edition.
- Chapter 9 updates MST outcomes for juvenile offending and overviews outcomes of MST adaptations for treating substance abuse, sexual offending, serious emotional disturbance, and chronic health conditions.
- Chapter 10, on MST quality assurance and improvement, was added to provide MST therapists, supervisors, and administrators with a framework for understanding the strategies used to improve youth outcomes through enhanced treatment and program fidelity.

We sincerely appreciate your interest in MST and hope that this volume facilitates your work.

Acknowledgments

First, we thank the many families who have opened their doors and worked side-by-side with us to effect change with their children, loved ones, schools, and community. These families are the true unsung heroes of multisystemic therapy (MST).

In addition, although many local, state, national, international, and foundation sources have supported MST worldwide, we are particularly appreciative of those sources that have funded our own research. These include the National Institute of Mental Health, National Institute on Drug Abuse, Annie E. Casey Foundation, National Institute on Alcohol Abuse and Alcoholism, South Carolina Department of Health and Human Services, Office of Juvenile Justice and Delinquency Prevention, Administration for Children and Families (U.S. Department of Health and Human Services), Center for Substance Abuse Treatment (Substance Abuse and Mental Health Services Administration), and Missouri Department of Social Services. The extensive validation of MST clinical and quality assurance protocols would not have been possible without the generous support of these funding sources.

Further appreciation goes to MST Services and its Network Partners, who represent the leading and often messy frontier of technology transfer. These organizations are key architects of strategies used to navigate the gray zones between procedures implemented on a small scale in a randomized trial and those required to support effective implementation on a larger scale. Without them, the validation of quality assurance protocols and several adaptations of MST could not have occurred.

Finally, this book is dedicated to the children in our own families: Jay, Lauren, Lee, Noelle, Phillippe, Russell, Santos, Sterling, and Waylon. They inspire us every day and keep us focused on what is really important in life.

Contents

CHAPTER 1

The Multisystemic Therapy Theory of Change

Conceptual and Empirical Bases

IN THIS CHAPTER

■ The theory of social ecology
providing the conceptual framework
for multisystemic therapy (MST).

■ The MST theory of change.

■ Research supporting the MST theory
of change.

Every day, families seek help for the treatment of their seriously troubled
teens; and every day, clinicians try to provide that help. Not all treatment is
created equal, however. Some treatments are more effective for a particular
set of problems than others; and, some are not effective for those problems
at all. This book focuses on a treatment shown to be effective with youth
experiencing serious antisocial behavior and their families: multisystemic
therapy (MST). The book details the logic underlying the design of interventions used within MST; the content and process of those interventions; and
the training, support, and feedback strategies used to support the implementation of treatment and attainment of treatment goals. For therapists and
supervisors working in the hundreds of MST programs worldwide treating
youth with serious antisocial behavior and their families, this volume serves
as a treatment manual—guiding the design and delivery of clinical interventions. For practitioners not formally working within MST programs, we
hope that the treatment principles and processes described herein can con-

1

tribute to the success of your work. For all others, this book aims to convey our optimism about the power of well-reasoned, scientifically tested, and well-implemented family- and community-based interventions to alter the life course of adolescents presenting serious antisocial behavior.

This first chapter presents the theoretical bases of MST. All treatments have an underlying theoretical framework that guides how the therapist conceptualizes and intervenes with clinical problems. At its simplest level, this framework suggests that if Problem B is caused by Variable A, then improving Variable A should lead to reductions in Problem B. From a cognitive-behavioral therapy (CBT) perspective, for example, if excessive negative thinking is hypothesized to lead to depression in adolescents, then implementing interventions that reduce negative thinking should decrease depression. This sequence—reducing a problem by treating its causes— defines the *theory of change* that underlies the intervention. Importantly, theories of change can be tested, and the results can support or refute the theory and its corresponding treatment approach.

Theory of Social Ecology

The MST theory of change is based primarily on several aspects of Bronfenbrenner's (1979) theory of social ecology.

Multidetermined Nature of Human Behavior

A central feature of the theory of social ecology pertains to the multidetermined nature of human behavior. Bronfenbrenner (1979, p. 3) likens the individual's ecological environment to "a set of nested structures, each inside the next, like a set of Russian dolls. At the innermost level is the immediate setting containing the developing person." Each concentric layer is then seen as representing a system (e.g., family, peer, school, neighborhood) or subsystem (e.g., siblings, extended family) that plays an integral role in the person's life. The theory of social ecology, therefore, differs from more traditional family systems theory in its focus on the influences of broader and more numerous contextual influences within a person's life, including settings and persons who do not come in direct contact with the adolescent (e.g., the mother's employer, the school board).

From a clinical perspective, this feature of the theory of social ecology suggests that adolescent functioning, including behavior problems, is influenced by the interplay among important aspects of the youth's life, such as family, friends, school, and neighborhood. That is, the social ecological model contends that adolescent behavior problems are multidetermined, and that the specific risk factors can vary from individual to individual. Logically, then, to be accurate and complete, clinical assessment must take into account a wide variety of possible contributors to behavior problems both within systems (e.g., lax parental supervision, association with deviant peers) and between systems (e.g., lack of caregiver knowledge about the youth's friends, conflictual caregiver interaction with school professionals). As detailed in subsequent chapters, the multifaceted MST assessment process drives the initial design and implementation of interventions to ameliorate the youth's identified problems. Moreover, therapists continue this assessment throughout the course of treatment as they identify factors contributing to observed intervention success or, when interventions fail, design subsequent strategies to address identified barriers to treatment success.

Ecological Validity

Another important aspect of social ecological theory is the emphasis placed on *ecological validity* in understanding development and behavior. The basic assumption of ecological validity is that behavior can be fully understood only when viewed within its naturally occurring context. This assumption is also vital to MST assessment and intervention design and delivery. Ecologically valid assessments require that the clinician understand the youth's functioning in a variety of real world settings (e.g., at home, in the classroom, during community activities) and that such understanding come from firsthand sources (e.g., caregivers, siblings, extended family, teachers, coaches) as much as possible. Similarly, therapeutic interventions are conducted with as much ecological validity as possible, which is one of reasons that the home-based model of service delivery, described in Chapter 2, is used exclusively in all MST programs. With MST, treatment services are provided where problems occur—in homes, schools, and community locations.

Reciprocal Nature of Human Interaction

A third clinically relevant emphasis of the theory of social ecology is the reciprocal nature of human interaction. The coercion mechanism (Patterson, Reid, & Dishion, 1992) provides an excellent example of reciprocal influences in parent–child relations. The father asks the teenager to do the dishes. The teenager argues and complains. The father decides it is less hassle just to do the dishes himself. The teenager stops arguing and complaining. The teenager has learned that arguing and complaining gets her out of work, and the father has learned that giving in to his daughter avoids an immediate headache. This notion of reciprocity is central to both MST assessment and intervention. At the assessment level, for example, reciprocity helps the therapist to understand why a caregiver might have given up attempting to discipline his or her adolescent—not out of a lack of love, but from a learned hopelessness. Likewise, and as discussed extensively in Chapter 3, therapists' design of treatment strategies takes into account the likely responses and counterresponses of all participants in the planned interventions.

The MST Theory of Change

Consistent with Bronfenbrenner's (1979) theory of social ecology, a primary assumption of the MST theory of change is that adolescent antisocial behavior (i.e., criminal activity, substance abuse, conduct problems) is driven by the interplay of risk factors associated with the multiple systems in which youth are embedded (i.e., family, peer, school, and neighborhood). Thus, to be optimally effective, interventions should have the capacity to address a comprehensive array of risk factors, though on an individualized basis (i.e., not all youth and families will have the same risk factors), while concomitantly building protective factors.

A second critical assumption in the MST theory of change is that caregivers are usually the main conduits of change. MST interventions, therefore, focus on empowering caregivers to gain the resources and skills needed to be more effective with their children. Then, as caregiver effectiveness increases, the therapist guides caregiver efforts to, for example, disengage their teenagers from deviant peers and enhance school performance. Thus, the family is viewed as critical to achieving and sustaining decreased adolescent antisocial behavior and improved functioning.

A simple depiction of the MST theory of change is provided in Figure 1.1. The therapist collaborates with the family, using family strengths (e.g., love of the adolescent, indigenous social support) to overcome barriers (e.g., caregiver substance abuse, debilitating stress, hopelessness) to caregiver effectiveness. As caregiver effectiveness increases (e.g., ability to monitor, supervise, and support the children), the therapist helps the caregivers design and implement interventions aimed at decreasing antisocial behavior by youth and improving their functioning across family, peer, school, and

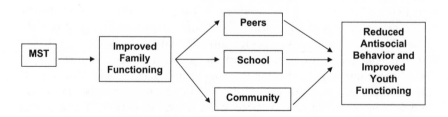

FIGURE 1.1. The MST theory of change.

community contexts. The ultimate aim is to surround the youth with a context that now supports prosocial behavior (e.g., prosocial peers, involved and effective caregivers, supportive school), rather than a context that is conducive to antisocial behavior. Similarly, as discussed in Chapter 7, treatment aims to surround the caregivers with indigenous (i.e., extended family, friends, neighbors) support to help sustain the changes achieved during treatment.

Support for the MST Theory of Change

As noted previously, the validity of the conceptual framework and theory of change underlying a treatment approach can be tested. The results of such tests might, or might not, support the treatment's theory of change. Fortunately for present purposes, the MST theory of change seems to be standing the tests of time, as evidenced by findings across several areas of investigation.

State-of-the-Art Family Therapies

In a recent overview of the field of family therapy, Lebow (2005) concluded that the most prominent of the new generation of family therapy approaches, including MST, share core attributes. Foremost, and consistent with the pioneers in family therapy, the new generation of methods maintains a systemic focus (e.g., importance of ongoing reciprocal influence, view that the whole is more than the sum of its parts). In addition, this new generation shares features that were not necessarily emphasized by the pioneers of family therapy. These features are relevant to the discussion of MST because they are consistent with the MST theory of change and clinical emphases described throughout this volume.

- *Consideration of biological basis of behavior.* The integration of pharmacotherapy with MST in treating youth with co-occurring attention-deficit/hyperactivity disorder (ADHD) provides a good example of the integration of biological and psychosocial interventions (see Chapter 6).
- *Emphasis on building the therapeutic alliance.* MST devotes considerable attention to cultivating and maintaining family engagement in treatment, which is critical to therapeutic progress. Similarly, engagement of others in the family's natural ecology who can influence what happens in treatment is also important. Engagement strategies and barriers to engagement are examined and addressed for every family receiving MST (see Chapters 2 and 3).

- *Shaping intervention strategies to knowledge about specific difficulties.* MST interventions target the risk factors for serious antisocial behavior in adolescents that have consistently been identified in research. Similarly, as discussed briefly in Chapter 9, MST adaptations for other behavioral difficulties (e.g., child maltreatment, chronic health problems such as diabetes and HIV infection) have also been developed, and changes in the MST treatment protocol made for these adaptations are based on empirical knowledge of the factors that contribute to those particular problems.

- *Maintaining a multisystemic focus.* Crediting the influence of MST, Lebow (2005) noted that state-of-the-art family therapies often focus on multiple levels of the youth's ecology and sometimes the family is not even the primary target of interventions.

- *Enhancing the sustainability of change.* MST places great emphasis on changing the youth's social ecology in ways that will sustain prosocial behavior in everyday life (e.g., engaging the youth with prosocial peer networks such as sports teams, church youth groups, and other adult-supervised activities) and in developing an indigenous support system that can help the family maintain treatment gains (see Chapter 7).

- *Emphasizing family strengths.* MST views family (and extrafamilial) strengths as key levers for therapeutic change. All aspects of MST interventions and quality assurance/improvement are explicitly strength focused.

- *Considering client goals.* As detailed in Chapter 2, MST uses a well-specified process to identify and articulate the exact goals of treatment, and family members (as well as, for example, teachers and court personnel) are essential to defining such goals.

- *Tracking outcomes.* MST has played a leadership role in promoting increased provider accountability through the tracking of client outcomes. The continuous tracking of targeted outcomes is one of the central principles of MST (see Chapter 2). Moreover, outcome assessment is an integral component of the MST quality assurance/ improvement system, and we are continually trying to improve the efficiency and validity of outcome tracking in MST programs worldwide (see Chapter 10).

- *Attending to culture.* The cultural context of children and their families is fundamental to the social ecological model. Thus the design and implementation of MST interventions take into account the cultures of the family and its social ecology. In addition, every effort is made to recruit and retain therapists who understand, or reflect, the cultures of the families and communities being served. Indeed, as reviewed by Huey and Polo (2008) and Schoenwald, Heiblum, Saldana, and Henggeler (2008), MST has been implemented successfully with youth and families from many different cultural backgrounds (e.g., African American, Hispanic, Pacific Islander, Scandinavian, Maori, Native American).

Research on the Determinants of Antisocial Behavior in Adolescents

A major impetus for the original development of MST in the late 1970s was the fact that existing treatments for delinquency, which had little empirical support, focused on a limited subset of the variables known to be associated with adolescent criminal behavior. Although researchers had clearly shown that delinquency and other aspects of child psychopathology were associated with child, family, peer, school, and neighborhood variables across the youth's social ecology, the prevailing treatments typically focused on a very limited subset of these risk factors. Logically, it seemed reasonable to hypothesize that such a narrow clinical focus doomed these treatments to failure, even when delivered by talented therapists. In light of these findings (i.e., current treatments of delinquency were ineffective, and adolescent behavior problems were multidetermined), Henggeler and his colleagues argued in *Delinquency and Adolescent Psychopathology: A Family–Ecological Systems Approach* (Henggeler, 1982, with Borduin contributing chapters in this volume) that to be effective, treatments must consider the multiple determinants of serious clinical problems, with the family viewed as primary.

Treatment developers in the areas of conduct disorder, delinquency, and adolescent substance abuse owe a great debt to the many talented researchers who have explicated the causes and correlates of antisocial behavior during childhood and adolescence. Among a host of important investigations, the major longitudinal studies conducted by Elliott (e.g., Elliott, 1994a), Loeber (e.g., Loeber, Farrington, Stouthamer-Loeber, & Van Kammen, 1998), and Thornberry (Thornberry & Krohn, 2003) stand out. Although some differences in risk factors for different populations (e.g., males vs. females, whites vs. African Americans, early vs. late adolescence) have emerged, findings from these and other studies of antisocial behavior in adolescents have been remarkably consistent throughout the past decades. *Antisocial behavior in adolescents is multidetermined by factors within the youth and across his or her social ecology (i.e., family, peers, school, and neighborhood).* Based on several excellent literature reviews (Biglan, Brennan, Foster, & Holder, 2004; Hoge, Guerra, & Boxer, 2008; Loeber et al., 1998), Table 1.1 provides a brief overview of those factors that are amenable to treatment (i.e., risk factors that are not amenable to interventions, such as genetic loadings and prenatal exposure to toxins, are not included).

TABLE 1.1. Key Causes and Correlates of Antisocial Behavior in Adolescents

Youth level

- ADHD, impulsivity
- Positive attitudes toward delinquency and substance use
- Lack of guilt for transgressions
- Negative affect

Family level

- Poor supervision
- Parental substance abuse and mental health problems
- Inconsistent or lax discipline
- Poor affective relations between youth, caregivers, and siblings

Peer level

- Association with drug-using and/or delinquent peers
- Poor relationship with peers, peer rejection

School level

- Academic difficulties, low grades, having been retained
- Behavioral problems at school, truancy, suspensions
- Negative attitude toward school
- Attending a school that does not flex to youth needs (e.g., zero-tolerance policy)

Neighborhood level

- Availability of weapons and drugs
- High environmental and psychosocial stress (e.g., violence)

Empirical Tests of the MST Theory of Change

Even for treatments of youth emotional or behavioral problems with demonstrated effectiveness, theories of change have rarely been tested (Kazdin, 2007). Yet, as noted previously, such evaluation is central to examining the validity of the conceptual basis of a psychosocial treatment. Several areas of research converge to support the MST theory of change articulated in Figure 1.1.

Results from MST Clinical Trials

First, as detailed in Chapter 9, rigorous evaluations (i.e., randomized clinical trials—the gold standard of research) with juvenile offenders have shown that MST can significantly reduce youth antisocial behavior (i.e., criminal offending, substance use) in comparison with other types of interventions. Important for examining the MST theory of change, many of these same studies also showed that MST was effective in changing key family (e.g., improved parenting) and peer (e.g., decreased association with deviant peers) variables that are linked with adolescent antisocial behavior.

Although these findings do not demonstrate that improved family relations and decreased association with deviant peers directly caused the reductions in youth antisocial behavior, such findings are consistent with this possibility.

Direct Tests of MST Mechanisms of Change

A second line of research tests the MST theory of change directly through advanced statistical methods. Using data from separate MST clinical trials with serious juvenile offenders (Henggeler, Melton, Brondino, Scherer, & Hanley, 1997) and substance-abusing offenders (Henggeler, Pickrel, & Brondino, 1999), Huey, Henggeler, Brondino, and Pickrel (2000) showed that, across both studies, therapist adherence to MST was associated with improved family relations and decreased association with delinquent peers, which, in turn, were associated with reductions in delinquent behavior. Figure 1.2 depicts the combined findings from these studies.

More recently, as part of a randomized trial of MST with juvenile sexual offenders, Henggeler et al. (in press) found that favorable MST effects on reducing youth antisocial behavior were mediated by increased follow-through on discipline practices as well as decreased caregiver disapproval of and concern about the youth's deviant peers over a 12-month follow-up (see Figure 1.3). These findings suggest that MST empowered caregivers to better identify friends that were having a negative influence on their adolescents, advise them to stop associating with such friends, and follow through on planned discipline. These behaviors, in turn, led to decreased antisocial

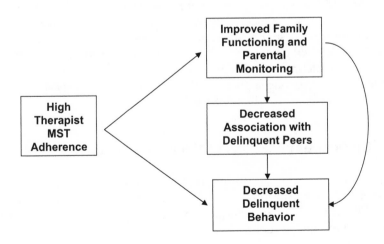

FIGURE 1.2. MST mechanisms of change with serious and drug-abusing juvenile offenders.

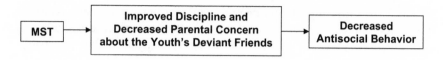

FIGURE 1.3. MST mechanism of change with juvenile sexual offenders.

behavior on the part of the juvenile sexual offenders. Thus, the three outcome studies produced similar results that were consistent with the MST theory of change. *MST (or adherence to MST) altered key family and peer risk factors for criminal behavior, and these changes in risk factors resulted in decreased adolescent antisocial behavior.*

Mechanisms of Change for Other Evidence-Based Treatments of Youth Antisocial Behavior

The third line of research supporting the MST theory of change pertains to the few studies that have examined mechanisms of change for other evidence-based treatments of youth antisocial behavior. In a study of Multidimensional Treatment Foster Care (MTFC; Chamberlain, 2003) in which juvenile offenders received either MTFC or group home care, Eddy and Chamberlain (2000) showed that the positive effects of MTFC on adolescent criminal activity were mediated by caregiver behavior management practices and adolescent association with deviant peers. Similarly, in an indicated prevention trial of the *Coping Power* program with at-risk preadolescent boys, Lochman and Wells (2002) found that inconsistent parental discipline was a key mediator of subsequent youth antisocial behavior outcomes.

In summary, these three lines of research—state-of-the-art work in the field of family therapy, research on the causes and correlates of antisocial behavior in adolescents, and empirical tests of the MST theory of change— provide relatively strong support for the MST theory of change and the theory of social ecology on which MST is based.

Clinical Implications of the MST Theory of Change

Together, social ecological theory, research on the causes and correlates of antisocial behavior, the MST theory of change, and research supporting this theory of change have several clear implications for the treatment of serious antisocial behavior in adolescents.

- *Adolescent antisocial behavior is multidetermined.* Thus, effective interventions must have the capacity to address a comprehensive array of risk factors across the multiple systems in which adolescents are embedded. For reasons of efficiency (i.e., not all youth have the same risk factors), these risk factors are addressed on an individualized basis. Moreover, consistent with a strength-based focus, considerable attention is also devoted to building protective factors such as parenting competencies (see Chapter 3), youth problem-solving skills (see Chapter 6), and social support (see Chapter 7).

- *Families should be empowered to address youth problems.* Caregivers are viewed as the keys to obtaining sustainable outcomes for the youth, and improved parenting is often the key mechanism in achieving favorable youth outcomes. MST identifies and then addresses the barriers to improved parenting, such as caregiver substance abuse (see Chapter 8). Then, caregiver skills and competencies are enhanced to address identified problems (see Chapter 3).

- *The negative influence of deviant peers must be addressed.* As noted previously, association with delinquent and drug-using peers is a powerful predictor of youth behavior problems. With the therapist's guidance, caregivers must do everything possible to decrease youth association with deviant peers and promote youth bonding with prosocial peers (see Chapter 4).

- *School or vocational performance must be enhanced.* School provides excellent opportunities for prosocial development, and education and job skills are critical to future economic and social functioning of the youth. Employment in a position that can lead to a legitimate career is a major predictor of desistance of criminal behavior (Sampson & Laub, 2005) (see Chapter 5).

- *An indigenous support system should be developed to help the youth and family sustain treatment gains.* Many families referred to MST programs have few indigenous resources (e.g., friends, neighbors, and extended family they can count on for help) that can be accessed in times of heightened stress. MST strives to help families develop social support networks to sustain prosocial behavior (see Chapter 7).

In conclusion, we hope that our discussions of the theory of social ecology that underlies MST, the MST theory of change, and the several substantive areas of research that support these perspectives have provided a strong rationale for the conceptual foundations of MST.

CHAPTER 2

Clinical Foundations

WITH ELENA HONTORIA TUERK

IN THIS CHAPTER

■ Clinical foundations and processes of MST
and conceptual aids that support use of these
processes during treatment.

■ The role of safety assessment
and interventions.

■ Integration of the quality assurance/
improvement system with the clinical process
and structure of MST.

■ Strategies for engaging families in treatment.

The purpose of this chapter is to describe the clinical foundations of MST
and the administrative structures, clinical supervisory processes, and quality assurance/improvement mechanisms that underlie and support MST
clinical interventions. MST is an intensive home-based treatment that is
grounded in social ecological theories and operationalized through adher-

Elena Hontoria Tuerk, PhD, is Assistant Professor at the Family Services Research Center
(FSRC) in the Department of Psychiatry and Behavioral Sciences at the Medical University of
South Carolina. She received her doctorate in clinical psychology from the Curry Programs in
Clinical and School Psychology at the University of Virginia in 2007 and completed her postdoctoral research and clinical training at FSRC as project coordinator for a study examining MST for
co-occurring child maltreatment and parental substance abuse. Dr. Tuerk's research interests
include the implementation and evaluation of community-based interventions for families.

ence to nine treatment principles. Interventions delivered within MST are grounded in research and delivered in a well-specified treatment approach supported by specific conceptual aids, supervisory processes, and quality assurance/improvement mechanisms that support the fidelity of implementation.

Central Role of the Family

As specified in this volume, MST is designed to treat youth with serious antisocial behaviors and their families. Families are the central focus of MST, and caregivers are seen as full collaborators in treatment and crucial change agents for their children. Thus, therapists are encouraged to find family and caregiver strengths and to use these strengths as leverage for clinical change. In turn, therapists are discouraged from labeling families in negative ways, blaming them, or giving up on them. Indeed, as described at the end of this chapter, MST has a long and substantial track record of engaging families; retaining them in treatment, and gaining their trust and satisfaction (see treatment completion rates described in Chapter 9).

Implementation Tools

Consistent with its grounding in social ecological theory discussed in Chapter 1, MST interventions encompass the entire ecology in which the family is embedded. As a result, therapists are expected to possess or develop the capability of assessing, understanding, and intervening with the youth's family, extended family, peer, school, and neighborhood systems. Because intervening successfully across these complex systems can be challenging, MST therapists are guided by several strategies and tools. These include:

- Nine treatment principles.
- Home-based model of service delivery.
- Ongoing training and support.
- An analytical process that maintains a focus on youth and family outcomes.
- Conceptual aids that support clinical aims.

MST Treatment Principles

The design of MST interventions is based on nine treatment principles. These principles serve as the foundation for the model and a template against which all MST interventions can be compared to judge fidelity. In fact, MST adherence measures that are part of the quality assurance/improvement system (see later section of this chapter and Chapter 10) were based largely on these principles. Table 2.1 provides brief definitions and examples of the use of these principles, and their relevance is noted in case examples throughout the text. Detailed explication of the principles is provided in the first edition of this volume (Henggeler, Schoenwald, Borduin, Rowland, & Cunningham, 1998).

Clinical Process of MST

As the nine principles provide a foundation for the design of interventions used in the model, so the MST clinical process provides the underlying structure and framework on which therapists build their interventions. This structure includes the makeup of the MST team, training and ongoing quality assurance/improvement, and conceptual aids that facilitate the ongoing organization and implementation of interventions.

Basic Team Structure

MST is provided by treatment teams consisting of two to four therapists and a supervisor embedded in licensed MST programs. MST therapists are typically master's-prepared clinicians trained in social work, psychology, counseling, or marriage and family therapy; and the teams are usually part of private service provider organizations contracted by public juvenile justice, child welfare, and mental health authorities (Sheidow, Schoenwald, Wagner, Allred, & Burns, 2006). Each therapist within the team works with four to six families at a time, providing intensive home- and community-based services over a period of 3 to 5 months. Although the duration of MST treatment is relatively brief, the intervention process is intensive and often involves 60 hours or more of direct contact between the therapist and family.

Home-Based Model of Service Delivery

The home-based model of service delivery, with 24-hour-a-day, 7-day-a-week availability of the MST team, is used for several purposes, including:

- Remove barriers to service access.
- Enhance therapeutic engagement.
- Provide more ecologically valid assessment data from which to base intervention design.
- Respond in a timely fashion to crises that threaten desired outcomes.
- Provide more ecologically valid clinical outcome data.
- Improve generalization of outcomes, as clinical changes are made directly in the settings in which the problems occur.

TABLE 2.1. The Nine Principles of MST with Examples from the Naaves family's treatment

1. Finding the fit

   The primary purpose of assessment is to understand the "fit" between the identified problems and their broader systemic context.
   Example: The therapist developed fit circles hypothesizing the roles played by school, caregiver, peer, individual, and community factors in contributing to each of Rick's referral behaviors.

2. Positive and strength focused

   Therapeutic contacts should emphasize the positive and should use systemic strengths as levers for change.
   Example: The therapist leveraged Mr. Naaves's commitment to his son and Rick's desire to gain his father's respect to facilitate their participation in interventions.

3. Increasing responsibility

   Interventions should be designed to promote responsible behavior and decrease irresponsible behavior among family members.
   Example: The overarching goals of MST treatment focused on getting Rick to attend school, stop using drugs, and comply with his father's rules. Interventions also focused on helping Mr. Naaves become a more effective parent.

4. Present focused, action oriented, and well defined

   Interventions should be present focused and action oriented, targeting specific and well-defined problems.
   Example: The goals for treatment were clearly defined and could be measured by objective means such as school attendance records and urine drug screens. The therapist targeted factors for intervention that dealt with the present situation, such as caregiver monitoring, rather than past events, such as Rick's anger over his mother's absence.

5. Targeting sequences

   Interventions should target sequences of behavior within and between multiple systems that maintain identified problems.
   Example: The therapist hypothesized that the poor home–school link involved interactions between father and son (i.e., ineffective monitoring, conflict), father and school (i.e., father's avoidance of school, school's negative assumptions about father) and youth and school (i.e., youth was not well supervised at school; youth misrepresented information to father). The therapist then developed interventions targeting each of these interactions.

6. Developmentally appropriate

   Interventions should be developmentally appropriate and fit the developmental needs of the youth.
   Example: The youth's behavioral plan contained rewards and consequences that were meaningful for a teenager, such as access to music, video games, cell phone use, transportation, food, and money.

7. Continuous effort

   Interventions should be designed to require daily or weekly effort by family members.

(continued)

TABLE 2.1. *(continued)*

Example: The home–school daily report card and home behavioral plans required daily effort on the part of youth and caregiver.

8. Evaluation and accountability

Intervention efficacy is evaluated continuously from multiple perspectives, with providers assuming accountability for overcoming barriers to successful outcomes.

Example: The therapist monitored drug use through frequent urine drug screens, school attendance through school records, and curfew compliance through father, son, and probation reports.

9. Generalization

Interventions should be designed to promote treatment generalization and long-term maintenance of therapeutic change by empowering caregivers to address family members' needs across multiple systemic contexts.

Example: Mr. Naaves learned to communicate with school personnel, better access indigenous social supports, obtain urine drug screens to monitor Rick's substance use, and develop and implement behavioral interventions to promote Rick's psychosocial functioning.

Thus, treatment is provided in the home and community, and treatment sessions are held at times that are convenient for family members.

Training and Support

Because providing such intensive services effectively can become daunting to the therapist, several processes and structures are set up within the MST model to support therapists and to help ensure treatment fidelity. The most important of these processes is the multifaceted and ongoing training and clinical support provided to MST therapists. As detailed in Chapter 10, MST training begins with a 5-day orientation to the treatment model. This orientation aims to ground therapists in the clinical process of MST, provide a common background in evidence-based treatment approaches, shift the therapists' focus to more family-based and systemic conceptualizations of problems, and help practitioners learn to include the family's key ecological systems (e.g., peer, school, neighborhood) when developing and implementing interventions.

While the 5-day orientation provides grounding in MST, the majority of MST clinical learning occurs as therapists work with families and receive weekly structured supervision and feedback both from an on-site MST team supervisor and an off-site MST consultant. The MST team meets weekly with the supervisor, as a group, and the supervisor follows a specified protocol for reviewing and addressing the issues in each case with the team. The entire team, in turn, discusses cases with an MST expert consultant once a week to obtain additional feedback and direction as needed. The overriding purpose of these supervision and consultation sessions is to provide the therapist with the support needed to facilitate attainment of targeted treatment goals and to enhance therapist fidelity to MST treatment protocols. More detailed descriptions of these processes and the roles of the supervisor and consultant are provided later in this chapter.

MST Analytic Process

The MST analytic process, also referred to as the MST "do-loop," serves as a broad road map for treatment planning and intervention. Figure 2.1 illustrates the sequential and recursive process that MST teams use to concep-

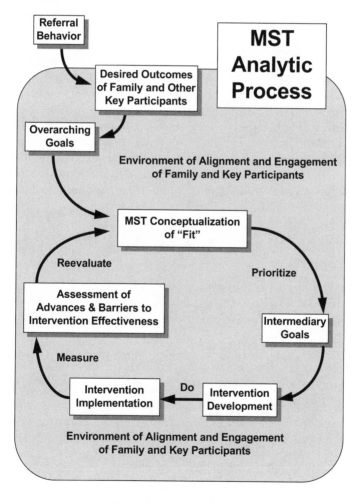

FIGURE 2.1. MST analytic process.

tualize and intervene with families. The components of the analytic process guide the Case Summary for Supervision and Consultation Form discussed subsequently. This form provides the details therapists need to use the analytic process with each case on a weekly basis, whereas Figure 2.1 depicts the treatment planning and implementation process more generally.

1. First, the therapist aligns with the family and works with family members and key stakeholders to develop a clear consensus of the overarching goals.
2. Second, the therapist works with the family and other sources of information, taking care to look within and between systems, to understand the "fit" of the referral behaviors (i.e., how they make sense) within the context in which the youth and family are embedded.
3. Next, the team and family members prioritize hypothesized drivers of the identified problems and develop interventions to address the drivers.
4. These interventions are implemented, and any barriers to effective implementation are identified.
5. Next, following the do-loop back up toward the top, therapists assess the outcomes of their interventions from multiple perspectives to determine if they are having the intended effects. If not, the information gained during this process is fed back into the loop, and therapists work to develop new hypotheses and modified interventions based on these revised hypotheses.

This reiterative process reinforces two important features of the MST model:

1. MST teams strive to never give up on youth and families; rather, teams do "whatever it takes" to help families reach treatment goals.
2. When interventions are not successful, the failure is the team's, rather than the family's.

In other words, when the team develops accurate hypotheses, identifies barriers, and implements correspondingly appropriate interventions, families will achieve their goals.

Conceptual Aids

A system of communication has been developed to help therapists convey important clinical information to supervisors, which, in turn, the MST team passes along to the team consultant. To help therapists save valuable time, the conceptual aids are designed to convey essential case information in formats that support the underlying MST clinical process while minimizing the amount of written text. The conceptual aids help therapists maintain a clear focus on treatment goals and progress while helping supervisors and consultants maximize the usefulness of their feedback. In completing these aids, therapists should glean information not only from the caregivers, youth, and family, but also, to the extent possible, from other stakeholders such as teachers and probation officers. Examples of these forms, completed for the forthcoming case example of Rick, are provided in corresponding figures.

BACKGROUND INFORMATION FORM

The Background Information Form is completed at intake and updated periodically as needed. As shown in Figure 2.2, this form starts with a genogram, which is especially useful for conveying a quick overview of the extended family members, their relationships, and their potential to serve useful roles in the treatment of the youth and family. The next section of the form asks therapists to describe the reasons for the youth's referral to the MST program. As MST teams serve primarily youth at risk of out-of-home placement due to antisocial behaviors, therapists are asked to focus on serious problem behaviors in this section. These behaviors are described using brief, specific behavioral terminology, and care is taken to provide information concerning the frequency, intensity, and duration of the behavior as well as the systems that have been impacted. Next, the therapist meets with as many stakeholders in the youth's ecology as possible, such as caregivers, siblings, extended family, teachers, and probation officers, and describes in each stakeholder's own words the outcomes they want the youth to achieve during treatment.

STRENGTH AND NEEDS ASSESSMENT

The Strengths and Needs Assessment is also completed at intake, and is updated periodically as new information surfaces during treatment (see Figure 2.3 for an example). In this form, therapists identify both strengths (protective factors) and weaknesses (risk factors) in each of the systems in which the youth and family are embedded (individual, family, school, peer, community). The MST team reviews this information periodically as a tool to help develop interventions that will leverage systemic strengths while mitigating or eliminating weaknesses.

CASE SUMMARY FOR SUPERVISION AND CONSULTATION

The Case Summary for Supervision and Consultation Form consists of six sections, serves as the reference for MST supervision and consultation, and

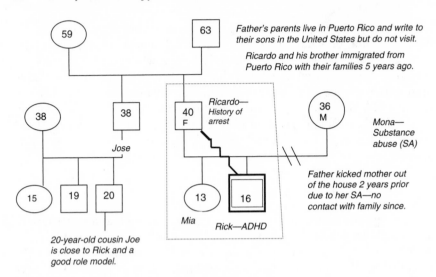

Referral Behaviors

Behavior	Frequency	Intensity	Duration
Marijuana use	3–4 times a week	1–2 blunts shared with 2 peers	Approx. 16 months
Truancy	2–3 times/ week	Skips entire day	Started last school year (12 months ago)
Physical aggression, fights with peers	Two known incidents	The client had to receive stitches for laceration, black eye	Incidents were 3 and 8 months prior to intake
Father–son conflict—both are verbally aggressive	1–2 times per week	Both scream, youth uses rude language, lasts 1–2 minutes	Approximately 2 years

Desired Outcomes

Participant	Goal
Rick	Get off probation, get Dad to stop nagging me
Ricardo Naaves (father)	Rick to go to school, get a job, make me proud of him
Mia (sister)	Do good, stop getting into trouble, stop fighting with Dad
Jose Naaves (uncle)	Stay away from bad kids, stop smoking dope
Mr. Johnson (probation officer)	Stay in school, stop using drugs, no violence

FIGURE 2.2. Background MST case information for Rick Naaves.

Family: R. Naaves   Therapist: T. Doe   Date: October 4

Systemic Strengths	Systemic Weaknesses/Needs
Individual	
Athletic, enjoys baseball	Impulsive—acts before he thinks, quick temper
Social—can be a leader in his group of friends	Verbal and pwhysical aggression
Wants to find a job	Endorses violent attitudes
Wants to get along better with father	Failing most classes
Admits that he has a problem with marijuana	Does not believe that he can stop using
History of responding well to ADHD meds	marijuana (can't get away from his
	delinquent peers)
	Does not readily admit his role in conflict
Family	
Father is very committed to his son	Father has authoritarian parenting style
Sister, Mia, is well-behaved	Father and son demonstrate high conflict at
Uncle is supportive of father and client	times
Cousin, Joe, also supportive, has job, potential	Father has history of arrest, unknown charge
as role model	Mother has history of substantial drug use
	Mother's location unknown for 2 years
School	
Willing to work with R. as long as he	Many of R.'s negative peers are at school
demonstrates efforts to improve	Low supervision of youth during free time
Has a baseball team	School has negative attitude about families
PE teacher/coach expresses interest and	from youth's apartment complex
concern for R. (doesn't want him to drop out)	R. may not be eligible for sports because of
	grades
	School not in regular contact with father
	Father avoids interfacing with school
Peers	
Father recalls positive friends from 2 years	Most of R.'s friends are not in school or skip
ago that still go to R.'s school	school often
One current friend has a job (Sam)	Most of R.'s friends use marijuana and alcohol
Cousin Joe may serve as good role model; has	Two of R.'s friends were also involved in the two
job and is willing to help	fighting incidents (Mike and A. J.)
R. is able to identify one prosocial peer that he	Mike and A. J. consistently involved when youth
would like to spend time with. This peer plays	breaks curfew, skips school, gets in trouble
baseball (J. R.)	
Community	
Recreation center in neighborhood with	Apartment complex known for high crime
baseball league and other sports	Drugs readily available in apartment complex
Little sister goes to church with aunt and	Police know R. and don't like him—per youth
uncle	
Lady next door in apartment complex is	
potential social support for father, helps	
watch Mia sometimes	

FIGURE 2.3. Strengths and needs assessment for Rick Naaves.

is completed/revised weekly. This form is based on the aforementioned MST do-loop, and an example is provided in Figure 2.4.

   I. The therapist starts by describing the *overarching/primary MST goals*. These are goals that (1) have been set jointly by the therapist/MST team and family/stakeholders; (2) are clearly connected with the youth's referral behavior; (3) aim to greatly reduce the frequency and intensity of the referral behavior; (4) are written in an objective, specific, behavioral manner; and (5) can be measured directly.

   II. The therapist lists the *previous intermediary goals* and whether these were met or not during the past week. Intermediary goals are smaller treatment goals that the therapist and team set on a weekly basis as intermediary steps toward reaching the larger or *overarching MST goals*.

  III. In the *barriers to intermediary goals* section, therapists explain any problems or barriers that were experienced while trying to reach intermediary goals.

  IV. Conversely, in section IV, therapists describe advances or gains in treatment.

   V. Section V is central to MST treatment fidelity. Therapists review the referral problems and overarching goals of treatment, and, taking into account any new information encountered during the week, describe how the therapist's conceptualization of the "fit" (Principle 1) of the problems being addressed might have changed or been modified. To complete this aspect of the form, therapists complete "fit circles" (described next), which are a tools used by MST teams to understand the causes, or drivers, of problem behaviors.

  VI. Finally, therapists state new intermediary goals for the next week of treatment. Often, the MST team, supervisor, and consultant will work with therapists during supervision and consultation to further develop or modify these goals and to think through the process of how to best implement interventions in the coming week, taking into account the team's knowledge of the strengths and barriers of the family and its ecology.

FIT CIRCLE

The term "fit" or "fit circle" is derived from the first principle of MST, which states that the primary purpose of assessment is to understand the fit between the identified problems and their broader systemic context. Hence, "fit circle" is the term applied to the process therapists and teams use to develop hypotheses concerning possible causes or drivers of referral problems, other behaviors, or interaction patterns. Fit circles are critical to assessing and understanding problems, and are developed during structured brainstorming exercises that therapists complete with family members and the MST team. The hypotheses concerning the primary drivers of behav-

Family: R. Naaves   Therapist: T. Doe   Date: November 2

Weekly Review

I. Overarching/Primary MST Goals

1. R. will demonstrate school success as evidenced by no unexcused absences, no removals due to disruptive behavior, completion of assignments, and passing grades, per school records.
2. R. will stop using marijuana as evidenced by clean urine screens for 10 consecutive weeks, per report of parents, therapist, and probation officer.
3. R. and Father will reduce conflict and arguments as evidenced by reports from family members (youth, sister, father, uncle, and cousin).
4. R. will eliminate all verbal and physical aggression at home and in the community as evidenced by no further charges, and parent report of no verbal or physical altercations at home or in the community.
5. R. will comply with terms of probation as evidenced by probation officer's report.

II. Previous Intermediary Goals

	Met	Partially	Not
1. Therapist and father to attend the school IEP conference to try and get joint home–school interventions in place	met		
a. Strategize how to approach teachers with father	met		
b. Develop school daily report card for teachers	met		
c. Get all teachers to buy into completing card		partial	
d. Get teachers to brainstorm concerning plan to help youth catch up, with academics		partial	
e. Set another meeting to follow up	met		
f. Get teachers to return Conner's ADHD scales to use with psychiatry consult (set for next week)	met		
2. Father to collect urine drug screen w/test cup following the protocol reviewed last week		partial	
3. Father and R. to try three strategies developed last week when indicators of conflict arise		partial	
4. Cousin J. to take R. to job interview at car repair shop			not
5. Review peer worksheet with father			not

III. Barriers to Intermediary Goals

1. English teacher, Ms. Smith, was not in the IEP conference, so unable to get her buy-in to completing daily report card or her help thinking of plans to help R. catch up in school. As R. has a problem with both behavior and grades in English class, her input and buy-in still need to be obtained.
2. R. left school early on Tuesday and Thursday last week (new information discovered during school meeting).

(continued)

FIGURE 2.4. Case Summary for Supervision and Consultation Form for Rick Naaves.

    3. Father collected urine screen but was unsure of how to read the results. Father did not call therapist for help and allowed youth to have privileges as if the screen were clean.

    4. Father reports that R. was disrespectful and did not follow through with his part of conflict management plan.

    5. Cousin was called in to work unexpectedly on his day off.

    6. Therapist did not have time to review peer worksheet with father due to other prioritized interventions.

IV. <u>Advances in Treatment</u>

    1. Coach Ramirez attended the IEP, seems fond of Rick, got along well with father. He is willing to attend future school meetings and be potential resource for family.

    2. Teachers and father agree that youth may need to switch to a more vocational track in school; guidance counselor is investigating this option. Teachers seem willing to fill in the brief report card each day and sign. Next school meeting is set for November 19.

    3. R. was able to set up another time to go with his cousin for the job interview.

    4. Therapist noted that father accessed social supports from next door neighbor more this week (called her twice to check on whether R. was home when he had to work late).

    5. Therapist noted evidence that father implemented behavioral plan last week. He rewarded Rick for making curfew each night as planned per youth and father report.

V. <u>Assessment of "Fit" between Identified Problems and Their Broader Systemic Context</u>

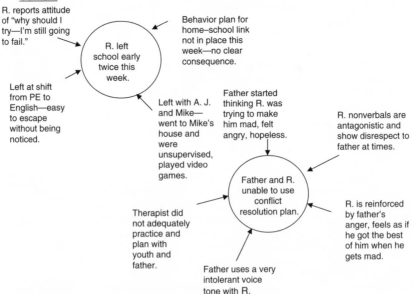

FIGURE 2.4. *(continued)*

VI. New Intermediary Goals for Next Week

1. Therapist to follow up with English teacher to complete communication concerning the daily report card and potential change to vocational track.
2. Therapist to check in with father concerning school daily report card this week.
   a. See if teachers and R. comply with plan.
   b. Check to see if father is able to follow through with consequences if indicated.
   c. Check to see if father is able to provide reward if indicated.
   d. Help father problem solve if difficulties arise.
3. Go with family to psychiatry consult, take teacher and parent Conner's scales. Purpose of consult is to see if diagnosis of ADHD is appropriate and to facilitate obtaining medication if indicated.
4. Father to call and ask Coach Ramirez to talk with R. about not skipping out after P.E. class.
5. Continue peer worksheet with father. Find out if father is willing to call Mike's mother and ask her not to allow R. to be at her house unsupervised due to his risk of probation violation.
6. Father to check in with cousin J. and make sure he is still able to take R. to the interview.
7. Therapist to continue to work with R. and father on conflict resolution skills.
   a. Help father and R. discuss what happened when they failed to implement plan well last week. Try to help them perspective take with each other and work toward shared goals. Leverage father's commitment to his son and youth's desire to get his father to respect him again.
   b. Consider having father and R. switch roles with each other during the role play.
   c. Practice thought replacements for father to use when he feels angry and hopeless.
   d. Practice better nonverbal cues for the youth to use.
   e. Reward the family (including sister) with pizza after this session to facilitate engagement and encourage positive interactions with youth and father.
8. Therapist to collect random UDS (urine drug screen) this week with father present. Will problem solve the collection process as well as address any barriers that arise to follow through on the behavioral consequences if dirty.
9. Continue to monitor implementation of behavior plan for curfew and house rules.

FIGURE 2.4. (*continued*)

iors derived from these fit circles are used to make decisions about which clinical interventions should be implemented and in what order. Initially, therapists complete fit circles on each referral behavior as well as any other important or concerning behaviors that are discovered during the intake process. Subsequently, MST therapists update past fit circles or provide new ones on a weekly basis as indicated in treatment. Several examples of fit circles are provided (see Figure 2.5) in the case example that follows.

Case Example: Rick Naaves

The following case highlights the clinical process of MST and demonstrates the ways in which the conceptual aids support fidelity to the model.

Background Information

Rick Naaves was a 16-year-old Latino male of Puerto Rican descent who was at immediate risk of out-of-home placement in a juvenile justice facility for repeatedly violating the orders of his probation. Specifically, Rick was not meeting his curfew and had recently obtained a new charge of possession of marijuana. At intake to MST, Rick's referral behaviors included marijuana use, truancy, and fighting with peers in the community. Rick also carried a diagnosis of ADHD and had a history of difficulties with impulsivity and anger management. Rick lived with his father and 13-year-old sister in an urban apartment complex.

The female therapist, Terri, started by meeting with and beginning to engage the youth and his family members in treatment. One of Terri's first objectives was to meet as many stakeholders as possible and to find out their goals for Rick's treatment. She also collected information from these individuals concerning the frequency, intensity, and duration of each of Rick's referral behaviors and obtained a genogram to help the team better understand the family history and potential sources of support. As seen in Figure 2.2, Rick's father had a brother, sister-in-law, nephews, and a niece who lived nearby and were potential resources for social support. Terri was able to obtain information concerning desired treatment outcomes from Rick's uncle and probation officer as well as his family. Based on this information and the referral behaviors, the therapist assessed the frequency, intensity, and duration of the behaviors that would likely be primary targets for intervention: Rick's marijuana use, truancy, fighting with peers, and the verbal aggression between Rick and his father.

Strengths and Needs Assessment

As part of her intake assessment, Terri also developed a list of the various strengths and needs she discovered as she assessed Rick and his family,

Family: R. Naaves   Therapist: T. Doe   Date: October 4

Fit Circles on Referral Behaviors Completed at Intake, page 1

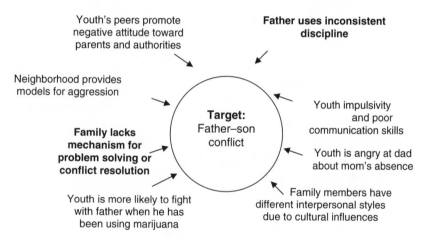

(continued)

FIGURE 2.5. Fit circles.

Fit Circles on Referral Behaviors Completed at Intake, page 2

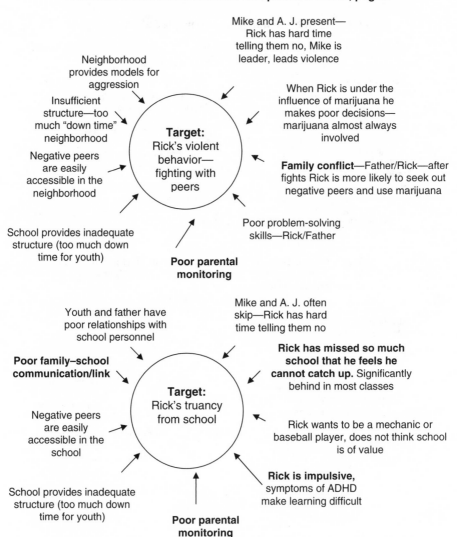

FIGURE 2.5. *(continued)*

school, peer, and community contexts. Terri collected this information via firsthand observation and through interviews with family members, teachers, and the probation officer. The Strengths and Needs Assessment serves to (1) help therapists see strengths that can be leveraged for change (Principle 2), and (2) highlight weaknesses or barriers that might need to be further assessed or treated. For example, although Mr. Naaves had an authoritarian parenting style and frequently fought with Rick, Terri found that he was very committed to his son and Rick seemed to genuinely want to get along better with his father. This information was helpful later when Terri started to design interventions to address parental monitoring difficulties and high father–son conflict.

Fit Circles on Referral Behaviors

Once the frequency, intensity, and duration of the referral behaviors are generally understood, the therapist develops fit circles on these behaviors. Terri introduced Rick and his sister, father, and uncle to the concept of fit circles at this time. These family members worked with Terri to think of factors that might be contributing to each of the referral problems and to list them as drivers of that problem. In Figure 2.5, for example, the first fit circle addressed Rick's marijuana use. Notice that the drivers listed around the circle included factors from individual (poor impulse control), peer (drug-using peers easily accessible), neighborhood (drugs easily available in neighborhood), and family (family conflict) systems. Notice also that the therapist highlighted (bold font) three drivers she felt were the most powerful and proximal causes of the problem (i.e., drug-using peers, poor parental monitoring, and family conflict) for the first as well as the other fit circles. This process of completing fit circles for referral behaviors served to (1) help establish common therapeutic goals and visions for the team and family, thus promoting engagement; (2) develop an understanding of the ways that several systems were contributing to the problem (Principle 1); and (3) provide specific well-defined targets for future interventions (Principle 4).

Case Summary for Supervision and Consultation

Figure 2.4 provides an example of the weekly paperwork submitted by Terri to the MST consultant and supervisor at approximately 1 month into treatment. The roman numerals in the following outline reflect the corresponding roman numerals on the paperwork.

I. *Overarching/primary MST goals.* After Terri completed the intake paperwork and fit circles, she did several things to prepare for team consultation. First, she developed a preliminary set of overarching or primary

MST goals. As described earlier, these are goals that are vetted with the family and designed to guide treatment. In Figure 2.4, notice that a goal was established to specifically address each of the four referral behaviors as well as an additional goal to ensure focus on compliance with the probation officer's concerns. The goals encompassed the desired outcomes listed by participants at intake, and were stated in such a way that progress could be easily monitored. Once approved by the family and clinical team, these goals recur weekly at the top of the paperwork.

II. *Previous intermediary goals.* In this section Terri listed her goals from the prior week and whether they were met, partially met, or not met. Notice that the goals for treatment were present focused, action oriented (Principle 4), developmentally appropriate (Principle 6), easy to measure (Principle 8), and required frequent or daily work on the part of therapist, caregiver, and youth to complete (Principle 7). Importantly, each intermediary goal was derived from a prioritized driver on a fit circle (see Figure 2.5). For instance, the goal of working to improve family–school communication was developed due to the significance of this driver in contributing to Rick's truancy. Also, intermediary goals were put in place to address most or all of the overarching goals, helping to ensure that progress was being made in all areas of concern.

III. *Barriers to intermediary goals.* This section is used by the therapist to explain why certain goals were not met or only partially met. In Rick's case, Terri discovered that Mr. Naaves did not know how to read the results on the urine drug screen cup, and that this resulted in Rick not receiving the appropriate consequences or rewards for a dirty or clean screen. Also, Terri did not receive a call from Mr. Naaves when this problem occurred, suggesting a potential lack of engagement concerning this aspect of treatment. Section III of the paperwork ties in nicely with the part of the MST analytic process (Figure 2.1) that describes the importance of assessing advances and barriers to intervention effectiveness and with Principle 8, which emphasizes the importance of continuously evaluating the efficacy of interventions. Information in this section was used to inform the fit circles in the next sections of the paperwork.

IV. *Advances in treatment.* The therapist lists information concerning advances in treatment or other positive information that might prove helpful. For instance, Terri found a coach at school who got along well with Mr. Naaves and was willing to be a potential school resource for Rick and his father. As in section III, this information helped the therapist track the effectiveness of her interventions and was used to inform the fit circles in the next section (V) of the paperwork. Keeping track of advances also helps the therapist and team remain strength focused (Principle 2).

V. *Assessment of "fit" between identified problems and their broader systemic context.* Here, the therapist lists the barriers noted earlier during the assessment of intervention effectiveness and develops hypotheses concerning the potential causes of these problems. In the present case, two such problems were identified (i.e., Rick left school early twice, and Mr. Naaves and Rick were unable to implement their conflict resolution plan). As depicted in Figure 2.4, hypotheses were developed concerning the potential causes or drivers of these barriers (Principle 1), thus creating fit circles for these two problems. This material was then used in the following section of this paperwork (VI) to guide the development of new intermediary goals.

VI. *New intermediary goals for next week.* At this point, the therapist prioritizes the drivers of problem behaviors listed on the fit circles in section V to determine which are most appropriate for intervention. In Rick's case, Terri developed new intermediary goals based on the drivers of identified barriers. For example, Terri and Mr. Naaves suspected that a primary driver of Rick's skipping school was that the home–school communication link and behavioral plan were not yet established. Accordingly, they developed several intermediary goals targeting this problem. First, Terri would check with Mr. Naaves daily to see if Rick and his teachers were following through with their respective roles in completing the Daily School Report Form (see Chapter 5). Then, anticipating Mr. Naaves might have difficulty following through with consequences or rewards, Terri made goals to check with him on such follow-through daily and to provide on-site assistance for him if needed.

The Course of Treatment for Rick's Family

The MST therapist continued with this clinical process, submitting weekly case summaries for supervision and following the MST do-loop throughout the course of treatment. The Naaves family's treatment lasted approximately 5 months and included more than 70 therapeutic contact hours. The family experienced one major difficulty in the middle of treatment (described in the next section on safety), but eventually all overarching goals were at least partially met. One of the most clinically significant outcomes was that Rick's father developed substantially better skills and resources for supervising and monitoring Rick. Mr. Naaves enhanced his parenting competence by learning to (1) give Rick rewards and consequences based on his behavior; (2) access social supports, including his nephew, brother, and neighbor, to help monitor and supervise Rick in his absence; and (3) communicate with schoolteachers and set up consequences at home for school attendance and behavior. Terri and the Naaves family also made substantial progress in getting Rick involved in more prosocial activities (e.g., two jobs) and limiting his unsupervised time with deviant peers. By the end of treatment, Rick's father and family members were able to carry out these tasks independently with little help from the therapist and clinical team.

Safety Assessment and Interventions for MST Families

Given the nature of the MST referral population and the community-based focus of interventions, all MST therapists and supervisors are encouraged to closely monitor and address the clinical safety needs and concerns of families on a frequent and ongoing basis. Safety needs most often pertain to intra-family violence (e.g., youth-to-family violence, marital violence, child abuse); risks posed to the youth by dangerous individuals in the community (e.g., serious juvenile offenders have extremely high rates of death by gunshot; Teplin, McClelland, Abram, & Mileusnic, 2005); risks the youth poses to the community (e.g., many youth in MST programs are violent offenders); and occasionally, suicidal behavior.

Administrative and Clinical Approaches

Safety concerns are addressed at both administrative and clinical levels.

Organizational

At the administrative level, MST teams are prohibited (through exclusion criteria for standard MST programs) from accepting youth who are actively suicidal, homicidal, or psychotic. That is, while MST is an appropriate intervention for youth with willful misconduct who are at risk of out-of-home placement for criminal behavior, MST is not an alternative to psychiatric hospitalization; nor is it an alternative to judicial placement if the youth poses a substantial and specific safety risk to people in the community. Because many judges and prosecutors believe that such a risk exists for all serious offenders, care is taken prior to MST program start-up to ensure that the team is treating appropriate referral populations as described in Chapter 10.

At the team level, as described later in this chapter and in Chapter 10, therapists have access to the MST supervisor, or a backup for that supervisor, 24 hours a day, 7 days a week to assist with emerging treatment needs and clinical crises. In addition, an expert MST consultant (a person who provides critical ongoing training and quality assurance/improvement to the program) is available for consultation during working hours. The other therapists on the team are also a resource. Thus, the MST therapist should never have to address a clinical crisis alone. He or she can collaborate with and obtain support and advice from several like-minded colleagues.

Clinical

In general, the MST team approaches safety using the same conceptual tools that are used to address other clinical issues and concerns.

SYSTEMIC CONCEPTUALIZATION—FIT CIRCLES

Safety risk is conceptualized in an ecological and systemic manner as a problem driven by the interaction of factors within and between systems. As a result, when the concerning behavior is identified (e.g., history of assault with a weapon), the therapist and team strive to better understand the causes or "fit" of that behavior from a multisystemic perspective (i.e., deviant peer affiliation, disorganized neighborhood that models and supports crime, poor parental monitoring, school expulsion, access to firearms, impulsivity). Next, based on the prioritized drivers of that behavior, the therapist and family put interventions into place to address these risk factors (e.g., supervision and monitoring of peers and weapons access, increase in prosocial activities, linkage with appropriate vocational opportunities).

EXPERT SUPPORT

Importantly, and as indicated previously, supervisors and consultants serve as key participants in the process of supporting safety. These professionals (1) are a resource for information (e.g., describing factors that are important to assess when trying to determine risk for violence), (2) provide clinical assistance or support to ensure that assessments and interventions are carried out well (e.g., go with therapist to complete the assessment), and (3) help determine when risk factors are too high and other interventions need to be put into place (e.g., placing youth in inpatient facility).

SAFETY TOOLS

MST tools specific to helping therapists address safety concerns are available to therapists. For example, MST Safety Checklists (see Henggeler, Schoenwald, Rowland, & Cunningham, 2002) can be used to help ensure that potentially dangerous items (i.e., knives, firearms) have been removed from the home. Likewise, MST Safety Plans (Swenson et al., 2005) can be specified with family members to provide a plan of action in the event that a predictable safety risk (e.g., a violent caregiver loses his or her temper) occurs.

An example of a crisis that occurred in the Naaves family is provided next to highlight how MST teams conceptualize and intervene with safety issues.

Case Example of Rick Naaves Continued: Safety Concerns

Approximately 6 weeks into treatment, Terri received an urgent call from Rick's father. The school had just contacted Mr. Naaves to tell him that Rick and two friends, A. J. and Mike, were in the principal's office being questioned about an incident at school involving a knife. When Mr. Naaves and Terri arrived at the school, they were told that a hunting knife was found in Mike's locker during a random school-based police search. A. J. and Rick had been pulled into the office as well due to their known connection to Mike and the guidance counselor's concern that the three of them might have been planning a fight with another group of boys with whom they often argued. While Mike was immediately expelled from school for the remainder of the academic year, Terri and Mr. Naaves convinced the school to allow Rick to return, provided that the MST team put a formal safety plan in place and worked proactively with the school to help prevent further incidents. The fit circles and MST Safety Plan that were completed concerning this incident are provided in Figures 2.6 and 2.7 respectively.

Safety Fit Circles

Terri responded to Mr. Naaves's call by traveling to the school immediately to meet with him as well as Rick, his teachers, and Coach Ramirez. She then developed fit circles on the two problems that she thought were most concerning and central to safety. These were the fact that a knife was found in Mike's locker and that Rick was continuing to have frequent access to two peers who were known to be significant drivers of his delinquent behavior, Mike and A. J. This assessment suggested that the crisis situation was the result of several factors involving the school, peer, family, and individual systems and the connections between these systems that should be amenable to interventions.

Examining the two safety fit circles in Figure 2.6 and reviewing drivers by system, the therapist and team noticed the following. At the individual level, Rick's impulsivity was highlighted as a prioritized driver (**bold font**) in both fit circles. During this crisis situation, Terri learned that although Rick had seen a psychiatrist several weeks prior and received a prescription for medication to treat his impulsivity and ADHD, the prescription had not been filled. At the family level, inadequate parental monitoring of Rick's access to deviant peers in general, and Mike and A. J. in particular, was hypothesized to be a strong driver of the safety concerns. In turn, the various systems were not fully supporting Mr. Naaves in his attempts to better structure Rick's access to peers. For example, the school had not yet followed through with promoting Rick's transfer to the vocational track that would isolate him from current negative peers and potentially provide him with a more appropriate career path. Also, the structure and supervision

Family: R. Naaves   Therapist: T. Doe   Date: November 16

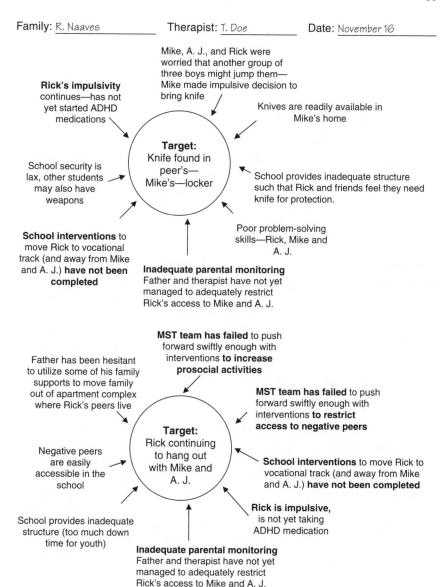

FIGURE 2.6. Fit circles on safety concerns.

of youth at this school was poor, making it easy for Rick and his friends to plan and carry out antisocial activities. Finally, the MST team had failed Mr. Naaves in several ways. Despite the team's understanding of the powerful influence of peers on adolescent behavior, they had failed to ensure the sense of urgency and consistent implementation of family and school interventions needed to restrict Rick's access to negative peers and promote prosocial activities.

Terri worked with Mr. Naaves and school personnel to come to a consensus on the importance of these prioritized drivers and ways to address them. The action steps for intervening with these drivers to promote safety were spelled out for each participant and system in the MST Safety Plan (see Figure 2.7). All participants signed the plan and kept a copy so that each was aware of his or her role in the process.

MST Safety Plan

Notice that the plan starts by summarizing the tasks or events that need to take place for Rick to stay safe. This summary provides a broad plan for prevention of another incident at school. Again, each system has a role to play, and the plan is designed to promote responsible behavior on the part of all participants (Principle 3). To summarize the plan, Rick was expected to take his medication, stay away from negative peers and drugs, and participate in prosocial activities that would be created in the new plan. Mr. Naaves was expected to continue to work to better supervise and monitor Rick and help the therapist step up interventions to increase prosocial and diminish antisocial peers and activities for Rick. Mr. Naaves also agreed to increase his use of family and neighbor supports. The school in turn agreed to more closely supervise Rick and to accelerate the process of getting him into a more appropriate educational track. Terri agreed to help guide and facilitate the interventions for each system and coordinate the process across participants.

Consistent with all MST interventions, the safety plan spelled out specific details of how each of the broader goals would be accomplished. The steps were concrete, action oriented, and amenable to evaluation (Principle 4). For instance, the school agreed to (1) continue to complete the Daily School Report Form for Mr. Naaves, (2) call the therapist and family immediately if a problem occurred, (3) work to find more suitable educational resources as soon as possible, (4) perform random searches of Rick's locker for weapons, and (5) provide Rick the opportunity to volunteer with Coach Ramirez after school 2 days a week. This behavioral approach to safety was easily tracked and modified as needed. To round out the communication process, the therapist submitted the completed *safety fit circles* and MST Safety Plan as part of her MST paperwork to her supervisor and consultant

Family: <u>Naaves</u>   Date Started: <u>11/18</u>   Date Stopped: _____

To be safe: Rick needs to stay away from friends who get into trouble (Mike, A. J., and any other friend listed by therapist, father, or teacher), as well as drugs and weapons. Rick also needs to take the medication prescribed by his doctor. Father will help Rick by following the monitoring plan and working with Rick to develop new friendships and to stay busy doing healthy things. School personnel will help Rick stay safe by filling out the daily behavioral report cards, encouraging Rick to develop prosocial activities, and calling Mr. N. or therapist immediately if problems arise.

WHAT I WILL DO:

PARENT—I will help my child be safe by (1) Following the behavioral and monitoring plan for home and school every day; (2) performing a room search with the therapist today and whenever indicated to make sure that my son is not harboring knives or other weapons; (3) talking with my brother and sister-in-law to get them to help me monitor Rick after school on afternoons when I am working; (4) talking with my neighbor to see if she can help monitor Rick if my brother is not able to do so; (5) making sure Rick takes his medication each day; (6) continuing to work on school interventions with the therapist; (7) continuing to work on peer interventions with the therapist; (8) calling our therapist if I need help with any of these actions.

YOUTH—I will help myself be safe by (1) following the behavioral and monitoring plan for home and school everyday; (2) staying away from Mike, A. J., and anyone else who gets in trouble at school or in the neighborhood—using the plan I developed with my dad and therapist; (3) not using drugs and cooperating with my dad by giving a drug screen each week to prove I am clean; (4) working with Dad, therapist, uncle, and cousin to find things to do with my time after school that will help me stay out of trouble; (5) taking the medication as prescribed by my doctor; (6) contacting Coach Ramirez if I need help at school.

SCHOOL—We will help Rick be safe by (1) completing the report card daily for Mr. N.; (2) calling Mr. N. or therapist immediately if Rick has problems at school; (3) immediately attempting to find more suitable educational resources for Rick (vocational classes); (4) performing random locker searches to make sure Rick does not have a weapon; (5) Coach Ramirez will allow Rick to do volunteer work with him after school on Mondays and Wednesdays for the P.E. Department; (6) Coach Ramirez will be available to help Rick if he needs assistance with problems.

THERAPIST—I will help Rick be safe by (1) dropping by the school each week at random times to check on Rick and see how he is doing, and make sure he is in class and that no friends who get into trouble are around; (2) helping Rick look for a job; (3) being available 24 hours a day, 7 days a week for calls to help Rick and his father if they argue or need help (or my backup team therapist will be available and will know the plan); (4) helping everyone on this list follow through with these interventions if they need help.

(continued)

FIGURE 2.7. MST safety plan for Rick Naaves.

WHOM I WILL CALL:

PARENT—I will call [Terri] at this phone number <u>123-4567</u> if Rick and I start to fight, or if I cannot find Rick or if he is not following rules and I don't know what to do.

YOUTH—I will call [Terri] at this phone number <u>123-4567</u> if Dad and I start to fight, or if I need help in any way.

TEACHER—I will call Mr. N. at this phone number <u>876-5432</u> or [therapist] at this phone number <u>123-4567</u> if anything happens at school that I believe they should know about—such as behavioral problems or skipping school.

CONTACTING OUR THERAPIST: Our therapist is Terri Doe. Her phone number is 123-4567.

I AGREE TO FOLLOW THE TERMS OF THIS SAFETY CONTRACT.

_____ Date _____   _____ Date _____
Parent/Guardian   Teacher

_____ Date _____   _____ Date _____
Youth   Teacher

FIGURE 2.7. (*continued*)

and incorporated the action steps on the plan into intermediary goals on the weekly Case Summaries for Supervision form for this family.

Safety Resolution

The MST Safety Plan created for the Naaves family served important functions both as an official document to help meet the school's administrative requirements for a formal written plan and as a way to solidify everyone's commitment to an organized systemic approach to the problems. The school incident helped bring clinical urgency to the case both for Mr. Naaves and Terri, prompting Mr. Naaves to follow through more completely with therapeutic interventions while motivating Terri to stay more clinically attuned to peer risk factors in this and subsequent cases. As described earlier, this case ended well with Rick being placed in a vocational track at school and becoming more involved with prosocial activities (e.g., volunteer job with Coach Ramirez, working with cousin at a local garage) and much less involved with deviant peers. Mr. Naaves played an important role in this process as he developed substantial skills in supervising his son at home, school, and in the neighborhood, and gaining family supports to help him with this process.

Supporting the Clinical Processes of MST: The Roles of the MST Supervisor and Expert Consultant

The MST supervisor and expert consultant are responsible for developing the clinical competence of the team and identifying and addressing any practitioner-, organizational-, and system-level barriers to the operational and clinical success of the MST program. This section of the chapter describes the characteristics of these professionals and their clinical roles. Chapter 10 describes how they are trained, supported, and evaluated in their work.

Supervisors

MST therapists are held accountable to achieve clinical outcomes and do "whatever it takes" to help families. To succeed in these responsibilities, therapists need support from skilled clinicians well versed in MST. Hence, the role of the on-site MST supervisor is crucial in the overall functioning and development of each MST therapist and team.

MST supervisors are expected to work full time in the organization operating the MST program, and supervising two teams is a full-time endeavor. Due to the intensive nature of both MST fidelity procedures and the home-based model of service delivery, supervisors are discouraged from having additional jobs that might distract from their availability to the MST team. The vast majority of MST supervisors hold a master's or doctoral degree and, like MST therapists, have usually been trained in social work, psychology, counseling, or marriage and family therapy (Schoenwald, Letourneau, & Halliday-Boykins, 2005; Sheidow et al., 2006). Many MST supervisors were recruited from the ranks of effective MST therapists and, consequently, bring much relevant experience to their position.

The responsibilities of MST supervisors are conceptualized as falling into five areas:

1. *Acquire ongoing knowledge and develop skills.* MST supervisors are expected to understand and stay current on the knowledge base relevant to MST (e.g., research findings on causes and correlates of delinquency, literature on evidence-based treatments), demonstrate strong clinical skills in evidence-based practices utilized in MST, and collaborate actively with the MST consultant to advance their own clinical and supervisory learning and development.

2. *Support therapist implementation of MST.* Supervisors are responsible for ensuring, on a case-by-case basis, the fidelity of all aspects of MST implementation—the multisystemic nature of assessment, the development of appropriate intermediate and overarching goals, adherence to the nine

treatment principles, and tracking of the analytic process—all of which aim to achieve the most favorable youth outcomes possible.

3. *Ensure weekly MST team supervision and consultation meetings are conducted as intended.* Supervisors are responsible for making sure that all of the administrative and clinical aspects of the MST supervision and consultation process and paperwork follow the procedures that have been specified and demonstrated to enhance fidelity and improve outcomes.

4. *Promote the clinical growth and development of each MST therapist.* MST supervisors work alongside MST consultants to strengthen therapist skill sets. These efforts involve the ongoing assessment of therapist competencies and barriers to effectiveness as well as the corresponding creation, implementation, and modification of therapist development plans.

5. *Represent the program to stakeholders.* The supervisor represents the needs of the team to the organization and the organization's requirements and resources to the team. Similarly, the supervisor is often the face of the program to community stakeholders (e.g., school personnel, probation, judges).

Consultants

Clinically, the MST expert consultant's primary responsibility is to do "whatever it takes" to help MST supervisors fulfill their roles and augment the support therapists need to help families reach their clinical goals. Hence, consultants must have expert-level knowledge of MST, substantial background and experience with evidence-based practices for the problems that arise in youth and families in MST programs, and demonstrated ability to transfer knowledge and skill sets to others. Consistent with these demands, early MST expert consultants were primarily doctoral-level clinicians, chiefly with backgrounds in clinical or counseling psychology. Recently, as MST has become more widely disseminated, a group of well-trained master's-level professionals with substantial experience as MST therapists and supervisors have become MST expert consultants based on model-based performance criteria. Generally, the duties of the MST consultant fall into three categories.

1. *Support therapist implementation of MST.* The consultant teaches clinicians to implement MST with fidelity and helps the team address internal and systemic barriers to achieving this. Thus, clinical progress for every case treated by the team is evaluated each week, and the consultant advises on resolving barriers and all other aspects of treatment design and implementation.

2. *Promote clinical competence of therapists and supervisor.* The consultant assesses development of competence in MST and MST supervision by

clinicians and supervisors. He or she assists the supervisor in creating strategies to facilitate the development of clinician competence and works with the supervisor to enhance his or her supervisory skills.

3. *Address organizational and system threats to fidelity.* The consultant helps identify organizational and interorganizational factors that might compromise implementation of MST and consults with the team and administrative leadership to develop and implement strategies to address these factors.

The MST Quality Assurance/ Quality Improvement System: Putting It All Together

The MST quality assurance/quality improvement (QA/QI) system has been designed to help ensure the dissemination of MST with fidelity to the key aspects of the model that are essential for youth and family outcomes. The process underlying this system has been worked out through more than 15 years of experience assisting community-based agencies in developing and maintaining sustainable MST teams. Chapter 10 describes the components of the MST QA/QI system in detail, and Figure 10.1 in that chapter provides a pictorial representation of the complexity of this system. As discussed in Chapter 10, many aspects of this system have been validated in ongoing research. The most important set of findings discussed in that chapter, however, pertains to the demonstrated linkages of various aspects of the QA/QI system to improved youth outcomes. These associations between strong program (e.g., therapist, supervisor, consultant) fidelity and favorable youth outcomes substantiate the value of the MST QA/QI system.

The broad components of this system, detailed in Chapter 10, include:

Training

- Initial 5-day orientation training
- Quarterly booster training
- Weekly on-site supervision
- Weekly consultation

Organizational Support

- Program development—extensive assistance to community stakeholders interested in establishing MST programs
- Ongoing organizational support—semiannual program reviews, problem solving of organizational and stakeholder barriers to implementation, support for program directors

Implementation Measurement and Reporting

- Measuring therapist adherence to the nine MST treatment principles
- Measuring supervisor adherence to the MST supervisory protocol
- Measuring consultant adherence to the MST consultation protocol
- Youth outcome measurement

In many ways the MST QA/QI system mirrors the clinical method of MST, following the MST analytic process or do-loop (Figure 2.1). That is, the MST consultant, agency, and supervisor work together and align to set overarching goals for the team. These goals often fall into organizational (e.g., number of families served per year, rearrest rates, average length of treatment), clinical (e.g., booster training needs), and QA/QI (e.g., fidelity scores, outcome data collection) categories. The supervisor and consultant then develop hypotheses concerning how best to meet these goals and start to implement interventions that are structured by the MST QA/QI process. Data are collected concerning outcomes in all of these areas (e.g., average caseload and length of treatment, rearrest rate, out-of-home placement, and therapist and supervisor fidelity scores), and feedback is provided on a routine basis to therapists, supervisors, and agency administrators. This information is then used to help all participants better understand the strengths of the MST program as well as the barriers to more effective implementation. Interventions are then developed that leverage agency, supervisor, and therapist strengths to effect better and more sustainable outcomes for youth and families receiving MST.

Summary

MST is an empirically grounded intervention with a comprehensive quality assurance/improvement protocol that is delivered using the home-based model of service delivery. MST therapists are expected to do "whatever it takes" to help families achieve favorable clinical outcomes. A multifaceted QA/QI system provides therapists with support via (1) comprehensive clinical tools and materials based on research, (2) training in evidence-based practice, (3) constant support and leadership provided by an on-site supervisor and an off-site consultant to help ensure the delivery of MST with optimal fidelity, and (4) agency-level support to facilitate model adherence. Hence, MST strives to leverage the strengths of therapists, supervisors, agencies, and systems to help families with youth experiencing serious behavioral and emotional problems create lasting changes for themselves and their children. As the engagement and retention of family members in treatment is central to this process, the final section of this chapter describes some of the approaches taken by MST therapists when working to establish and maintain family engagement.

Engaging Families in Treatment

This segment of the chapter illustrates common strategies MST therapists use to engage families in treatment—especially families that might feel coerced to enter treatment by their referral source (e.g., juvenile justice system). Therapy cannot progress unless key family members (i.e., the youth's caregivers, those adults who control family resources or who have decision-making authority) are engaged—defining problems, setting goals, and implementing interventions to meet those goals. From the MST perspective, parents and other family members are essential to achieving positive treatment outcomes, and such outcomes are almost always accomplished through hard work by those family members.

As illustrated in the do-loop (Figure 2.1), cultivating and maintaining engagement throughout treatment is fundamental to MST. Hence, MST therapists invest significant energy toward developing and maintaining family commitment to treatment. The continuous focus on engagement has paid off as evidenced by the excellent rates of treatment completion achieved by practitioners in MST research projects (e.g., greater than 90%; see Chapter 9) and MST programs in community settings (e.g., 85% on average as reported by therapists to the MST Institute, at *mstinstitute.org*). Such success in engaging and retaining families in treatment has been facilitated by many of the implementation processes and tools discussed throughout this chapter. For example:

- The home-based model of service delivery removes barriers to service access.
- Low caseloads allow therapists the time to engage challenging families.
- Treatment principles emphasize family strengths and the importance of the family's cultural context.
- Family collaboration in the development of treatment goals and the nature of therapeutic interventions is central.
- Clinical support (e.g., supervisor and consultant) and tools (e.g., fit circles, do-loop) provide resources for identifying barriers to engagement and designing interventions to overcome those barriers.

Although these tools and processes are helpful in fostering family engagement, they are not sufficient by themselves. Effective use of these tools requires implementation by therapists who possess certain basic clinical skills.

☆ Core Clinical Skills for Engagement

Most clinical and counseling training programs identify several core clinical skills and behaviors as critical to building a therapeutic alliance and sustaining client engagement in treatment. These skills and behaviors are central to cultivating and sustaining engagement throughout MST.

Empathy

Clients often identify empathy as one of the most helpful aspects of treatment. Given its importance, MST therapists strive to maintain an "empathic stance" throughout treatment. Unlike sympathy, in which a person reacts to and feels compassion for another's experience while still maintaining his or her own frame of reference (e.g., "I feel sorry for him that his car was repossessed, that must be hard on the family"), empathy requires a vicarious experiencing of another's internal world (e.g., "I feel as though my car were repossessed, and that feels awful"). An empathic stance helps the therapist develop interventions that are congruent with the family's current state of being, an experience some therapists describe as "meeting them where they are."

Maintaining authentic compassion is fairly easy when a person or situation appears deserving (e.g., a victimized adolescent, a disabled caregiver). Therapists can feel frustrated, however, when working with individuals who do not seem to be trying hard enough or who often seem to put their own desires before their children's needs. Such therapist frustration can be conveyed as judgment, and no client wants to work with someone who does not like them or judges them harshly for their decisions. Thus, MST practitioners are encouraged to actively monitor and reinvigorate their empathy for family members throughout treatment, and supervision and ad hoc discussion with team members are often helpful in this regard. Therapists might also find the following strategies useful in reducing frustrations and refreshing empathy.

NONCLINICAL TIME

Just as perspective taking can be difficult for conflicting family members, therapists can have trouble appreciating a family member when engagement or clinical progress seems hampered by that person's behavior. Such situations might call for what has been coined the "cup of coffee" intervention. Here, the therapist suspends clinical assessment and intervention activity to spend time in informal settings with the family member with whom it is difficult to empathize (e.g., a perpetrator of domestic violence). The therapist's goal during this time is to gain an understanding of that person's view of the world and to examine the fit of the behavior that is distasteful to the therapist. Usually, as the therapist appreciates the caregiver's own social ecology, negative affect decreases and the development of a therapeutic alliance is promoted.

COGNITIVE ASSISTS

Therapists can also engage in a cognitive exercise aimed at representing the family member at an earlier age or in a situation for which the therapist experiences compassion. For example, the therapist might visualize what the father might have looked like as a 10-year-old boy, when it would have been easier for others to feel empathy for his experience. The therapist might imagine him at that young age, going to school, playing outside, wanting adult approval. What things might the therapist have wanted for him at that younger age? What would be different for the father if he had experienced a different caregiving or educational environment? What might the youth in this family look like when he or she is the father's age if things don't get better? What might be improved by compassion from others at this point in the father's life?

Warmth

Most therapists choose clinical careers because they want to help others, and they often possess personality characteristics that are helpful in the human services field. Interpersonal warmth is one such characteristic and is critical to the development of collaborative therapeutic relationships. Warmth is communicated in various ways, depending on the family and circumstance. For example, therapists who experience genuine pleasure when seeing clients naturally convey this in their manner. Similarly, observing client patterns of interaction can help therapists select appropriate ways to convey affection and concern (e.g., accommodating a parent's preference to greet the therapist with a kiss on the cheek rather than a handshake, if appropriate). Moreover, a therapist's appearance, posture, and facial expressions can have the effect of either bringing the therapist–client relationship closer or creating more distance. For example, sitting far away from a client or having a closed-off posture (e.g., positioned at edge of seat, arms tightly crossed across chest) conveys discomfort. A relaxed but interested manner (e.g., seated 3–5 feet away, leaning forward slightly with hands loosely clasped) suggests that the therapist is at ease in the family's home.

Reflective Listening

Reflective listening is a basic therapeutic skill that demonstrates understanding of another person's experience. Skillful reflective listening requires the therapist to accurately summarize both content and meaning in a way that conveys acceptance of and respect for a client's experience, without the therapist necessarily agreeing with the client's current perspective. In a simple reflection, the therapist (1) repeats back a critical word or phrase to encourage the client to elaborate further ("Tell me more about feeling 'desperate.'") or (2) repackages the central theme of the communication in fresh language to demonstrate understanding of the underlying message ("You're feeling really frustrated right now and don't know what else to try."). More sophisticated reflections, in which certain statements or themes are selectively chosen to direct conversation in a particular direction, increase the utility of the reflective listening strategy (Miller & Rollnick, 2002). For example, a therapist who reflects, "You really dislike everyone at the school," will likely continue to hear about the negative experiences the mother has had in her teen's various academic settings. In contrast, if the therapist is aiming to facilitate the family–school interface, he or she might reflect, "The school has been a real problem; I wonder if there is anything they can do better to help us out?"

Reframing

A youth's problems are often sustained, in part, by negative attributions family members have of one another's behavior. For example, a mother might view her son's delinquent behavior as an attempt to "get back" at her for being strict on him. The son might perceive his mother's discipline as a sign of hostility and rejection. As described in classic structural and strategic family therapy texts (see Chapter 3), reframing is a technique that provides an alternative (and less negative) explanation for a situation. Reframing is designed to decrease negativity and refocus family members on joint problem solving.

Reframing has been described as a three-step process (Alexander & Parsons, 1982) in which the therapist:

1. Reflects the perspectives of the family members (e.g., "I can see why you would think he [she] is doing this to hurt you").
2. Provides an alternative perspective that puts the behavior in a more benign or even positive light (e.g., "I wonder if this behavior is his way of trying to become more independent"; "Perhaps your mom is so strict because she loves you and is trying to protect you.").
3. Checks with family members to see how the reframes fit and reformulates them accordingly.

A reframe sometimes requires a significant shift in thinking, especially if the previously held belief is long-standing or entrenched (e.g., "My mom doesn't care about me."). Because it can be hard for family members to accept a new perspective at first pass, the therapist often offers reframes tentatively and provides family members an opportunity for "partial buy-in" (e.g., "Could this be a small part of what's going on here?").

Flexibility

Flexible people adjust to changes quickly and make the best of less-than-ideal circumstances. Along with empathy and warmth, therapist flexibility is needed to demonstrate to families that the therapist can handle the many problems they face. Therapists working in the homes and neighborhoods of client families are likely to face a wide range of situations requiring flexibility and an unflappable attitude. Such circumstances can include physical limitations (e.g., lack of seating in living room, no air conditioning during summer) or situational changes (e.g., family needs to move immediately). Managing situations with a "can do" attitude and good humor demonstrates the therapist's willingness to "roll with the punches."

Nonclinical Strategies to Increase Engagement

Several pragmatic, nonclinical strategies can also be used to initiate the therapeutic alliance and sustain engagement throughout treatment.

Family Photos

When completing a genogram or family tree with a family, the therapist can suggest looking at family photos. Such photos can help cue caregiver recollections of people and times in family history that might provide useful information for treatment planning. Reviewing photos also gives the therapist an opportunity to show interest in the *family*, not just the family's problems. Showing curiosity about the people, locations, and customs that appear in photos has the added advantage of eliciting information in a nonthreatening way. For example, viewing a photo of the referred youth at an earlier age can help a parent remember more positive feelings toward and hopes for the child.

Food

One of the most popular strategies therapists use to "get in the door" is to bring food for the family to the treatment session. Bringing food has several advantages: hard-to-reach family members are more likely to join the session, family members observe that the therapist is attentive to their needs (e.g., by lightening the load on caregivers who might be tired after work), and therapeutic intimacy is increased by sharing in a nurturing ritual. Although time-strapped therapists often provide pizza or other takeout foods, one seasoned clinician recommends the "chicken soup approach" during particularly difficult times in treatment: bringing homemade comfort food to families in crisis. Similarly, therapists should be cautious about refusing food or drink from families, particularly when such refusal might be misunderstood as a form of distancing from the family or the family's cultural background. Practitioners should appreciate the honor of being admitted into the family's home and take care to convey comfort with and respect for the family's practices.

Help with Practical Needs

When practical needs seem to overshadow clinical work, treatment is not likely to progress until these concerns are addressed. Going "above and beyond" to help families access information and goods can be a critical step toward motivating families for change. The more that family members perceive the therapist as accessible, interested in helping, and savvy at negotiating bureaucratic systems, paperwork, and so forth, the more likely they will be to reach out at times of need. Opportunities to help abound: therapists are likely to have easier access to computers, for example, to download forms to secure housing, find an inexpensive but serviceable sofa on the Internet, or format a professional-looking resume for the client. Similarly, a family moving to safer housing might need help finding boxes or locating a truck. A therapist who finds creative ways to achieve outcomes can be a refreshing surprise for families who are accustomed to uphill battles with social service professionals.

Five-Minute Sessions

Five-minute sessions are especially useful for engaging when family members want to cancel sessions or do not seem motivated to participate on a given day. The therapist acknowledges that the caregiver is tired and asks that they complete one task together, with the understanding that the therapist will come back the next day for the full session. When the 5 minutes are up, the therapist asks whether the caregiver prefers to finish today or meet again tomorrow. More often than not, the family member chooses to continue a session once it has begun.

Ongoing Therapist Self-Assessment to Maintain Engagement

As discussed previously, the MST quality assurance/improvement system provides considerable structure and support to help therapists achieve favorable outcomes, including successful engagement with the youth and families they are serving. In addition to this external support, therapists can engage in a self-assessment to evaluate whether a negative cognitive bias might be interfering with developing a strong therapist–family alliance. Warning signs of possible negative cognitive bias, for example, include thoughts such as:

- "I care more about this child than his mother does" or "If I were in that position, I would.... "
- "I don't need this. I'll go work with someone who wants my help."
- "She has a raging personality disorder."
- Disparaging, "below the belt" thoughts about a client's appearance, home, manner, habits, or community, which might be shared with colleagues under the pretense of "gallows humor."

The following strategies can be used to attenuate therapist negative cognitive bias.

Social Perspective Taking

Therapists think of a particular incident or client statement that produced a negative reaction in them and consider:

- What underlying message was the client trying to convey when this occurred? What was he or she feeling? What got in the way of the client communicating the message in a way that would make me feel more positively?
- How did the client get to this point today (this month, in her lifetime)? How has communicating in this way (or doing this thing) been useful in the past? Where did the client learn this?
- How does this situation demonstrate the client's strengths? How does this demonstrate his or her suffering? How can I show the client that he or she does not need to do this anymore to get help from others?

Data Log

Therapists seek evidence of client strengths and efforts.

- Write down the thought that needs to be disconfirmed (e.g., "The client doesn't care about her son.").
- Write down client statements and behavior that suggest effort, motivation for change, or positive feelings—anything that could disconfirm that thought or suggest a way to leverage strengths toward disconfirming the thought.
- Remain patient with the process of finding evidence by having real-

istic goals (e.g., "I was able to find one piece of evidence yesterday, today I might find two"). Recall that clients are moving targets. For example, the mother might show little evidence that she cares about her son right now, but the therapist should be open to the possibility that the situation is temporary, not permanent.

Opposite Action

Opposite action (Linehan, 1993) is a behavior that elicits emotions that are incompatible with the original thought or emotion. For example, a person who is feeling sad might watch a frightening movie to induce physical and emotional sensations (e.g., racing heart, feelings of anticipation, relief) that are incongruent with sadness. By engaging in opposite action, the therapist can counteract the original emotion (e.g., "I am dreading this session; I hope they cancel") by performing a behavior that promotes the opposite feeling (e.g., "I've spent a lot of time coming up with a plan for this session and feel motivated to accomplish these tasks. They'd better not cancel!"). One therapist reported, for example, that she brought flowers to a client when "it was the last thing I wanted to do." Rather than an insincere gesture, the therapist's action was an attempt to acknowledge the difficult time she and the client were having together, while orienting her (the therapist) toward positive feelings. Clients who are used to bringing out negative reactions in others may be particularly affected by such a gesture. The therapist noted, "It was the best session we ever had together," likely because the therapist surprised both the client and herself.

Summary

The capacity to engage family members and to maintain that engagement throughout treatment is an important skill for MST therapists to acquire and nurture as part of their ongoing clinical development. As engaging families in treatment is a necessary foundation for all effective interventions, the clinical process of MST, conceptual aids, and QA/QI system described earlier in this chapter help to ensure that engagement is always assessed and that therapists are provided with appropriate supports as needed to attain and maintain engagement.

CHAPTER 3

Family Interventions

┌───┐

IN THIS CHAPTER

- Key dimensions of family relations.
- Assessing family strengths, subsystems, and social ecology.
- Family interventions commonly used in MST.
- Guidelines for applying parent–child, marital, and systemwide interventions.
- Strategies for overcoming barriers to intervention success.

└───┘

Families come in many forms. They may be headed by two biological or adoptive parents, one biological and one stepparent, a single parent who is divorced or who has never been married, one or more grandparents, or a relative acting as a parent. The diversity of family forms has broadened in recent years, and more and more children are raised by divorced, remarried, and/or never married caregivers. Regardless of the particular form a family takes, the relationship between the developing child and his or her caregivers probably represents the most significant influence during the course of the individual's life. Indeed, most theories of socialization view parents as the primary facilitators of children's self-concepts, emotional well-being, interpersonal skills, and achievement motivation. Moreover, research suggests that children and adolescents who evidence problematic relations with their parents or other caregivers are more likely to exhibit emotional and behavioral difficulties, including antisocial and delinquent behavior (Cummings, Davies, & Campbell, 2000; Mash & Barkley, 2006). Thus, the family relations of adolescents presenting serious antisocial behavior are almost always a critical target for interventions in MST.

This chapter describes assessment and intervention strategies that are commonly used in MST with families of juvenile offenders and provides guidelines for assessing which strategies might be needed to make changes with a particular family. MST family intervention strategies do not reflect a single therapeutic modality, but include several different types of interventions integrated from structural and strategic family therapies, behavioral family systems approaches (Robin & Foster, 1989), behavioral parent training (Wierson & Forehand, 1994), behavioral family intervention (Sanders, 1996), and cognitive-behavioral therapy (CBT) (Kazdin, 2003; Weisz, 2004). Interventions to change parenting styles can range from simple, focused behavioral interventions that some caregivers can implement with little assistance from the therapist, such as setting and monitoring a curfew, to more complex series of interventions organized by the therapist to simultaneously address multiple problems such as marital conflict, maternal depression, and parent–child discipline practices.

MST therapists and supervisors who have limited familiarity with the family therapy strategies outlined in the present chapter may find several texts by prominent strategic (Fisch, Weakland, & Segal, 1982; Haley, 1987, 1993) and structural (Minuchin, 1974; Minuchin & Fishman, 1981; Minuchin, Nichols, & Lee, 2007) family therapists to be instructive. To facilitate therapists' acquisition and implementation of family therapy skills, we strongly recommend that MST supervisors allocate some time during group supervision meetings to review selected segments from videotapes of therapists' sessions in which family therapy interventions are used. Although periodic videotaping of family treatment sessions requires extra time and effort from therapists, reviewing therapy tapes can contribute substantially to the development of their intervention skills. Therapists should always ensure that families understand the purposes of videotaping (i.e., to help therapists do a good job) and complete the appropriate forms providing their permission.

The first section of this chapter describes the ongoing assessment process used in MST to identify the specific combination of systemic, caregiver–child, and marital factors that compromise effective functioning and contribute to referral problems in a particular family. The second section describes interventions used to improve family functioning, including both parent–child and marital relations. Throughout this chapter, case examples are discussed to illustrate family assessment strategies and family interventions used in MST.

Assessing Family Relations

General Overview

Assessment of family relations is an ongoing process that begins when the therapist first meets the family and continues throughout treatment as interventions are implemented and their effects are observed. Together, the therapist and family members observe and try to tease out the specific family interactions that are the most powerful, proximal predictors of the identified problems. Throughout this process, the therapist follows the iterative process of MST case conceptualization and intervention implementation described more fully in Chapter 2.

1. *Develop hypotheses* (e.g., explanations, hunches, or beliefs) regarding the relative contributions of familial factors to problem behaviors. Consistent with MST Principles 4 and 5 (present focused, targeting specific, well-defined problems; targeting sequences of behavior within or between multiple systems), hypotheses focus primarily on observable interactions and behaviors. For example, a therapist might hypothesize that the punitive and emotionally distant relationship between Ms. Jones, a single mother, and her teenage son, Joe, plays a primary role in Joe's verbal aggression and hostility toward female adults, including Ms. Jones and school teachers.

2. *Gather evidence* (i.e., information that was observed, self-reported, or concretely monitored, such as checklists, charts, check-in phone calls by stakeholders) to support or refute the hypotheses. Information gathered by the therapist about the Jones family might reveal that a combination of witnessing domestic violence between Mr. and Ms. Jones, Ms. Jones's inexperience as a disciplinarian, her social isolation following her recent divorce, and Joe's involvement with aggressive and hostile peers are as important as Ms. Jones's emotional distance from Joe in maintaining his verbally aggressive behavior toward female adults. Thus, the therapist's original hypothesis that mother–son emotional disengagement was a primary driver of Joe's behavior would be refined to incorporate domestic violence, social support, and other extrafamilial (i.e., youth peer relations) factors.

3. *Implement interventions* that target the key hypothesized contributing factors. In the example just used, such interventions might include helping Ms. Jones develop nonviolent relationships with men, identify and cultivate sources of support within her indigenous environment, facilitate Joe's involvement with prosocial peers, develop effective discipline strategies, and increase positive reciprocity in her relationship with Joe.

4. *Observe* whether the interventions result in changes in problem behaviors. The therapist checks with multiple informants and uses multiple methods to evaluate the ongoing effectiveness of family interventions. Therapists can interview and observe caregivers, the youth, siblings, teachers, peers, classmates, possibly neighbors and family friends, and other professionals working with the family. When behavior problems continue, therapists generate additional hypotheses about factors contributing to the fit.

5. *Identify* barriers to intervention success. Here, the therapist gathers information to support or refute additional hypotheses about factors contributing to identified problems. Returning to the Jones example, the therapist might learn that Ms. Jones's ongoing conflict with her ex-spouse is

interfering with interventions aimed at changing her discipline strategies, cultivating her social support network, and improving her relationship with Joe.

6. *Design interventions* to overcome these barriers. In the prior example, the therapist might need to develop one or more interventions to promote cooperation between Ms. Jones and her ex-spouse regarding childrearing strategies in order to accomplish other important interventions with Ms. Jones and Joe, such as increasing mother–son warmth.

Key Dimensions of Family Relations

To develop hypotheses about the relative contributions of familial factors to identified problems, the therapist must be able to organize his or her observations about family relationships (e.g., caregiver–child, marital) in a way that is easily communicated and understood by the supervisor, other members of the treatment team, and the family. These familial factors are described below.

Dimensions of Parent–Child Relations

Affect and control are the major dimensions along which parent–child (or caregiver–child) relations vary (Maccoby & Martin, 1983; Seaburn, Landau-Stanton, & Horwitz, 1996). Therapists need to have a clear understanding of the main functions of parental affect and control in children's social and emotional development. This understanding can contribute substantially to the therapist's ability to "make sense" of a particular youth's offending behavior and to develop a comprehensive conceptualization of fit.

WARMTH

The affect dimension of parent–child relations reflects verbal and nonverbal behaviors that are emotional in tone and that range from warmth to rejection. Warm caregivers are relatively accepting and nurturing and use frequent positive reinforcement (e.g., praise; verbal encouragement; humor; play; imitation; affectionate tones; a smile, hug, or pat on the back) when interacting with their children. On the other hand, neglecting caregivers are low in nurturance, and rejecting caregivers are both low in nurturance and relatively hostile, using criticism and even aggression when interacting with their children.

Caregiver warmth contributes to child development in two important ways:

1. Caregiver warmth affirms the emotional bond between caregiver and child in a way that can be understood by both. This affirma-

tion provides emotional security for the child and contributes to the development of a secure attachment.

2. Caregiver warmth also establishes and maintains a positive mood during interactions with the child. The induction of positive mood states in the child is crucial because it sets the stage for the development of empathy and teaches the child to value interactions with other people.

All of this helps to explain why children who experience low levels of positive affection (i.e., emotional neglect) and high levels of negative affection (i.e., emotional rejection) are at risk for the development of emotional and behavioral difficulties. Indeed, emotionally neglected and rejected children frequently lack the requisite developmental experiences for learning to trust and to respond empathetically to others. Thus, these children often view interpersonal transactions in a negative light and may lack the skills that are needed for initiating and maintaining positive interactions.

CONTROL

Caregiver control strategies can range from permissive to restrictive. Permissive caregivers provide their children with little structure and discipline, make few demands for mature behavior, and take a tolerant attitude toward their children's impulses. Restrictive caregivers, in contrast, are more directive, overcontrolling, and intrusive in regard to their children's activities.

Caregiver control strategies have several important functions in child development:

1. Caregiver controls teach the child to tolerate frustration.
2. Caregiver controls teach the child socially acceptable norms of behavior, including the avoidance of aggression, cooperating with others, and showing respect for authority.
3. By teaching the child to manage emotions and behavior, parental control prepares the child for interactions with peers and other adults throughout the life span.

When caregivers allow their child to behave aggressively toward them (or toward other family members) or when they often give in to the child's demands, they are teaching the child social norms that can promote aggression and noncooperation in the child's relations with peers. Similarly, when caregivers do not teach the child to respect their authority, the child is likely to have considerable difficulty interacting with adults outside of the home. The child's lack of respect for authority (or the belief that he or she has the same rights and privileges as do adults) can lead to problems in the child's interactions with teachers, with adult leaders of youth groups (e.g., coaches, band directors, scout leaders), with neighborhood residents, and, eventually, with the legal system.

PARENTING STYLE

Different configurations of affect and control in parent–child relations can be used to define different styles of parenting (Baumrind, 1989, 2005). These parenting styles include:

- *Authoritative* (high-control, high-warmth) caregivers:
  —Are responsive to the reasonable needs and desires of the child.
  —Make maturity demands appropriate to the child's developmental stage.
  —Have clear and well-defined expectations and rules regarding the child's participation in household chores, school performance, and interpersonal behavior with family members, peers, and adults outside the home.
- *Authoritarian* (high-control, low-warmth) caregivers:
  —Are directive and overcontrolling.
  —Require that children have an unquestioning obedience to parental authority.
  —Use fairly severe punishment (often physical) when the child deviates from parental rules.
  —Use a directive teaching style (i.e., physically taking over, or giving direct verbal orders) and do not invite the child's participation in decision making.
- *Permissive* (low-control, high-warmth) caregivers:
  —Provide their children with little structure and discipline.
  —Make few demands for mature behavior.
  —Tolerate even those impulses in children that meet with societal disapproval.
  —Are typically warm and responsive, but not demanding.
- *Neglectful* (low-control, low-warmth) caregivers:
  —Provide little discipline or affection to their children.
  —Appear to have little concern for or interest in parenting.
  —Are not responsive to the reasonable needs and desires of their children.
  —Do not expect responsible child behavior with respect to tasks or social relationships.

In general, research findings show that the *authoritative parenting style is associated with positive outcomes in youth* (e.g., high academic achievement, social responsibility, positive peer relationships), especially youth from European-American and middle-class families. The development of an authoritative parenting style, therefore, is often a target of family-based interventions in MST. In contrast, authoritarian, permissive, and neglectful parenting styles are linked with negative outcomes on various indices of youth functioning (Baumrind, 1991; Bornstein, 2002; Steinberg, Lamborn, Darling, Mounts, & Dornbusch, 1994). However, the negative consequences of authoritarian parenting might not be as severe among minority youth living in economically disadvantaged circumstances; these youth might benefit from a relatively more authoritarian parenting style (Steinberg et al., 1994) in which caregivers are more strict, vigilant, and controlling.

Although ineffective parenting style (e.g., permissive, authoritarian, or neglectful) is often identified as part of the "fit" of the referral problem, the factors that sustain a particular caregiver's style can vary from family to family. For some caregivers, a combination of work schedule, caring for younger siblings, and marital problems contributes to permissive parenting practices. For others, permissive parenting might be sustained by a lack of knowledge about effective discipline practices for adolescents and concern that warm parent–child relations will be damaged if the caregivers set limits. One authoritarian parent might implement harsh and arbitrary punishment because he or she believes such punishment to be effective and necessary, while another authoritarian parent verbalizes that he or she has tried to reason with the child to no avail, and thus resorts to physical punishment.

Dimensions of Interaction among Family Members

The present-focused and solution-oriented nature of MST is particularly consonant with structural (Minuchin, 1974; Minuchin et al., 2007) and strategic (Fisch et al., 1982; Haley, 1987) models of family therapy.

STRUCTURAL FORMULATIONS

Minuchin (1974) has suggested that *family structure*, or the repeated patterns of interaction that regulate family members' behaviors, can be discerned only by observing the family in action. In his structural model, the family's preferred patterns of interaction are reflected in the membership and boundaries of its subsystems.

- *Subsystems* can include one or more family members and are developed to perform essential functions (e.g., providing emotional support, socializing a child) in the family. Each family member belongs to several different subsystems, and membership is most commonly along generational and role lines (e.g., marital, parental, and sibling subsystems).
- *Boundaries* of a subsystem are the implicit rules defining (1) who participates and (2) what roles the participants take toward each other and

toward nonparticipants in carrying out the specific functions of the subsystem. *Clear boundaries* allow subsystem members to carry out their functions without undue interference while also allowing for communication across subsystems. Clear boundaries facilitate the development of healthy levels of individuality and mutuality in all family members. Subsystem boundaries that are too *diffuse* (i.e., "enmeshment") or *rigid* (i.e., "disengagement") are linked with child emotional and behavioral problems. Diffuse boundaries, for example, entail overinvolved and overdependent parent–child interactions and can fail to promote children's mastery of problems, independent achievements, and emancipation from the family. Rigid boundaries impede communication across subsystems, thereby limiting the family's capacity to respond to environmental stress and meet the affective needs of family members.

STRATEGIC FORMULATIONS

Strategic conceptualizations also inform the MST clinician's assessment of family functioning. To design interventions that effectively address interactions within and between systems (Principle 5), the therapist undertakes assessment of the "recursive sequences of behavior" (Haley, 1987) associated with an identified problem. The clinician's assessment of the family power hierarchy, or "who tells whom what to do" (Haley, 1987), is seen as a key step in understanding and mapping problematic patterns of interaction. For example, when a child refuses to comply with a reasonable request from his or her caregiver, the strategic model views the power hierarchy in the family as "confused" because the child occupies a more powerful position than the caregiver does. Constructs such as triangulation and parent–child (or cross-generational) coalition describe transactional patterns that confuse parent–child and spousal relationships, often in ways that involve the youth in the negotiation of marital conflicts.

Dimensions of Marital Relations

Generally speaking, successful marriages require that partners be able to love and feel loved, to honor their commitment to monogamy, and to experience the marital relationship as one in which they receive at least as much as they give. Over time, couples must deal with transitions associated with the development of each of their children, with work, with financial circumstances, community changes, and so forth. When major crises occur, families need to be adaptable, but not so adaptable that they are disorganized and unstable. Thus, marital partners must balance the need for stability and structure with the need for flexibility. Just as the major dimensions of parent–child interactions are warmth and control, so the major dimensions of marital interactions involve intimacy and power (Emery, 1994).

INTIMACY

Intimacy refers to the strength of the emotional bond between adults, and a positive emotional bond is important to the longevity of intimate relationships. When the emotional bond of marriage is strained by conflict, distance, or chronic imbalances in power, all family members can sustain deleterious outcomes. On the other hand, when couples are emotionally bonded and have the ability to resolve conflicts, family members are more likely to have secure emotional attachments, and stressors and crises are less likely to threaten the integrity of the family system.

POWER

Power refers to the relative influence of each member of the couple on the affective and instrumental aspects of the relationship. On the instrumental level, couples need to make decisions about financial concerns (earning, budgeting, spending), household tasks, parenting tasks, and obligations to families of origin and civic institutions. When marital roles are not clearly defined or couples lack the skills or motivation needed to successfully resolve conflicts about affective and instrumental aspects of the relationship, the marriage suffers. Moreover, marital conflict is associated with a host of emotional, behavioral, and relationship problems in children (Cummings et al., 2000); it can interfere with caregivers' abilities to deliver consistent discipline, model poor conflict resolution skills, and be very stressful to children.

How to Assess Family Relations

This section of the chapter describes and illustrates the MST approach to assessment of family functioning. The assessment of family functioning in MST is part of a broader assessment, introduced in Chapter 2, that identifies the strengths and weaknesses/needs that characterize each system in the youth's ecology. The broader assessment is conducted by the therapist in multiple settings (home, school, and neighborhood) using multiple sources, including family members, teachers, and extended family. The therapist's assessment of the family and other systems is updated as needed to reflect additional information obtained throughout the treatment process.

Assessing Caregiver–Child Relations

The therapist begins the assessment of parenting styles and family interactions during the first meeting with the family at their home. The therapist usually meets with the caregivers (e.g., parents, stepparents, grandparents, or other adults responsible for the youth's well-being), the identified "problem" youth, and his or her siblings. Typically, the therapist introduces himself or herself and briefly explains how MST works. The therapist usually explains, for example, that he or she is available as needed, will meet with family members wherever the action is (usually in the home, school, or neighborhood), may meet with other persons important to the youth and family, and can meet at different times during the day or evening. The therapist also explains the limits to confidentiality and ensures that the family has completed confidentiality forms and releases required by the provider agency. Then, the therapist speaks to each family member to obtain his or her name and family role (stepfather, grandmother raising the children, etc.). The therapist can also take the opportunity to briefly ask individual family members about their interests (e.g., a mother's flower garden, a teenage boy's skateboard). The therapist tries to get a direct response from each family member in order to define the situation as one in which everyone is involved and important. Following this brief social interchange with the family, the therapist can tap information about family relations in three distinct ways.

DIRECT QUESTIONING

Therapists ask family members questions about their own behavior and their perceptions of other family members' behavior. To begin, the therapist can ask each family member to give his or her view of the youth's presenting problem(s). To affirm the authority of the caregiver, the therapist gives top priority to obtaining the caregivers' responses. It is important, however, for the therapist to get each family member's perspective to learn about areas of agreement and disagreement in the family. Therapists are advised not to ask questions that probe for insight (these questions often begin with the word *why*) because such questions tend to elicit explanations from family members that focus on intrapsychic factors and the past. Although the therapist does need some information about how long a problem has existed and whether the family has tried treatment before, the therapist should always keep in mind that he or she cannot help the family to change the past. Questions that inquire about the "what" (e.g., What does your teenager do that presents a problem for you?) or "how" (e.g., How do you respond when your adolescent breaks a rule?) of parent–child relations are usually more productive because such questions keep the family members and therapist focused on present circumstances.

Parental Control Strategies. The therapist can ask a wide range of questions to assess control in parent–child relations. To assess parental control strategies, the therapist asks about:

- Rules in the home for the youth and his or her siblings.
- Parental expectations for the youth's school performance, participation in household chores, and interpersonal behavior.

- Parental responses (i.e., discipline) when the youth breaks a rule.
- The perceived effectiveness of parental disciplinary strategies.

Michael Miller was a 15-year-old ninth grader who lived with his mother and stepfather. Michael was referred for MST treatment because of delinquent activities, runaway incidents, drug use, and school misconduct. Mr. Miller had lived with Michael and Ms. Miller for 3 years at the time of referral. Michael's biological father was in prison, as was his 19-year-old brother. Mr. Miller had a disability that prevented gainful employment, yet he provided financial support for two children from a previous marriage. He also had intermittent problems with alcohol abuse. Ms. Miller worked rotating shifts at a local paper factory. Michael was arrested four times while committing acts of vandalism and car theft, and one of these arrests included an assault charge. Some of the arrests occurred when he stayed out all night after major family altercations.

During the clinician's first visit with Michael and his family, Ms. Miller reported that Michael's runaway incidents were precipitated by intense stepfather–stepson conflicts punctuated by mutual threats of physical violence. Neither Michael nor his stepfather volunteered their perspectives on the problem. Ms. Miller also reported that Michael's delinquent activity occurred primarily while Michael was on runaway status, though Mr. Miller disagreed with this assessment. The MST therapist had not yet obtained independent verification of this information (e.g., from police records, schoolteachers, neighborhood sources, family homework assignments tracking conflicts and behavior problems).

After obtaining the perspectives of the mother, stepfather, Michael, and later the school personnel, the therapist began to appreciate that variations of the following sequence of interactions within and between systems were critical to understanding the "fit" of Michael's school misconduct and his runaway and delinquent behavior. In recent months, the sanctions usually issued by the school for serious misconduct were in-school or out-of-school suspensions. When issued an out-of-school suspension, Michael did not go home, nor did he inform his mother or stepfather of the suspension. Thus, the school's perception was that Michael's parents were unresponsive to school efforts to sanction Michael's behavior. When the school and Ms. Miller did connect, she became angry and frustrated with Michael and with the school. Seeking support from her husband, she complained to him about Michael's behavior and about the school's apparent inability to control Michael and to contact her when problems arose. Mr. Miller responded by blaming Michael's behavior problems on his wife's lenient parenting practices. Marital arguments invariably ensued. If Michael was at home or returning home as these events were occurring, he would interrupt the marital disagreement and defend his mother verbally, which angered his stepfather and brought mixed responses from his mother, who was now angry with Michael and with her husband. The conflict between Michael and his stepfather escalated until the two threatened one another with physical harm. At that point, Michael often stormed out of the house and did not return until the next day or evening. Thus, the recursive sequences of family interaction that sustained Michael's behavior were part of a longer, more complex chain of interactions among participants within and outside of the family. The reports of the family members and key informants outside the family were necessary to understand this complex chain.

Warmth and Affection. To assess affective relations in the family, the therapist obtains information about:

- Verbal and nonverbal messages exchanged between the caregivers and youth in everyday interactions around instrumental issues (e.g., taking out the trash, completing homework on time).
- Caregiver praise in response to the youth's successes or positive behaviors (e.g., bringing home a good grade on a test, helping a sibling complete a chore).
- Caregiver expressions of interest in the youth's experiences at school, with peers, with other family members, and regarding hobbies or extracurricular activities.
- Expressions of concern regarding things that are not going well for the youth.

In some families, strong negative affect arises in the context of parent–adolescent conflict, as occurred frequently in the Miller family.

Although Ms. Miller initially voiced anger and frustration about Michael, the therapist obtained ample evidence of a positive mother–son bond (e.g., frustration gave way to concern once a therapeutic alliance was established; mother–son heart-to-heart talks occurred occasionally). In addition, the therapist learned that while Michael and his stepfather had grown very distant during the past 18 months, they reported that they had initially spent a few afternoons together (e.g., fishing at a local lake, attending a stock car race) when Mr. Miller moved into the home and reluctantly admitted that they might be willing to do so again. At the same time, however, arguments often escalated into shouting matches among all family members and threats of violence between stepfather and son.

The therapist should be alert to the expression of strong negative parental affect toward a youth. Expression of negative parental affect may be evidence of a poor caregiver–child bond if the negative affect occurs in the context of ongoing parent–child interactions that should be neutral or positive in affective tone. When this is the case, the therapist should assess whether emotional neglect or rejection is occurring, as evidenced by minimal parental responses to the youth's positive behaviors, rejection of youth efforts to engage in verbal interactions or parent–child activities, minimal awareness of the youth's concrete and emotional needs, and, in the case of a rejecting parenting style, consistently critical, belittling, or hostile responses to the youth even when he or she is engaged in neutral or positive activities.]

OBSERVING FAMILY INTERACTIONS

[What the therapist observes during early meetings with the family also represents an important source of information about how family members relate to each other. In fact, the therapist should never rely solely on the family's verbal self-description to assess family relations. Only by observing how the family members behave with each other can the therapist support or disconfirm hypotheses based on family reports.]

Beginning with the first meeting, the therapist should watch for non-verbal clues that confirm or contradict what the family is telling him or her. The therapist observes how the caregivers and youth speak to one another. For example, the caregivers might be too severe with the youth and his or her siblings or might pay little attention to them. What does the youth do in response to parental efforts to express affection or to gain compliance? The therapist might observe that one of the caregivers enters into a coalition with the youth against the other (e.g., by siding with the youth around discipline issues) or that the caregivers do not agree with each other about how to raise their teenager. As tentative hypotheses are formed about which aspects of parent–child relations are problematic, the therapist should not offer advice or share his or her observations with the family at this time to avoid arousing defensiveness. Instead, the therapist engages family members by showing helpful interest while listening to and observing the family.

During the first or second meeting with the family, the therapist should also arrange to observe the caregivers and youth interact long enough to obtain a sample of caregiver–youth affective relations and parental control strategies. During this "interaction stage" (Haley, 1987) or "family enactment" (Minuchin, 1974), the therapist gets family members to engage in interactions with each other rather than with him or her. That is, the therapist directs certain family members to interact with each other in a clearly delineated framework, in order to learn by listening to and watching how the family handles one or more types of situations. Typically, the therapist directs the family members to transact various aspects of parent–child relations that have been identified as problematic, such as trying to establish control over a disobedient youth, or attempting to resolve a parent–youth conflict. No matter how hard the family members try to involve the therapist in their interactions (e.g., by ignoring the therapist's directive and continuing to talk to the therapist) or object to discussing the problem among themselves (e.g., by telling the therapist that they have already discussed the issue and don't see the need to do so again), the therapist should direct them to talk with each other to demonstrate their typical interactions. The therapist might also wish to move the family members physically next to each other to facilitate their enactment. In all cases, the therapist's task is to bring the parent–youth relationship problems into the room rather than simply having the family members engage in a discussion about the problems.

> Jana Johnson, a 14-year-old eighth grader, was the eldest of three children living with her mother, Ms. Johnson, who had been divorced from Jana's father for 3 years. Mr. Johnson lived in another state, and Jana and her 10-year-old sister saw him once or twice a year. Jana was referred to MST by her probation officer for possession of marijuana and a misdemeanor charge related to a shoplifting incident. She was failing the eighth grade and had barely passed the seventh grade. When she did attend school, she often fell asleep, argued with teachers, and skipped classes. Jana's mother, Ms. Johnson, worked as a waitress in a local restaurant. Teachers reported that Ms. Johnson did not respond to school communications regarding Jana's behavior. When initially contacted by the MST therapist, Ms. Johnson announced that she planned to "send Jana off if she doesn't straighten up." Ms. Johnson also stated that the help offered to date by counselors, probation officers, and school personnel had been "useless."
>
> The therapist's initial assessment of strengths and needs in the Johnson family illustrated the importance of her observations of family processes in MST case conceptualization. One of the weaknesses identified by the therapist in her assessment of family functioning was "unclear intergenerational boundaries." To support the hypothesis that parent–child boundaries were blurred in this family, the therapist observed that when Jana and Ms. Johnson spoke to each other, conversations often revolved around Ms. Johnson's frustrations with her ex-spouse. Next, the therapist identified the possible impact of the boundary transgression on all family members (Jana, her mother, her younger sister, her father) and on the relationships between them. One apparent benefit was a momentary increase in intimacy between mother and daughter, whose interactions were generally highly conflictual. On the other hand, the mother's credibility as an authority figure and her capacity to execute effective discipline strategies for Jana was low. Given Jana's problems in school (truancy, failing grades, problems with authority figures) and with antisocial peers (drug and alcohol use, shoplifting), the benefits of increased mother–daughter intimacy obtained by transgressing generational boundaries did not appear to outweigh the costs.
>
> The MST therapist recognized that other factors within and outside the family system might also be maintaining Jana's behavior problems and gathered evidence regarding the relative impact of these factors in compromising Ms. Johnson's parental effectiveness. Identified factors included lack of knowledge of parenting strategies for adolescents;

lack of skill enforcing discipline because the father had been the disciplinarian prior to the divorce; lack of energy due to the demands of working while raising two children; and relative social isolation since the divorce. The therapist's observations of family interactions (including an enactment in which the therapist asked Ms. Johnson to talk with Jana about her truancy and other problem behaviors), examination of Ms. Johnson's work schedule, and conversations with Ms. Johnson confirmed the therapist's hypotheses about the importance of these factors in maintaining Jana's behavior problems. In trying to make sense of the "fit" for Ms. Johnson of the mother–daughter discussions of her marital problems, the therapist noted that Ms. Johnson experienced both emotional distress and increased social isolation after the divorce, and that these factors contributed to her initiation of conversations about her ex-spouse with Jana. Thus, the therapist's original systemic hypothesis regarding the primacy of inappropriate boundaries in maintaining Jana's behavior problems was refined to incorporate practical (work schedule), parenting, and social support factors.

ASKING FAMILY MEMBERS TO MONITOR AND RECORD PARTICULAR BEHAVIORS

The therapist can also obtain information about parent–child relations by having caregivers document specific behaviors and interaction sequences. To assess parental control strategies, therapists can ask caregivers to document all discipline attempts and responses to them. Specifically, the therapist can request that caregivers keep a daily record of:

- Youth misbehaviors.
- Each caregiver's response to those misbehaviors.
- The youth's compliance or noncompliance with each disciplinary attempt.
- Each caregiver's response to the youth's compliance and noncompliance.

The therapist then examines the caregivers' records to assess their disciplinary strategies, perceived effectiveness of these strategies, and parenting style (i.e., authoritarian, permissive, neglectful, or authoritative) reflected in these strategies.

Over a 2-day period in Michael Miller's family, for example, four out of five interactions about chores that occurred between Michael and his stepfather involved Mr. Miller issuing a command, shouting the command, and physically grabbing Michael to redirect him if the command was unheeded. The frequency and consistency of similar interactions and the complete absence of efforts to explain the rationale for the commands or to negotiate the activities on the chore list led the therapist to conclude that Mr. Miller had an authoritarian parenting style. Other evidence of authoritarian parenting included the following: punishment was often harsh or physical, punishment was not calibrated to the seriousness of the infraction (i.e., the punishment was excessive relative to the "crime"), and discussion or negotiation regarding rules was absent or rare, even when such discussion would be developmentally appropriate, as is the case in families with adolescents.

In contrast, therapist observations and a checklist completed by Ms. Johnson regarding her efforts to discipline Jana indicated that, outside of clearly established expectations regarding Jana's babysitting for her sister when Ms. Johnson was at work, no other rules regarding curfew, homework, or chores existed. Moreover, Jana was left to make decisions for herself that, at her age, typically require adult guidance (e.g., when to come in on weeknights, whether to get into cars with older boys). This and other evidence prompted the therapist to identify permissive parenting as a factor potentially contributing to Jana's problems.

Caregivers can also be asked to monitor and record behaviors reflecting the affective dimension of parent–child relations. To assess parent–child affective relations, the therapist might request that the caregivers keep daily track of:

- The youth's good behaviors and other successes at home, school, and elsewhere.
- Each caregiver's response to those good behaviors and successes.
- The youth's response to each effort by the caregivers to recognize positive youth behaviors.

Such monitoring can provide the therapist with a sense of the emotionally positive interactions between the caregivers and youth. As described in more detail later, the therapist should be precise (i.e., give clear instructions) when explaining the monitoring task to the caregivers and should have the caregivers review the task before completing it, particularly if the task is relatively complex.

Assessing Marital Relations

Couples treated in the context of MST may not immediately identify marital difficulties as a primary concern because the serious behavior problems of their children were the cause for referral for treatment. Often, couples will allude to marital difficulties only in the context of conversations about other topics, such as discipline. When describing a child's behavior problems, for example, a husband might report that he punishes the child for "back talk" while his wife does not. Or, a teenager might report that when her mother says she can't go out on Friday night, she asks her father, who will give her permission. Both of these examples signal interparental inconsistencies in discipline strategies, which, in turn, are often part of the "fit" of referral problems. In many instances, disagreements about parenting practices occur in the context of a troubled marriage. In some cases, other aspects of marital functioning are adequate and the couple does not consider disagreement about parenting practices important until they are able to appreciate that such disagreement contributes to the child's behavior problems. Finally, complaints about the way a spouse spends money or about how much or little time is spent with children, at work, or in leisure activities away from the home can also signal marital difficulties.

MARITAL INTIMACY AND POWER

When the therapist suspects that marital difficulties are contributing to the referral problem, he or she should arrange to interview the couple about their marriage when the children are not present. The therapist should use the initial interview with the couple to assess the level of intimacy and extent to which affective relations are positive or negative. A modicum of a positive bond is needed to motivate the couple to work toward the resolution of what often turn out to be long-standing problems and conflicts. The therapist can obtain information about affect from both verbal and nonverbal cues:

- How closely the partners sit
- Whether they make eye contact
- The tone of voice used
- Whether a question is sincere or rhetorical
- Whether a request is really meant as a command
- Whether an attempt is made to understand the spouse's perspective about a given issue

The therapist can also obtain information about marital affect by asking the spouses to describe each other's positive characteristics. Therapists must be aware that sociocultural differences sometimes influence the types of qualities listed by partners during this exercise. While highly educated and relatively affluent individuals might state that a spouse's humor or caring are positive qualities, less advantaged spouses might value the fact that the husband is a good provider or that the wife is a good cook. Because MST interventions are tailored to the unique strengths and needs in a marriage, the therapist must understand the marriage from the perspective of the couple's sociocultural context.

If either spouse has extreme difficulty describing positive qualities of the other, that spouse might truly feel that the other has little redeeming value. On the other hand, prolonged conflict in the marriage might have temporarily biased the spouse's view of the relationship. Couples who have experienced prolonged conflict have usually devoted considerable attention to the negative aspects of their relationship and little or no attention to the positive aspects. Caregivers whose children have a chronic history of behavior problems might also view the relationship negatively because the majority of their marital interactions, and interactions between the couple and the institutions (e.g., schools), agencies (e.g., juvenile justice, mental health, social services) and individuals (e.g., neighbors, parents of their child's peers) involved with the family, are negative. The following case example exemplifies this point.

> Mr. and Mrs. Rodriguez were referred to MST because they were having difficulty controlling their 15-year-old daughter, Angela. According to Mr. Rodriguez, Angela had become increasingly defiant of family rules (i.e., regarding curfew, chores, grades, and school attendance) over the past few years, and the police had recently found her drinking liquor with a 19-year-old boy late one evening in a local park. Mrs. Rodriguez described her husband as a harsh disciplinarian who had difficulty relating affectionately to Angela. She noted that her husband seldom spoke to Angela except to criticize her appearance and behavior. Mr. Rodriguez, on the other hand, stated that he did not believe his daughter should be coddled. He also stated that he felt hurt and betrayed because his wife often sided with Angela and against him on various family matters, including discipline. Mr. and Mrs. Rodriguez agreed that they were not sure if their marriage would last because they now spent so much of their time together arguing with each other and with school and juvenile authorities about Angela's behavior, and so little time doing anything that was fun.

When spouses have difficulty describing the positive aspects of their mates, the therapist should attempt to determine whether feelings of optimism can be generated about the relationship. To do so, the therapist might ask the couple to describe:

- What the relationship was like when they first dated.
- What attracted them to one another.
- What they used to do for fun.
- What their wedding day was like (ask to see wedding pictures if any are readily available).

The quality of a couple's sex life is also an indicator of the affective relationship in a marriage. The therapist can assess the quality of the couple's sex life by asking direct questions about the frequency of, and each spouse's satisfaction with, lovemaking. Although couples who rarely make love tend to be distant and those who have an active love life tend to be more intimate, there are many exceptions to this rule of thumb. An active sex life can occur within the context of a marriage characterized by serious disagreements. Again, sociocultural sensitivity should be used in assessing sexual aspects of the marital relationship.

MIXED MESSAGES

Couples who have experienced months or years of hostile interactions often have grave doubts about whether their marriage will improve. Since practitioners of MST are apt to be assessing the marital relationship in a family context characterized by multiple stressors and serious adolescent behavior problems, doubts about the marital relationship might not surface in the initial family interviews. Should such doubts become apparent, the therapist might decide to investigate the issue with the doubting spouse before meeting with the couple, as that spouse is more likely to tell the therapist how he or she really feels when the mate is not in the same room. During the interview, the therapist should state directly that he or she senses such doubt. The therapist should ask about the spouse's investment in marital therapy and in the marriage itself. During such an interview, the therapist can help clarify mixed messages in a way that opens the spouse to consider marital therapy.

PREDOMINANTLY NEGATIVE MESSAGES

Sometimes when therapists probe apparent ambivalence, they find that the spouse no longer wants the marriage. This is usually an implicit decision that has been made over the course of one or more years. Typically, the spouse has not acted overtly on these feelings for a number of reasons (e.g., fear of losing custody of the children, economic support, the social support of in-laws or relatives). As discussed later in this chapter, learning that one spouse aims to leave the marriage has important implications for the design of interventions.

Assessing Adjustment to Family Transitions: Divorce, Remarriage, Single Parenthood

In a significant percentage of families with a youth presenting serious antisocial behavior, the children have experienced one or more sets of difficult family transitions related to divorce, remarriage, and/or living in a single-parent family.

MARITAL SUBSYSTEM CHANGES

Divorcing spouses must accomplish several overarching tasks, including:

- Redrawing boundaries around intimacy (i.e., which areas of a former spouse's life the other spouse is allowed to access, under which circumstances, and for how long).
- Redrawing boundaries around power (influence over the events that occur in one another's lives with respect to children, finances, etc.).
- Separating marital roles from parental roles.

The therapist should be attentive to communications signaling role confusion, for example, disagreements regarding such issues as the clothing a child is wearing upon returning from one parent's home, leisure activities provided by one parent but not the other, and visitation schedules. Such disagreements may signal a parent's reluctance to relinquish control over the parent–child relationship between the ex-spouse and the child, or over the ex-spouse. Frequent unplanned phone calls to a former spouse, ostensibly regarding child-related matters, might also signal reluctance to accept the reduction in marital intimacy between spouses that occurs as a function of divorce. As the following case example suggests, the ex-spouses might also use the child to hurt the other in revenge for past grievances.

> Bobby Giordano, 13 years of age, was referred for MST because he had physically assaulted several peers in school, was frequently truant, and had run away several times, presumably in response to his mother's strictness. Bobby's mother and father had been divorced 6 years earlier. The divorce was extremely bitter, and neither parent had remarried. Each parent actively and covertly sought the youth's alliance and lobbied against the other parent. Mrs. Giordano referred to her ex-husband as a "drunken, no-good bum who doesn't care about anyone except himself." Although she "encouraged" Bobby to love his father, she also communicated indirectly that it was foolish to trust such a man. Mr. Giordano, on the other hand, was extremely permissive during Bobby's visits, encouraged Bobby to "punch out" any peers who got in his way, and periodically lavished him with gifts. These actions served to accentuate the mother's strictness and lower standard of living. Mr. Giordano also gave Bobby the message that he desired full custody. However, this message was intended more to provoke his ex-wife than to acquire increased access to Bobby.

PARENT–CHILD SUBSYSTEM CHANGES

When it appears that parenting practices contribute to referral problems in a family affected by divorce, the MST therapist should assess whether current practices predated the divorce or emerged after the divorce occurred, as interventions might vary accordingly. In Jana Johnson's case, for example, several aspects of parent–child relations contributed to the referral problem: Ms. Johnson had a permissive parenting style, was unable to monitor Jana's whereabouts consistently, and relied periodically on Jana for emotional support. The permissive style predated the divorce, while the monitoring and emotional support issues emerged as a result of the divorce.

CONCRETE AND PRACTICAL CHALLENGES

The therapist should also assess whether concrete and practical issues raised by the divorce are drivers for the youth's behavior problems. These challenges might include:

- Moving to a different home.
- Accommodating parent visitation schedules.
- Interacting with the legal system regarding divorce and custody issues.
- Working longer hours to compensate for financial losses associated with the divorce.

Increased work hours for the custodial parent, typically the mother, can reduce adult monitoring of the children and negatively influence the mother's own adjustment. The mother might also become isolated from her social support network when all her time is spent at work or engaging in child-care responsibilities, as was the case for Ms. Johnson.

PARENTAL DISTRESS

A caregiver's coping strategies can also contribute to the development of child behavior problems. Some ways of coping, such as depression or chronic hostility and anger, are particularly likely to interfere with the caregiver's capacity to engage in appropriate parenting practices. The second part of this chapter and Chapter 6 describe interventions to address parental depression, anxiety, and social isolation.

REMARRIED FAMILIES

Because the adults and children in most remarried families have experienced divorce, the therapist might also need to assess and address the divorce-related issues identified previously when working with remarried families. In addition, the formation of a new family group presents new challenges, and the therapist should understand the extent to which remarriage enhances or compromises effective family functioning. For some families, such as Michael Miller's, the potential benefits of the stepparent's presence (e.g., relieve financial stress, bolster the effectiveness of the custodial parent, increase the availability of adult supervision and monitoring) are mediated by the stresses of that parent's previous financial obligations (to children from a previous marriage), by mental health or substance abuse problems, or by persistent conflict that arises out of unclear expectations and role relationships.

As with families in which divorce has occurred, the therapist working with remarried families should assess the extent to which the problems in question predated the remarriage, were exacerbated after the remarriage, or first emerged after remarriage. If, for example, a youth's aggressive behavior and the permissive parenting style that appeared to maintain such aggression predated the current marriage, then a hypothesis suggesting that the new stepfather's authoritarian parenting is the primary factor contributing to the youth's problems would miss the mark. On the other hand, the youth's preexisting problems and parent–youth interactions that maintained them might be currently exacerbated by the stepfather's attempt to become the chief disciplinarian in the absence of an adequate affective bond with the youth, as occurred in the case of Michael Miller.

SINGLE-PARENT FAMILIES

When single-parent status occurs as the result of a divorce, the therapist should be sensitive to the potential contribution of divorce-related factors to the referral problem. In addition, when a single parent begins to date, the therapist might need to assess the role that significant others play in the life of the family. In many cases, the impact of parental dating is minimal, as the parent draws appropriate boundaries around the intimate relationship and parenting responsibilities. The extent to which the children experience the relationship as beneficial or detrimental is likely to vary in accordance with the factors that come into play in families reconstituted through marriage, including the quality of the relationship with the custodial parent, the quality of the relationship with the significant other, and the clarity of parenting roles. If a positive bond exists between the child and significant other and family functioning has been enhanced by virtue of the adult relationship, the end of the dating relationship might be experienced as a loss at instrumental and emotional levels for the child. If, on the other hand, the end of the dating relationship returns family functioning to a more positive pattern for the child, the loss might be welcomed with relief. In any case, when the pattern of relationships established by an adult caregiver regularly alters the experiences of children in the family, the children are likely to experience multiple transitions. As with children in remarried families, such experiences can result in diminished willingness to accommodate each successive transition.

In some cases, a parent's intimate relationships negatively influence family functioning, either because the boundaries between the adult and parent–child relationships are too porous (e.g., mother's boyfriend is allowed to discipline the children), or because the parent focuses on the adult relationship at the expense of the parent–child relationship. Sometimes, the parent becomes involved in successive relationships and the nature of parent–child and family interactions changes each time a relationship starts or ends. When the MST therapist suspects that a parent's intimate relationships with others contributes to the "fit" of the referral problem, he or she should identify the factors that contribute to a pattern in which the parent becomes involved with successive partners and allows that involvement to compromise effective family functioning.

- Is the parent's struggle to make ends meet eased when a partner is found?
- Does a single mother obtain relief from the stresses of monitoring and disciplining her children when the boyfriend steps in?
- What are the parent's sources of social and emotional support?
- Does he or she have the requisite social skills to develop a support system that does not involve an intimate partner?
- Is this a parent who first became a mother while still a teenager, and whose social development in the realm of adult relationships was compromised?

KIN AS PARENT FIGURES

For many families in MST programs, grandparents or other relatives are the surrogate parents, often assuming guardianship, if not legal custody, of the youth. In some of these cases, surrogate parents (e.g., foster parents) have had substantial involvement with the youth prior to assuming primary parenting responsibility. In other cases, several relatives have previously shared parenting responsibilities simultaneously or in succession. As with all families, the MST therapist assesses the family ecologies of kin acting as parents for the child. *When the child and his or her kin have not lived together for extended periods of time, the therapist should pay careful attention to assess the affective connections between the caregivers and the youth.* The therapist should also identify adult relationships within the kin network that can be used to support the caregiver and child, or that might present barriers to the development of a stable kin-and-child family group.

Treating Family Relations

General Overview

This section describes interventions that therapists can use to improve family relations. First, however, three considerations that apply across all family interventions are noted.

Interventions Are Individualized

Discussion of family interventions does not readily lend itself to a step-by-step or "cookbook" approach because MST interventions are individualized to address the specific constellation of intrafamilial and extrafamilial factors that sustain a particular adolescent's behavior problems. In all cases, however, decisions of where and how to intervene are informed by the continuous MST assessment process, through which evidence regarding multiple possible explanatory factors are "ruled in" or "ruled out," and judged to be more or less proximal (as opposed to distal) contributors to behavior problems on the basis of ongoing observation, implementation of interventions, and assessment of intervention outcomes (see Chapter 2).

Interventions Are Often Multifaceted

With most families referred for MST, we have found that simply giving advice and assigning homework rarely suffice. Interventions addressing parent–child and marital interactions, skill deficits, and social and practical barriers to effective parenting generally require the implementation of several techniques with ongoing monitoring of progress toward desired treatment goals. Some of the more complex interventions targeting parent–child relations in MST are derived from the structural and strategic models of family therapy. Although each of these models has its own language for describing relationship problems and therapeutic techniques, the intervention strategies used in these models have much in common (see Peake, Borduin, & Archer, 2000) and are readily integrated within the MST approach. As we discuss, therapists and their supervisors need to plan carefully to develop interventions that disrupt dysfunctional sequences of family interaction and replace them with more effective interaction patterns.

Interventions Must Be Prioritized

The flexibility of MST and the array of interventions available to the MST therapist can lead to confusion in determining the specific foci and sequence of intervening. The therapist's decision to use a particular family intervention is influenced by:

- A comprehensive MST assessment of the "fit" of the particular problem with the ecology (MST Principle 1).
- The other eight principles of MST.
- Empirical literatures regarding the effectiveness of the modality or technique with a particular problem.
- The therapist's good clinical judgment.
- Therapist skill level regarding the treatment technique.
- Therapist creativity.

Consistent with MST Principles 4, 5, and 9 (interventions are present focused and action oriented, targeting specific and well-defined problems; interventions target sequences of behavior within and between multiple systems; interventions should promote treatment generalization), the therapist's decisions regarding the nature of interventions, and the order in which they are implemented, are most often guided by "first-order" factors. First-order factors are immediately observable events in the everyday interactions within families and between families and external systems. Thus, for example, with a family characterized by practical challenges (e.g., lack of transportation, inadequate and overcrowded living conditions, caregiver's evening work schedule), limited parental knowledge and skill, and caregiver social isolation, the therapist would likely implement interventions targeting the practical and caregiver knowledge and skill problems prior to implementing interventions designed to increase social support, though the latter might follow soon thereafter.

Changing Parent–Child Relations

When it becomes apparent that a child's behavior problems are being maintained by ineffective parenting styles (e.g., permissive, authoritarian, neglectful) or parent–child interaction patterns, the therapist and caregiver(s) identify factors across the family's social ecology that might be sustaining the ineffective style or interaction pattern (see Figure 3.2, discussed later in this chapter), as intervention strategies vary depending upon the role each of these factors plays. Then, the therapist tailors interventions to the particular strengths and needs of the parent, family, and social ecology. First, however, the caregivers must be engaged in the treatment process.

*Sustaining Rapport and Motivating Parents to Change
(Building Parental "Buy-In")*

Caregivers are often frustrated with their child's problematic behavior and with the challenges of trying to control such behavior. Caregivers may also feel that they have somehow failed their child. The therapist who indicates, implicitly or explicitly, that the caregivers are responsible for the youth's problems will have difficulty establishing a cooperative relationship with the caregivers and is unlikely to facilitate favorable change. Thus, as described in Chapter 2, therapists generally should align with the caregivers (e.g., by providing emotional support and highlighting any positive aspects of parenting) while assessing family factors that might be linked with identified problems. Following the development of a therapist–caregiver alliance, many caregivers are able to acknowledge their frustration and openly ask for help. For other caregivers, frustration can lead to angry blaming of the teen and to rejection of others' suggestions that change is possible and may require effort on the part of the caregiver.

In light of the variety of ways that caregivers can respond to the suggestion that parenting practices might need to be changed, therapists should have several strategies in their response repertoire. The goal of each strategy is to avoid unnecessary confrontation with the caregiver while ensuring that the importance of change is understood. Therapists may find one or more of the following strategies useful for clarifying the importance of change by caregivers:

- The therapist can explain the negative effects of continuing current parenting practices for the youth. The therapist can tell permissive caregivers, for example, that impulse control problems and antisocial behavior can be a result of giving in to the youth's demands or allowing the youth to behave disrespectfully toward authority. Similarly, to authoritarian caregivers, the therapist might explain that extreme punitiveness toward the youth can evoke anger and resentment toward the caregiver. To those authoritarian caregivers who use physical discipline with the youth, the therapist should also explain that, aside from being ineffective, such discipline is likely to be viewed by most youth as an invasion of their personal space and a sign of disrespect for their physical integrity. Thus, physical discipline can be humiliating to the youth and have a negative effect on the youth's relationship with caregivers.

- For those caregivers who are not very concerned about the negative consequences of current parenting practices for the youth, the therapist can point out the negative consequences of those practices for the caregivers' own lives (e.g., frequent absences from work to deal with the youth's school and legal problems; aversive interactions with school, neighbors, and police; parenting-related stress that may exacerbate physical health problems).

- The therapist can also ask the caregivers to talk about everything they have tried to do (including current parenting practices) that failed to solve the youth's problems. This discussion gives the therapist the opportunity to emphasize what has not worked before and to make a list of those strategies. If the caregivers notice that everything they have tried to do has failed, they may be more likely to listen to what the therapist has to offer.

- The therapist can also project the caregivers into the future and have them talk about possible long-term, negative consequences for the youth (e.g., incarceration, failure to develop employment skills) and family if something does not change. The caregivers might decide that they would like to alter their parenting practices to increase the likelihood that their child will mature into a responsible adult.

Once the caregivers understand that change is necessary, the therapist can help the caregivers develop alternative parenting practices and make important changes in parent–youth relations. When caregivers show continuing reluctance or outright refusal to agree to engage in parenting interventions, the therapist and team should consider and address a number of potential barriers to engagement (e.g., substance abuse, psychiatric disturbance, marital problems, faulty beliefs about parenting, practical challenges, and low commitment to parenting) and address those barriers directly, as described in later sections of this chapter.

Changing Discipline Strategies

When a youth's behavior problems are being maintained by a caregiver's discipline strategies, the therapist has three general tasks in providing caregivers with alternative strategies:

- Caregivers must learn to set clearly defined rules for the teen's behavior.
- Caregivers must develop sets of consequences that are inextricably linked to the rules. That is, when an adolescent complies with the rule, positive reinforcement occurs; and when he or she does not comply, a negative consequence (i.e., punishment) occurs.
- Caregivers must learn to effectively monitor a teenager's compliance or noncompliance with rules, even when the teen is not in the caregiver's presence.

Munger (1993, 1999) has detailed the steps in accomplishing these three tasks in two simple (but not simplistic) books for parents, entitled *Changing Children's Behavior Quickly* and *Rules for Unruly Children: The Parent Discipline Bible,* respectively. The key concepts and practices that MST therapists should be able to teach are summarized below.

RULES

Consistent with MST Principle 4 (target well-defined problems), the primary purpose of rules is to clearly define desired and undesired behaviors, which often become goals of treatment. The therapist should adhere to the following guidelines when helping caregivers make and enforce rules:

1. The expected behavior should be defined so clearly and specifically that anyone else can tell whether or not the behavior has occurred.
2. Rules should be stated in terms of positive behaviors (e.g., Jim will be inside the house at 9:00 P.M. on school nights, as opposed to Jim will not be late).
3. The privilege that will be given or withheld when the rule is kept or broken should be listed with the rule.
4. Rules should be signed, dated, and posted in a public place in the home (e.g., refrigerator door, cupboard, near family calendar).

5. Rules should be enforced 100% of the time.
6. Rules should be enforced in an unemotional manner.
7. Privileges should be dispensed or withheld every time a teen complies with, or breaks, a rule.
8. Praise should be used in addition to the dispensation of the privilege.
9. When two parents are involved, rules should be mutually agreed upon and enforced by both parents. (Factors underlying a couple's apparent inability to collaborate as parents, and potential remedies, are discussed later in this chapter.)

REWARDS AND PUNISHMENTS

To teach their children good behavior, caregivers need to identify and control belongings and privileges the adolescent wants and enjoys. Caregivers should not manipulate "basic privileges" (e.g., shelter, food, clothing, and love), however (Munger, 1993, 1999). Note that basic food refers to meals, not to snacks, desserts, chips, and so on, which caregivers can use as optional privileges. In addition, caregivers should not generally withhold "growth" activities that contribute to the child's prosocial development (e.g., church groups, athletic teams, scouts). On the other hand, playing video games, going out on Saturday night, and using the phone are not growth activities.

Any reinforcer that is not a "basic" or "growth" privilege is considered an "optional" privilege. Caregivers can use such privileges as a reward for good behavior or withhold them as a punishment for problem behavior. To be effective, the punishment must be experienced as aversive by the youth, and the reward must be highly desired. Many activities and items fall into the optional category, and caregivers will likely need help identifying them. Consistent with MST Principle 6, effective rewards and punishments will vary with the child's developmental level. *For younger teenagers*, optional privileges might include such activities as playing with the X box, watching TV, or having a favorite snack. Younger teens also generally find activities with a caregiver, such as going to a park or baseball game, rewarding. *For older adolescents*, optional privileges might include going to the mall, non-basic clothing, telephone time, or watching TV. Adolescents also generally enjoy spending time with their peers.

Several guidelines should be followed for the effective dispensation and withdrawal of privileges:

1. As noted above, the privilege must be highly desired by the child/adolescent.
2. The younger the child, the more frequently the desired behavior must be rewarded.
3. For youth of all ages to see that good behavior "pays off," the behavior must be rewarded frequently.

4. The privilege must be tied to a specifically stated rule about a behavior that is desired. The link between the rule and the positive or negative consequence is critical to changing the behavior.
5. The age of the child is an important consideration when making rules. Caregivers might need help with matching their expectations and demands to the cognitive, emotional, and physical capacities of their children.
6. Caregivers must discuss the nature of the rules and privileges with their children before the structure is implemented. Children and adolescents should understand what is changing, what will be expected of them, and what to expect from their caregivers when strategies designed to change their behavior are put in place.
7. When a teen is being raised by two parents, the parents must develop rules and consequences jointly and enforce them consistently.

To help caregivers effectively implement effective rules, privileges, and consequences, it is usually necessary to articulate them on paper so the caregivers and youth can track daily whether the rule has been followed. As noted above, these rules should be clearly defined, enforceable 100% of the time, and posted in a public place in the home. The sample chart shown in Figure 3.1 is based on the case of 15-year-old Tia, who had been arrested for

Date: Week of November 2–8

Rule	Privilege	Consequence	Day	Rule followed? (Yes/No)
1. Tia stays in all classes in school all day each school day.	Tia can go out until 8:00 P.M. after homework is done.	Tia cannot go out after homework is done. No cell phone or computer use that day.	Mon. Tues. Wed. Thurs. Fri.	Yes Yes Yes No
2. Tia is in the house on school nights (including Sunday night) by 8:00 P.M.	Use of cell and home phone until 10:00 P.M. Leisure use of computer until 10:00 P.M.	No cell or home phone use. No computer leisure time (can use computer for homework only).	Sun. Mon. Tues. Wed. Thurs.	Yes Yes Yes Yes No
3. Tia is in the house by 10:00 P.M. Friday and Saturday nights.	Extension of weekend curfew to 11:00 P.M. the next weekend.	Weekend curfew set back to 9:00 P.M. the next weekend	Fri. Sat.	

FIGURE 3.1. Sample behavior chart with rules, privileges, and consequences.

disturbing the peace with older, drug-using peers at midnight on a school night and whose referral problems included truancy. The week after establishing this chart, the therapist and caregivers had gathered enough information about Tia's peers to identify three deviant peers. Thus, for the following week, they modified the chart to add a rule that Tia could not call or see any of these three peers, with associated privileges and consequences.

IMPLEMENTATION: INCREASING CHANCES FOR SUCCESS

After the behavioral chart delineating rules and consequences has been developed, it is time to implement these changes in behavioral expectations. Developing a chart is one thing, but monitoring behavior and implementing consequences are quite another. Therapists should assure that the caregivers are prepared for implementation.

Prepare for Conflict. Although always hopeful for a smooth resolution of the problem, the therapist should prepare caregivers for the likelihood that their adolescent will react negatively to increases in family structure, and caregivers should expect that youth will "test" the new rules. In anticipation of such testing, the therapist should be prepared to support the caregiver in "sticking with" the program and finding support for appropriate parenting from other adults (spouse, relatives, other parents) in the natural environment (see Principle 9). Permissive caregivers are particularly likely to need support when their children test new rules. Such caregivers sometimes feel they would rather live with the youth's obnoxious behavior than with the negative reaction the adolescent displays in response to new rules. To address this understandable feeling, the therapist should help the caregivers to appreciate that the consequences of giving in are likely to extend beyond their home and negatively affect their child.

> Barbara Walker had considerable difficulty controlling her 16-year-old son, David, who was referred to MST after a long history of delinquent offenses, including stealing and wrecking his neighbor's car and selling his mother's jewelry to pay for new stereo equipment. Mrs. Walker, who also had two younger boys (ages 9 and 11 years), told the therapist that she loved David and would rather live with his irresponsible behavior than have to establish rules for him and listen to the "constant whining and complaining" that would follow. The therapist needed to remind Mrs. Walker multiple times that although she was willing to live with the abuse that her son directed toward her, doing so supported his antisocial behavior outside the home (with concomitant risks of injury and incarceration) and set a poor example for his younger siblings. The therapist devoted considerable time throughout treatment working with Mrs. Walker and David in negotiating rules that he was able to follow and Mrs. Walker was willing to enforce.

Enforce Rules Unemotionally. Caregivers should try to enforce rules in an unemotional way. Caregivers should avoid badgering the youth to follow the rules and allow the decision regarding compliance to be made by the youth. If rules are well written, there should be little argument about whether the rules were followed. Thus, the caregiver should not respond to the youth's attempts to argue about this issue. Families are not courts of law, and caregivers should feel free to run the household as benevolent despots, especially when dealing with youth who are presenting serious behavioral problems. Moreover, caregivers are more likely to enforce rules if punishments provide some payoff to the caregivers. With adolescent antisocial behavior, for example, punishments might include washing the caregiver's car, scrubbing the bathroom, and cleaning windows.

When Well-Implemented Consequences Are Not Working. Occasionally, when treating a youth who engages in serious antisocial behavior, the therapist will find that the youth's behavior does not change even when the caregiver has learned and consistently exercised appropriate control strategies (e.g., use of rules and concomitant provision and withdrawal of privileges, use of punishments aversive to the teen and helpful to the parent). In such cases, the therapist and caregivers may consider implementing more drastic consequences for behavior. For example, the caregivers might inform the youth that failure to meet curfew will result in being locked out of the house. Although such a consequence deprives the youth of a "basic" privilege (shelter), the therapist and caregivers might need to use such an extreme approach to increase the probability that the youth will begin to respond to treatment efforts. The therapist and caregivers should undertake radical strategies only after other approaches fail, after supervision is sought, and after local law enforcement and social service agencies are informed of the caregivers' plan. Such strategies are occasionally used in MST, are generally successful in changing the youth's behavior, and do not result in harm to the child or in legal difficulty for the therapist. Again, the therapist should carefully consider and discuss the ethical and legal implications of such strategies with the clinical supervisor, provider agency, and community agencies that have legal mandates either to protect or to prosecute youth or their families.

Stay Positive. Finally, given the likelihood that the youth will react negatively to increases in family structure, the therapist might need to provide the caregiver with frequent reminders to maintain a positive perspective about his or her parental role. Indeed, as the therapist helps the caregiver adopt more effective discipline strategies, the caregiver may begin to equate parenting solely with enforcing discipline and lose sight of the fact that being a caregiver is first and foremost an emotional connection with the youth. Caregivers should set limits on their children's behavior out of love and concern for their children's psychosocial development. Yet, some caregivers need to be reassured that they can be *both* loving and firm with their children. It is easy for the caregiver (and sometimes the therapist) to lose sight of the positive emotional connection between the caregiver and youth when the caregiver is struggling to establish control over the youth's misbehavior and the youth is doing everything in his or her power to make the caregiver feel miserable about using discipline.

> Peter Davis, age 17 years, had dropped out of school two years earlier and had a long history of delinquent offenses involving unruly conduct, habitual disobedience, vandalism, and theft. A few months earlier, he had driven his mother's car without her permission to visit a friend who had moved almost 200 miles away. More recently, he had taken and cashed a check from a neighbor's mailbox to obtain money to buy concert tickets. Although charges for the latter offense had been dropped, it was only a matter of time before Peter would be convicted of an even more serious offense. Indeed, several members of his current peer group had been incarcerated during the past year for burglary and grand larceny.
>
> Mrs. Davis, Peter's mother, was a successful real estate agent who had been divorced almost 6 years at the time that Peter was referred to MST. In addition to Peter, she had two daughters, ages 16 and 20 years, both of whom also lived at home. Mrs. Davis was a warm and nurturing parent to all of these children, but she lacked disciplinary skills. Fortunately, with the exception of Peter, Mrs. Davis's other children were well behaved, helped with various household tasks, and had productive lives outside the home (i.e., the youngest daughter did well in school, and the oldest daughter had a full-time job). All of the children were extremely courteous and well mannered. Peter was an attractive, interpersonally skilled adolescent who related warmly to everyone, including the therapist. When asked about his mother's complaints, Peter stated that he had been looking for a job and was willing to follow any rules that his mother established for him.
>
> During the next 2 months, the therapist worked closely with Mrs. Davis and Peter in negotiating rules regarding curfew, peers, household chores, and obtaining a job. However, despite Peter's verbal acknowledgement of the rules, he consistently ignored them and failed to comply with Mrs. Davis's disciplinary efforts. Peter was an apparent master at excuses, blaming his continued noncompliance on a poor memory and other circumstances that were beyond his control (e.g., he could not keep curfew because he did not have a watch to keep track of the time). Similar excuses were offered for Peter's failure to remain employed, despite the fact that the therapist and one of Peter's aunts had helped him to obtain two different jobs. The situation was further complicated by Mrs. Davis's own job, which demanded long and irregular hours and limited her ability to closely monitor Peter's behavior.

It was clear to everyone that Peter was a relatively bright, interpersonally skilled adolescent who had few intentions of using his abilities productively, though he apparently wanted to be treated as an adult. Moreover, in the absence of further intervention, Peter was headed for a life of crime and might seriously injure himself or others. Thus, with the therapist's assistance, Mrs. Davis established a timetable during which Peter was to obtain a job and assume greater household responsibilities. Mrs. Davis allowed Peter 5 weeks (until his 18th birthday) to accomplish these tasks. Failure to accomplish the tasks would result in Peter's expulsion from the home. Because it seemed unlikely that Peter would comply with his mother's requests, plans were established to assist Mrs. Davis in expelling and keeping Peter out of the home (e.g., locks on the doors were changed, and Mrs. Davis informed Peter that she would call the police if he tried to force his way into the home). In addition, criteria were established for Peter's possible return into the home following his expulsion.

As expected, Peter was forced from the home on the date set by Mrs. Davis. For approximately 3 weeks, Peter lived in the homes of various friends. However, because neither these friends nor their parents wished to feed and clothe an 18-year-old adolescent who refused to provide financial reimbursement, Peter quickly wore out his welcome. Peter soon decided that it was in his best interests to obtain employment and to assist his mother with other household responsibilities. Peter returned home for a month, quit his job, and was again expelled from his mother's home. Two weeks later he again obtained employment and was permitted to move back into the home. One year later, he remained employed and was still living in the home. He was also attending night school in an effort to earn his high school equivalency diploma.

Changing Family Relations during Treatment Sessions (Family Therapy)

After the therapist (1) has identified patterns of parent–child interaction that contribute to the identified problems and (2) has persuaded the family that change is necessary, the work involved in altering and improving parent–child relations can begin. One of the most effective strategies that the therapist can use is to implement changes in parent–child relations while the family members are communicating with each other during the session. This strategy is especially effective because it allows the therapist to intervene directly in a problematic interaction sequence and to immediately observe the impact of the intervention on family relations. As noted earlier, there is considerable value in having the family enact instead of describe their interactions. This holds true whether the therapist is attempting to assess problems in family relations, intervene in family relations, or assess the impact of an intervention on family relations.

Assigning Tasks within the Session: Encouraging Communication

The therapist can use a variety of tasks to create a framework for intervening with family members during sessions. Tasks can range in complexity and should be closely linked with treatment goals established collaboratively by the family members and the therapist. The following list includes some widely used techniques that the therapist can use to encourage intrafamilial communication:

- The therapist can simply *ask the family members to talk among themselves about a given topic*. For example, the therapist might begin a session by asking the caregivers and youth to talk with each other about the youth's recent behavior problems in school.
- The therapist can *find opportunities to direct two or more family members to talk with each other* during the natural flow of conversation during the session. For example, when a youth complains to the therapist that the father never spends any time with him, the therapist can tell the youth, "Talk with your dad about that, and give him some suggestions about things you would like to do with him." After the youth has spoken directly to the father, the therapist can encourage the father to respond to the youth and, in doing so, can begin to open lines of communication between the two. In subsequent instances in which one family member is talking about the behavior of another member, the therapist may only need to point or look at the other member before the speaker begins to talk directly with him or her.
- The therapist can *use a task* to draw attention to certain family interactions and to suggest changes. For example, in a family with an older, domineering sibling and a younger, submissive sibling, the therapist might ask the caregiver to prevent the older child from interrupting the younger child during the session.
- The therapist can *manipulate position and space* to emphasize the need for communication between two or more family members. For example, the therapist might ask a mother and father to sit next to each other as they talk with their son about a family plan to reduce his drug use. When asking the caregivers to talk with their son, the therapist might also move his or her chair further away from the family to emphasize the need for the family members to talk with each other and not to the therapist.
- In those families in which a caregiver lacks effective communication skills or has difficulty controlling his or her emotions, the therapist can *use role play* with the caregiver (i.e., to rehearse what the caregiver will say) prior to meeting with the entire family. The role play allows the therapist to shape the content and delivery of the caregiver's communication and helps the caregiver anticipate and plan for possible responses from the youth.

Thus, the likelihood the caregiver will be successful in communicating with the adolescent is increased.

Changing Family Structure

The therapist can make use of structural interventions to alter maladaptive transactions in the family to improve (1) individual boundaries and/or (2) subsystem boundaries. In both cases, the therapist can employ tasks (i.e., directing family members to interact with each other in a clearly delineated framework) to mark boundaries.

SUPPORTING DIFFERENTIATION

To promote individual boundaries, the therapist (and eventually the caregivers) can introduce and enforce simple rules during sessions, such as:

- Family members should listen to what another family member says and acknowledge his or her communication.
- Family members should talk directly to each other, but not about each other.
- Family members should not answer questions directed to another family member or act as the memory bank for the entire family.

Such rules should be introduced at times when they are immediately relevant to the family members' current interactions with each other or with the therapist. By blocking the flow of communication along its usual channels, the therapist can begin to alter the family's recurrent sequences of interaction in a way that promotes individual autonomy.

The therapist can also work with the caregivers to insure that the children in the family are differentiated, receiving individual rights and privileges according to their age and position in the family. For example, as noted earlier, the caregivers should consider the children's ages when assigning household chores and developing rules for everyday activities such as eating, watching television, taking baths, getting dressed, going to bed, and the like. When the autonomy of children in a family seems to be hampered, the therapist should help the family to recognize and celebrate differences between the children (e.g., hanging one child's artwork and another child's poem or essay on the refrigerator door for everyone to see). The therapist can also help the caregivers to assign responsibilities and provide rewards that are consistent with each child's developmental stage. Problems with individual boundaries are often an issue in families with an authoritarian caregiver, and the therapist should be alert to the need for interventions in this area.

CHANGING SUBSYSTEM BOUNDARIES

The therapist might also need to use interventions that target subsystem boundaries. In single-parent families, the therapist might need to promote stronger affective bonds in one or more parent–child subsystems while also strengthening the boundaries around the executive (i.e., parental) subsystem in ways that support parental authority over the youth. Likewise, in two-parent families, the therapist might need to support decision making in the executive subsystem, particularly with regard to childrearing. In addition, in two-parent families in which one parent forms a stable coalition with a child against the other parent (i.e., a father–mother–child triangle), the therapist must often work to redefine the boundaries around several subsystems: strengthening the spouse subsystem boundary so the couple can negotiate marital issues without involving a child (or another third person), weakening the boundary surrounding the overinvolved caregiver and child, and strengthening the boundary around the underinvolved caregiver and child. In some families, the therapist might also need to develop interventions that protect the sibling subsystem from undue parental interference so that the children have the opportunity to learn skills for living with peers. The therapist can accomplish these and other boundary changing interventions using a wide range of in-session strategies, including:

Blocking Transactional Patterns. The therapist can block the usual sequence of interactions in a family to strengthen the boundary around one subsystem and to weaken the boundary around another. For example, when an older child consistently interrupts his mother to translate her communications to the other children in the family, the therapist can block the child's interference, thus allowing for increased contact between the mother and the other children and appropriately weakening the older child's position of authority in the family. Using this and other interventions (e.g., role play, coaching), the therapist can help the mother take charge of parenting with all of her children.

Assigning Tasks to Subsystems. The therapist can assign a task to one or more subsystems in the family to address the affect and/or control dimensions of parent–child relations. For instance, the therapist might ask an emotionally distant stepfather and stepson to plan a mutually enjoyable activity for the forthcoming week. At the same time, the boy's mother and the therapist can sit in another room and discuss parenting issues, thus drawing a boundary around the mother as primary disciplinarian for her son. The task of planning an enjoyable activity can help to improve the stepfather–stepson relationship and can also have a positive effect on the marriage, such that the mother feels supported by her husband for her parenting efforts.

Changing the Group Composition. The therapist can also strengthen boundaries by working selectively with different subsystems in the family. For example, the therapist might begin a session with an entire nuclear family consisting of two parents and their four children so that parent–child affective relations can be generally addressed. Later in the session, the therapist might send the children to another room so that the therapist and parents can discuss parenting or marital issues. In the next session with the same family, the therapist might meet with the parents and only the two oldest children to discuss discipline problems that do not involve the younger children.

Revealing Underlying Conflict. In families in which conflict is hidden and not productively resolved, the therapist might need to probe for differences between family members on a given issue and encourage them to discuss their differences. This strategy is most likely to be useful with caregivers around issues pertaining to parenting strategies or marital relations. For example, in families in which one caregiver does most of the talking about parenting (or the marriage) and states (or implies) that the other caregiver is in complete agreement, the therapist should always explore whether this is actually the case. The therapist can empower the less talkative caregiver (e.g., by pointing out that the caregiver seems very intelligent and undoubtedly has his or her own ideas about the issue under discussion) in an effort to encourage the caregiver to express his or her own opinion. Caregivers of youth presenting serious antisocial behavior are almost never in complete agreement about parenting strategies or their own relationship, and the therapist should always encourage each caregiver to express his or her own views so that underlying conflicts can be identified and resolved.

Joining in Alliance or Coalition. The therapist might temporarily join one or more family members or subsystems against another in an effort to draw subsystem boundaries. This strategy is often useful with families or couples that rigidly deny or defuse conflict (even though it is apparent to the therapist that family members are not working together to solve problems). Joining in a coalition can also be used with highly enmeshed families (those with weak boundaries) to enable family members to develop differentiated rules and appropriate support. When using this strategy, it is crucial for the therapist to convey some support to non–coalition members to avoid alienating them. The entire family must always sense that the therapist is ultimately allied with them. For example, during a session in which a stay-at-home mother and her teenage son continue to convey to the father that he is a failure (i.e., by criticizing the father's low paying job and the family's general lack of resources), the therapist might align with the father by telling him that he seems to be doing the best that he can for his family at the present time and asking him to talk about his hopes for the future. By focusing on the father's good intentions, the therapist attempts to elicit support from the mother for the father. If successful, this effort weakens the mother–youth coalition and temporarily strengthens the parental dyad until more direct marital interventions can be provided.

Reframing Behavior or Symptoms. The therapist can relabel a family member's behavior to change the way that other family members perceive and respond to that family member. For example, when a mother's behavior is described by her husband and children as overcontrolling and intrusive, the therapist might comment that the mother seems to be very concerned about the welfare of her children and is trying to demonstrate her concern. By highlighting a positive and previously hidden motive behind the mother's behavior (i.e., a strength-focused intervention), the therapist begins to create a context for new transactions between the mother and the other family members.

Achieving Intensity. Changing parenting strategies or parent–child interactions is often difficult and requires a good deal of practice. Thus, the therapist should expect to engage the family in within-session practice around a given issue over the course of several or more sessions and to assign homework that requires practice between sessions. Issues related to the assignment of homework tasks in such situations are discussed later in this chapter.

Strategy and Sequence in Family Interventions: An Extended Example for Enhancing Affective Relations

The structural and strategic models of family therapy both emphasize the role of therapist planning in the development of interventions to change family transactional patterns. This emphasis is particularly consonant with the iterative process of MST case conceptualization and intervention implementation. When developing plans for changing family transactions, the therapist and supervisor should carefully consider how to sequence interventions *both within and across sessions.* Planning for a session should not be done at the last minute and should be given enough time and discussion within weekly supervision meetings for the team to reach a general consensus about the nature of the treatment strategy and its implementation. In the absence of careful planning, the therapist can waste a lot of time during sessions, and the family might lose interest and motivation to change. Of course, even the best developed session plans are sometimes disrupted by unexpected events (e.g., a family crisis) or new information that the family reveals to the therapist during the course of a session. Nonetheless, the therapist should not be easily steered away from the plan and goals for the session. And, the session plan and goals should be consistent with the goals for treatment that have been collaboratively developed by the family and therapist.

The following transcript illustrates how the therapist can sequence interventions within a single session to help meet an important goal of treatment with the family of a chronic juvenile offender. The youth, Ryan, had a history of 10 arrests for theft, burglary, and physical assault (against male peers, a police officer, and a school principal). Ryan was incarcerated in a juvenile detention setting for approximately 2 months following the most recent assault (school principal), at which time the charges were dropped and Ryan returned home. At the time of his referral to MST, Ryan was again running the streets with his deviant peers and had just been kicked off the school baseball team because of truancy and poor grades. The therapist's assessment revealed, however, that Ryan was very bright and socially skilled. The therapist hypothesized that Ryan's antisocial behavior and involvement with deviant peers were fueled by several salient family factors, including permissive parenting, a strained mother–son emotional bond, and an incarcerated father who modeled violent behavior.

During the first three sessions with the family, the therapist had spent considerable time alone with Ryan's mother addressing her reluctance to set limits on her "out of control" son. Shortly after the fourth session, by which time the mother had begun to develop rules and set limits on Ryan's behavior (including a curfew), several of Ryan's friends came to the family's home, broke down the front door with an ax, and threatened the mother to "leave our boy alone or else." The mother called the police, and the boys were arrested shortly thereafter. The mother, however, was understandably shaken and hesitant to set further limits on Ryan's behavior. Nevertheless, the therapist persuaded the mother during the fifth session to stick to her new rules at least temporarily. In the meantime, the therapist and supervisor concluded that Ryan's mother would have difficulty controlling her son as long as he remained more attached to his deviant peers than to his mother. Thus, the plan for the sixth session was for the therapist to use a sequence of interventions *designed to increase mother–son warmth.*

The following excerpt begins about 2 minutes into the sixth session. The therapist starts the session with Ryan, his mother (who is divorced from Ryan's father), and his 8-year-old sister. The therapist included the younger sister in the first part of the session to obtain an additional source of information (besides Ryan and his mother) about Ryan's recent behavior around the home.

THERAPIST: (*to Ryan*) So, it sounds like you decided not to argue with your mom about going out with your friends?

RYAN: (*to therapist*) I didn't want to fuss about it. I just went to my room and went to sleep.

MOTHER: (*to therapist*) Uh-huh. He did.

THERAPIST: (*to Ryan*) Why didn't you want to fuss about it?

RYAN: (*to therapist*) I don't know why I didn't.

THERAPIST: (*to Ryan*) You're slipping, Ryan.

RYAN: (*to therapist*) What?

THERAPIST: (*to Ryan*) You're slipping.

RYAN: (*to therapist*) What do you mean?

THERAPIST: (*to Ryan*) Well, you've got to huff and puff if you are going to get your mom to give in on this.

MOTHER: (*to therapist*) I had to go back twice and check myself. You know, I said, "Ryan, you went out Friday night, that should have been enough...."

RYAN: (*to therapist*) Well, I went outside and she thought I was leaving. I said I had to get my bike. I came in, shut the door, and just went in the room and then I fell asleep.

THERAPIST: (*to sister*) What do you think about this change in your brother?

SISTER: (*to therapist*) I think it is pretty good since he's leaving me alone now. Last night I had to give him the last piece of my pizza for a necklace. And my mom said, "You should be ashamed of yourself, you two...."

MOTHER: (*laughing, to sister*) " ... greedy asses."

(*Therapist and family laugh together.*)

SISTER: (*to mother and therapist*) No, "Two crazy child I have."

THERAPIST: (*to sister*) So your brother is leaving you alone?

SISTER: (*to therapist*) Uh-huh.

THERAPIST: (*to sister*) He's not giving you a hard time?

SISTER: (*Shakes her head no.*)

THERAPIST: (*to sister*) Are you giving him a hard time?

RYAN: (*to everyone*) Sometimes.

SISTER: (*to therapist*) Mostly.

The therapist is satisfied that Ryan is beginning to follow his mother's rules for curfew and appropriate behavior in the home. The therapist now sends the two children from the room and meets privately with the mother to draw a boundary around the parental subsystem. The therapist also begins to lay the groundwork for a subsequent intervention involving the mother–son subsystem.

THERAPIST: It sounds like the past several days, actually the last week or so, has gone really well. I know you were feeling really frustrated for a while.

MOTHER: I sat down with him and told him that I'm just going to have to cut everything off. No going this or there. He's going to have to come straight home from school, no more weekends, no more nothing. Just start staying at home until he learns. Then I told him when he got 16, I'm going to get him in the service (*laughing*). And he says, "I ain't quitting school." I said, "Well, if you can't learn to behave, then I'm going to get you in the service." (*long pause*) Hey, something has changed! Now I say, "Ryan why don't you go on to your room." And he says, "Can't I stay here?" So....

THERAPIST: What do you think about that?

MOTHER: Well, it's a big change. At least he is getting out, coming in with the family. He's not being a loner like he was, you know, hanging to himself. He's starting to come out and be with us more. The other night, we all sat in the living room watching cartoons, just laughing. I had made popcorn and he's sitting right beside me and he kind of nuzzled up to me. And I said, "What's that for?" And he said, "You got the popcorn." (*Shares laugh with therapist.*) I'm kind of proud of him now. He minded me! Yeah ... me! (*Laughs.*)

THERAPIST: So what does that tell about you?

MOTHER: Did I do this, or was he just tired?

THERAPIST: No, I don't think that's it, Melinda.

MOTHER: So, but he's been asking me now, "If I go out tonight, am I allowed to go out?" (*pause*) He has edges that need to be curved off. Least we've got some parts of it shining. I just am hoping that when the summer comes up, he won't say, "Oh heck, I don't have school, I don't have to keep these rules now."

THERAPIST: I think that is totally up to you. I have no doubt that he'll test it.

MOTHER: Yeah.

THERAPIST: He'll push the limit and he'll be outside staying out until 2 or 3. You'll need to hang tough. I think you can do it. He will challenge in every possible way. You can really hang in there and really show him where those limits are.

MOTHER: He has to test me quite a while before I give up ...

THERAPIST: Have you told Ryan all of these good things?

MOTHER: Yeah. Ryan's been hearing them.

THERAPIST: Does he?

MOTHER: That what? What people been saying?

THERAPIST: That you're proud of him?

MOTHER: Oh yeah.

THERAPIST: That you're proud of him and it's nice to have a nice atmosphere at home. And there's a lot less tension.

MOTHER: Well, not so much I've told him, but he knows, you know.

THERAPIST: What's going to happen if you don't tell him?

MOTHER: Well, when I try to tell him, he goes, "Oh Mom, God, I don't want to hear this."

THERAPIST: Well, you know that's the way he is. Is he grinning while he's doing it?

MOTHER: Yeah, he's grinning.

THERAPIST: So, what does that tell you?

MOTHER: And then if I don't come in [to his room], he says to me, "What did you say about the room?" I say, "It looks nice, looks OK." And he says, "I thought you'd say that. Nobody can do it like I can do it."

(*Mother and therapist laugh together.*)

THERAPIST: In the past you've said he has Marvin [his father] as a role model. And how a man is supposed to work or he ends up in prison and stuff. You told him that a lot. And sometimes that can become what they call a self-fulfilling prophecy, which means you say it often enough and it becomes true. I don't think Ryan has to be like his dad. You know in some ways it would be neat to be like his dad, but his dad is . . .

MOTHER: They are just like two peas in a pod, though.

THERAPIST: He has a chance not to go to prison. I think when you tell him, "You are just like your dad," he gets a picture in his head that is what his life is going to be like.

MOTHER: Yeah.

THERAPIST: Even if you see a lot of similarities that's OK, but I think he has to start having a different picture of who he is.

MOTHER: (*Nods.*)

THERAPIST: "That picture of my life is not the way I want it. It doesn't have to be that way." So, how might you go about telling him that?

MOTHER: Oh, just telling him, "Try not to be like others. Do things what you feel like you want to do yourself, not cause anyone expects it of you." Naturally, it's an old saying, "You're just like your daddy. You're just like . . . " It's just a cliché. It's been going on for years.

THERAPIST: It's an easy one to follow.

MOTHER: I guess I've been led in that pattern. "You're just like so and so" (*points at her head*), and that's kind of what we are supposed to say, and we just sort of carry on the tradition.

THERAPIST: Pretend I'm Ryan.

MOTHER: (*Laughs.*) Here we go again.

The following sequence is a role play in which the therapist is slouching in her chair and pretending to be Ryan. The therapist is preparing the mother to talk with Ryan later in the session. The mother's last comment ("Here we go again") implies that she has participated in role play with the therapist before and that she did not relish the experience. Although parents may be reluctant to engage in role play because it usually demands new skills from them, this is exactly the reason that role play can be used to facilitate parent–child relations.

MOTHER: OK, Ryan, you know, I said a lot of things, "You are like your daddy" and all. You got good qualities about yourself, and you know who you are and you know what you want to do. I think you ought to try to find Ryan and do what Ryan wants.

THERAPIST: God, Mom!

MOTHER: I know you don't want to hear this, but … you got to do for yourself. You can't do what everybody else wants you to do and expects you to do.

THERAPIST: I know! God, Mom!

MOTHER: If you expect you want to play ball or whatever, you got to go for Ryan. You got to make yourself believe you can do it and work towards it. That's all you got to do is work for what you want.

THERAPIST: OK, OK.

MOTHER: And you just can't be like everybody else. You got to be like what you want to be.

THERAPIST: But you tell me that I'm like my dad all the time.

MOTHER: Well, I know I do. I shouldn't do that. I should tell you different. I should tell you to be yourself.

THERAPIST: Do you think I am like my dad?

MOTHER: No, you're not like him.

THERAPIST: How am I different?

MOTHER: You're Ryan. You have Ryan's ways.

THERAPIST: What does that mean?

MOTHER: What's that? It means that Ryan wants things out of life and Ryan wants to work for things, but Ryan thinks it should be handed to him. Ryan should work for his goals.

THERAPIST: Do you think I'm going to go to prison like Dad?

MOTHER: Well, if that what Ryan wants, Ryan's going to get it. But if Ryan doesn't want that, Ryan won't get it. Ryan's got to work for what he wants. If Ryan wants to be a street walker, Ryan will be a street walker. If he wants to be the mayor, then he's going to have to work for the mayor's position. Don't follow behind everybody else. Be a leader, not a follower.

(The role play ends at this point and the therapist sits up in her chair.)

THERAPIST: Good job. You are really great at coming up with ideas. Really emphasize with him that "Hey, I see a lot of ways that you are different than your dad. You really try hard, you really care. I don't think you're going to have the same life as your dad." Really emphasize that.

The therapist leaves the mother in the room, returns with Ryan, and sits next to the mother to provide support and encouragement as the next task begins. The therapist asks the mother to begin by letting Ryan know that she is proud of his recent efforts to follow her rules. As noted earlier, the overarching objective of the session is to increase mother–son warmth.

MOTHER: Ryan, Momma wants you to know ... that I have been very pleased with you and the way things have been going with you asking and around home, and I feel that there has been a lot of tension let off of you and me, and we kind of enjoy being around each other a little bit more than what's necessary. It's a real nice pleasure to have you home again, son. (*Laughs.*) And, I want you to also know that, you know, in the past I always said, "You are just like your daddy" and stuff like that which, you know, I really shouldn't be saying because you are you, Ryan.

RYAN: Huh?

MOTHER: You are you, and you might do things, but I think it's because I just keep saying it. I really should be saying that you are your own self. You know, you've got your own mind, your own ways, and you can do what Ryan wants to do instead of following in everybody else's footsteps. It's you ...

RYAN: I want to play baseball.

MOTHER: You want it. You've got to go for it. You've got to reach out and touch it. AT&T. (*Laughs.*) This is AT&T here—reach out and touch somebody.

The therapist moves and sits next to Ryan to encourage him to respond to his mother and to provide him with support during this difficult task.

THERAPIST: What do you want to say back to your mom?

RYAN: What?

THERAPIST: Do you want to say anything back to her?

RYAN: I don't have anything to say but thanks for the compliment.

THERAPIST: Has it been nice for you at home?

RYAN: Yeah.

THERAPIST: What's it been like having your mom not yelling at you all the time?

RYAN: It's a nice feeling.

THERAPIST: It's a nice feeling not having her yell at you? How does it feel to sit and talk and laugh with your mom?

RYAN: It's OK. Except sometimes when we're laughing, she messes with me.

THERAPIST: (*Laughs.*) She teases you?

RYAN: Yeah, I don't know.

THERAPIST: Do you think she cares about you?

RYAN: Yeah, I'm not used to it.

THERAPIST: So it sounds like your mom cares about you.

RYAN: Yeah.

THERAPIST: Do you care about your mom?

RYAN: (*Pauses.*) Yeah.

THERAPIST: Can you tell her that?

RYAN: I don't know.

THERAPIST: Ready?

RYAN: No.

THERAPIST: Mom ...

RYAN: No, I can't.

THERAPIST: Come on.

RYAN: No, I can't. Mom ... (*long pause*)

THERAPIST: I really care about you.

RYAN: I know.

(*Everyone laughs.*)

THERAPIST: Well, tell her then so she knows.

RYAN: Mom, I really care about you.

MOTHER: Thank you.

The therapist's encouragement and persistence with both Ryan and his mother led them to reach out to each other in a warm and affectionate way at the end of the session. The sequence of interventions within the session reflected careful planning and execution on the part of the therapist and also set the stage for interventions across subsequent sessions. Indeed, as the relationship between Ryan and his mother continued to improve over the next month, the therapist was able to guide the mother in implementing interventions that removed Ryan entirely from his deviant peer group and that encouraged his association with peers who valued academic achievement and athletic success.

Designing Homework Tasks

To expedite treatment gains and enhance generalization of favorable changes in family relations, the therapist should also develop and assign "homework" tasks for the family members to complete outside of treatment sessions. In most cases, these tasks are designed in ways that are consistent with interventions that the therapist and family members have enacted during sessions. That is, these tasks should address the same boundary issues and transactional patterns that are the targets of within-session interventions. The therapist can use homework tasks to reinforce within-session changes or as a vehicle for initiating changes that the family has struggled to make within sessions. In either case, the therapist's development of such tasks requires careful planning and should not be done hastily at the end of a treatment session. The following guidelines (Haley, 1987) can help the therapist ensure that homework tasks are well designed, and therefore more likely to be effective in altering family relational patterns.

PERSUADE THE FAMILY TO COMPLETE THE TASK

The motivational strategies described earlier for building parental "buy-in" are relevant to both within-session tasks and homework assignments. In addition, the way in which the therapist presents the homework task to the family can help elicit cooperation. For example, the therapist can tell families who enjoy challenges or are more energetic that the task will be relatively large or difficult, whereas the therapist can tell families who are more reluctant or less energetic that the task is relatively small or easy. Similarly, if the family is orderly and logical in their manner, the therapist can present the task as one that is orderly and logical. It should be emphasized, however, that the therapist should not anticipate noncompliance from a family when designing a task. If the therapist works collaboratively with the family in setting goals, focuses on family strengths, and provides a reasonable explanation as to why a task is necessary, family cooperation is likely.

KEEP IT SIMPLE

The therapist should make the assignment simple enough so that the family can carry it out. The task should not add to the concrete or practical challenges faced by the family members and should be possible for them to accomplish in their situation.

FIT THE TASK TO THE FAMILY

The task should require an organizational change in how the family members behave toward each other. For example, with an underinvolved father and son who would like to improve their relationship, the therapist can use the father and son's mutual interest in basketball to design a task that fits the family. The therapist can ask the father and son to visit the local recreation office to inquire about opportunities for the youth to play on a team and perhaps for the father to serve as a volunteer assistant coach. To promote parental cooperation in the same family, the therapist might design another task requiring the mother and father to travel to the son's basketball games together and to jointly plan and cook dinner on days when the youth is playing basketball. Whatever the nature of the task, the therapist must design the task in a way that takes the usual problematic sequence of behavior into account and interrupts that sequence.

BE PRECISE

The therapist should give clear instructions to the family members about what is to be accomplished. Rather than making a suggestion (e.g., "Maybe you might be willing to do … ") or asking a question (e.g., "Why don't you try doing … ?"), the therapist should be direct and precise about what is to be done (e.g., "I would like you to … " or "I want you to … "). If the therapist is not sure that someone in the family understands the task, the instructions should be clarified. By being clear and precise, the therapist can help to ensure that the task will be completed.

INVOLVE EVERYONE

The therapist should involve everyone in the family in accomplishing the task to put the emphasis on the entire family unit. One member can be directed to plan the task, two others to carry it out, and another to help or supervise. For example, if the task is that a stepmother and stepson should talk about some issue during the week, other family members (e.g., father) can be given various responsibilities such as reminding the stepmother and youth that it is time to talk. Depending on the purpose of the task, the therapist might also decide to exclude one or more family members (e.g., a same-age sibling) from the task.

REVIEW THE TASK DIRECTIONS

In general, the therapist should have the family members review what they are expected to do. The therapist should include all of the family members in the discussion and should anticipate possible problems in completing the task, including ways that the family members might try to avoid the task. In many cases, family members will mention likely barriers to task completion. By discussing possible barriers to completing the task and helping family members generate solutions to those barriers, the therapist can increase the likelihood that the family will commit to and complete the task.

DISCUSS TASK OUTCOMES DURING THE NEXT SESSION

After the task has been assigned, the therapist should ask the family to report on the task during the next session. If the family has completed the task, the therapist should congratulate the family members and the session can continue. Depending on the family's overall progress in changing their transactional patterns, the therapist might decide to assign similar or new homework tasks to the family in the future. On the other hand, when the family has only partially completed the task or has not done any of the task, the therapist should determine the reasons. In some instances there are practical reasons for the family's failure to complete the homework as assigned. Once the therapist helps the family address these practical barriers, it is often possible for the family to complete the task and move ahead in meeting treatment goals. In other instances, however, the family might not be able to provide the therapist with a valid excuse for not completing the task. The therapist should not ignore or easily excuse failures to complete an assigned task and should attempt to determine the barriers to the intervention. As these barriers are identified, the therapist can revise the conceptualization of fit and design interventions to address the barriers.

Addressing Factors That Contribute to Problems in Parent–Child and Family Relations

A schematic tool often used by MST therapists to clarify barriers to effective parenting is illustrated in Figure 3.2. Common barriers include concrete needs (housing, heat, transportation, etc.); knowledge, beliefs, and skills specific to childrearing; commitment to childrearing; parental depression or anxiety, mental illness, or substance abuse; child characteristics; and problems in the marital (divorced, remarried) subsystem. If the therapist does not take these factors into account when initially designing interven-

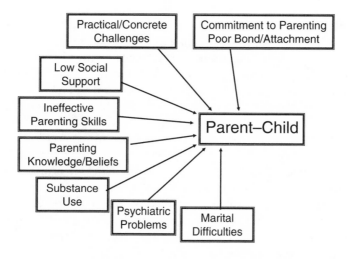

FIGURE 3.2. Barriers to effective parenting.

tions, the factors can emerge as barriers to intervention success. Thus, the therapist and team should examine the following potential barriers to successful outcome in the initial design of interventions and when trying to understand why an intervention might have failed.

Cognitions about Child Rearing (Knowledge and Beliefs)

When assessing the role of beliefs and cognitions in maintaining ineffective parenting practices and problems in caregiver–youth relations, the therapist should attend to caregiver language signaling unrealistic expectations about the youth's capacities and motivations and should collect evidence regarding the correspondence between these beliefs and parenting behavior. A caregiver might state, for example, that an 11-year-old should "know better" than to loiter near gang territory after school or that a 14-year-old can decide for himself whether attending school is in his best interest. Some caregivers, often those with authoritarian parenting styles, protest that rewards are "bribes" and that youth should comply with caregiver requests and demands simply on the caregiver's authority, as the caregiver did when he or she was an adolescent. Other caregivers might believe that their teen's misbehavior is motivated by malicious intent aimed at the caregiver.

UNDERSTAND THE BASES OF BELIEFS

When evidence indicates that caregiver misconceptions or faulty beliefs are helping to sustain caregiver–youth relationship problems, the therapist should attempt to understand the bases for the beliefs prior to making attempts to change those beliefs. For example, a caregiver's continued use of harsh physical punishment might be associated with a belief that "it was good enough for me." That is, the caregiver points out that he or she was raised similarly and "turned out fine." If the MST therapist has developed a strength-based approach to treatment, he or she, indeed, is likely to recognize many ways in which the caregiver has "turned out fine." Thus, we have rarely found it useful to dispute the caregiver's stance, appeal to changing times, or cite facts and figures about the deleterious effects of harsh physical punishment. Instead, we often point out ways in which this particular youth appears to be suffering difficulties (e.g., suspensions, involvement with the law, and whatever other problems resulted in the youth's referral for MST) that may warrant alternative, perhaps even radical-sounding, approaches to discipline. Such an approach might increase caregiver receptivity to the idea that different types of discipline might be needed to benefit this particular youth. By focusing on the caregiver's ability to help the youth and on the long-term negative consequences of the youth's present behavior, the therapist is more likely to promote caregiver cooperation.

ADDRESS COGNITIVE DISTORTIONS

The therapist might also find that both the caregiver and youth possess cognitive distortions that contribute to parent–child conflict. The following case provides a good example of how such distortions might be addressed (also see Chapter 6).

> Mr. Hill believed that his 15-year-old son, Robert, should respond to all parental requests with absolute obedience, while Robert was convinced that his father's limit setting would ruin his life. To assist Mr. Hill and Robert in changing distortions that contributed to the fit of the identified problem targeted for MST treatment (in this case Robert's burglary of several homes in his neighborhood), the therapist reframed the distorted cognitions and helped the family members identify various aspects of unreasonable thinking. Thus, the therapist described (reframed) Mr. Hill's hotly contested efforts to set an age-appropriate curfew for Robert as arising out of concern for Robert's safety and well-being, rather than as a deliberate attempt to control Robert's every move. Moreover, for Robert to develop a more objective understanding of what motivated the behavior of his father, the therapist taught more effective communication (e.g., listening, stating the problem in nonblaming terms) and interpersonal problem-solving skills to father and son. In addition, the therapist implemented interventions that monitored and tested the validity of faulty beliefs. The therapist asked Robert to list specifically how his life might be ruined by a curfew, and relevant observers (i.e., Robert and Mr. Hill) monitored how frequently

those things occurred within a week and what consequences ensued. In this and other cases, the ruinous consequences anticipated by the youth or parent seldom come to pass (i.e., the cognitions are distortions); thus, the therapist then helps the youth and parent to recognize that the beliefs were not confirmed and designs interventions that support more accurate appraisals. In the present case, Robert's curfew had prevented him from attending a valued extracurricular event (i.e., a high school football game), and the therapist modeled for Mr. Hill (1) how to calmly interrupt Robert's predictable complaint that his life had been ruined and (2) how to acknowledge that Robert was disappointed about missing the event. The therapist also pointed out that missing the game did not lead to Robert being rejected by peers—the dire consequence predicted by Robert.

FLEX TO CAREGIVER STRENGTHS AND WEAKNESSES

The therapist should develop strategies to increase caregiver knowledge regarding effective childrearing practices. The therapist's selection of strategies should be based on a careful assessment of the amount of teaching, practice, and therapist involvement needed to increase the likelihood that a particular caregiver will be able to implement the new practices. Therapists might need to remind authoritarian caregivers that children and adolescents *learn* to behave correctly, and that such learning occurs when good behavior is rewarded. Such learning requires *both* explanation and caregiver action. Caregivers who use reasoning alone (as permissive caregivers often do) to try to change the behavior of a child are not likely to be successful. On the other hand, children have considerable difficulty learning what is appropriate and what is inappropriate behavior when consequences are delivered without explanations (as sometimes occurs with authoritarian caregivers, described earlier). Thus, therapists should aim to support an authoritative style of child rearing—providing both explanations and consequences—among caregivers.

Just as interventions implemented with caregivers should be sensitive to the developmental needs of the child or adolescent (Principle 6), so, too, the therapist should assess the level of cognitive development of caregivers when designing interventions. We have worked with many families in which the primary caregivers had stroke-related memory problems, were characterized by very concrete thinking, or were borderline or below in intellectual functioning. In these cases, expert consultation has usually been sought from professionals in neuropsychology and adult developmental disabilities to assist in translating the objective of an intervention (e.g., increasing parental monitoring) into intervention plans that could be effective given the caregiver's memory problems or developmental disability. In one case, for example, a system was used in which colored stickers differentiated calendar days to prompt a grandmother to call the school. In another case, an alarm clock was set for 6:00 P.M. daily and the phone numbers of two neighbors were placed on the clock to facilitate a mother's ability to retrieve her 13-year-old son at curfew time and seek assistance from neighbors if she could not find him.

Social Support

The availability of social support is consistently linked with positive marital adjustment, effective management of parent–child problems, and a host of other positive family outcomes (Pierce, Sarason, & Sarason, 1995). Indicators of a lack in social support include caregivers who engage in few social interactions outside of work and childrearing, are unaware of the experiences other caregivers might be having with their children, or complain that there is no one to talk with. By virtue of the MST therapist's frequent contact with multiple aspects of the neighborhood and community in which the family is embedded, she or he is in a strong position to assess the quantity and quality of social support available to family members. Chapter 7 devotes considerable attention to the assessment of social support and to the development of interventions that enhance the support that families need to sustain favorable treatment gains.

Psychiatric Disorders

Caregiver mental health problems such as depression, anxiety, or more serious psychiatric disturbance can clearly interfere with the caregiver's capacity to effectively nurture and supervise his or her children. Chapter 6 guides the therapist in the identification of such problems and provides protocols for delivering evidence-based psychosocial interventions (e.g., cognitive-behavioral therapy) and supporting caregiver access to evidence-based pharmacological interventions. Because well functioning caregivers are viewed as critical to the effective treatment of youth behavior problems, significant attention is devoted to the identification and treatment of adult psychopathology by the MST therapist.

Caregiver Substance Abuse

Likewise, caregiver substance abuse is often a critical barrier to treatment effectiveness in families receiving MST. Caregivers with substance abuse disorders are often unable to provide the stability and consistency in parenting needed to ameliorate the serious antisocial behavior presented by adolescents. Fortunately, effective treatments of adult substance abuse have been developed during the past 15 years, though few have been transported to community-based providers. In light of this treatment development research as well as our own extensive experience in the area of substance abuse treatment during this same time period, a new chapter has been added to this MST treatment text. Chapter 8 focuses on the delivery of evidence-based substance abuse interventions that can be integrated into MST for the treatment of substance abuse disorders in adolescents and adults.

Practical Challenges and Basic Needs

Family members have great difficulty learning, growing, and changing when their physical, health, and safety needs are not being met. When practical problems in living interfere with a caregiver's capacity to meet the youth's needs, therapist strategies typically focus on helping the family to connect with people who can provide additional services and support. If, for example, a caregiver works long hours for subsistence-level wages and is, therefore, both unable to monitor her teenage son's whereabouts and too exhausted to cultivate positive affective interactions with him, the therapist can implement several possible strategies. One course of action might be to determine whether neighbors, members of the extended family, or friends are able and willing to assist with monitoring the son after school so that he is not "on the streets" while the mother is at work. Note that consistent with Principle 9 and the more extensive description of building social support in Chapter 7, emphasis is placed on developing indigenous family supports versus agency supports. The therapist might also assist the mother in find-ing higher-paying employment or in accessing sources of financial support made available through public service agencies. In such a case, mother–youth affective relations might improve when financial stressors are attenu-ated and monitoring strategies are sufficient to reduce the son's troublemak-ing in the streets. In either case, the therapist's primary responsibility is to help the family develop and implement strategies to overcome identified barriers to change.

Lack of Commitment to Parenting

In some cases, multisystemic strategies to change caregiver–youth interac-tions are met consistently with halfhearted attempts, inadequate follow-through with homework, or sheer lack of response from the caregiver. Usu-ally, such caregiver responses are related to the factors described previously (knowledge, beliefs, concrete needs, depression, etc.) or occur because the MST clinician is pursuing goals not shared by the caregiver, has not imple-mented interventions properly, or has implemented interventions that do not match the nature of the problem. Periodically, however, assessment of the factors that sustain ineffective parenting and present barriers to change indicates that a substantive lack of commitment to parenting is present. As always, assessment and subsequent interventions require that the therapist understand the caregiver's perspective: Why has this caregiver decided to raise children but not attend to their affective and instrumental needs adequately? For some caregivers, career aspirations or economic necessity are the first priority, and the long hours devoted to income generating activities sap the time and energy needed to attend to their children. Alternatively, the demands associated with caring for other family members such as a chronically ill child or an older caregiver may render the needs of the youth referred for treatment less pressing in the eyes of the caregiver.

When evidence clearly suggests that lack of commitment is a primary barrier to meeting a youth's emotional and developmental needs, therapist strategies typically focus on helping the caregiver change his or her attitudes and behaviors. Such change can sometimes be accomplished by helping the caregiver understand the youth's need for affection, focusing on the importance of the caregiver's love and guidance for the youth, and examining the long-term costs of ignoring the youth.

Laying the groundwork for change might require the therapist to identify aspects of the caregiver's life that can be enriched by increasing involvement with the youth. For example, Mr. Watson perceived that his business, reputation, and marriage suffered considerably due to his son's criminal behavior and the demands of court appearances, attorneys' fees, and restitution. Thus, Mr. Watson did not wish to engage in activities related to his 16-year-old son and stated that if the boy was "old enough to be a criminal," he was "old enough to be on his own." In this case, the therapist's appeals for Mr. Watson to salvage his son's future fell on deaf ears. Instead, the therapist promoted engagement by focusing on the father's self-interest. The therapist pointed out that Mr. Watson's increased involvement with his son might reduce the youth's criminal behavior and, therefore, the father's need to leave work, pay legal fees, and prop up his own reputation in the community. Once Mr. Watson agreed to work with the therapist, subsequent discussions focused on the ways in which Mr. Watson's "hands-off" approach and angry stance toward his son failed to have the desired impact on the son's behavior, on alternative strategies that might be effective, and on the many ways in which the boy needed his father's guidance.

In summary, and as delineated in the initial chapter of this volume, the development of effective parenting is a critical component of MST and the MST theory of change. Yet, several barriers to parental effectiveness emerge frequently among families receiving MST. The present section provided guidelines for reducing the negative effects of these barriers. The next section focuses on a related barrier, one that warrants considerable attention in its own right—marital distress.

Changing Marital Relations

In some families headed by two caregivers, the therapist obtains evidence from the initial assessment that marital (or adult relationship) problems contribute to the youth's antisocial behavior. In other families, marital problems not evident in the initial assessment present barriers to treatment progress. In either scenario, the MST therapist's task is to design and implement needed marital interventions. Although discussion of the research on marital therapies and their outcomes is beyond the scope of this chapter, therapists might find recent reviews and source materials cited in these reviews helpful (Sexton, Alexander, & Mease, 2004). In general, the four models of marital therapy most often tested in empirical studies are behavioral marital therapy, emotion-focused marital therapy, cognitive-behavioral marital therapy, and integrated systemic marital therapy. Reviewers have concluded that improvement rates are relatively consistent across all types of therapy and studies, only about 40–50% of treated couples are happily married at the end of therapy, and that continued research is needed to increase the short- and long-term effectiveness of marital treatments (Sexton et al., 2004). The intervention strategies described in this section are consistent with those common to behavioral and integrated systemic marital therapies and conform to the principles of MST.

We have observed that therapists new to MST often use less structured supportive or insight-oriented techniques when the focus of intervention shifts from caregiver–child problems to marital difficulties and that even experienced MST therapists are sometimes reluctant to implement marital interventions. The "fit" of therapist reluctance to implement marital interventions or to use more active interventions often is related to one or more of the following factors: limited practice with marital interventions and a related lack of confidence in the skills needed to implement such interventions; concern about how to effectively intervene in verbal conflict between adult partners (vs. caregiver–child conflict); and perceptions that few empirically supported intervention techniques exist.

To increase therapist opportunities to practice marital intervention skills, group supervision for cases requiring such skills should include more frequent (1) review of videotaped intervention sessions to reinforce effective strategies and alter ineffective strategies and (2) role plays to practice interrupting and effectively redirecting marital conflict. If needed for a particular case, ad hoc supervision can be scheduled at a time when enough members of the team are available to enact a role play and provide constructive feedback. When several therapists on the same MST team struggle with marital interventions, we recommend that the consultant and supervisor provide (1) a quarterly booster training focused on this domain and (2) a follow-up to assess the team's implementation of marital intervention strategies that were practiced in the booster session. The remainder of this section describes common challenges and strategies that therapists can use to address them when implementing marital interventions.

Setting the Stage for Marital Interventions

In light of the pressing problems of youth referred for MST, caregivers understandably focus on these problems rather than on possible marital difficulties. Before attempting marital interventions, then, MST therapists (1) introduce the idea that the couple's relationship problems are relevant to fixing the youth's problems and (2) cultivate the willingness of each partner to work together with the therapist to address these relationship problems. That is, the therapist seeks to establish the couple's initial engagement in the marital intervention process.

DEMONSTRATING RELEVANCE TO THE PROBLEM AT HAND

To introduce the relevance of marital problems to the situation at hand, the therapist clearly describes specific incidences or sequences of behavior, linking marital problems to the youth's behavior problems (e.g., a youth stays out all night and gets into trouble) or to the failure of interventions designed to help solve those problems (e.g., marital conflict interferes with enforcing the youth's curfew). A therapist might note, for example, that 14-year-old Lucas was twice able to play video games for an hour during the past week rather than going straight to his room with homework (the agreed-upon consequence for being late to school) while the parents argued about who should have been responsible for Lucas being at school in the first place. The therapist can use previously completed fit circles to show the couple how specific marital interactions seem connected to the failure of specific intervention strategies for youth behavior problems. By describing hypotheses about links between relationship problems and youth problems in an objective way, the therapist helps the couple to join together as they view and consider the hypotheses of the therapist. This experience frequently represents a change in the interaction pattern of couples with marital problems, who often feel that they are starting an interaction from "opposite sides of the fence."

CULTIVATING INITIAL ENGAGEMENT IN THE MARITAL INTERVENTION PROCESS

For some couples, recognizing how particular relationship problems negatively affect their youth or limit his or her progress in MST is enough to facilitate initial engagement in marital interventions. In other families, one partner might acknowledge that marital problems exist, while the other might not. In such circumstances, the therapist might need to interview the partners separately to understand how each evaluates the quality of the marriage in order to establish a common framework for addressing the marital problems. In the individual meeting with the partner perceiving no problem, the therapist might take a "one-down" stance, asking for help in understanding how to make better sense of information the therapist sees as indicating that marital problems exist and interfere with treatment progress. Based on information obtained from each partner, the therapist generates and asks the couple to "try out" different frameworks that might help establish a common ground for addressing relationship issues in conjoint sessions. For example, if each partner acknowledges in the individual meeting that the couple does not see eye to eye on how to raise the children, the therapist can reframe marital problems as pertaining primarily to conflicts about parenting, at least initially.

WHEN BREAKUP IS IMMINENT

Unfortunately, sometimes when the therapist is engaging the spouses in marital therapy, one spouse indicates that there is little likelihood he or she will remain in the marriage. In such circumstances, if the therapist has determined that the marital or parent–child interactions sustaining behavior problems are related to this stance, the treatment goals established for the couple and for the family must be adjusted accordingly: Developing joint marital goals is unjustified if one spouse is not likely to extend considerable effort on behalf of the marriage. When children have serious behavior problems that require immediate attention, even the spouse who is leaving a marriage might need to change his or her behavior with respect to the partner so that parenting can be more effective.

In such cases, the therapist should help couples clarify the differences between marital and parenting functions and assist in enhancing the latter. Of course, the emotional distress that typically accompanies the ending of a relationship will complicate efforts to engage in collaborative parenting. Issues related to the continuation of parenting in such situations are discussed in the subsequent section on divorce.

Intervention Guidelines and Strategies to Enact Them

After the partners have agreed to address their relationship problems, at least in the interest of the problem adolescent, the therapist uses language tailored to the couple to convey a few key guidelines originally described by Henggeler and Borduin (1990) about marital interventions:

- As with other interventions in MST, addressing relationship problems will likely require daily effort, "behavioral" homework (i.e., changing what each person says and does, even between sessions), and sacrifice (i.e., providing and giving up some things each person might not have otherwise done).
- The couple and the therapist are jointly responsible for the success of the interventions; the therapist has the primary responsibility of designing and implementing appropriate interventions and supporting the partners' efforts to change, and each of the partners is responsible for changing his or her own behavior.
- In addressing relationship problems the therapist will work with the couple to:
  —Emphasize mutual giving and cooperation, rather than competition.
  —Learn how to resolve conflicts, resentments, or frustrations as they arise, rather than letting them build up.
  —Recognize the positive efforts made by each partner.

IDENTIFY DESIRED CHANGES

Having explained the aforementioned guidelines and addressed questions or concerns about them, the therapist typically invites the couple to list changes they would like to see regarding the affective or instrumental nature of their relationship. To facilitate the process, the therapist might suggest completing in session a Strengths and Needs Assessment (see Chapter 2) for the marriage, as the caregivers, therapist, and relevant others did for all domains of the social ecology during the initial MST assessment process. Or, the therapist might suggest that each partner identify aspects of the relationship that he or she used to enjoy and might now miss as a strategy to identify desired changes. Alternatively, some couples find it easier to work from fit circles to identify relationship changes they would like to make. For example, a mother might point out that when she alone tries to enforce 16-year-old Johnny's curfew, he continues to rebel and get into trouble, and that she would like her husband to help enforce the curfew. The therapist could reframe the mother's statement as an appeal for more teamwork in the marriage, checking the acceptability of that reframe with the couple. At any rate, the therapist helps the couple define the types of changes they would like to see (e.g., more emotional support, help with the housework, more frequent sex) and helps operationalize the changes (e.g., "I'll cook five times a week, and you do the dishes") so that, per standard MST protocols, outcomes can be tracked.

UNDERSTAND META-LEVEL MESSAGES

Throughout the course of marital therapy, the therapist must attend to the "meta-level" messages about the relationship that partners convey to one another. That is, the therapist must attend not only to the content of a statement, but also to what the statement conveys about the speaker's perceptions, expectations, and feelings about the relationship. Put simply, what is said—the content of a statement—is only part of the message. *How* the message is said, both during a particular interaction and over the course of time, conveys important information about what the message means in the broader context of the relationship. The therapist's ability to correctly interpret meta-messages between spouses helps guide his or her identification of appropriate marital intervention goals and techniques, as illustrated next.

> Gary and Tonya Rawlings were happily married for the first 11 years of their relationship. Their overt problems began when Tonya decided that she was tired of being a housewife and wanted more out of life. She found a job and planned to enter a management training program. Gary was very dissatisfied with this change and demanded that Tonya stop working and start devoting more time to the household and the three children, the oldest of whom had been referred for MST. Tonya refused to comply, thus intensifying the conflict between her and Gary. On a content level, the central issue was Tonya's job versus household responsibilities. At a meta-level, however, Gary's underlying concern was that Tonya was moving away from him emotionally, and that he and the family were no longer a high priority. Gary was afraid that Tonya would become increasingly independent and self-sufficient and that she would eventually leave him. Therefore, the therapist decided that the most productive solution would be to help Gary feel more secure in the relationship, but not to ask Tonya to drop her new interests. The meta-level issue was commitment to the marriage, not the performance of housework.

AVOID TRIANGULATION

The therapist can become triangulated with the marital partners during conjoint treatment sessions. Sometimes triangulation occurs because the therapist has held individual meetings with one of the partners and has formed an alliance with that partner to the exclusion of the other partner. In this situation, the therapist might have trouble effectively conceptualizing and changing marital interaction patterns. One or both partners might raise concerns about the therapist's credibility as a trustworthy source of help for the marriage or the family when triangulation occurs. In such cases, the therapist should acknowledge the concerns, ask the partners to describe the words and behaviors that are fueling them, and discuss what the therapist can do in future sessions to demonstrate trustworthiness and effectiveness.

Other times, clues that triangulation may be occurring are not obvious to the therapist or the couple but emerge in case summaries or tapes of sessions that are reviewed in clinical supervision. When this happens, the team and supervisor can help the therapist to conceptualize the interaction pattern signaling the triangulation (e.g., "It sounds like you are defending Bob's behavior to Mary, rather than reflecting to both of them they are starting an argument and then interrupting that argument"). The team can also role-play how the therapist can realign himself or herself with the couple rather than with one of the partners.

Dealing with Negative Affect and Promoting Compromise

To promote marital satisfaction, the therapist must help the couple interrupt the repeated cycles of negative interaction that frequently occur in unhappy and unsatisfying marriages. To successfully interrupt such behavioral sequences, the therapist may first need to convey that the problem and its solution lie with the couple, not with a particular individual. Then, the therapist helps the spouses to learn, practice, and implement some basic skills. The following steps, originally described by Henggeler and Borduin (1990), are useful in helping couples interrupt cycles of negativity and diminish the intensity and longevity of marital conflicts. The therapist coaches each partner to do the following:

1. *Recognize that a negative behavior that is part of the cycle has occurred.* This first step requires partners to recognize the precursors of conflict. To help partners do this, the therapist can assess whether they experience a sense of "here we go again" during the early stages of a conflict. The therapist can demonstrate in sessions how to use those "here we go again" cues to stop the sequence and consider what has set off the feeling of impending conflict. These cues (e.g., sensing "tension in the air," hearing a comment muttered under the partner's breath) should not be ignored in sessions or outside of sessions. Neither should the cues provoke an escalation. Instead, partners need to learn that the cues represent an early warning system for a conflict. The therapist might assign homework asking each partner to track every time each perceives the cue and whether the negative interaction (defined clearly) occurred, thereby providing a baseline on how often and in what situations the early warning system goes off.

2. *Inform the spouse that the negative behavior has occurred.* This step requires that the speaker communicate in ways that minimize defensiveness. Therapists will likely need to teach spouses how to state concerns about a partner's negative behavior without blaming the partner. Even so, partners smarting from the pain of marital problems may have a hard time listening to their mate's comments about their own negative behaviors, so the therapist

should establish realistic expectations about how much can be conveyed at one time and to what end. The therapist models in session how to give and respond to such feedback, using a real example from the life of the couple. Then, the therapist provides opportunities for each spouse to speak and receive the feedback in sessions, providing praise and corrective feedback about the interaction. Therapists can coach partners to try several strategies when informing one another about a negative behavior. These include:

- *Take a one-down position.* For example, Jim might tell his wife, Jan, that he feels she is upset with him for some reason and that he is afraid that another conflict is brewing. Jim's tone of voice and his body language should reflect the one-down verbalization. Accordingly, if Jim stands above Jan's chair so he cannot see her face and speaks sharply, the therapist might ask him to sit, meet her gaze, and speak clearly but not sharply.
- *Take a 5- to 10-minute time-out when tension is beginning to develop.* The therapist explains that a time-out is useful because it can (a) break the couple's usual cycle of negative reciprocity and (b) signal each partner's willingness to put the relationship above personal interests. The therapist can also suggest the couple develop a signal that a time-out is needed. For example, some couples have used the time-out hand signal used in sports, and another drew a miniature stop sign on construction paper. During the time-out, each partner goes to a separate room to try to understand the situation from the perspective of the other spouse. Strategies to facilitate such perspective taking are elaborated in step 4, below.

3. *Explain the behavior and its corresponding meaning to the spouse in a nonattacking way.* Immediately after the time-out, the couple should come back together to accomplish this task. When teaching couples to address their concerns in a more productive fashion, the therapist will need to help spouses recognize the meta-level concerns raised by the conflicts, as in the following examples:

- Complaints about a messy house may actually reflect a spouse's fear that the partner does not care about him or her enough to help with household chores.
- Negative comments about the friend of a spouse may represent fear that the spouse in more interested in spending time with the friend than with the mate.

As with previous steps, the therapist should (a) engage the couple in within-session practice over several sessions and (b) assign and review homework requiring daily practice between sessions (Principle 7).

4. *Gain an understanding of the spouse's perspective regarding the negative behavior and the underlying circumstances that might have prompted the behavior.* In marriages characterized by repeated cycles of negative interaction,

partners often feel their perspectives are not understood or valued. Shifting the pattern in which spouses do not listen to one another requires each spouse to use perspective-taking skills. Perspective taking requires that a person set aside his or her own view of a situation long enough to understand that another views the situation differently and the nature of that person's perspective. Because partners with a long history of negative interaction often devote more energy to defending their own behavior and point of view than to understanding the spouse's perspective, engaging couples in perspective taking usually requires that the therapist:

- Model the concept in session, using real examples from the life of the couple.
- Provide multiple opportunities for practice within sessions, offering specific praise and corrective feedback.
- Assign homework that requires practice between sessions and discuss homework outcomes during subsequent sessions, including any barriers to practice.
- Consider each partner's level of cognitive development, as individuals who think very concretely will have difficulty developing social perspective-taking skills.

5. *Work out a mutually agreeable solution to the negative interaction.* This last step requires negotiation skills and willingness to compromise. The therapist must help spouses shift from a mode of dealing with conflict that emphasizes "winning" to a mode in which conflict situations are resolved in ways that allow both spouses to feel that they gave as much as they received. Priority is placed on each spouse doing whatever is reasonable to make the other comfortable with the outcome. The therapist's responsibility is to help the couple develop a cognitive set in which each partner can say "I believe I am right, but I understand my spouse's perspective, too." When couples can reach this level of cooperation, teaching negotiation skills is fairly straightforward. When a couple has difficulty compromising, however, the therapist may need to serve as an arbitrator. In the arbitrator role, the therapist helps each partner identify concessions he or she is willing to make. The arbitrator role, unfortunately, does not promote the long-term maintenance of therapeutic change (Principle 9), because the spouses are not learning to resolve issues themselves.

Changing Instrumental Relations

When marital conflict centers on instrumental issues such as household tasks, child-care responsibilities, or financial issues, the therapist will often need to help partners develop shared expectations regarding one another's roles. In doing so, the therapist should help the couple to develop the cognitive set that marriage is a 50–50 proposition that requires equal effort, time, and energy from each partner. Although many couples will agree with this proposition, translating the concept into an equitable distribution of tasks often requires that marital partners reconceptualize their ideas about the amount of effort they are required to devote to such tasks. Once reconceptualization has occurred, desired behavioral changes must be defined so that they can be observed and monitored (Principles 4 and 8). Examples include doing the dishes 3 nights a week (as opposed to just "doing the dishes"), picking the children up from school 5 days a week, and so on.

Spouses should be instructed to provide daily feedback to one another regarding their performance of instrumental tasks. The following guidelines might be helpful to therapists when working with spouses on providing feedback to each other:

- Feedback can occur at the end of the day, when the spouses discuss each other's efforts to change.
- The spouses should provide each other with positive recognition to help break cycles of negativity.
- The spouses should also provide each other with accurate negative feedback about their performance.
- Daily feedback helps to put "bad" days in perspective, because couples have a more objective way of tracking how frequently bad days occur and can place their occurrence in the context of "good" days.
- One useful technique for providing feedback is to have spouses use a "report card" or "grade" approach.
- The spouses should track one another's performance on paper, as is done when interventions designed to change the behavior of children are implemented, so that the therapist can be continuously and accurately informed of the spouses' efforts (Principle 8).

The Burke family was referred for MST after Jerry, age 15, was arrested for the third time and found to test positive for cocaine. Jerry was the youngest of three children; his 17-year-old sister was pregnant and finishing her GED, and his 20-year-old brother was unemployed and living at home. The Burkes had been married for 20 years and had abused alcohol and narcotics intermittently for the first 12 years of their marriage. Neither parent had used substances for 3 years at the time of referral. Ms. Burke attended Narcotics Anonymous meetings consistently, and Mr. Burke attended intermittently after repeated urging from Ms. Burke.

Assignments given early in treatment revealed that, although the couple rarely disagreed or argued openly, they never spent time together without their children. In addition, Ms. Burke was unhappy in the marriage and believed that the family's goals for treatment (getting Jerry back into school, off cocaine, out of trouble with the law, and engaged in prosocial activities) would not be met if Mr. Burke did not participate. Mr. Burke, however, indicated that while the marriage was not ideal, he had made his peace with it and did not see the need for change. The therapist, unsure of the role of marital problems in the marriage, and having never conducted marital therapy before, proceeded with interventions targeting permissive parenting, monitoring of Jerry's whereabouts, mending fences with school personnel, and establishing expectations for household contributions to be made by the 17- and 20-year-olds.

Assignments that required participation from both Mr. and Ms. Burke were rarely completed, little progress was made, and Ms. Burke, increasingly frustrated with the lack of progress, began to doubt the therapist's competence. At this juncture, the therapist met with the couple and introduced the notion that marital interventions might be needed to help the couple help their children. For 1 week, the therapist met several times with the couple to assess the strengths and needs in their relationship (e.g., what first attracted them to one another, to what extent they still cared for one another, whether they could engage in perspective taking and hear one another) and put previously implemented interventions "on hold." Thereafter, marital sessions were held twice each week, and sessions targeting parenting interventions and meetings with school personnel and neighbors were scheduled separately.

The therapist's early attempts to help the couple reach compromises regarding a new division of household labor failed, primarily because neither individual felt the other appreciated his or her efforts. Thus, the therapist engaged the couple in perspective-taking exercises before and while attempting to help them reach compromises about instrumental issues. In addition, Ms. Burke complained that she needed more affection from Mr. Burke, while Mr. Burke complained that the couple hadn't had sex for over a year. In response, Ms. Burke complained that she was too exhausted to make love after spending all her energy on their children and family crises, and suggested that she might have more energy if Mr. Burke did his fair share of parenting and supported her emotionally. The therapist quickly averted an argument, validated both partners' concerns, and added increasing intimacy to the intermediary goals. The couple agreed that going on a date might be a reasonable step toward increasing intimacy and agreed to make the first date one on which discussion of household tasks and child-related problems was not allowed, and sex was not to be expected. The couple agreed to these terms and planned a date for the following Friday night.

On that Friday evening, the couple took their 17-year-old daughter along because she was distraught after an argument with her boyfriend. The therapist used this incident to illustrate the porous nature of boundaries between the couple and their children, the date assignment was revisited, and more specific terms of the date (no children allowed) were established. Eventually, after many starts and stops, the couple came to function as sober marital partners (they had been primarily substance abusing buddies the first 12 years of marriage). They helped each other out, came to express understanding and love, and resumed sexual relations. Though the relationship was far from perfect, improved marital satisfaction and more clearly defined marital bound- aries enabled more effective collaboration in addressing their children's difficulties.

Whether the therapist in this case was discussing the importance of spousal flexibility in completing housework responsibilities or the hus- band's love for his dissatisfied wife, it is important to note that the underly- ing therapeutic process is the same: to convince the couple that they will need to alter their conceptualizations of the relationship in order to resolve their difficulties. This meta-level process, rather than the specific content of the argument, is a critical component of marital interventions in MST. The therapist frames the rationale for this change in a way that is most useful for motivating the particular couple. The reframing has direct and logical implications for behavior change. Thinking about the situation in a new way does not necessarily result in behavior change, but it does set the stage for such change.

Enhancing Effective Functioning during and after Family Transitions

In most communities, more than 50% of families receiving MST are headed by single parents. Many of these parents have never been married, but many others have experienced divorce. As reviewed by Emery and his col- leagues (Emery & Sbarra, 2002; Pryor & Emery, 2004), separation and divorce can present family members with significant emotional and behav- ioral challenges—challenges that further complicate therapeutic efforts to decrease the adolescent behavior problems that resulted in the referral to MST. This section provides guidelines for therapists to consider when treat- ing families with single parents and families that have experienced transi- tions such as divorce and remarriage.

Families Affected by Divorce

The MST therapist should consider several intervention aims when miscon- ceptions about the divorce, inappropriate expectations about adaptation to divorce, or unsuccessful role negotiation contribute to the identified prob- lems.

1. The therapist might need to *educate family members about norma-tive behavioral responses* to divorce. Those normative responses vary in accordance with the child's age and level of development. Thus,

for example, preschoolers of divorced families experience fears of abandonment by both parents more frequently than do school-age children, but even adolescents may need reassurance that both parents still love them.

2. To *help fill the void in instrumental family functioning* (e.g., household tasks), the therapist can assist parents and children in developing reasonable expectations about the kinds of tasks that each child can perform, given his or her age and cognitive and physical capacity.

3. Previously *effective parenting practices should be reinforced or reinstated*, and the therapist might need to help one parent develop new parenting skills to compensate for those previously implemented by the other parent.

4. The therapist might need to *assist parents in garnering the social and financial support* required to sustain effective practices during emotionally and practically difficult circumstances.

5. Therapists might *assist parents in renegotiating their relationships with their ex-spouses* in ways that are conducive to coordinated parenting.

6. Finally, the therapist might need to *help the parent to manage personal distress* if that distress interferes with effective family functioning.

PARENT–CHILD SUBSYSTEM

Residential and nonresidential parents often have difficulties maintaining authoritative childrearing practices following separation and divorce. Emery (1994, 1999, 2004) has identified a specific and problematic pattern of parent–child interaction that can emerge after divorce as a result of parental guilt about the impact of the divorce on the child. In this pattern, the parent mistakenly attributes mild aberrations in a child's mood or behavior to the effects of divorce, rather than to normal influences. Such attributions can prompt parents to minimize or focus excessively on negative child behaviors, attempt to appease the child, and relax appropriate parental disciplines. Consequently, a coercive cycle of parent–child interaction develops in which misbehavior that would have been punished previously is positively reinforced (e.g., appeasing the child), and parents are negatively reinforced for giving in to children's demands (i.e., parents experience relief from the child's negative behavior by giving in). As a result, children quickly learn the power of provoking parental guilt to achieve their aims.

If parents and teenagers are caught in such a cycle, debating and gaining insight into the teen's motivations (i.e., is the child being deliberately manipulative, or not?) is rarely useful. If the youth's guilt-inducing comments and behaviors succeed in making his or her life easier because the parent fails to enforce rules or behaves more attentively, the adolescent is likely to continue such behaviors. Rather than take up issues of teen motivation in such cases, the MST therapist should help the parent to consistently enforce rules of conduct and provide support as the parent builds confidence in his or her capacity to manage guilt-inducing and problem behavior. Generally, such confidence increases as the parent experiences success in maintaining consistent rules in the face of the youth's guilt-evoking behaviors, and as these behaviors decrease in frequency when they are no longer reinforced.

MST therapists frequently use role plays to ensure that interventions will be implemented successfully, but doing so is particularly necessary when parents face guilt-evoking complaints from their children. The divorced parent might harbor concerns about the youth's love for and loyalty to him or her relative to the other parent, and such concerns sometimes present barriers to the parent's ability to exercise authority in the face of the youth's comments comparing one parent with the other (e.g., "Dad doesn't make me do this."). For parents who have great difficulty ignoring the content of the youth's comments, the therapist might suggest that the parent:

- Focus on the behavior in question (e.g., the youth won't follow curfew) rather than on the content of the youth's comment (e.g., "Dad doesn't make me do this.").
- Discuss any realistic fears (e.g., concerning conflict between parents, divided loyalties, and uncertainty about the future) at a later time, not during a parent–child interaction that revolves around limit setting, the completion of chores, and so on.

Again, the therapist might need to use repeated practice, initially in the context of role plays, to help the parent remain steadfast in effective parenting practices following divorce.

Finally, noncustodial parents who have contact with their children must be equally mindful of boundary issues. Disagreements between the parents should be addressed directly by them and not through the child, and the therapist might need to help the parents communicate effectively with each other. Similarly, noncustodial parents might try to compensate for the diminished amount of time they have with their children by planning special outings and activities each time the child visits. The therapist might need to educate the noncustodial parent about the importance of engaging in everyday activities with children. That is, the important lessons of a youth's life (e.g., caring for others, generosity, the value of hard work) are learned through everyday behaviors rather than through trips to amusement parks. Although the noncustodial parent might feel that his or her limited time with the children provides little opportunity to convey such lessons, the therapist should encourage the parent to take a long-term perspective. That is, much can happen during the coming years, and eventually, as the children reach late adolescence and young adulthood, decisions about whom they spend their time with will be theirs.

RELATIONS BETWEEN FORMER SPOUSES

When evidence clearly indicates that negative interactions between former spouses or the inability of former spouses to exercise interparental consistency contribute to a youth's behavior problems, the therapist's overarching goal is to enable the divorced spouses to act in the best interests of the youth despite difficulties in renegotiating the affective and instrumental aspects of their personal relationship. Recognizing that the renegotiation of intimacy and power between former spouses is an ongoing task, and one often fraught with emotional anguish and practical challenges, the therapist should have realistic expectations of the parents when designing interventions. Emery (1994) has observed that it is not necessary for parents to have an integrated, highly cooperative relationship to achieve the goal of redefining family relationships in a manner that will best promote children's well-being. Former spouses must, however, be able to make and keep agreements about parenting tasks. Thus, the MST therapist might have to help the ex-spouses to:

- Devise acceptable means of communication regarding such day-to-day issues as homework, doctor visits, birthday parties, and vacations.
- Agree upon visitation schedules and avoid spontaneous violations of the schedule for the children's sake.
- Resolve conflicts that directly involve and affect the children.

Accomplishing each of these tasks often requires the therapist to conduct a series of individual meetings with each parent prior to, and sometimes instead of, joint meetings.

CONCRETE AND PRACTICAL CHALLENGES

Divorce usually gives rise to concrete and practical challenges for parents, such as working longer hours to compensate for financial losses associated with the divorce, moving to a different dwelling following divorce, accommodating parent visitation schedules, and interacting with the legal system regarding divorce and custody issues. When divorce significantly reduces family income, the custodial parent, typically the mother, might return to full-time employment outside the home or, if already employed, obtain a second job. Increased work hours might reduce adult monitoring of the children and negatively influence the mother's personal adjustment. The mother might also become isolated from her social support network when all of her time is spent at work or engaging in child-care responsibilities. Thus, intervention strategies might be needed to address the family's financial needs:

- In the short term, the therapist might help the parent to coordinate social services that will attenuate the family's financial needs.
- The therapist might also need to help a parent navigate the court system to obtain adequate child support payments, although this legal process is often time-consuming, stressful, and unlikely to address the family's immediate financial crisis.

ADDRESSING PARENTAL DISTRESS

When a parent's distress (grief, anger, anxiety) about the divorce interferes with his or her ability to parent effectively or to engage in appropriate communication with the ex-spouse about parenting tasks, the therapist might need to:

- Provide emotional support before engaging the parent in strategies to parent or communicate more effectively.
- Identify individuals who can help the parent grapple with the emotional and practical impact of the divorce and reinforce appropriate parenting practices (see Chapter 7).
- Assure that any individuals (e.g., parent's friends, other adult family members) who provide instrumental support (e.g., child care) refrain from discussing the ex-spouse, marital issues, and so forth with (or in front of) the children.
- Recommend more formal sources of support (e.g., church groups, community organizations such as Parents Without Partners) when social support is needed but not available from adults in the indigenous environment (family, friends, coworkers).

Prior to making such suggestions, however, the therapist should attempt to address potential practical (e.g., scheduling, transportation, child care), social (e.g., discomfort with groups, concern about stigmatization), and cultural (e.g., religious, ethnic practices) barriers to increasing social support. Moreover, if the distress precipitates depressive or anxiety-related disturbances or disorders, the therapist might need to implement pertinent intervention strategies for these problems, as described in Chapter 6.

Remarried Families

NORMALIZING STEPFAMILY EXPERIENCES

When the therapist obtains evidence that unrealistic expectations about the family system (e.g., the expectation that the current family group is a re-created nuclear family) are contributing to behavior problems, he or she might need to explain the developmental process of family reconstitution in terms that all members can understand. That is, the family members might need to hear that:

- It takes time to develop an identity as a family.
- Conscious effort is required to cultivate positive affective relationships and workable instrumental arrangements (e.g., how chores are divided and money is spent).
- Conflicts about preferred ways of doing things are normal.

If the thoughts and behaviors of the parents and children are reframed as natural occurrences in the development of a reconstituted family system, unrealistic expectations can be altered and a sense of cooperation among family members can be fostered.

When stepsiblings are housed under one roof, conflicts often occur about the manner in which parents spend resources, affection, and time on the various children. If such conflicts appear to contribute to a youth's behavior problems, the therapist should conduct a thorough assessment of the factors sustaining the real or perceived disparity. If real and significant disparities do exist that are not inappropriate to the developmental needs of children of different ages (e.g., infants should receive more parental attention than adolescents), the therapist should address the basis of these disparities with the parents. On the other hand, if the disparities are more perception than reality, such stepsibling conflicts should be normalized. Parents often hope or expect that children from different nuclear families will develop positive affective bonds with one another simply because the parents love one another and the children live together. The children, meanwhile, must adjust to changes in their relationship with the custodial parent while being asked to develop a new positive relationship with the stepparent and stepsiblings. Parents with unrealistic expectations about stepsibling bonding might need to be reminded that although they chose to marry, their children did not choose to have additional siblings. Although parents should develop and enforce rules for respectful behavior among all children in the household and encourage activities that might stimulate positive affective experiences among stepsiblings, they should not expect the children to experience or express positive affection for one another initially.

CLARIFYING PARENTAL ROLES

When either lack of clarity regarding parental roles or inappropriate assignment of such roles contributes to the youth's behavior problems, the therapist should arrange to meet with the marital partners without the children present. The purpose of the meeting is to determine:

- Whether the spouses have, overtly or covertly, agreed upon the responsibilities each will have in caring for the biological and stepchildren.
- How they came to this agreement.
- Whether differences of opinion emerged.
- How such differences were handled.

Such meetings often reveal that little time and attention have been devoted to the overt negotiation of parenting issues, as the primary source of the spouses' concern was stabilizing the new marriage in the presence of children.

Generally, stepparents are more successful if they first establish a relationship with the child as a friend and assume the role of disciplinarian later. That is, a positive affective relationship should be established first, while the stepparent follows the biological parent's lead in enforcing discipline strategies (Henggeler & Borduin, 1990). This sequence of parenting tasks (i.e., first affective, later guidance) can be particularly difficult if the biological parent married, in part, to obtain help with parenting responsibilities. For example, during the MST therapist's second meeting with the Rios family, Mrs. Rios openly admitted that one of the main reasons she had married her current husband of 2 years was that she needed "a man to control my son," who had a long history of delinquent behaviors. In such cases, the therapist should empathize with the biological parent regarding the many demands of single parenting, particularly when a child with serious behavior problems is involved. The therapist should also, however, dispel the myth that the stepparent can and should become the primary source of parental control in the household. To accomplish this goal, the therapist will most likely need to:

- Teach the biological parent effective parenting strategies.
- Create opportunities to practice those strategies that afford the parent success experiences.
- Solicit the stepparent's support for the biological parent.
- Support the stepparent's efforts to develop a positive affective relationship with the child.

The biological parent's belief that the stepparent should be a disciplinarian is not likely to be dispelled unless (a) the biological parent has been able to engage in effective parenting practices and (b) the stepparent is willing to support the biological parent but not rescue him or her when asked to intervene in discipline efforts. The therapist's task is to design and implement interventions that create such experiences.

Single-Parent Families

Many of the interventions for families affected by divorce are applicable to families headed by a single parent. When the intimate relationship of the single parent appears to contribute to the referral problem, however, the therapist might need to use additional interventions. In these cases, interventions focus on clarifying parent–child and subsystem boundaries in much the same way as must occur in remarried families. In contrast with remarried or nuclear families, however, adults who have not made a commitment to a lasting relationship might have difficulty discussing such issues because doing so would require defining, constraining, or changing the developing relationship just when its novelty is most exciting.

If the MST therapist obtains evidence that the single parent's involvement in intimate relationships alters family interactions in ways that contribute to a youth's behavior problems (e.g., the mother spends considerable time at her boyfriend's home, while leaving her adolescent in charge of the younger children, or the boyfriend lives with the family and serves as the primary disciplinarian for the children), the therapist seeks to help the parent meet legitimate needs for adult intimacy, financial support, or assistance with parenting tasks in ways that do not radically alter the children's experiences. We have worked with many families in which a parent with a long-standing history of successive relationships was able to identify, with the therapist's assistance, economic, emotional, and parenting needs that her various partners had helped to meet.

> Debbie was the 29-year-old mother of a 15-year-old son and 7-year-old daughter, each by a different father. The son had been referred for MST shortly after his mother had been released from a residential substance abuse treatment program. During the previous 3 years, Debbie had lived with several men who provided financial assistance and acted as surrogate parents to her children. At the first family meeting, Debbie introduced the MST therapist to Al, a man she met in the treatment program. Debbie complained that her son, Erwin, would not mind Al, while her daughter "loved" him. Debbie's affection for Al and enthusiasm about his being a father figure for the children was immediately apparent to the therapist. The therapist empathized with Debbie's enthusiasm in terms that emphasized Al's value to her (e.g., adult intimacy and

companionship) and deemphasized his value as a potential parent to the children. Over the next week, the therapist gathered evidence via direct observation of family interaction and family responses to homework assignments that indicated the adult relationship was contributing to Erwin's behavior problems. Armed with this evidence, but still validating Debbie's positive experiences of Al as an intimate partner, the therapist was able to engage Debbie in a conversation in which she could begin to consider some ways in which involving Al so immediately and pervasively in her children's lives might be associated with the problems her children were experiencing. Next, a combination of interventions was implemented (including obtaining child care, enrolling Debbie in a GED program so that she could obtain a job, identifying non–substance-abusing adults as sources of social support, and teaching parenting skills) to enable Debbie to draw appropriate boundaries around her relationship with Al.

During the treatment, Debbie continued to defer frequently to Al for parenting help. Thus, the therapist met with the couple often to (1) reinforce the importance of Al as a source of emotional support, intimacy, and companionship to Debbie; (2) establish and reinforce ground rules about his nonparticipation as a parent; and (3) assist the couple in discussing their plans for the relationship and what implicit or explicit agreements about financial support and parenting tasks had been made between them. These discussions made both Debbie and Al uncomfortable, as they had agreed not to make a long-term commitment when Al moved in, each having been "burned" in previous relationships. Moreover, Al saw his financial support as tantamount to permission to parent, and Debbie had implicitly agreed to this arrangement. In the end, Al moved out approximately 3 weeks prior to the scheduled termination of MST. In subsequent weeks, the therapist worked daily to assist Debbie in practicing parenting skills, developing sources of social support, and obtaining public assistance to address concrete needs.

Conclusion

MST is first and foremost a family-based intervention model. As described throughout this volume, family empowerment is the key to decreasing adolescent antisocial behavior and improving functioning. Hence, this chapter serves as the clinical bedrock of this volume. Research on family relations and family interventions is extensive and complex. We have attempted to distill the aspects of this research that are most relevant to the conceptualization and design of the family-related interventions used in MST. Clinical success will be determined largely by the therapist's capacity to draw on family and ecological strengths to address roadblocks and barriers to effectively altering the life course of youth in MST programs.

CHAPTER 4

Peer Interventions

Peer interactions and friendships have primary roles in the cognitive, moral, emotional, and social development of children and adolescents. Critically for the purpose of this volume, peer relations can have powerful effects on youth antisocial behavior, and the family–peer interface can play a critical role in decreasing these problems.

Peer Influence on Child Development

Peers influence the development of emotional security and self-esteem by providing children and adolescents with loyalty, affection, and a sense of belonging (Bukowski, Newcomb, & Hartup, 1996; Prinstein & Dodge, 2008). Similarly, peer interactions promote cognitive growth and learning and contribute to acquisition of behavioral norms and moral values (Prinstein & Dodge, 2008; Roseth, Johnson, & Johnson, 2008). Thus, peer interactions provide a proving ground in which children and adolescents with incomplete but roughly comparable interpersonal skills can develop and enhance their skills through mutual exploration and feedback (Berndt, 2002).

Types of Skills Needed for Positive Peer Relations

A variety of skills developed in the context of social interaction between youth of similar age are necessary to sustain positive peer relations (Bukowski et al., 1996). These include:

- Perspective taking.
- Empathy.
- Collaboration in activities and tasks.
- Initiation and reciprocation of interactions.

In general, youth who achieve positive status among their peers display these skills across multiple social situations. In contrast, youth who have difficulty initiating or sustaining interactions and mutual give-and-take in relationships with peers often experience peer relationship difficulties. Some of these youth are simply *neglected* by their peers, while others are actively *rejected*. Neglected youth often appear inept during social interactions and are at risk for subsequent internalizing problems. Rejected youth often engage in aggressive and obnoxious behavior in social contexts and are at risk for subsequent externalizing problems, school failure, and delinquency (Becker & Luthar, 2002; Hoza, Molina, Bukowski, & Sippola, 1995).

Importance of Peer Relations in the Treatment of Antisocial Behavior

Two consistent findings from developmental and criminology research are highly pertinent to the treatment of antisocial behavior in adolescents.

1) Research consistently shows that problems with peer relations (e.g., high association with deviant peers, poor relationship skills) are powerful predictors of antisocial behavior in youth (Dodge, Dishion, & Lansford, 2006; Lahey, Moffitt, & Caspi, 2003; Loeber & Farrington, 1998) (see also Chapter 1).

2) Most youth commit criminal offenses in the context of peer activities (Howell, 2003). For such youth, strong emotional ties usually reinforce involvement in criminal behavior with deviant friends.

Therefore, in addition to the importance of peer relations to normative adolescent development, developing expertise in peer-related interventions is especially pertinent for clinicians working with the types of youth referred to MST programs.

Importance of the Interface between Family and Peers

Caregivers can influence their adolescents' peer relations in several positive ways.

- Caregivers teach their children to value interactions with other people, including peers, and to successfully initiate and maintain relations with them. In general, children and adolescents whose families are cohesive and interpersonally positive have more opportunities to learn the types of interaction styles that are needed for positive peer relations.
- Caregivers serve as instructors or coaches regarding desirable behavior in social interactions by providing feedback on how to handle, for example, bullying, teasing, rejection, or aggression from peers.
- Caregivers help manage their children's social lives, providing opportunities for social contact with youth outside the family (e.g., suggesting that the youth share a video game or invite an acquaintance over to play basketball, signing the youth up for a sports team or church youth group).

In light of the strong influence of caregivers on their children's peer relations, it is not surprising that certain problems in caregiver–child interaction (e.g., high conflict, low positive affect) and childrearing practices (e.g., harsh and inconsistent discipline; poor monitoring; authoritarian, permissive, and neglectful parenting styles) are frequently associated with youth involvement with deviant peers (Kim, Hetherington, & Reiss, 1999; Reid, Patterson, & Snyder, 2002; Vitaro, Brendgen, & Tremblay, 2000). On the other hand, caregivers who do not allow their children to engage in age-appropriate activities (e.g., are overprotective) can stifle the adolescent's pursuit of normal levels of emotional and behavioral autonomy—thereby interfering with the development of successful peer relations as well.

When considering the linkages between the youth's family relations and peer relations, the therapist should also recognize that the youth's peers are members of their own family contexts that can indirectly influence the youth. For example, in an effort to obtain parental approval for participating in some new or previously disallowed activity, the youth might attempt to bring the influence of peers' parents to bear on his or her own parents' decision making (e.g., the youth might comment, "Jeff's parents let him do it."). Similarly, a youth who is regularly hanging out and getting in trouble on the streets with other youth at 2:00 A.M. probably has peers whose parents are not monitoring or seem unconcerned about their children's whereabouts and, consequently, are helping to maintain the peer group's problem behavior. Thus, systems that are external to the developing youth (i.e., peers' families) can indirectly influence the youth's behavior and family relations, and therapists should always appreciate the possibility of these influences.

Assessment of Peer Relations

The initial section of this chapter describes the assessment process used to identify the specific combination of factors that compromise effective peer relations and contribute to antisocial behavior. The remaining sections describe interventions used to improve peer relations—including removing youth from deviant peer groups and helping them develop friendships with more prosocial peers.

Key Aspects of Peer Relations

To develop hypotheses about the relative contributions of peer factors to identified problems, the therapist must be able to organize his or her observations about peer relations in a way that is easily communicated to the supervisor and treatment team. Information obtained through a comprehensive assessment should shed light on the following two key aspects of the youth's peer relations.

Sociometric Status

Sociometric status reflects the relative acceptance of the youth by his or her peers.

- High social status youth are well liked (i.e., popular), are often considered leaders by their peers, and evidence a preponderance of friendly behaviors.
- Neglected and socially isolated youth are neither most nor least popular among their peers and generally fall in the middle to lower (but not lowest) range of peer social status. These youth tend to be somewhat shy and less interactive than higher status youth.
- Low-social-status youth are disliked (i.e., unpopular), are actively rejected by their peers, and evidence low rates of prosocial behaviors and high rates of aggressive and uncooperative behaviors.

Involvement with Deviant Peers

As described later in this chapter, the extent of the youth's involvement with deviant peers has important implications for treatment. In general, the therapist should distinguish between the following:

- Youth who associate exclusively with prosocial peers
- Youth who associate with some prosocial and some deviant peers
- Youth who associate exclusively with deviant peers

In sum, a clear understanding of the youth's relative social status among peers and of the extent of his or her involvement with deviant peers should be developed. This understanding can contribute substantially to a comprehensive conceptualization of the fit of identified problems and the design of corresponding interventions.

How to Assess Peer Relations

Therapists can use several strategies to assess the youth's peer relations. Such assessment, however, should always go hand in hand with the broader and ongoing assessment of the youth's individual characteristics (e.g., cognitive skills), family relations, and school environment.

Direct Questioning

Information about the youth's peer relations should be obtained and synthesized from several different sources.

CAREGIVERS

When conducting the first or second therapy session with the family, the therapist should assess each member's perceptions and beliefs about the youth's social functioning. A good way to begin is to ask the caregivers about:

- The number and nature of the youth's acquaintanceships versus friendships (i.e., similar-age peers with whom the youth has close emotional ties).
- Their impressions of the youth's acquaintances and friends. What are the reputations of these teenagers? How well are they functioning socially? How well are they achieving in school?
- Their interest in the youth's peer activities. How much contact do the caregivers have with the acquaintances and friends? How much

contact do the caregivers have with the caregivers of these peers, and what is the nature of that contact?

- What is the quality of the youth's peer relations in school versus outside of school? Some youth have close friends whom they see only after school or on weekends, or they might have friends in their church or on a recreational sports team.

These initial questions will usually reveal the extent to which the caregivers are informed and concerned about the youth's peer relations. If these relations represent a source of concern for the caregivers, it is often helpful to assess:

- The caregivers' attributions about the causes of the youth's peer difficulties. The caregivers might believe, for example, that the youth is easily led by peers to engage in antisocial activities or is unfairly ridiculed by peers.
- Whether the caregivers have attempted any interventions on their own to resolve the youth's problems with peers. The therapist might find that caregiver behavior is inadvertently preventing a productive solution to the youth's peer difficulties (e.g., by allowing a youth to stay at home from school to protect him from the cruel remarks of a few classmates).

YOUTH

After obtaining information from the caregivers, the therapist asks the youth to describe his or her acquaintances and friends. The therapist can ask about:

- The activities and interests of the friends.
- Their level of achievement in school.
- The quality of the peers' relationships with their own parents.
- Whether the youth is satisfied with his or her peer relations and, if not, how he or she would like them to improve.

Although most youth are open about their friends, some are hesitant to discuss their friendships (or their difficulties with peer relations) during the therapist's meeting with the family. Such hesitation (or complete silence) usually indicates that the youth is distressed by the quality of his or her peer relations or has friends that the caregivers do not like. In such instances, the therapist can use information caregivers have already provided about the youth's peer relations as a starting point for a private discussion with the youth.

TEACHERS

Although caregivers are often aware of problems in the youth's social relations in school, such problems are often of secondary importance to them (unless the referral was initiated by school personnel). Understandably, the caregivers' attention is usually focused on problem behavior at home and in the neighborhood that has an immediate and direct effect on the family (e.g., drug use, stealing, aggression, and noncompliance). Thus, we strongly recommend therapists evaluate the youth's peer relations in school. Teachers can provide valuable and relatively objective views of the youth's peer relations. Because youth often have friends in a number of different classes as well as friends whom they see only at lunchtime or during extracurricular activities, the therapist meets with as many of the youth's teachers as possible to obtain a comprehensive assessment of peer relations. This strategy also provides a more balanced view of the youth's interpersonal strengths and weaknesses than might be obtained from only one or two teachers.

Several types of information should be obtained from the teachers regarding the youth's peer relations.

- Does the youth have friendships with other youth in the school? The therapist should distinguish between getting along well with peers (i.e., peer acceptance) and having close emotional ties with one or more classmates (i.e., having friends). A youth can maintain friendships despite generally low peer regard; on the other hand, a youth can have no close friends and still be accepted by most peers.
- If the youth has friends, what are their levels of social and intellectual functioning? This information will provide a general idea of the youth's level of social competence. For example, if a youth has few friends or associates primarily with socially rejected adolescents, he or she likely possesses significant deficits in social competence.
- If the youth has friends, what are their social reputations and interests? If a youth associates primarily with friends who have reputations for drug use, then drugs probably play an important role in the presenting problems. Alternatively, a youth who is popular and highly regarded by his or her peers probably possesses significant interpersonal strengths that can be used subsequently as levers for therapeutic change.

OTHER SOURCES OF INFORMATION

Members of the youth's extended family, peers, parents of the youth's peers, coaches, and neighbors who know the youth and family all represent potential sources of information regarding the youth's peer relations.

Observing Peer Relations

If the information provided by multiple sources suggests the youth's inter-actions with peers are not problematic, direct observations of the peer system are seldom necessary. On the other hand, when the information about the youth's peer relations is contradictory or difficult to obtain, such direct observation is likely needed. Therapists seeking direct access to the youth's interactions with peers look for opportunities to observe the youth with peers at home, in school (in class, at lunch, on school grounds), in the neighborhood, and at other sites where the youth participates in activities with peers.

In some situations, information about the youth's peer relations might best be obtained through direct interaction with the youth and his or her friends or acquaintances. For example, the therapist might wish to assess an unpopular youth's level of social competence or resolve conflicting reports about the prosocial/antisocial nature of a youth's peer group. To accomplish these tasks, the therapist will need to interact with the youth and peers on the basis of their interests or skills and in a setting that is comfortable to them. For example, the therapist can determine whether a youth and a friend are interested in learning some card tricks, in meeting the therapist's pet dog, or making a 15-minute movie with the therapist's video camera. Then, with the caregivers' cooperation and assistance (this includes having caregivers obtain consent from the friend's caregivers), the therapist can arrange to meet at the family's home with the youth and his or her friend and share the selected activity with them. By engaging the youth in a meaningful activity, considerable information can be obtained about the cognitive and behavioral skills and everyday interests of both the youth and his or her friend. For example, a therapist will formulate different intervention strategies if he or she observes that a youth is skillful when interacting with a good friend than if the youth does not get along even with adolescents identified as friends.

Translating Assessment Information into Fit Circles

As with all MST intervention planning, understanding the fit of a behavior through assessment is an essential step in the design of effective interventions.

Understanding Association with Deviant Peers

The factors that sustain a youth's involvement with deviant peers can vary from family to family; Figure 4.1 illustrates several of these. As noted earlier in this chapter, several different aspects of family interaction (e.g., family

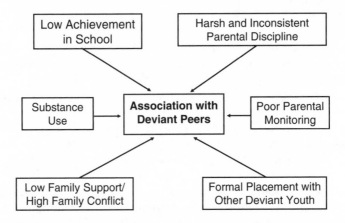

FIGURE 4.1. Factors contributing to involvement with deviant peers.

conflict, parenting style, parental monitoring) can contribute to a youth's involvement with deviant peers, and the initial MST assessment of family relations should provide clues regarding the potential contribution of such factors. In addition, a youth's low achievement in school and use of alcohol and drugs can contribute to association with like-minded peers who devalue school achievement and value substance use. Once a youth is involved with a deviant peer group, his or her antisocial behavior is often reinforced via group collaborative participation in antisocial acts as well as peer support and acceptance for engaging in such acts. Moreover, adolescents with behavior problems are unlikely to voluntarily extract themselves from a deviant peer group because they are often as closely attached to their friends as are nondelinquent youth to their nondeviant friends.

Understanding Peer Estrangement or Rejection

When an adolescent is socially isolated, actively rejected, or simply neglected (left alone) by same-age peers, aspects of the youth's interpersonal behavior that might be contributing to the lack of peer bonding and social isolation should be assessed. Common factors to consider when clarifying the particular constellation of influences on a youth's peer estrangement or rejection are illustrated in Figure 4.2.

WHEN AGGRESSIVE BEHAVIOR IS A KEY FACTOR

If aggressive behavior appears to be a primary contributor to disrupted peer relationships, the therapist should assure that family and family–school interventions are addressing all the factors that sustain the youth's aggressive behavior. If these interventions are being well implemented but aggressive behavior continues, then the therapist should examine possible contributions of the individual factors discussed in Chapter 6 and redesign interventions accordingly. In some cases, cognitive deficiencies and distortions contribute to inept or aggressive peer interactions. In addition, problems with hygiene (e.g., dirty clothes, body odor), physical appearance (e.g., unusually tall, short, thin, or heavy), or lack of conformity with peer norms for dress are linked with negative attention from peers and increased self-consciousness, which, in turn, can lead to conflictual peer interactions.

WHEN AGGRESSIVE BEHAVIOR IS NOT A KEY FACTOR

If, on the other hand, aggression does not appear to be a primary obstacle to the development of positive peer relationships, the therapist should work with the youth and family to identify which of several areas of interaction associated with successful peer relations might be problematic for the youth. In general, socially neglected or rejected youth withdraw from social situations, have difficulty initiating and sustaining positive give-and-take in conversations, and act in ways that are not accepted or valued by same-age peers.

Withdrawal and failed efforts at maintaining social give-and-take often result in peer avoidance, which, in turn, minimizes the positive peer contact necessary for the unskilled youth to learn alternative prosocial behaviors. Similarly, socially awkward or intrusive youth also elicit negative responses from peers, and, gradually, peers might develop negative labels for such youth and ridicule or ostracize them. Compounding the situation, social

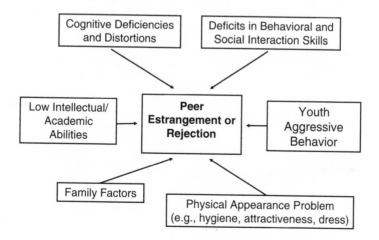

FIGURE 4.2. Factors contributing to peer estrangement or rejection.

rejection and negative labeling by peers can increase the antisocial, awkward, or withdrawal behaviors of some youth in that peers come to expect and selectively attend to inappropriate social behavior in a particular youth. When such negative expectancies occur:

- Peers are less likely to notice and respond positively to the youth's prosocial behavior.
- Continued negative feedback from peers can seriously compromise the adolescent's poor self-image, thereby contributing to increased social isolation.

Thus, negative responses from peers inhibit establishment of the types of positive interactions needed to improve the youth's social appropriateness at each successive step in development.

Treatment of Peer Relations

Interventions to address problems in a youth's peer relations (e.g., association with deviant peers, peer estrangement or rejection) must be sustainable in the absence of the MST therapist. Thus, *MST interventions draw on caregivers as key agents of change in the realm of peer relations*. Therapists will often need to assist caregivers to become:

- Experts in the interests and talents of their sons and daughters, even if those interests and talents have been eclipsed by behavior problems.
- Sources of advice and guidance about friendships when problems in peer relations are contributing to behavior problems.
- Sources of structuring, monitoring, and discipline needed to reduce opportunities to affiliate with deviant peers.
- Facilitators of exposure to community activities that include prosocial peers.
- Liaisons with the parents of their youth's friends.
- Adult supervisors, on occasion, of their youth's peer activities.

Decreasing Association with Deviant Peers and Increasing Affiliation with Prosocial Peers

When a youth's association with deviant peers contributes to a pattern of antisocial behavior, interventions are needed to reduce this affiliation and increase his or her association with prosocial peers. Often, interventions will be needed to help the caregiver accomplish each of the following tasks:

Monitor the Youth's Whereabouts

Those factors that are maintaining a lack of monitoring by the caregivers should be addressed first. Chapter 3 details factors commonly linked with low caregiver monitoring and interventions that are effective in increasing monitoring and supervision.

Increase Caregiver Contact with the Youth's Peers and Their Caregivers

Caregivers can use several strategies to increase the amount of contact that they have with the youth's peers. The therapist should be prepared to help caregivers understand when and why it is necessary to increase the amount of such contact.

FACILITATE PEER ACTIVITIES AT HOME

The therapist can help caregivers identify how to make the home a welcome place for peers to visit. Caregivers can provide one or more locations inside (e.g., family room, living room) or immediately outside the home (e.g., rear patio, basketball court in the driveway) where the youth and his or her peers can talk, play a game, watch a movie, or engage in some other age-appropriate activity with just enough (but not too much) caregiver supervision. "Just enough" means caregivers can see and hear what the youth and his or her peers are doing without constantly being in the immediate environment or interfering with peer interactions (unless a problem arises that requires parental intervention). Having refreshments available when the youth and his or her peers visit the home is another way that caregivers can make their home a welcome environment. Therapists should ensure caregivers provide the youth with reasonable guidelines about how often and for what length of time friends can be invited to the home and about what types of activities are allowed or prohibited when peers visit. With input from the youth, caregivers should also decide in advance how to handle unplanned visits from peers. Caregivers who provide a welcoming yet structured environment in their home for the youth's friends will find many opportunities to interact with those peers and learn about their interests and activities.

TAKE ADVANTAGE OF EVERYDAY OPPORTUNITIES

Therapists can help caregivers identify routine practical activities that present opportunities to observe and/or manage peer interactions. For example, a caregiver can transport several adolescents to and from the movies, to the mall, or to the ballpark. Caregivers lacking transportation can recommend (or require) that the youth's friends meet at the family's home in advance of a scheduled bus departure or cab ride to an afternoon or evening event.

STAY IN TOUCH WITH CAREGIVERS OF YOUTH'S FRIENDS

An important component of increasing caregiver monitoring of the youth's peer interactions involves regular contact with caregivers of the youth's friends. The therapist should encourage the youth's caregivers to talk with the peers' caregivers by phone or in person whenever peer activities are planned that require monitoring by adults. For example, prior to permitting the youth to visit another youth's home for a "party" on a Friday evening, the caregivers should talk with the peers' caregivers (including but not limited to the caregivers in whose home the event will be held) to ensure that the planned activities are appropriate and will be supervised by one or more responsible adults. By staying in regular contact with the caregivers of the youth's friends, the youth's caregivers can determine whether the teen is generally socializing with a responsible (i.e., prosocial) group of peers whose parents are equally concerned about monitoring peer group activities. This contact also enables the youth's caregiver and caregivers of these peers to begin to trust each other's judgment, share effective monitoring and disciplinary strategies with each other, and develop a network of parenting support for prosocial peer interaction. Importantly, the adolescent's caregivers also learn which of the other caregivers do not adequately monitor and supervise their own children or otherwise enable antisocial behavior (e.g., allow adolescents to drink or smoke marijuana in their home).

MEET OTHER COMPETENT PARENTS

Therapists might also need to help caregivers recognize or create opportunities to meet and develop relationships with other responsible caregivers at structured youth activities where caregiver attendance is encouraged (e.g., a school athletic event or play, parent-teacher conferences). When youth participate together in organized extracurricular activities, their caregivers can develop relationships that extend beyond the activities themselves and begin to play an important role in monitoring youth peer relations.

Sanction Youth Contacts with Antisocial Peers and Reward Contacts with Positive Peers

Caregivers should establish very unpleasant consequences for the youth's continued involvement with deviant peers. As suggested in Chapter 3, sanctions should include those that the youth finds especially aversive and that, under more normal circumstances, might seem quite unreasonable. For example, after establishing a set of procedures and guidelines for monitoring the who, what, when, and where surrounding the youth's activities, the caregivers might respond to *any* violation of the guidelines by restricting the youth to the house and having him or her perform a 5-hour work detail that includes the most unpleasant household tasks (e.g., cleaning the toilet, bathtub, sinks, and kitchen floor). The caregivers must ensure the youth's compliance by inspecting his or her work and by having the youth redo any work that does not meet the caregivers' standards. Other relatively aversive activities, such as washing and waxing the car, or vacuuming and dusting the entire house, can also be added to the youth's list of tasks should the youth continue to violate the caregivers' rules.

Help the Youth Identify Areas of Competence and Interest

Talents and activities that were apparent earlier in the youth's life are some-times eclipsed by involvement in antisocial activities, school failure, and involvement with the law. These talents and interests can provide important vehicles for promoting the youth's involvement with nonproblem peers. For example, caregivers can encourage youth with musical talents to participate in organized musical groups (e.g., the school jazz band); adolescents with literary talents can be encouraged to join the staff of the yearbook or school newspaper; mechanically talented youth can be enrolled in special voca-tional programs and perhaps work as apprentices in certain employment settings; and athletically gifted youth can be encouraged to participate in organized sports. Other examples of prosocial activities include commu-nity-based service organizations, church groups, recreation center activi-ties, and after-school volunteer or paid employment. Although it is impor-tant for caregivers to require that the youth become involved in prosocial activities, the choice of the specific activity should be left to the youth (thus providing a sense of control), and therapists might need to facilitate initial family discussions about these choices.

Facilitate the Youth's Participation in Prosocial Activities

Whatever the prosocial activity, caregivers should reinforce the youth's par-ticipation. For example, the caregivers might need to provide the youth with certain resources (e.g., a musical instrument, athletic equipment), assure that he or she has transportation to and from the activity, and show interest in those activities at which their attendance is encouraged. Indeed, caregiver attendance at the youth's activities makes a powerful statement—providing concrete evidence of the caregiver's commitment to the youth and pride in his or her talents.

Suggestions for Helping Caregivers Accomplish These Tasks

The specific intervention strategies used by the therapist to accomplish each of the aforementioned tasks will vary in accordance with the strengths of the particular youth, family, school, neighborhood, and community. Nevertheless, therapists helping caregivers take a proactive role in rearranging a youth's peer ecology can follow several guidelines that increase the likelihood that these often difficult tasks can be accomplished.

1. *Prepare the caregivers for battle.* Minimizing a youth's contact with valued but deviant friends and increasing his or her contact with unfamiliar but prosocial peers can be an extremely arduous process and will likely be met with considerable resistance from the youth. Thus, caregivers must be well prepared for the likely challenges associated with this process. To aid in this process, therapists convey in no uncertain terms that caregiver efforts to change the youth's peer affiliations will probably:

- Require a major investment of their time, energy, and emotion.
- Elicit angry responses and various ploys from the youth in an attempt to change their decisions.

Moreover, with caregivers who are reluctant to become involved in changing the youth's peer affiliations, the therapist might need to:

- Point out the probable long-term negative consequences of the youth's continued involvement with deviant peers (e.g., incarceration, drug addiction, getting shot while committing a crime).
- Help the caregivers weigh these consequences against the short-term but unpleasant task of preventing the youth's continued affiliation with deviant peers.

Caregivers must have the support and assistance of other family members, friends, co-workers, and other significant adults (e.g., teachers, neighbors) prior to implementing interventions designed to minimize the youth's contact with deviant peers. Even when such support is forthcoming, the therapist should be prepared to provide substantial assistance initially (e.g., taking phone calls at midnight when the youth does not return home, arriving on the scene when the youth does return and the caregivers try to implement sanctions). If peer interventions require such extreme measures as tracking a youth's whereabouts when he or she is with problem friends who temporarily house or hide the youth, the therapist might need to help caregivers enlist the help of more formal community supports such as probation officers, community police, and social service staff.

2. *Help the youth see the disadvantages of associating with deviant peers.* Typically, the therapist uses (and coaches caregivers to use) a cognitively oriented approach to introduce a youth to the idea that his or her peer group affiliation needs to change. This approach uses strategies similar to those used in motivational interviewing (Miller & Rollnick, 2002). The therapist can help the youth identify his or her educational and occupa-

tional goals as well as the necessary steps for achieving those goals. After the goals and steps have been identified, the therapist and caregivers help the youth examine some of the likely discrepancies between the goals and the youth's current lifestyle. For youth who argue that they have plenty of time to start pursuing their educational or occupational goals and would rather wait, for example, until age 25 to do so, the therapeutic task becomes one of convincing the youth that this strategy has little chance of success. This discussion provides an opportunity to examine some of the probable differences between the youth's goals and those of the current peers. Once the youth recognizes that these discrepancies exist, therapists and caregivers can examine productive ways that the youth can go about meeting his or her goals. At this point, the issue of forming friendships with peers who are pursuing similar goals can also be explored.

The therapist can also help the caregivers discuss the type of social reputation the youth would ultimately like to develop in the broader community (assuming that the youth would not like a reputation as a criminal and is experiencing some negative consequences as a result of hanging out with deviant peers). Again, discrepancies between the youth's social goals and current behavior can be examined, and ways to better meet these goals can be addressed. Given that most youth hold positive occupational and social goals for themselves, the idea of beginning to work toward (and not in opposition to) these goals can sometimes be used as a lever to convince the youth that withdrawal from the current peer group (or the most deviant peers) is necessary. If other individuals in the natural ecology of the youth and family (e.g., an uncle, coach, or neighbor) are more credible sources of information for the youth initially (because, for example, such individuals have not previously engaged in arguments about the peers), the therapist encourages the caregivers to solicit the help of these individuals.

3. *Avoid berating, belittling, or insulting peers who are valued by the youth.* Caregivers should avoid trying to convince the youth that his or her friends have no redeeming personal or social attributes. Therapists may need to help caregivers understand such an approach is seldom effective and will likely fuel caregiver–youth conflict because it ignores the fact that these friends are likely to be providing the youth with emotional support and a sense of belonging. Thus, therapists should help caregivers acknowledge the youth has positive feelings about the deviant peers while focusing on the negative consequences of affiliating with those peers.

Special Considerations When Peers Are Mixed versus Exclusively Deviant

Therapists and caregivers take into account the extent and intensity of the youth's association with deviant peers when designing and implementing interventions.

INTERVENING WHEN PEERS ARE MIXED

When a youth has some prosocial and some antisocial peers, the therapist and caregivers can attempt to steer the youth toward the former. When a youth has peers the caregivers regard as questionable (i.e., on the border between desirable and undesirable), but whom the youth regards as close friends, caregivers can set and enforce firm limits regarding the youth's contact and interactions with those peers. The following case exemplifies the second type of situation.

> Erik Graham was an eleventh-grader who had been referred to MST following two arrests for physical assault of a peer in school and three suspensions from school for truancy. During a conference with the caregivers and three of Erik's teachers, the therapist learned that Erik had an excellent academic record (A's and B's) until the past year, when he began to skip school with a number of his friends on the football team. Some of the same friends had also encouraged Eric's fighting, which had been directed toward another male student who had made derogatory remarks about Erik's former girlfriend. Although Mr. and Mrs. Graham had disciplined Erik appropriately (i.e., grounding him for several weeks, assigning a long list of extra chores to complete each weekend, and removing his television and music privileges), their efforts had not produced any positive changes in Erik's grades or discouraged his association with his problem teammates. Mr. and Mrs. Graham were especially concerned that one of Erik's friends had recently dropped out of school, and they feared that it was only a matter of time before Erik would do the same.
>
> After meeting several times with Erik and his parents, the therapist concluded everyone in the family (including Erik) valued academic achievement and occupational success. Moreover, Erik was well aware of the negative consequences associated with fighting and performing poorly in school, including being grounded, being temporarily suspended from the football team, dropping off the honor roll, and disappointing not only his caregivers but also his teachers. Nevertheless, Erik adamantly refused to meet his caregivers' request to give up his friends, whom he had known since elementary school. Erik argued that he had a right to choose his own friends, regardless of what his caregivers thought of them.
>
> The therapist and parents decided that prohibiting Erik's association with his current peers and encouraging his association with non-problem peers was not a viable treatment strategy for several reasons. First, Erik's strong long-term alliance to his friends, with whom he shared common talents (i.e., football and athletic skills), greatly reduced the likelihood that he would shift his allegiance to a new group of peers. In fact, Erik had already proven that he was willing to endure whatever punishments his caregivers might use to discourage this allegiance.

Second, when meeting with Erik and three of his friends one day after school, the therapist learned that Erik's friends were hard workers even if they were not academically inclined. Each of the boys had a part-time job and engaged in a rigorous physical conditioning program. Furthermore, these boys begrudgingly admired Eric for his ability to get good grades in school. Third, although Erik's friends teased him about being a "mama's boy," it was clear they cared a great deal about him and that they were aware he was under much pressure from his parents not to skip school or fight.

In light of the preceding factors, the caregivers and therapist decided the family's interests would best be served by teaching Erik to cope with peer pressures aimed at devaluing academic achievement and encouraging fighting. The therapist arranged a "brainstorming" session during which Erik, his caregivers, and the therapist generated a number of possible strategies that Erik could use to respond to negative pressure from his peers. Then, Erik gave his favorite strategies a "test drive" in a series of role plays in which his caregivers played the role of high-pressure peers. Based on these role plays, the caregivers and Erik decided that the most effective strategy would be for Erik to (1) ignore the peers' negative requests and, if that was not successful, (2) tell his friends that he did not want to hurt the football team again by risking suspension, (3) point out that he was already in trouble with his caregivers and did not want to spend the next year being grounded, or (4) change the subject to something humorous that had happened in one of his classes or that he had seen on television.

Thus, although Mr. and Mrs. Graham would have preferred that Erik find a new group of friends, they gradually came to appreciate the fact that Erik's current friends met important emotional needs in his life and that Eric feared being rejected by these friends. Because Erik already recognized the long-term benefits of receiving an education and did not enjoy the consequences imposed on him by his parents for his problem behaviors, he was willing to follow his caregivers' suggestions (with input from the therapist) regarding ways of responding to negative peer pressure. Although Erik skipped a few more classes during the course of therapy, his grades improved dramatically and he noted that his peers no longer hounded him about skipping school. At a 1-year follow-up, Mr. and Mrs. Graham reported that Erik's grades remained quite high and that he had expressed an interest in attending the local community college after graduating from high school.

When a youth such as Erik shares prosocial interests or talents with an otherwise deviant group of peers, it is sometimes possible to reduce the likelihood that the youth will continue to engage in deviant behavior without being removed from the current peer group. Moreover, depending on the case, strategies other than helping the youth to cope with deviant peer pressure can also be used. The following example shows how the therapist and mother used indigenous resources to restructure a teenage girl's activities in ways that promoted prosocial behavior.

> Brenda Ellis was a 16-year-old high school student who was referred to the MST program following a series of arrests for shoplifting and late-night loitering with her friends, as well as punching and kicking a female classmate who had made fun of Brenda's out-of-date clothes. Brenda's father had abandoned the family 3 years earlier, leaving Mrs. Ellis with the difficult task of raising Brenda and her five younger siblings. Although Mrs. Ellis was concerned about Brenda's behavior, she was clearly overwhelmed by her parenting and financial responsibilities and had no immediate or extended family members on whom to rely for emotional or instrumental support. Mrs. Ellis stated that she had neither the time nor the energy to keep close tabs on Brenda's behavior, and that Brenda would need to be placed in a foster home or some other place if her problem behavior continued.
>
> After meeting with Brenda and two of her closest female friends, the therapist concluded that the girls' problematic behavior was largely motivated by their desire to have certain types of "in" clothes and other basic provisions that their families could not afford. None of the girls received an allowance, and their families could not afford to provide them with one. During a subsequent meeting, the therapist and Mrs. Ellis reached an agreement with Brenda, her two closest friends, and their caregivers that everyone was happy to accept. Specifically, the parents would help the girls find part-time jobs with local neighborhood merchants if the girls would agree to stop shoplifting, loitering, and fighting. With the help of Mrs. Ellis and another parent, the therapist taught the girls how to fill out employment applications and suggested likely places of employment. One month later, each of the girls had obtained a part-time job that did not interfere with their responsibilities at school or at home. During subsequent sessions with Mrs. Ellis and Brenda, the therapist helped them negotiate rules regarding the management of Brenda's paycheck, performance and attendance in school, household and babysitting responsibilities, and time spent with friends. Eighteen months later, Brenda had graduated from high school, obtained full-time employment at a better job, and not been rearrested.

INTERVENING WHEN PEERS ARE EXCLUSIVELY DEVIANT

When an adolescent is exclusively involved with deviant friends, the therapist and caregivers will need to rearrange the youth's everyday ecology in ways that provide powerful positive reinforcers and negative sanctions to compete with the perceived benefits of affiliation with the deviant peer group. The aforementioned intervention strategies and guidelines should be attempted before making the decision to extract the youth entirely from a deviant peer group. This decision is usually made when four conditions are met:

1. Members of the youth's peer group have little interest or involvement in *any* type of prosocial activity (e.g., maintaining passing grades in school; participating in an extracurricular club, team, or organization; holding down a part-time job).
2. The peer group has a history of *continued and extensive* participation in illegal activities, especially those involving violent behavior or drug abuse.
3. Interventions designed to change the youth's peer affiliation have been unsuccessful.
4. The peers have caregivers who provide little structure and monitoring and possibly engage in illegal behavior themselves.

The following case provides an example of the concerted effort by caregivers and others in the family's support network needed to disengage a youth from deviant peers.

Jasmine Campbell was a physically mature 15-year-old female whose deteriorating grades, repeated arrests for minor thefts, vandalism, and disorderly conduct, and increased sexual activity over the past 18 months were of considerable concern to her parents. To deal with these problems, they had implemented a series of increasingly restrictive punishments. By the time the family was referred to MST, Jasmine was essentially a prisoner in her home and her parents functioned as guards. She had no phone privileges, was not allowed out after school, and was confined to her home during weekends. Despite these restrictions, Jasmine had managed to sneak her 18-year-old boyfriend through a second story window into her bedroom one night. Another night, she had crept out of the home at 1:00 A.M. to spend several hours drinking and vandalizing new cars at an auto dealership with her boyfriend and several other older male and female peers.

In discussing the situation with the family, the therapist obtained several indications that removal from the peer group was needed. First, neither Jasmine's boyfriend nor her other older peers (who were friends of her boyfriend) had any positive direction in their lives. They had all dropped out of high school, were unemployed, and lived with caregivers who were extremely permissive. Second, Jasmine was deeply committed to her boyfriend. He was her first love, and he met emotional needs that had not been met by her parents, who had relatively distant emotional styles. Third, if Jasmine were forced to choose between her family and her peers (especially her boyfriend), then she would probably choose her friends. Fourth, the parents were bright, competent individuals who were concerned about their daughter's welfare. And fifth, although Jasmine was physically mature, her level of emotional functioning was not yet at age level.

Before deciding on a course of action, the therapist and parents reached a consensus about several important issues. First, they decided that a home should not be a prison and that it was not in the best interest of any family member to live in such a restrictive environment. Jasmine needed to have friends with whom she could spend time, but her parents' concern about her sexual activity, problems in school, and criminal behaviors needed to be addressed. Second, although the therapist and parents understood why Jasmine was in love with her boyfriend, they did not believe this was a positive relationship in the long run. The boyfriend had some serious problems, and Jasmine had many strengths that would enable relationships with more responsible young men. Since Jasmine was now only 15 years old, she was legally bound to comply with her parents' wishes. Although everyone could appreciate Jasmine's feelings, the parents could not allow her to continue the relationship with her boyfriend or his friends.

Next, the therapist and parents designed a plan to return the home to normal, to terminate Jasmine's relationship with her boyfriend and other older peers, and to allow Jasmine the freedom that an adolescent needs. First, Jasmine's parents would grant her age-appropriate privileges and freedoms. However, if she continued to see her boyfriend and his friends, her parents would file a criminal complaint (statutory rape, contributing to the delinquency of a minor) against these older youth and would consider placing Jasmine in a more restrictive environment that allowed peer interactions only with girls (a single-gender boarding school). The parents and therapist emphasized that this was not a course that they wanted to take, but that it was preferable to converting the family's home into a jail and to constantly worrying about Jasmine's welfare. Thus, if Jasmine chose to continue to see her boyfriend and/or his peers, the consequences would be extremely unpleasant. On the other hand, if she terminated the relationships (with her parents' assistance), her freedoms would be restored.

The therapist used cognitive, family-based, and peer-based interventions to help Jasmine make and maintain her decision to terminate the relationship with her boyfriend. At a cognitive level, the therapist helped Jasmine appreciate that she had many positive intellectual and personality characteristics and would have ample opportunities to develop relationships with boys who had as many positive qualities as she did. The therapist also addressed emotional aspects of family and marital relations, such that the parents were able to (1) express their love and concern for Jasmine more openly and (2) provide more support for each other as parents and marital partners. Finally, the therapist helped the parents develop ways for Jasmine to establish nonproblematic relations with youth her own age. For example, they provided Jasmine with the resources to engage in extensive activities with her church's youth group as a way to develop ties with prosocial peers and eventually form new friendships. Jasmine already knew a few of the adolescents in this group because she had been in classes with them at school. She also joined the staff of her high school newspaper and met several new male and female peers through her participation in that activity every day after school. Although Jasmine's former boyfriend tried to visit her at school several times during lunch hour and made numerous phone calls to the home (including threats against the parents), the parents, with cooperation from school officials and police, were able to prevent him from seeing Jasmine and he eventually disengaged from her life.

Helping Socially Rejected or Neglected Youth

As with interventions that target youth association with deviant peers, therapists make every effort to include caregivers in interventions that target youth rejection or neglect by peers to ensure that changes in peer relations are sustained in home and neighborhood settings. Importantly, when family interaction patterns contribute to peer rejection or neglect of the youth, the therapist helps families change those interaction patterns. For example, the family itself might be socially isolated, or the caregivers might be socially anxious or relatively unskilled in their own social interactions. In addition, the caregivers might not be aware of the important role that they can play in arranging opportunities for their youth to engage in social interactions (e.g., by seeking out community activities, enabling peers to visit, providing rides to the mall). *When family interaction patterns contribute to the youth's deficits in peer interaction skills, interventions directed solely at the youth are unlikely to be successful.* Thus, before and while implementing the individualized social skills training techniques described in this section and Chapter 6, the therapist implements interventions to address the family factors believed to contribute to the peer problems.

Intervention Targets: Specific Skill Deficits

Treatment programs for youth with social skills deficits typically focus on the individual youth and his or her interactions with peers in a single natural setting such as a classroom. Within the context of MST, the therapist and caregivers can design and implement individually oriented procedures with the youth at home, while seeking opportunities for the youth to practice in the context of school and neighborhood settings in which same-age peers can be observed. The therapist considers the nature of the youth's social interaction problems and his or her level of cognitive development when identifying the specific targets of intervention. Common problem areas include the following:

1. *Weak acquaintanceship skills.* Some youth have particular difficulties initiating interactions with peers. They might be unsure how to:
- Approach others (e.g., greeting others, giving compliments).
- Get a conversation going (e.g., making an appropriate comment, asking a question).
- Join a group (e.g., listening and then engaging with the group).

When youth resort to either obnoxious show-off behavior or anxious behavior (e.g., withdrawal, seeking sympathy, whimpering, fidgeting), they might need instruction in positive methods of acquiring peer attention and engaging in peer interactions.

2. *Deficits in communication skills.* Socially isolated and neglected youth often lack skills such as:
- Telling about themselves (i.e., self-disclosing) to promote intimacy and friendship.
- Making suggestions or giving advice to promote extended friendly interactions.
- Asking for help or making requests (i.e., asking directly and calmly, showing appreciation if granted).
- Expressing their feelings directly, rather than complaining or withdrawing.
- Appropriately asserting their wishes (e.g., saying no appropriately).
- Becoming empathic when others talk (e.g., perceiving others' feelings and expressing understanding).

3. *Deficits in sharing and cooperation skills.* Many youth are not liked by peers because they do not play well—they cheat, have trouble sharing, and are generally no fun. Often these youth have never really learned the principles of cooperation or how to balance a give-and-take relationship. Whether they are overly dominant or overly passive in peer interactions, these teens are basically lacking in the skills necessary for cooperative and reciprocal interaction.

4. *Deficits in problem-solving and conflict resolution skills.* As described in more detail in Chapter 6, deficits in the cognitive problem-solving abilities that mediate social interaction can reduce a youth's interpersonal effectiveness. When presented with interpersonal problem situations, socially unskilled youth often find it difficult to consider and appraise alternative courses of action.

Addressing Peer Relationship Problems

During meetings with the youth, the therapist and caregivers can draw upon several types of instructional strategies that have been used effectively in social skills training and problem solving interventions for youth. These strategies, which are also described in detail in Chapter 6, include instruction in the particular skill to be learned, modeling the skill, providing opportunities for the youth to practice the skill, and giving verbal reinforcement and corrective feedback after observing the practice. Instructional strategies are explained to caregivers so that they can reinforce the newly developing skills and become involved in coaching the youth in the absence of the therapist.

INSTRUCTION IN THE SKILL TO BE LEARNED

The therapist should be familiar with the common problem areas listed above and with the specific problems or deficits in social interactions experienced by the particular youth. As the case of Justin illustrates, one or more of these skill areas may present greater difficulties than others.

> Justin was able to greet classmates with accepted slang and was sometimes greeted in return. However, he rarely participated in even casual conversations about the most obvious topics (e.g., homework assignments, television shows, after-school activities, sports). During the assessment process in the home and while observing Justin at an after-school activity, the therapist learned that Justin often disclosed inappropriate information about himself and his family (e.g., that his older brother was in prison). Moreover, even when he did ask a question of a peer, Justin rarely followed up with additional questions, launching instead into comments about his dirt bike, his cousins, and the first school he attended when his family lived in another state.

Once a specific skill deficit has been identified, the therapist should provide a clear description of the skills to be learned, one at a time, and explain why each is important. In Justin's case, starting a conversation with a same-age peer was the first target of intervention. To introduce this concept, the therapist explained that Justin's desire to get to know someone at his school would not likely be met unless he could learn to start conversations. The therapist also explained that the ability to start conversations would help Justin obtain information about other things he cared about, like whether any of his classmates were interested in dirt bikes and whether the local library or recreation center had information about motocross camps and programs.

As described in more detail in the Social Skills Training section of Chapter 6, another important aspect of coaching social skills is verbal instruction regarding the specific verbal and nonverbal behaviors involved in the skill (e.g., making eye contact, standing close enough to be heard but not so close as to make others uncomfortable). For relatively simple skills, such as learning to give a compliment, relatively few behaviors are involved. However, when providing instruction on more complex skills, such as starting a conversation or asking someone on a date, the therapist or caregiver might have to describe and model several different behaviors, such as making eye contact, greeting the other person by name, asking an open-ended question, following up if the person responds, asking another question, and so on.

MODELING

Modeling occurs when the youth observes the social behavior of others. Models are more powerful when they are similar to the youth in age, gender, and race. A variety of such models appear on television programs and in movies. Together, the therapist and youth can review recorded scenes of adolescents engaging in positive, realistic, and nonviolent social interactions. Watching and discussing these scenes together can serve two important purposes. First, the scenes can help to clarify the concept of the desired behavior. Second, the scenes illustrate that there are many acceptable ways to engage others in positive interaction.

Exposure to real-life prosocial models should also be arranged by identifying activities and locations in which positive youth peer interactions are likely to occur. To maximize the teaching value of observational outings, the therapist should point out specific interactions and skills that contribute to positive and reciprocal social interaction. Comments such as "Notice how well they are getting along" are not likely to help the youth develop a clear concept of what it takes to get along. On the other hand, observations such as "He said he liked the other guy's jacket, and the guy with the jacket said 'thanks' and asked him something back," provide specific information that can be conveyed to the adolescent as teachable, and therefore learnable, skills.

BEHAVIORAL REHEARSAL AND PRACTICE

A third instructional strategy used in social skills training includes behavioral rehearsal and practice. Behavioral rehearsal helps to ensure that the teenager will be able to perform the target behavior in appropriate situations. For youth who have the cognitive ability to imagine situations in which they are attempting to employ new skills, the steps in behavioral rehearsal might be as follows:

- The youth begins by visualizing a particular situation and his or her response to the situation.
- The therapist then encourages the adolescent to talk through the situation by describing the scene, how she or he would behave, and the possible consequences.
- The therapist, teen, and his or her caregivers then role-play the situation.

- Next, the therapist and caregivers observe the youth, initially in the context of role plays, and provide feedback to the youth about her or his performance so that necessary corrections can be made.
- The therapist and caregivers should also obtain the adolescent's evaluation of her or his behavior in these role plays to ensure that the youth can accurately assess his or her performance and not engage in overly harsh self-evaluations (e.g., "I completely blew it") or overly optimistic ones (e.g., "I really did a great job," when several corrective statements from the therapist or caregiver were required to elicit the desired behavior).

An extended example of the importance of behavioral rehearsal and practice in teaching social skills is provided in the problem-solving section of Chapter 6.

ECOLOGICAL SUPPORT FOR NEWLY ACQUIRED SKILLS

The final component of effective social skills training interventions is to encourage performance of newly developing skills in real-world contexts. Ecological support for newly acquired skills is essential, as individuals rarely perform new skills if they are not reinforced. If, for example, siblings ridicule the youth's efforts to give a compliment (a beginning step in creating positive interactions) or refuse to respond to requests to share (a more advanced skill), the teenager might decide not to practice the skills as needed. In such a case, the therapist would work with the caregivers to alter sibling interactions to be more supportive. Similarly, if the majority of a youth's classmates ignore, ridicule, or actively reject him or her, then the therapist and family would try to identify other settings (e.g., neighborhood, church youth group, recreation center) in which the youth could begin to practice skills mastered in role-played sessions with the therapist. When successes are experienced in these settings, the therapist, caregivers, and adolescent together design and try strategies that increase the likelihood that classmates will respond positively.

The following case incorporates each of the instructional strategies discussed in this section.

> Derrick Earl was a tall, muscular 16-year-old boy referred to MST following two arrests for physically assaultive behavior in school. According to his high school principal, Derrick had a long-standing reputation for his quick temper and aggressive behavior toward other boys. Over the past 6 months, he had severely beaten up at least three of his male peers, one of whom required eye surgery. It was only a matter of time before Derrick's violent behavior would result in incarceration.
>
> During the first few weeks of treatment, several pertinent aspects of Derrick's peer relations became clear. The therapist learned that

Derrick was an exceptional athlete whose basketball and track skills had earned him substantial recognition and had made him the envy of many of his male peers. On the other hand, Derrick had relatively low intellectual abilities (a Verbal IQ of 79), had a lisp for which he received speech therapy, and was near the bottom of his class academically. According to Derrick's teachers, both his academic performance and his speech impediment were targets of verbal taunts from several of his male peers. It was these taunts that usually provoked Derrick's aggressive outbursts. Derrick's school counselor reported that the majority of these peers had emotional and family problems, and that all of them had marginal academic and athletic skills.

As a next step, the therapist decided to role-play a number of different scenarios with Derrick to learn more about the peer interactions that were contributing to his aggressive behavior. After Derrick described some of the interactions with peers that angered him, including the specific statements that his peers made to him, the therapist asked Derrick to role-play a situation that involved verbal taunting about his academic abilities. The therapist explained that Derrick should indicate when he was becoming angry at the therapist, who played the role of a peer, so that the role play could be stopped at that point. Although Derrick initially thought that the idea of a role play was silly, the therapist enacted the role of a peer effectively enough to engage Derrick in a series of angry interchanges.

Following each angry exchange, the therapist talked with Derrick and Mrs. Earl about Derrick's responses to the "peer's" statements. This discussion revealed that Derrick did not recognize how readily he was baited by his peers, nor did he see that his peers might be envious of his athletic skills. Although he was unable to generate any positive alternatives to fighting with his peers, he reported that he did not enjoy fighting, nor did he like the fact that he had developed a reputation as a bully. The therapist and Mrs. Earl also learned that Derrick tended to interpret many signs of affection from peers (e.g., a pat on the back, a hand on the shoulder) in a hostile light. He stated that he did not want anyone "messing' with him, even if the person was someone he liked.

The therapist's initial intervention was to help Derrick identify some of the likely reasons behind the taunts of certain peers, and to understand some of the positive motives behind other peers' signs of friendship. Next, the therapist asked Derrick's uncle (Mrs. Earl's younger brother), a former college basketball player whom Derrick greatly admired, to assist with the next set of interventions. The therapist, Derrick, and his uncle met together on several occasions and jointly developed some nonaggressive strategies for responding to both the negative and positive behaviors of Derrick's peers. For example, in response to peers' taunts about his academic performance and speech difficulties, the therapist taught Derrick to kindly ask whether they would like some help in developing their basketball and track skills—effectively silencing these nonathletic peers. In response to physical shows of affection from his peers, Derrick's uncle taught him the "fist bump," used by many professional athletes that Derrick admired, to convey his acceptance of them. These strategies were rehearsed and refined over a period of 2 months, and Derrick's reputation as a bully gradually diminished.

Barriers to Change and Strategies to Overcome Them

Common barriers to the success of peer interventions are described next, and possible strategies to overcome these barriers are discussed.

Gangs

Extraction from a deviant peer group can be particularly difficult for gang-affiliated youth. However, findings from youth gang studies are relevant to MST treatment of such youth (see Howell, 2003).

- Many types of adolescent peer groups violate laws together but are not gangs.
- Gang membership is not stable, with nearly two-thirds of gang-involved youth remaining members for only 1 year.
- Previous gang members are able to develop prosocial peer associations following departure from the gang.

The central implication of these findings for therapists and families is that a youth's proclaimed or actual involvement in a gang need not be seen as an insurmountable barrier to the success of peer interventions. On the other hand, if serious threats on the life of the youth or family members ensue following efforts to extract the youth from a gang, these threats should be taken seriously by therapists, family members, and law enforcement officials, and a safety plan (see Chapter 2) should be devised.

Group Therapy and Other Juvenile Justice or Substance Abuse Interventions That Aggregate Youth

For a variety of reasons (e.g., availability, low financial cost, convenience to service systems), many traditional juvenile justice and substance abuse interventions bring antisocial youth together in group treatment, special classrooms, and in other ways. However, in light of the mutually reinforcing effects of deviant peers upon one another, school, juvenile justice, and community efforts that aggregate troublesome youth often exacerbate, rather than ameliorate, deviant behavior (Dodge et al., 2006). Indeed, it seems unreasonable to expect that a group of youth with behavior problems will somehow generate prosocial values and group norms by interacting with one another. Moreover, time spent in group treatment with other deviant youth cannot be spent on building the types of academic and social competence with prosocial peers that are critical to sustaining positive behavior change for adolescents with serious antisocial behavior. Thus, MST program policies strictly restrict youth involvement in group treatments that involve deviant peers, and considerable efforts should be made to engage teenagers in educational and vocational settings that include successful and competent peers. MST programs that are having difficulties in sustaining these policies should seek assistance from their MST consultant.

Lack of Parental Buy-In

Some caregivers simply are not aware of the importance of peer relations to positive development or of the significant role that families play in facilitating peer relations. Thus, the therapist should be sure to obtain the caregiver's perspective on the contribution of peer issues to the referral problems and should have evidence linking the two if the caregiver does not see the connection (e.g., the youth steals and takes drugs only when he or she is in the presence of certain acquaintances). Alternatively, some caregivers appreciate the importance of peer relations but do not believe that they have the right to influence their youth's choice of friends. In such cases, the therapist should point out that (1) adolescents have every right to choose their friends as long as those friends have prosocial interests, and (2) teens who choose deviant peers as friends typically need caregiver guidance in finding new friends who are not deviant.

Inadequate Implementation

Inadequate implementation most often arises when caregivers are attempting to extract the youth from a deviant peer group. A common situation is that the caregivers were inadequately prepared for battle and gave in when the youth reacted negatively to their monitoring efforts by, for example, running away or threatening violence. In such instances, the therapist and caregivers should review the support plan, determine where support broke down in ways that contributed to the caregivers abandoning the intervention plan, and design strategies to prevent a similar breakdown in the future. Moreover, if significant adults in other areas of the youth's life (e.g., teachers, supervisor at the recreation center) had not previously been part of the plan but can provide reporting functions (e.g., he left class with the tough kids today) or support, they should be approached. In addition, the therapist and caregivers should ensure that the positive consequences for avoidance of negative peers and affiliation with prosocial peers are still salient to the adolescent, the negative consequences are powerful deterrents, and no familial (e.g., marital conflict, caregiver inconsistency, caregiver substance abuse or depression) or other barriers are interfering with the implementation of rewards and consequences.

Concrete or Practical Barriers

When caregiver interventions are thwarted due to limited economic resources, the therapist and caregiver will need to problem solve. For example, they might request that entry fees for enrollment in community activities be reduced or waived, apply for scholarships or financial assistance from community organizations to assist with payment, or engage in informal bartering of one service for another (e.g., a caregiver agrees to bake for a drive to buy uniforms, and the youth receives a uniform in return). Similarly, the youth might need to make do with clothing and equipment that are not brand new. Teens do not need to have the latest in designer athletic shoes, for example, to participate in a local track club or basketball league, and caregivers should be wary of claims to the contrary. Some communities, particularly isolated rural communities and highly impoverished urban neighborhoods, offer relatively few organized recreational options for youth and rely more heavily on church, neighborhood, or informal social networks to provide activities for youth after school and on weekends. In such communities, the therapist and caregiver should work diligently to find out how to access after-school opportunities and activities that are available to teenagers who are not engaged in antisocial behavior.

Conclusion

Association with deviant peers is a powerful predictor of antisocial behavior in adolescents. Consequently, MST places a high priority on disengaging teenagers from problem friends and supporting their relations with prosocial peers. Indeed, such changes in peer relations are central to the MST theory of change, and the value of limiting contact between antisocial youth and deviant peers has been supported in research on the mechanisms of evidence-based treatments for antisocial behavior (Chapter 2). Thus, this chapter provided strategies to help caregivers remove their adolescents from deviant peers, assist youth in developing the social skills needed for establishing positive relations with prosocial peers, and overcome barriers to such changes.

CHAPTER 5

Promoting Educational and Vocational Success

WITH CINDY M. SCHAEFFER

IN THIS CHAPTER

- Common school-related problems of youth in MST programs.
- Assessing school-related problems.
- Interventions for school-related problems.
- Preventing youth dropout.
- Promoting educational and vocational progress when youth have left school.

By the time adolescents with serious antisocial behavior are referred to MST programs, many have experienced repeated truancy, suspension, expulsion, and academic failure. The caregivers and teachers of these youth are often puzzled, frustrated, angry, and even hopeless about the youth's academic and behavior problems. Caregivers frequently blame the school for the youth's academic and classroom problems and report hearing either nothing or only bad

---

Cindy M. Schaeffer, PhD, is Associate Professor in the Department of Psychiatry and Behavioral Sciences at the Medical University of South Carolina and a member of the Family Services Research Center faculty. She received her doctorate in child-clinical psychology from the University of Missouri–Columbia and completed a postdoctoral fellowship in prevention science at the Johns Hopkins Bloomberg School of Public Health. Dr. Schaeffer's work involves understanding the development of antisocial behavior across childhood and adolescence, and developing new, ecologically based interventions for antisocial youth and their families.

news from teachers and principals. School personnel might blame the family for failing to help the youth succeed and often report that the family is not involved in the youth's schooling experience. Thus, a pattern of antagonistic interaction develops that, repeated often enough, can lead school personnel and caregivers to disconnect from one another completely. Facing situations such as these, MST therapists must engage teachers, other pertinent school personnel, and caregivers in developing and implementing interventions that help the youth progress academically and behaviorally in school.

The school-related outcomes most commonly desired by caregivers, school personnel, and therapists for adolescents in MST programs are:

- Keeping the youth in school.
- Improved grades.
- Eliminating truancy.
- Avoiding school disciplinary actions such as suspension and expulsion.

These are particularly high-stakes outcomes, as failure to achieve them increases the risk that youth will experience the many negative long-term economic (e.g., reduced wages, limited career opportunities) and social (e.g., housing restrictions, fewer opportunities for children) consequences of dropping out (Bridgeland, Diulio, & Morrison, 2006; U. S. Department of Education, 1998).

Addressing the problems of the youth in class and on school grounds that typically contribute to truancy, suspension, and expulsion is often a priority for MST therapists. The case examples of Erik Graham in Chapter 4 and Tim Clayton in Chapter 6 illustrate that several social ecological factors that contribute to criminal activity (e.g., association with deviant peers, lack of parental monitoring and ineffective parenting practices, a youth's lack of problem-solving skills) can also contribute to school-related problems. Often, when these systemic problems are resolved, as in the cases of Erik and Tim, school-related difficulties improve dramatically. In other cases, however, behavior problems in school reflect the interplay of the youth's cognitive and academic limitations with family, peer, and school factors. In such cases, interventions might be required in the classroom, home, and family–school interface to improve school-related problems. Accordingly, this chapter begins with guidelines and strategies MST therapists use to:

- Engage teachers, pertinent school personnel, and caregivers in the assessment, design, and implementation of interventions that occur in school.
- Engage caregivers in the design and implementation of interventions at home needed to support school interventions.
- Cultivate effective collaboration between the youth's teachers and caregivers to improve youth behavioral and academic performance.

Subsequent sections of the chapter describe strategies to assess the fit of youth problems in the classroom and interventions to address them, prevent school dropout, and promote educational and vocational progress among youth who leave school before graduating.

Engaging Teachers and Other School Personnel

The main question guiding therapist collaboration with school personnel is: What can I do to help this particular teacher (principal, coach, special education coordinator) support the academic and behavioral success of the youth? Therapists should keep the following guidelines in mind when seeking answers to this question.

Engage Teachers

The therapist's first step in engaging teachers is to understand the teacher's perspective on the nature and likely causes of the adolescent's presenting problems. Key components of engagement (see also Chapter 2) include:

- Understanding and using the language of the teacher.
- Identifying teacher goals that provide motivation to help solve the problem.
- Demonstrating the capacity of the teacher and therapist to make change happen.
- Changing one's own behavior if it creates obstacles to effective collaboration.

To facilitate engagement, therapists ensure their verbal and written communications with teachers and other school personnel are not critical or blaming, and acknowledge teacher efforts, even when those efforts are not particularly effective.

Engage Other School Personnel

In most instances, implementation of school-based interventions also requires buy-in from school administrators, counselors, or other well-respected teachers. The therapist can follow several guidelines to facilitate such buy-in.

Follow Established Procedures

Therapists can aid engagement by following established procedures and policies when making telephone and face-to-face contact with school personnel, observing youth on school grounds, and convening meetings between caregivers and school staff. Thus, therapists should learn the formal structure of school operations, reflected in hierarchy, rules, and procedures. In some schools, for example, a secretary or office manager is the conduit to all school personnel at all times; while in others, making a phone call or sending e-mail directly to a teacher is preferred.

Understand the School's Social Ecology

Therapists should also develop an understanding of the school's social ecology, such as which teachers are opinion leaders, how teachers get along with one another and the principal, and how they view the school and outsiders (like MST therapists). In larger cities, this process can be time consuming, as youth in the same MST program might attend many different schools. Thus, it can be helpful for MST teams to keep a school resource file in which therapists provide helpful information about the formal and informal policies and practices at particular schools.

Reinforce School Efforts

To sustain engagement, therapists should look for opportunities to affirm the importance and contribution of specific school staff (principal, teacher, aid, coach, custodial staff) to the success of an intervention plan. When a caregiver participates in or is aware of an intervention, the therapist encourages the caregiver to offer such acknowledgment. For example, therapists and caregivers can send a note to the principal highlighting the helpfulness of a particular teacher and provide a copy to the teacher. Such strategies not only help the youth and family, but also contribute to the likelihood that school personnel will welcome the involvement of MST therapists in the future.

Ensure Intervention Design and Selection Is a Collaborative Process

Just as MST therapists and caregivers together identify fit factors and implement interventions, so too therapists invite teachers to identify factors contributing to the teenager's problems in school and help select and implement corresponding interventions. Taking into account the times and methods of communication preferred by a particular teacher, MST therapists should obtain teacher feedback daily if necessary, but at least weekly (Principle 7) on the effects of specific interventions. Communication methods can include brief face-to-face meetings, phone calls, e-mails, and home–school communication tools such as the Daily School Report Form (see Figure 5.1).

Youth Name: _____   **Parent(s) Name:** _____

Today's Date: _____   **Parent phone:** _____

Period	Class	Teacher	Behaviors	No = 0 Yes = 1	Total (0–3)	Teacher's Initials
1			a. On time?	0 1		
			b. Behaved appropriately?	0 1		
			c. Homework recorded correctly? (see below)	0 1		
2			a. On time?	0 1		
			b. Behaved appropriately?	0 1		
			c. Homework recorded correctly? (see below)	0 1		
3			a. On time?	0 1		
			b. Behaved appropriately?	0 1		
			c. Homework recorded correctly? (see below)	0 1		
4			a. On time?	0 1		
			b. Behaved appropriately?	0 1		
			c. Homework recorded correctly? (see below)	0 1		
5			a. On time?	0 1		
			b. Behaved appropriately?	0 1		
			c. Homework recorded correctly? (see below)	0 1		
6			a. On time?	0 1		
			b. Behaved appropriately?	0 1		
			c. Homework recorded correctly? (see below)	0 1		
7			a. On time?	0 1		
			b. Behaved appropriately?	0 1		
			c. Homework recorded correctly? (see below)	0 1		

(continued)

FIGURE 5.1. Daily School Report Form.

Period	Class	Teacher	Behaviors	No = 0 Yes = 1	Total (0–3)	Teacher's Initials
8			a. On time?	0 1		
			b. Behaved appropriately?	0 1		
			c. Homework recorded correctly? (see below)	0 1		
			Total			

Class	Homework	Due Date

FIGURE 5.1. (*continued*)

Help Implement the Interventions in School Settings

MST therapists often help implement school-based interventions at least until other resources can be developed or the intervention is no longer necessary. If the intervention requires a teacher to use a new skill, such as ignoring a noxious behavior and rewarding a desired behavior, the therapist might need to help teach that skill, using the procedures for skill acquisition described in Chapter 6 (e.g., modeling, feedback, reinforcement).

Prepare Family and School for Communication and Collaboration

Interventions to address youth problems in school are often implemented by teachers in classrooms, caregivers at home, and conjointly, as occurs when the teacher and caregiver use the Daily School Report Form to convey information about the youth's attendance and behavior throughout the day. Until the therapist has evidence that school personnel and caregivers can effectively communicate about the implementation of an intervention plan for a youth, he or she facilitates meetings between the family and school. In preparation for such meetings, therapists might need to coach intervention participants in what to say and provide opportunities for practice, using role plays, before telephone or face-to-face meetings.

Assessing the Fit of School-Related Problems

As always in MST, the first step toward intervening in the problems of the youth is to conduct a "fit" assessment. Commonly identified fit factors for school-related problems are identified in Figure 5.2. These can involve the youth (cognitive abilities and deficits, academic abilities and skills, health or mental health problems), family (structuring the home to support academic activity, monitoring and rewarding academic and social competence at school), school (structure, resources, leadership, climate), classroom (type of classroom, classroom management, instruction effectiveness), family–school linkage (frequency and nature of contacts, interpersonal relationships), peers (low-achieving peers, drug-using peers), and neighborhood (transient residents, high crime).

The therapist gathers information about the factors contributing to the youth's school-related problems using interviews and direct observation. He

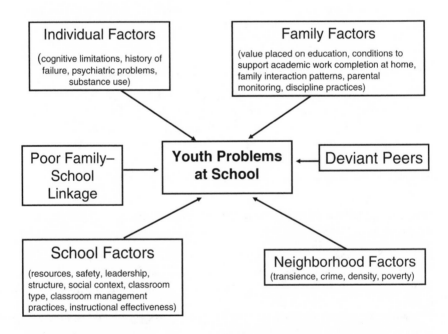

FIGURE 5.2. Common factors contributing to school problems.

or she interviews teachers, other school personnel who interact with the youth, caregivers, and the adolescent, and observes the youth in class, at transition times, and on the school grounds. In addition, with the permission and appropriate releases of information from the adolescent's caregivers and school, the therapist reviews the results of standardized intelligence and achievement tests and the youth's grades to detect patterns of relative cognitive and academic strengths and weaknesses that could be contributing to identified problems at school.

Assessing Classroom Behavior Problems

The therapist uses behavioral observation and interviews with teachers, other school personnel, and the youth to understand the fit of youth behavior problems occurring within the school. As also described in Chapter 8, which focuses on interventions for substance abuse, functional analyses are often useful in specifying fit factors. Indeed, functional assessment is increasingly recommended as a basis for the design of school-based interventions for children with behavioral problems (Individuals with Disabilities Education Act Amendments, 1997; Wilcox, Turnbull, & Turnbull, 1999–2000). Consistent with MST conceptualizations (Principle 1), the assumption underlying functional assessment is that the behavior "makes sense" given the pattern of positive and negative consequences the person experiences when engaging in it. Thus, in conducting a functional assessment, the task is to understand the ABCs of behavior—delineating the Antecedents that elicit the Behavior and effects of the corresponding Consequences on the future probability of that behavior. The MST perspective, however, extends the scope of how the youth's behavior "makes sense" in the immediate context to consider (1) the pattern of positive and negative consequences of that behavior to others in the adolescent's broader ecology and (2) interaction patterns in that broader ecology that might contribute to the youth's behavior.

Define Immediate Antecedents and Setting Events

Antecedents are the immediate proximal predictors of a problem behavior. These events happen right before the behavior and seem to "trigger" it. Antecedents can be particular times, places, people, activities, feelings, or situations, or a combination of these. For example, an outburst in school might be triggered by a teacher request or demand, the criticism of a classmate, or the youth not knowing how to do a math problem. Setting events "set the stage" for the problem behavior. For example, failure to take stimulant medication might increase the likelihood of acting out in school for a child with ADHD when he or she is asked to complete an academic task. Similarly, inadequate sleep might increase youth oppositional behavior.

Define the Behavior

The nature (e.g., cursing, slamming books), time (e.g., late afternoon), and frequency of the behavior are delineated.

Identify Consequences of the Behavior

The therapist identifies the consequences of the problem behavior for the youth and others in the social ecology. If a teacher, youth, or caregiver has difficulty identifying the consequences of the youth's behavior, the therapist can ask the following questions:

- What usually happens right after the behavior occurs?
- How do you respond to him or her?
- How do other students react to this behavior (e.g., laugh, encourage)?
- Does the student get out of doing something (e.g., classwork, homework)?

Identifying payoffs for the problem behavior provides clues about what teachers and caregivers can do to reinforce desired behavior.

Understand Previous Attempts to Change the Behavior

To understand the fit, one must appreciate previous school attempts to decrease or eliminate the youth's problem behavior. Typical school consequences include loss of privileges, referral to a school counselor or assistant principal, a note sent home, reprimands, in-school detention or suspension, and meetings with caregivers. Sometimes, teachers are surprised to learn that the consequences they designed to address a problem behavior (e.g., in-school suspension, being sent to the office) actually exacerbate the behavior. Just as MST therapists help caregivers to identify and evaluate the effects (or lack thereof) of their parenting efforts to change youth behavior using "fit circles," so too therapists might need to help teachers and other school personnel evaluate the consequences of their well-intentioned efforts differently.

Standardized Testing

Often learning disabilities, low intelligence, or other cognitive challenges of the youth have previously been documented in school records. The results of formal intelligence testing and achievement testing might even have formed the basis of an individualized education plan (IEP) for the youth. In other cases, MST therapists cannot discern whether such testing has occurred. When the therapist has evidence to suggest that cognitive limitations contribute to youth behavior problems, and records of previous testing are not available, the therapist collaborates with the caregiver and appropriate school personnel to identify a school psychologist or other qualified professional to conduct such testing. Most school systems have requirements regarding the use of testing data and professional qualifications of examiners. As occurs when MST therapists seek the professional consultation or collaboration of psychiatrists on behalf of youth and caregivers (see Chapter 6), the therapist might need to help empower the caregiver to obtain clear answers in advance to the following questions:

- What kinds of tests will be used?
- What will the results tell us?
- Who will conduct the tests?
- Who will interpret the test results for the caregivers and school personnel?
- How will the results be used?
- Who from the school will work together with the caregivers and youth to develop and monitor a plan informed by the results?

When evaluating the response to the first question, therapists might find it useful to know and share with caregivers which tests are most appropriate.

Intelligence Testing

Generally, assessment of a youth's intellectual strengths and weaknesses should include well-validated IQ tests such as the Wechsler Intelligence Scale for Children—Fourth Edition (WISC-IV; Wechsler, 2003); Woodcock–Johnson Tests of Cognitive Abilities—Third Edition (WJTCA-III; Woodcock, McGrew, & Mather, 2001a); or the Stanford–Binet Intelligence Scales—Fifth Edition (Roid, 2003). If mental retardation is suspected, the Vineland Adaptive Behavior Scales—Second Edition (Sparrow, Cicchetti, & Balla, 2005) should be included in the assessment battery.

Achievement Testing

Well-validated achievement tests include the Wechsler Individual Achievement Test—Second Edition (WIAT-II; Wechsler, 2001); the Wide Range Achievement Test—Fourth Edition (WRAT4; Wilkinson, & Robertson, 2006); and the Woodcock–Johnson Tests of Achievement—Third Edition (WJTA-III; Woodcock, McGrew, & Mather, 2001b).

Mental Health Testing

In addition, when therapists suspect that a mental health problem such as attention-deficit/hyperactivity disorder (ADHD), depression, or anxiety is contributing to the youth's problems in school, they should undertake the assessment and intervention strategies described in Chapter 6, which might include seeking consultation with a child psychiatrist.

Case Example: Javier Diaz

The case of Javier Diaz illustrates the assessment and intervention strategies used by MST therapists when the drivers of identified problem behaviors in class are elusive and might include a youth's cognitive or learning difficulties. Javier Diaz was 15 years old and repeating seventh grade in an inner-city middle school when he was referred to the MST program following a second arrest for vandalism. Javier's academic performance and classroom behavior troubles became apparent in second grade, and he was diagnosed with ADHD in third grade and placed on stimulant medication. By the time he reached middle school (sixth grade), Javier had failed two grades and had a record of truancy and fighting. The truancy and fighting resulted in suspensions and expulsions that pushed him even further behind academically than his same-age peers. Javier's academic instruction in most subjects occurred in one of two self-contained classrooms for youth with emotional and behavioral disorders.

Before Gloria, the MST therapist, made her first visit to Javier's teachers, she reviewed the IEP and prior testing results that had been obtained with the permission of Mrs. Diaz and the school principal and special education coordinator. Gloria saw Javier's ADHD was a matter of school record, and had formed the basis for the IEP in elementary school. The most recent standardized testing scores indicated Javier (at age 15) performed at an eighth-grade reading level and third-grade math level. Gloria developed the hypothesis that family and teachers were not sufficiently considering the potential implications of Javier's ADHD and math achievement level on his behavioral and academic difficulties. She therefore held at bay the idea of suggesting further testing, pending further assessment of the "fit" of Javier's disruptive classroom behavior using interviews and observational strategies.

In conducting the initial assessment of the school ecology, Gloria met with the teachers of Javier's two self-contained classrooms. They reported that Javier had a quick temper and short attention span and was disrespectful to them. Mrs. Smith, the math teacher, noted the behavioral problems were frequent and very disruptive to the class—cursing, slamming books, and yelling. Mrs. Jones, the English teacher, noted that Javier would often fall asleep in her afternoon class. Neither the physical education nor shop teacher was available to meet with Gloria during her first visit at the school.

To assist in the functional assessment of Javier's behavior problems in school, Gloria used the Classroom Behavior Observation Form (see Figure 5.3). Regarding the identified problem behavior, Mrs. Smith reported that Javier yelled and used obscenities at least three to four times per week. The yelling lasted anywhere from 5–10 seconds and was loud enough to be heard in the neighboring classroom. In addition, in one 2-hour observation session, Gloria observed Javier twice slam his work on the desk, and once refuse to open the book to the assigned problems. The consequences for all of these behaviors were similar—Javier was reprimanded and sent to the office. Gloria hypothesized that these problem behaviors enabled Javier to avoid doing his work—thereby "rewarding" him, as math was very difficult for him. In addition, Javier received attention from his teacher and classmates for his disruptions.

Gloria also examined whether classroom management and organization were contributing to Javier's behavior problems. She observed that Mrs. Smith sometimes ignored student talking and disruptive behavior until it escalated and other times repeated the same request frequently when Javier

Time	Behavior	Context	Task	Consequences	Possible function
9:00 A.M.	Curses. Slams books. Yells.	Math, self-contained class, all boys; female teacher	Mrs. Smith asks Javier to do a math problem aloud.	Mrs. Smith asks two more times, raising her voice. She sends Javier to office.	Javier avoids task he does poorly. Avoids embarrassment of doing poorly in class. Gets teacher attention. Gets classmate attention.
1:00 P.M.	Puts head on desk.	English, self-contained class, all boys; male teacher	Mr. Jones assigns in-class writing.	Mr. Jones "thumps" Javier on shoulders, gets him to sit.	Gets teacher's attention.

FIGURE 5.3. Sample Classroom Behavior Observation Form.

and other students did not comply. Gloria hypothesized that Mrs. Smith had a limited repertoire of classroom management skills, or had adequate skills but was unable to use them consistently. Although teaching classroom management skills is usually beyond the scope of MST, therapists are encouraged to help teachers use such skills with the particular youth they are treating if necessary.

To complete the assessment, Gloria also evaluated whether setting events (i.e., more distal factors) were contributing to the classroom problem behaviors. In Javier's case, the therapist obtained baseline data on the everyday behavior of the youth and his family. Gloria typed the hours from 7:00 A.M., Javier's typical waking time, until midnight, Javier's bedtime, on a piece of paper, providing several blank lines for each hour. She left one copy with Mrs. Diaz to complete based on home events from the time Javier woke up until he went to the bus stop for school and when he returned from school until bedtime. Gloria took another copy to school, where she obtained Javier's class schedule and transition times, and observed him in class and on school grounds. After 3 days, Gloria and Mrs. Diaz consolidated their information and noticed that Javier exhibited more problem behaviors in the morning, during math class with Mrs. Smith, and after lunch in Mr. Jones's English class. The evidence suggested that when Javier had slept poorly the night before, he argued with his mother when she tried to wake him, got up late, and in his haste to leave for the bus failed to take his stimulant medication. Peer conflict on the bus was also sometimes in play. Javier's academic difficulty in math was an important contributing factor as well. In addition, poor sleep and missed lunches were identified as possible contributors to Javier "zoning out" and putting his head on the desk in Mr. Jones's class.

In sum, the therapist used multiple methods (interviews, observations, test results) to determine the fit of Javier's school-related problems that threatened his ability to remain in school (see Figure 5.4). These fit factors, as discussed subsequently, served key roles in the design of interventions for Javier.

Interventions for Problems at School

The interventions typically required to address adolescent antisocial behavior such as truancy, suspension, and expulsion and the behaviors associated with them (e.g., fighting, cutting classes, threatening teachers, damaging school property) are described and illustrated in case examples throughout this book. The current chapter focuses specifically on problem behaviors in the classroom that are associated, in part, with cognitive and learning problems.

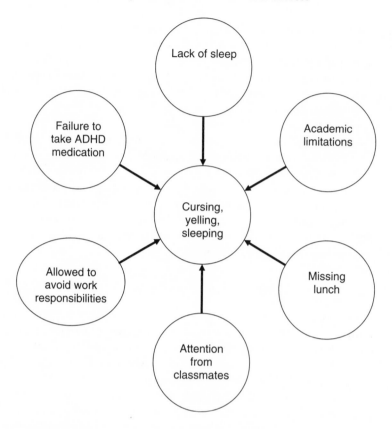

FIGURE 5.4. Fit circle for Javier's problem behavior in school.

Eliminating Problem Behavior in the Classroom by Managing It Effectively

When the fit analysis indicates problem behavior in the classroom is maintained by a combination of the youth's response to specific, challenging academic tasks and teacher–student interaction patterns, interventions are designed to change the way the academic task is approached by the student and teacher.

Interventions Targeting Immediate Antecedents

Manipulating immediate antecedents is a viable option for reducing problem behavior(s) in class. Javier's yelling in math seemed to occur under three circumstances: being called on to answers problems aloud, being asked to complete problems at the board, and being verbally corrected by Mrs. Smith when his answers were incorrect. Gloria and Mrs. Smith determined together that Mrs. Smith would try to avoid these triggers by asking Javier first to solve an easy problem (one she knows he can successfully complete); giving Javier the choice of completing the problem at his desk instead of at the board; and arranging the situation so he can ask for help without being publicly embarrassed.

In addition, Gloria learned from Mrs. Smith that Javier seemed to respond well to frequent rewards, encouragement, and playfulness in teaching situations. The classroom intervention plan for Javier, therefore, also included increased use of rewards and verbal encouragement in response to evidence that Javier was trying his best. Moreover, it was understood that if Javier did not make an effort to do a problem or ask for help when experiencing difficulty, Mrs. Smith would come to his desk to assess the situation instead of calling out to him in front of the class.

Replacing Problem Behavior and the Consequences That Maintain It

The odds of eliminating a problem behavior increase when individuals can use a different behavior to accomplish a similar goal. The therapist uses the identified strengths of the youth, teachers, others in the school ecology, as well as caregivers, to craft interventions that enable the youth to obtain the consequences (e.g., gaining teacher attention, avoiding embarrassment in front of classmates) produced by the problem behavior in more socially appropriate ways (e.g., asking for help). First, the therapist makes sure the youth has the knowledge and skills to engage in the alternative behavior. A more socially appropriate method for Javier to get out of math tasks in front of his classmates would be to say, "Mrs. Smith, I am not sure how to complete the assignment, but I think it would help if I first saw someone else solve the problem." Because Gloria had evidence from other contexts (e.g., in other classes, at the skate park when needing tips on how to do a trick) that Javier had the skills to appropriately ask for help, she and Mrs. Smith designed interventions to reinforce Javier's use of those skills. Gloria helped Mrs. Smith praise Javier's socially appropriate requests and quiet behavior with books, and ignore his book slamming and cursing. Because Javier's cursing functioned to allow him to get out of doing math problems, Gloria, his mother, and Mrs. Smith designed a strategy that required increased work when Javier disrupted the class.

Once acceptable replacement behaviors are identified and the therapist and school personnel have evidence the youth can execute them, ensuring they are reinforced is essential. Teachers often use a variety of activities or goods to reward appropriate youth behavior, including classroom activities such as free time or game time; food or beverages; tokens that can be redeemed by the teacher or at a school store; and social interaction the youth experiences as positive, like attention and praise. Gloria leveraged the strengths of Mrs. Smith's teaching expertise and experience with Javier to identify things that were reinforcing to him. And, Gloria and Mrs. Diaz together identified rewards and consequences Javier could receive at home for behavioral improvements at school. In a meeting with Gloria and Mrs. Diaz at school, Mrs. Smith and the other teachers agreed to use a Daily School Report Form to communicate with Mrs. Diaz about Javier's behavior.

Interventions Targeting Setting Events

Sometimes, a distinct intervention is needed for each setting event. Other times, the same intervention addresses several distinct setting events. For Javier, poor sleep contributed directly to morning arguments at home (when Mrs. Diaz tried to wake him) and to being too rushed to take his stimulant medication. Thus, a common set of interventions designed to ensure Javier gets enough sleep (e.g., going to bed earlier than midnight, turning off the video game earlier in the evening) could facilitate smoother functioning in the morning. In contrast, more effectively managing peer conflict on the bus would require understanding and addressing the factors precipitating those conflicts, and unless fatigue was the only fit factor (unlikely), interventions might include sitting in a different seat and increasing Javier's repertoire of social problem-solving skills (see Chapter 6).

To address the setting event of a history of academic failure, Gloria and Mrs. Diaz met with the special education coordinator and teachers to identify peers and adults who could provide effective tutoring to Javier in math. Given his concern about public embarrassment, Javier did not want to participate in peer tutoring. Gloria and Mrs. Diaz identified a retired teacher among members of her church to tutor Javier in math twice a week for a nominal fee. (See Chapter 7 for strategies to secure social support to meet specific needs.) It was hoped that if his math skills were improved, math-related frustration would become less frequent.

Cultivating Effective Family–School Collaboration and Communication

When a youth is first referred to MST, the caregiver and school rarely have a plan for how, when, and how often they will communicate about the youth's progress at school. There are numerous barriers at school, at home, and in the interface between these systems that can hamper the development and execution of such plans. For example, teachers are responsible for many students and are tightly scheduled during the school day. The caregiver's work demands during school hours might prohibit making contact when the teacher is available. When efforts to communicate have been limited

or characterized by conflict, each party might believe the other is not sufficiently committed to helping the youth. As with marital interventions
(Chapter 3) and individual interventions to increase social problem-solving
skills in adults and teenagers (Chapter 6), MST therapists often need to help
all parties increase their perspective-taking capacity and coach caregivers
and teachers in making requests of one another and managing frustrations
that arise when interactions do not go as planned. The goal is to cultivate
effective and sustainable collaboration between caregivers and school personnel. To this end, therapists try to:

- Help caregivers think of school personnel as partners in the process
  of helping their son or daughter by better appreciating the strengths
  and challenges of the particular school context and the positive motivations of school staff.
- Help teachers and school personnel better recognize the caregiver's strengths and commitment to school success by maintaining a
  strength focus, reframing youth behavior, and accentuating the positive.
- Identify and overcome barriers to collaboration and school success
  (e.g., history of adversarial interactions, skill deficits, anxiety and
  fear).

Develop a Good Home–School Communication Plan

A major focus of family–school collaboration and communication is behavior management. The therapist's goals are to ensure (1) all aspects of interventions occurring in school and at home to support the school are clear to
everyone involved, (2) a monitoring system is in place to track the youth's
behavior (e.g., Daily School Report Form, Figure 5.1), and (3) barriers to
intervention implementation are quickly identified and addressed. In addition, if behavioral emergencies are anticipated (e.g., the youth becomes
physically aggressive in school), a safety plan should be specified that identifies someone who can be available to remove the youth from the room and
deescalate the problem (see Chapter 2). This can help prevent the types of
incidents that prompt suspension and expulsion.

A good communication plan specifies who will contact whom, how,
and under what conditions. The communication plan takes into account
how a teacher prefers to be contacted (note, telephone, e-mail) and the
means caregivers have for making contact (not all families have telephones
or computers, and using a phone at work might be a problem). When only
the teacher and caregiver participate in the interventions planned, then the
therapist can help the two of them determine who will take the lead in
monitoring the school-related intervention plan and how this will happen

(e.g., the teacher completes the Daily School Report Form, and the caregiver will call the teacher on Thursdays right after school). When more intervention partners are involved (e.g., multiple teachers, aides, assistant principal), then the therapist should ensure they agree on who will serve as the point of contact when questions or problems arise and modifications to the intervention plan need to be made. Initially, this point of contact might be the therapist, although priming others to take this role relatively quickly is critical to ensure the plan is sustainable after therapy ends.

If the Daily School Report Form is used, the therapist works with the teachers, caregivers, and adolescent to ensure all view the student as responsible for getting teachers to complete the form, getting the form home, and returning it to school the next day. Rewards and consequences delivered by the caregiver and teacher might be needed to support youth execution of this responsibility.

Supporting School Performance and Behavior at Home

Caregivers can support improvements in academic and behavioral functioning in school in three substantive ways:

- Convey the importance of the youth's education by praising his or her effort, anticipating the positive future gains associated with finishing school, and identifying and discussing subjects or activities at school that align with the teen's talents and skills.
- Establish a routine for doing homework that includes providing a quiet space (television is off, other children are not playing in the room) and conditions and materials to do the work (sufficient light, clear surface, paper and pens).
- Provide rewards and consequences at home for academic effort and behavioral improvement, some of which are developed in conjunction with the teacher to support specific aspects of an intervention strategy used in class.

If the combination of classroom and other school-based interventions are particularly numerous or complex, therapists might find it useful to develop a behavioral contract the youth, teacher(s), and caregivers sign. The contract specifies the rewards and consequences at home and at school for compliance with specific strategies. Such contracts should be developed conjointly among the intervention participants, and be sufficiently straightforward that everyone can easily see what has and has not occurred. The caregiver and pertinent school personnel should have a copy of the contract. And, as described previously, it should be clear who will take the lead in monitoring the contract and communicating with others about progress, barriers, and successes.

When Dropout Seems Imminent or Youth Are Not in School

Adolescents in MST programs have averaged 15 years old when referred and usually have several (depending on number of grades failed previously) high school years remaining before graduation. Thus, therapists, caregivers, and school personnel can still chart a course of school attendance and performance that gets youth through graduation. For some older youth, and even for many 14- and 15-year-olds, aversive experiences in school, multiple academic failures, and conscription to alternative schools are among the factors that can conspire against the youth staying in school. In addition, because most states do not require youth to attend school after they turn 16 years old, many schools have little incentive to retain underachieving older youth until they graduate.

Preventing School Dropout

In some cases, well-conceived and well-implemented interventions to improve key school outcomes—truancy, suspension, expulsion, and in-class behaviors contributing to these problems—fail repeatedly. In assessing the fit of these failures, the therapist might learn that the youth, caregivers, and school personnel believe that certain alternatives to high school completion are viable, and perhaps even desirable. Although alternatives to completing high school might be viable for some youth (e.g., a 17-year-old ninth grader with family connections in a trade industry), the long-term interests of the vast majority of youth in MST programs are likely best served by completing high school before seeking full-time employment. Thus, when caregiver and youth are advocating for the teen to leave school, the therapist should clarify two issues with the family before examining the viability of dropping out.

Communicate the Lifelong Importance of Completing High School and the Downside of Dropping Out

As indicated previously, dropping out of high school is a critical life decision that has significant implications for the youth's future economic and social well-being. Most likely, the adolescent and caregiver have valued goals for the teenager's future that will probably be impeded by dropping out. The therapist should help caregivers identify these goals and assess how completing or dropping out of high school aligns with them. Therapists can suggest generating a list of the pros and cons of school completion for the youth, and can supplement this list as necessary with facts about the differences between high school graduates and dropouts. These differences include the odds of finding employment, level of pay, and increased risk for pregnancy, single parenthood, and spending time in prison. Therapists can find a more detailed list in materials published by the U.S. Department of Education (1998).

In addition, therapists can help caregivers appreciate the proximal costs of dropping out, costs that might not have been considered previously.

- Youth are likely to have more time on their hands, and thus to require increased adult monitoring.
- Caregiver–adolescent conflict can worsen when the youth becomes bored, restless, and irritable, and when caregivers begin to resent the fact that the teen is not engaged in productive activities.
- Younger siblings might feel that they, too, no longer have to attend school, thereby creating additional challenges for the caregiver.
- The youth's judge or probation officer will likely view the decision unfavorably, which could result in more hassles for the caregiver and adolescent in these systems (e.g., having to transport the youth to court programs).

The therapist, therefore, makes certain that the youth and caregiver completely understand the negative implications of dropping out.

Examine and Address Common Fit Factors for Wanting to Drop Out

Adolescents wishing to drop out of high school often say they find school boring, too hard, or aversive in other ways (e.g., the teachers are awful or out to get them; the other students are mean, arrogant, or otherwise lacking). Youth who have failed multiple grades often contend they are too far behind to finish anyway, or that an alternative plan, like passing a General Educational Development (GED) Test, seems more realistic than struggling through school for 3 more years. Just as MST therapists empathize when caregivers struggling to manage a youth's behavior problems say they have lost hope of effecting change, therapists can convey empathy for the adolescent's perspective about finishing school.

Then, the therapist should identify and address all factors in the social ecology contributing to the youth's perspective. Observation and interviews at school might reveal fit factors that were not identified when the teenager's school-related problems were assessed previously. For example, perhaps his or her desire to drop out began when a favorite teacher left, or when friends on the verge of leaving school were discussing their plans to make money and buy a car. Sometimes, a caregiver expects the youth will finish high school but has not clearly stated that expectation. More often, the expectation is clearly stated, but the caregiver has not taken action to support school completion (e.g., facilitating attendance and homework completion, tying rewards and consequences to attendance and performance).

Assuming that the adolescent and caregiver have at least some ambivalence about quitting school, the therapist should endeavor to address the key fit factors per standard MST intervention design and implementation (see Chapter 2 and do-loop).

- Develop clear goals.
- Engage key stakeholders in goals.
- Specify interventions to meet those goals.
- Monitor outcomes.
- Evaluate barriers to success.
- Redesign and implement new interventions.
- Repeat loop until goals are achieved.

In addition, school-specific interventions should be considered to support the youth's retention in school. For example, the therapist might work with the caregiver, teenager, and school personnel to develop an individualized "master plan" for how the youth will complete high school. The purpose of this plan is to get everyone on the same page regarding what it will take to get the credits he or she needs to graduate, to help the youth see that graduation is an achievable goal, and to address other school and peer drivers of the desire to drop out (e.g., school's reluctance to retain the problem student, a lack of friends in school). Similarly, the therapist and caregivers might ask school personnel to identify school-based incentives (e.g., providing early school release for the youth to attend work, easing restrictions on club or sports involvement) that increase the chances of success—and the family might provide incentives for school advancement as well.

Alternatives to Completing High School

Despite doing their best, the therapist and family sometimes are not able to retain or reenroll the youth in high school. In such cases, the therapist, caregiver, and adolescent should explore other educational and vocational activities. *The therapist's first task in this regard is to ensure the caregiver will expect and demand that the youth do something productive with his or her time and to support the caregiver in this stance.* Productive activities are those that will help the youth develop skills he or she will need for future independent living. Thus, although babysitting younger siblings all day while the caregiver works might be productive, it does not help the teen move toward independence unless paired with other supports such as continued education (e.g., a GED program) and a salary. Ideally, the activities arranged for the youth should involve some combination of continued education or training and legal employment that are compatible with the adolescent's interests, skills, and long-term goals.

Develop a Plan

To facilitate the development of a viable educational and vocational plan for a teenager who is leaving school, therapists typically help the caregiver and youth:

- Identify the youth's interests, skills, and goals.
- Explore options available for the teen in the community.
- Evaluate the pros and cons of each option in terms of the youth's interests, skills, and goals.
- Provide advice as to which of these experiences will be most valuable to the adolescent.
- Determine how the caregiver will monitor and support youth compliance with the plan (e.g., providing rewards and consequences, advice, problem-solving help if needed).

Therapists can also encourage caregivers to view themselves as experts on the youth's strengths and abilities. If, for example, the adolescent is not able to identify any vocational interests or goals, the caregiver can present the youth with a "menu of options" that lists opportunities available locally and discuss which option sounds best. A sample menu of options for Gina, age 17 years, could be:

1. Attend GED classes and work 20 hours/week.
2. Attend GED classes and begin taking courses at the community college.
3. Attend GED classes and enroll in cosmetology school.

Three ground rules should be kept in mind when helping caregivers develop such menus.

1. Any non-negotiable activities (in the above example, the GED program) appear in every option.
2. The caregiver should be prepared to allow the youth to pursue whichever option is chosen.
3. The caregiver should remain open to compromises the adolescent might propose.

Gina might choose options 1 and 3, insisting that she can juggle the demands of the GED program, cosmetology school, and work. Her grandmother might agree to allow Gina to "try it and see" for a specific time period with the understanding that if she does not study for and pass the GED, Gina will need to quit work until she does.

Find Productive Activities

Finding productive activities for a youth often involves enrolling him or her in formal educational or vocational programs provided by various community agencies (e.g., community colleges, career counseling centers) or businesses. However, less formal, more creative solutions can also sometimes succeed. For example, a teenager who would like to work in a day-care center but who is too young to be hired could work for an in-home day-care provider to "learn the ropes" and obtain a letter of recommendation, provided that the experience was structured and monitored by the caregiver. Keep in mind that experiences should minimize risks and maximize potential payoffs, as described next.

Beware of Deviant Youth

Help the caregiver look for opportunities that serve adolescents or young adults generally rather than those that target juvenile offenders or other high-risk populations such as substance users. As described in Chapter 4, grouping antisocial youth together puts each at risk for engaging in more deviant behavior (i.e., peer contagion). Thus, a GED program held at a local community college is preferred to one sponsored by juvenile probation. Also, when the majority of program participants are older than the referred youth, therapists and caregivers should ensure that the older individuals are relatively prosocial (e.g., a vocational program that involves recent graduates as instructional assistants).

Seek Highly Structured Programs

The risk for peer contagion in group-based programs is greatest when youth spend large amounts of unstructured time together (Dishion, Dodge, & Lansford, 2006). Unfortunately, many programs for young people have considerable "down time" during which negative peer associations can be established. Therapists and caregivers should obtain information about a program's schedule of activities. Some programs with long hours seem intensive but include many unstructured time periods. The therapist might need to help the caregiver strike a balance between the desire for intensive programs (i.e., those occupying many hours of the adolescent's day) and the need to not exacerbate the youth's problems. The therapist and caregiver usually need to spend a few hours observing programs and asking staff and participants to describe their typical day in order to evaluate the structure and intensity of the program.

GED Programs

The GED Test is an alternative to the high school diploma that, when passed, certifies that the individual has high-school-level academic skills. To take the test, an individual must be at least 16 years old (or, for many states, 17 years old) and not be enrolled in school. Some states set further restrictions before the test can be taken, such as proving residency or passing a pretest. The tests are administered at numerous locations throughout each state, usually at community colleges and adult education centers. A GED Test center locator is available at *www.acenet.edu/resources/ged/center_locator.cfm.* GED Test preparation courses typically are offered at community colleges and at the testing centers themselves, as well as through numerous private, for-profit (e.g., Kaplan test courses), community, and online test preparation programs.

GED Test preparation programs vary in their degree of structure and intensity, from completely self-directed Internet-based programs to multiple hours of intensive small group instruction. A youth who has not been successful in school is likely to need a great deal of individual instruction (as well as caregiver support and oversight) to pass the test. A typical small group program at a community college requires about 3 hours of classroom instruction twice a week for 12–15 weeks, with the expectation that participants study and practice skills on their own outside of class. The costs of such classes are approximately $70–$100, including materials.

Vocational Training Programs

The National Youth Employment Coalition, through its Promising and Effective Practices Network initiative has delineated the characteristics of effective youth vocational programs (National Youth Employment Coalition, 2005). Significantly, these characteristics are consistent with central conceptual and clinical emphases of MST (e.g., goal oriented, ecologically valid, comprehensive, strength focused, pragmatic, and able to engage stakeholders). Drawing from the characteristics identified in this review, MST therapists should guide caregivers to select vocational programs that help the youth:

1. Determine career interests, explore a variety of career options, set career goals, and create realistic plans to achieve goals.
2. Engage in work-based learning activities such as job shadowing and real-world work experience.
3. Make the connection between academic learning and work by pro-

viding some amount of academic programming (e.g., professional writing within medical technician training).
4. Exercise leadership skills and contribute to the program and broader community.
5. Develop competencies that are relevant to the local/regional labor market and/or the standards in the industry of choice.
6. Develop "soft" job skills (i.e., those that are relevant to any job), such as résumé writing, job searching, interviewing, and communication with supervisors.
7. Learn to manage their finances and develop other independent living skills (e.g., accessing health care, obtaining automobile insurance).
8. Graduate from the program with a credential that is recognized by employers, such as the Automotive Service Excellence certificate, a barber apprentice license, or the National Work Readiness Credential.
9. Link to real-world employment opportunities (i.e., not only those provided by the program) by networking with individuals actually employed in the trade.
10. Obtain ongoing support from program staff for job retention.

Also consistent with MST, effective vocational programs set high expectations for the youth and provide incentives for progress rather than punishments for not meeting program goals. Therapists and caregivers should look for evidence a program offers nurturing and sustained relationships with youth, communicates with the youth's family, and supports a positive peer environment in which cooperative work is valued. Although many vocational programs are tailored toward specific industries or careers (e.g., construction trades, auto mechanics), the best ones assess youth interests continuously throughout the training and provide linkages to alternative training opportunities if the adolescent decides that a career within the targeted profession does not interest him or her. Generally, because of the soft job and other life skills training inherent in high quality programs, the teenager's time will not have been wasted if interests change.

Youth Employment

When a youth has dropped out or been permanently expelled from high school, obtaining a job is typically a key identified goal of treatment. Although employment has potential benefits (e.g., learning soft job skills like attendance and punctuality), at least two substantive drawbacks are evident as well.

1. Without the benefits of a vocational training program, unskilled adolescents tend to be eligible only for menial jobs in the service sector that provide low incomes and little potential for advancement or skill development. Over time, youth often find such jobs boring and might become disillusioned about legitimate work and tempted by other life paths (e.g., pregnancy, selling drugs).
2. Caregivers of a teenager with a job and an independent source of income might find it more difficult to monitor and supervise his or her behavior. Restricting a youth to the home for a curfew violation is difficult if he or she is working every day.

Thus, *many types of work include significant costs*—such as lost opportunities to receive an education, learn marketable and lucrative job skills, link to high-quality employment, and receive benefits like retirement savings or health insurance (Larson & Verma, 1999). The MST therapist should help caregivers understand these costs in lost opportunities and develop a plan for the youth that balances work with other productive activities such as passing a GED Test and vocational training.

Family and Ecological Support for Youth Who Are Not in School

Adolescents who are not in school require a great deal of support to be successful. Any single program will not likely meet all of the youth's needs or keep the youth productively occupied around the clock. Also, most educational or vocational experiences will require much more self direction from the teenager than does traditional high school coursework. Accordingly, caregivers will need to provide a high level of structure/monitoring, resources, and incentives for their son's or daughter's success.

Structure and Monitoring

Therapists need to ensure caregivers do not expect that the adolescent will have the ability or motivation to locate and make good decisions about educational and vocational opportunities, or to coordinate a complex work and training schedule. Indeed, the teenager's situation will likely require comparable (or even greater) support from caregivers and others in the social ecology to be successful than was required when she or he attended a traditional school. Caregivers with limited engagement in their youth's school progress to date might not have the skills necessary to promote the adolescent's success and will require concrete assistance from the therapist. Fortunately, there are fewer barriers to facilitating the success of the youth in GED and vocational programs than exist for public school. For example, the teenager's reputation in the new setting is not yet established, and there is no history of caregiver–school conflict to overcome. Thus, the MST therapist can cultivate in caregivers and youth the perspective that this is a "fresh start," an opportunity to maximize his or her chances for success from the beginning of the new experience.

Caregivers should monitor adolescent functioning in ways virtually identical to those used to promote traditional school success.

- Maintain regular contact with program leaders/teachers.
- Have a clear understanding of program expectations.
- Verify attendance and youth progress.
- Set and reinforce study or practice time at home.
- Address any behavior problems that occur in the program.
- Provide resources necessary for program completion.

Caregivers also can enlist the help of employers or other members of the natural ecology to support their rules regarding work. For example, the caregiver can arrange for the employer to provide the caregiver with the adolescent's work schedule and can arrange for direct depositing of the youth's paychecks into a shared bank account that requires caregiver permission for withdrawals. In addition, the caregiver (and members of the natural ecology) can monitor the teen's work attendance and performance by giving rides to and from work or dropping in at the youth's place of employment unannounced.

Resources

In many cases, the program itself will cost money and require some costly materials (e.g., a tool kit for a construction trade vocational program, workbooks for GED Test preparation). Because such expenses are essential to the youth's success in the program, therapists encourage caregivers to view these as items that the adolescent is entitled to, like food and clothing, not as growth privileges to be earned, like video games. Caregivers might need to arrange or help provide transport to programs and jobs and work through other logistical issues that arise (e.g., getting the teen an ID or obtaining bus tokens).

Therapists also help caregivers leverage the strengths of their own job and life experiences when supporting the youth's new course. Most caregivers know what it's like to obtain and keep a job and the inevitable struggles that occur in the workplace, such as conflicts with coworkers or unfair supervisors. Caregivers can be encouraged to inquire with their children about these issues and to provide advice about how to manage difficult situations. The youth might require some of the social skills training components described in Chapter 6, and caregivers can assist the therapist in providing this training and reinforce the youth for using new skills. In addition, the caregiver and other members of the natural ecology (e.g., neighbor, coworker, and church member) can help link youth to individuals employed in professions the teenager is interested in for possible mentorship or job placements.

Incentives and Emotional Support

Therapists ensure caregivers provide incentives for program attendance and progress just as they would for high school completion. Rewards should be linked to specific regular behaviors that are associated with program or job success (e.g., attendance, engaging in study time at home), and adolescents should be able to earn rewards on a weekly basis. Larger milestones of success (e.g., receiving a certificate or getting a job promotion) also can be celebrated.

Incentives for older youth should reflect the developmental needs of an emerging young adult (Principle 6). Incentives that provide the youth with increasing levels of independence are likely to be the most motivating and communicate that the youth is becoming a responsible young adult. For example, a youth who has successfully taken the bus to his vocational training program every day for a month could be given the privilege of driving the family car to the program occasionally. Similarly, an adolescent who has abided by the rules set forth for working might be allowed more freedom in how he or she spends the earnings. In addition to tangible incentives, caregivers and other members of the natural ecology should convey their respect for the youth's efforts and take advantage of opportunities to validate his or her achievements (e.g., attending program graduation ceremonies).

Conclusion

Educational and vocational success are among the strongest predictors of favorable long-term outcomes for youth with serious antisocial behavior—such as those in MST programs. Consequently, MST therapists always devote considerable attention and effort toward facilitating viable youth educational or vocational aspirations. The methods used to identify goals, engage stakeholders, develop and implement interventions, and overcome barriers to success follow the same MST structures and processes as those for addressing any identified problem. Although school-related success might be considered a lower priority than avoiding rearrest, it's worth repeating that such success will largely influence whether the adolescent becomes a productive citizen in the community.

CHAPTER 6

When and How to Conduct
Individually Oriented Interventions

IN THIS CHAPTER

■ When to use individual interventions in MST.
   ■ Individual interventions most commonly
      used with adult caregivers.
   ■ Individual interventions most commonly
      used with youth.
■ When medications might make a difference:
   Empowering families to collaborate
   effectively with physicians.

This chapter describes when and how MST therapists might use individual interventions with either the youth's adult caregiver or the youth. The chapter focuses first on adult caregivers because they are the primary interventionists in the youth's natural ecology. In MST, caregivers help design and are the primary implementers of many strategies needed to change the particular family, school, and peer interactions that contribute to youth problems and to effectively manage future challenges. Therefore, any barriers to the engagement and effectiveness of caregivers must be successfully resolved to achieve desired progress in treatment.

The main caregiver barriers addressed in this chapter are depression and anxiety. The hallmark symptoms of depression in adults include sleep problems (i.e., sleeping too much, or not sleeping), being either restless and irritable or slow, feeling down all day, feeling worthless, feeling fatigue or loss of energy nearly every day, being unable to make decisions and finding it hard to concentrate, no longer having interest in favorite activities, and significant change in appetite. The hallmark symptoms of anxiety in adults include feeling fearful, worrying a lot about everyday things, having a hard time concentrating, problems with falling or staying asleep, being irritable, startling easily, and body symptoms such as muscle tension and headaches (American Psychiatric Association, 2000).

For youth, MST therapists most often use individual interventions to improve their ability to interact effectively with peers, in school, and in other community contexts. Thus, considerable attention is devoted to describing how to implement problem solving and social skills training interventions with adolescents. In addition, for youth correctly diagnosed with ADHD, suggestions are provided for empowering caregivers to be savvy consumers of information about medication and effective collaborators with physicians prescribing medication for their child. Finally, a small percentage of teenagers in MST programs have symptoms of posttraumatic stress disorder (PTSD), and effective strategies to address these symptoms are also described briefly. Resources for therapists that provide greater detail for all these interventions are listed at the end of the chapter.

Setting the Stage for Success: When and How to Suggest Individual Interventions

When

The possibility that individual intervention for caregiver depression is needed comes up at two different points in the do-loop: (1) as a critical barrier to initial engagement in MST; and (2) after treatment has been under way, when intermediary goals are consistently either not met or only partially met, and evidence suggests that individual problems of the caregiver are critical barriers to achieving those goals.

To determine if individual interventions for adult mental health problems are appropriate in a particular case, the therapist should be able to answer "yes" to the following questions and to describe the evidence that leads to the "yes."

1. Do I have good evidence that the problem (e.g., depression, anxiety, substance abuse) exists?
2. Have I used systemic interventions to address ecological factors that present barriers to engagement or treatment progress?
3. Do I have observations or self-reports that indicate the caregiver is unable or unwilling to make certain changes in behavior, even when he or she knows how to make the change and has the skills and help needed to do so?

4. Do I have evidence that the caregiver's failure to make the behavioral change helps to maintain or exacerbate the identified problems of the youth?
5. Do I have evidence that the depression, anxiety, or substance abuse, as opposed to other factors (e.g., marital problems, practical needs, skill or knowledge deficits, or a history of adversarial relations with school officials), is a powerful predictor of the youth's identified problems?

How

Families are referred to MST because an adolescent has serious problems. In contrast with adults seeking treatment for their own problems, caregivers of youth referred to MST are not often focused on their own depression, anxiety, or substance use. Before attempting individual interventions, then, MST therapists need to cultivate the caregiver's interest and his or her willingness to receive help for such problems. Such cultivation might take several attempts. A first conversation to introduce the idea that individual intervention might be helpful can take anywhere from 10 minutes to an hour or longer, depending upon a number of factors. Among these factors are whether the caregiver is aware of and distressed by the problem (e.g., caregiver might not be distressed by personal substance abuse) and perceives the therapist as genuinely concerned and able to help. To increase the odds that a first conversation will go well, therapists should consider the following suggestions, although all might not be necessary in each case.

1. Schedule a time to be alone with the caregiver.
2. Explain your purpose for this meeting as related to the caregiver's own well-being rather than to other aspects of treatment ongoing at the time.
3. Describe the problem (e.g., depression, anxiety, substance abuse) and:
    a. Your evidence that it is a problem.
    b. How you think the problem affects the caregiver, youth, and family.
4. Ask whether the caregiver sees this as a problem, and if so, how.
5. Describe how you can help.
6. If the caregiver agrees, together assess the current level of depression or anxiety, and brainstorm "fit factors" for these problems.
7. Schedule the next individual intervention meeting within 24–48 hours.

Therapists concerned about introducing the topic should make a fit circle that identifies the drivers of their concern and enlist the help of other therapists and the clinical supervisor to address the drivers and to role-play parts of the conversation expected to be most difficult.

Troubleshooting Engagement

In some cases, when the therapist talks alone with the caregiver about treatment for a mental health problem, the caregiver is relieved and eager to get help. Other caregivers are reluctant, and the therapist needs to understand the fit of the reluctance to receive treatment before proceeding. For problems with depression or anxiety, common fit factors include the caregiver thinking the focus of treatment should be on the youth; feeling overwhelmed and unable to make more time to deal with her or his own problems; and fearing that having a "mental health problem" means he or she is crazy, weak, or in some other way inadequate as a caregiver or person. Suggestions for addressing these barriers to engagement are provided next.

The Caregiver Says Treatment Should Focus on the Youth

When the caregiver is reluctant to consider an individual intervention because of concern that treatment should focus on the youth, the therapist's first step is to validate that concern. After all, the teenager was referred for MST for sufficiently serious problems that placement outside the home was imminent. Therapists should verbalize their appreciation of the caregiver's concern and efforts ("I'm impressed with how committed you are to getting Isaac's problems solved, given how often you feel down and hopeless.") and reiterate their own concern for the youth given the seriousness of the problems at hand ("I'm really concerned about Isaac, too, and I'm here to do everything possible to help him stay out of trouble and get back on track for a decent future."). Then, the therapist can emphasize how important the caregiver is in the life of the youth and in helping to manage the youth's problems ("I know it seems like Isaac is battling you tooth and nail lately, but let's think for a minute about all the ways you are important to him, and about the things you've done during the past 4 weeks to begin getting him back on track.") It is also helpful to provide specific examples of how the depression seems to be interfering with progress toward managing those problems effectively ("Despite these great efforts, I'm really afraid that you are running out of energy to keep on top of him every day. We need to figure out a way to get your energy up—and to make you feel happier too."). In the upcoming extended case example of this chapter, "Ellie and the Pesky 6 (Depression Rating)," the therapist—Tanya—used a fit circle she and the mother, Ellie, had put together to understand why it was hard for Ellie to monitor her son Isaac and enforce his curfew. Tanya pointed out that Ellie felt too hopeless to go find Isaac after arguments with him and with her own mother, and that this hopeless feeling is something Tanya might be able to help change by working individually with Ellie.

The Caregiver Is Overwhelmed

Again, the therapist's first response is to empathize with the feeling of being overwhelmed. Next, the therapist can suggest doing a fit circle on factors contributing to these feelings. A single caregiver with several children, a job, and difficulty making ends meet financially might be so busy trying to meet the concrete needs of the family that carving out time to make the changes needed at home, school, and in the social ecology to address the youth's problems consumes most waking moments of the day. The fit circle can help identify additional steps the therapist or others in the social ecology might take to help address some of the family's concrete needs. Tanya, the therapist in the forthcoming "Pesky 6" example, helped the caregiver deal with impending eviction by drafting letters and scheduling appointments with the housing authority. Similarly, a therapist might offer to stay at the home for 30 minutes after a session to watch a younger child so the caregiver can pay bills. Often, however, depression itself is contributing to the feeling of being overwhelmed. When evidence indicates this is the case, the therapist can provide concrete examples of how the feeling of being totally stressed out prevented the caregiver from doing things that were important to him or her. ("I know you wanted to get Ruby's supplies for school and get to the electric company to pay the bill, and I wonder if the call from Isaac's school left you feeling too down to do those things.") By using individual treatment to address the feeling of being overwhelmed, the caregiver can both feel better and be more prepared to accomplish tasks that are important.

Treating Depression or Anxiety Means the Caregiver Is Crazy or Weak

"I'm not crazy" is a protest therapists might hear when suggesting that an individual intervention might help address a caregiver's depression or anxiety. Despite public education and public relations efforts aimed at combating the stigma associated with mental health problems, many people continue to believe that such problems are rare and debilitating. That an account executive at a major insurance company could suffer from depression and still keep her job is unheard of to many outside the mental health professions. Unfortunately, rare but high profile media events involving individuals with diagnosed mental illness can contribute to the public perception that such individuals are crazy and dangerous. Since most people don't experience themselves as crazy and dangerous, the idea they might need help for a mental health problem can seem, well, crazy.

In this situation, the therapist begins by validating the caregiver's concern. ("Of course you're not crazy; look at all the things you do to take care of your family and in your job.") Then, strategies can be used to normalize and cut the problem down to size (i.e., helping the caregiver perceive the problem in specific, nonpejorative, and concrete ways). For example, rather than continuing to use the word *depression,* the therapist can describe a specific situation in which the caregiver had unpleasant thoughts and feelings that interfered with achieving treatment goals for the youth. The therapist might discuss situations that seem to lead the caregiver to feel depressed. For example, the therapist might observe, "It seems like you've had this problem of being yelled at by your aunt, feeling really down, and then going to your room for the night and getting none of your household tasks done. This happened three or four times last month and always seems to make you feel even worse—like nothing will change for the better. If this situation with your aunt really is making you feel depressed, we can work together to change things."

For some people, finding a label that isn't laden with stigma can also be helpful. For example, labeling depression as "having a bad case of the blues" or "dealing with the big D" can help reframe the problem and set the stage for change. For others, understanding the problem as an illness makes it more manageable, because they perceive that illnesses can be readily treated, if not cured. Here, individual sessions can be framed as providing the tools to help manage the illness, and the caregiver can be informed that other tools, such as medication, might also be helpful. Essentially, the aim of these strategies is to find language for the problem that is acceptable to the caregiver and that can be used to create a shared (caregiver–therapist) picture of why the depression or anxiety is a problem (e.g., it is distressing and interferes with valued goals such as getting a job or meeting an MST treatment goal desired by the caregiver) and convey the sense that ways to manage the problem are available from the therapist.

Treating Caregiver Mental Health Problems That Are Barriers to Achieving Youth Outcomes

The experience of therapists implementing MST throughout the United States and internationally indicates the most common caregiver-related barriers to treatment progress are *depression,* specifically depression in female caregivers, *anxiety* problems, and *substance abuse.* As interventions for substance abuse in youth and caregivers are described in Chapter 8, the caregiver treatment portion of the current chapter focuses primarily on interventions for adult depression and secondarily on interventions for adult anxiety.

Caregiver Depression

For most adults with nonpsychotic mental health problems, behavioral interventions are just as effective as medications, and the positive effects often hold up over time. Reviews of research on treating depression in adults (Hollon et al., 2005) have concluded that cognitive-behavioral therapy (CBT) is relatively effective, helping about 60% of clients. When the correct medication is combined with CBT, clients can get better faster and stay better longer. Importantly, similarities in the principles of MST and CBT (e.g., action oriented, present focused, addressing specific well-defined problems) facilitate the use of CBT interventions within MST for caregivers and youth. In addition to CBT, the use of social support to decrease symptoms of depression and anxiety is described here (see also Chapter 7).

Cognitive-Behavioral Therapy

CBT is based on the premise that faulty ways of thinking are a key factor contributing to such difficulties as depression, anxiety, poorly controlled anger, and problematic impulsive behavior. The following example shows a sequence of thinking, feeling, and behavior that is particularly amenable to CBT interventions.

> Mrs. Smith, the depressed mother of a son referred for MST, avoided job seeking because she thought she would never pass an interview. She also avoided answering the telephone when she saw the school number on the phone's caller ID because she feared bad news about her son. Mrs. Smith believed her unemployment confirmed her failure in life, and that calls from the school were certain signs of disaster. In response to these thoughts and feelings, she stopped looking for employment and avoided further contact with school personnel. These actions, in turn, reduced her odds of becoming employed as well as any ability to help school personnel manage her son's behavior more effectively.

In CBT, the therapist acts as a coach and helps the client detect and change ways of thinking that are linked with the bad feelings (depression, anxiety, anger) and the kinds of behaviors that often accompany those feelings. To do this, therapists engage the individual in a process that fits well with the types of problem analyses that underlie MST. Specifically, CBT therapists help people identify the bases for thoughts and feelings that are linked to depressed or anxious states (e.g., "Everyone should like me.") and check the validity of assumptions, beliefs, and thoughts by examining evidence that contradicts and supports them. In addition, the CBT process helps individuals think in terms of probabilities rather than certainties, because the behavior of others and events in the world are not entirely predictable. For example, a therapist might point out to Mrs. Smith that while there is no guarantee she will get a job if she starts applying, the odds are much better she'll get a job if she applies than if she does not.

Finally, the behavioral aspect of CBT provides valuable challenges to negative thoughts and examples of what happens when those thoughts are tested. For example, Mrs. Smith can find out whether talking with the school will be a disaster by actually having the conversation. To prepare for the conversation, however, the therapist would first help Mrs. Smith practice how to replace her automatic thought that the call will be a disaster with the possibility that the call could be at least a neutral, if not positive event. The therapist would also help Mrs. Smith practice in advance how to start a phone conversation to reduce the odds that she will feel blamed or attacked by the school.

COGNITIVE DISTORTIONS AND COGNITIVE DEFICIENCIES

Two constructs are central to most cognitive-behavioral interventions: cognitive distortions and cognitive deficiencies. Each represents a particular type of information processing problem, and research supports their relevance to difficulties in functioning associated with depression and anxiety in adults and children and with aggressive behavior in children.

Clues about cognitive distortions come in the form of statements such as "My boss didn't talk to me when I got to work so he must not like me" or "I am a failure" in response to criticism from a coworker or relative. These kinds of statements in response to relatively routine negative events can be indicators of faulty thinking, and adults with depression have this kind of thinking often. Cognitive distortions can also be a problem for adults and teens whose angry and aggressive behavior creates negative consequences for others and themselves. For example, 15-year-old Jimmy, who thinks, "He's out to get me," when pushed accidentally by another boy in the lunch line is demonstrating faulty thinking called a "hostile attribution bias."

Cognitive deficiencies refer to insufficient thinking in situations that require forethought prior to taking action. Jimmy might have developed a limited range of options in response to perceived provocations, such as being pushed in the lunch line. Consequently, he uses the one option he knows well and practices often—aggressive behavior—to solve the problem. CBT strategies would be used to help Jimmy by first working to correct his distorted thinking, for example, by examining evidence for and against Jimmy's conviction that the push was deliberate, and then introducing other plausible thoughts ("it was an accident") and examining the evidence for and against the alternate thoughts. Then, after gathering evidence that Jimmy has no or few other ways to respond to these types of situations, the CBT therapist would teach and practice skills to expand the range of problem-solving options Jimmy can use. In the context of MST, because the therapist is working in Jimmy's natural ecology, he or she can obtain needed information by observing Jimmy at home, school, and with peers, and by talking with Jimmy's mother, teacher, and neighbors. Most importantly, and as a clear advantage over using CBT by itself to treat serious antisocial behavior in youth, the MST therapist can also change interactions at home, in school, and with peers to support the more individually oriented CBT strategies.

FREQUENTLY USED CBT TECHNIQUES

For adults with depression and anxiety, several different CBT techniques have been shown to be effective (e.g., Leahy, 2003). In the context of MST, the techniques used most often with caregivers are identified in Table 6.1. This table identifies each technique and what it is designed to do, and provides examples of tools to help implement the technique. As with all other MST interventions, these techniques are tailored to the individual strengths and needs of the caregiver and his or her family and social support system. Use of these techniques is described later in the chapter, in the context of a case example.

Social Support Strategies

Social isolation often contributes to depression, and strategies to increase social support can help overcome that isolation. Chapter 7 describes how to identify different types of social support and strategies to help families cultivate the support needed to sustain family, peer, school, and community

TABLE 6.1. CBT Techniques Commonly Used with Adult Caregivers in MST

Technique	Purpose of technique	Examples of tools
Keeping daily records	Shows "What I think connects to what I feel" and that changing thoughts can change feelings and behavior	Daily Tracking Chart (see Figure 6.4 as example)
Examining evidence	Teaches how to evaluate thoughts in terms of evidence for and against	Evidence Examination Chart (see Figure 6.3 as example)
Problem-solving training	Increases repertoire of problem-solving skills, especially interpersonal problem-solving skills	Problem-Solving Steps Chart (see the section of this chapter on improving problem-solving skills)
Activity scheduling	Increases physical and social activity, tests negative thoughts (e.g., "I can't do anything")	Activity Schedule

interventions. For present purposes, MST therapists often use strategies to increase instrumental social support when intervening with caregiver depression (e.g., helping a mother get help with child care or transportation so she can engage in a pleasant activity). In addition, it is often useful to line up sources of appraisal support. Appraisal support provides affirmation or feedback, as illustrated by such statements as "You're doing the right thing, making Isaac get up for school, even though he curses you when you do" and "I know you feel bad about asking your mother to stay away from the kids when she's been drinking, but you are doing what is best for the kids."

Appraisal support is often needed from the therapist when a caregiver first attempts to use assertive behavior with a family member or relative with whom interaction consistently triggers depressed feelings. After practicing the new behavior in role plays, the therapist and caregiver predict how the target of the new behavior might respond. In sessions, the therapist provides much of the appraisal and emotional support needed to encourage the caregiver to use the new behavior in the face of negative feedback from the target. The therapist and caregiver should, however, quickly identify other sources of such support in the caregiver's natural ecology. Similarly, activity scheduling (i.e., explicitly increasing the caregiver's social and physical activity to counter depression) often requires the caregiver to try new things, like taking a walk with a neighbor, having coffee with a coworker, or signing up for a job-training class. Coaching the caregiver in how to talk with potential sources of support and what kinds of "quid pro quo" might be helpful to sustaining the support is essential (see Chapter 7). The subsequent case in this chapter illustrates the application of a few of these strategies for individual treatment for depression in adults.

Some caregivers, however, are reluctant to ask for social support from relatives, friends, neighbors, or colleagues. In some cases, particularly when a family member or relative is involved, long-standing interaction patterns laced with conflict or avoidance can prompt the caregiver's reluctance to ask for help. That history might also invoke feelings of anger or disappointment that interfere with the caregiver's capacity to effectively negotiate for help. In other cases, the caregiver might already feel beholden and embarrassed about having asked favors in the past. Sometimes, caregivers expect others to judge them negatively or to blame them for the problems of the youth and family for which help is being sought, in part because they, themselves, feel disappointed or embarrassed about being unable to manage these problems effectively. If, after having worked with the therapist as detailed in Chapter 7 to identify the type of support and sources of support needed to achieve specific treatment goals, the caregiver is unable or unwilling to attempt strategies to solicit that support, the therapist, as always, collects evidence regarding fit factors for that reluctance. If evidence indicates the fit factors include embarrassment, anger, or other distressing feelings and consequences, the therapist can use the cognitive-behavioral strategies described in this chapter to address these barriers to cultivating social support.

Case Example for Treating Caregiver Depression: Ellie and the Pesky 6 (Depression Rating)

The Sanders family was referred to the MST program after Isaac and two older peers were arrested at 2:00 A.M. on a weeknight in a stolen car. Isaac, age 15 years, had been arrested twice before and had a history of truancy, suspensions from school, and fighting in the neighborhood. Isaac lived with his divorced mother, Ellie, his sister, Ruby (11 years of age), and brother, Robbie (8 years of age) in a subsidized apartment complex in a rundown neighborhood.

When MST began, Isaac and Ellie argued almost daily, and Isaac sometimes threatened his mother with physical violence during these arguments. Isaac came and went as he pleased. Tanya was the therapist assigned to the case. Four weeks into treatment, Tanya had helped Ellie avoid eviction by appealing to the housing authority. With Tanya's help, Ellie had established and sometimes enforced a curfew for Isaac and gotten Isaac up and to school on time on 10 of the past 14 days. Importantly, unwanted and often disruptive visits from Ellie's alcohol-dependent mother were identified as one of several fit factors for inconsistent follow-through on Isaac's curfew, monitoring of his whereabouts, and mother–son arguing. For 2 weeks in a row, progress toward intermediary goals looked like Figure 6.1 on the MST Case Summary.

Tanya and Ellie together completed "fit circles" to identify barriers to meeting each goal, and during that process Ellie identified feeling "hopeless" about things ever changing and "exhausted," among several other barriers (see Figure 6.2). Ellie said she had felt this way for a while before MST started, and thought getting help for her family would make her feel better—and that it did, a little. Now, however, things were "back to normal"—mean-

Intermediary Goal	Met	Partially Met	Not Met
Limit evening visits mother			X
Get Isaac to school on time daily		X	
Get Isaac in by curfew weeknights		X	
Identify adults to help monitor Isaac			X

FIGURE 6.1. Sanders family intermediary goals at week 6.

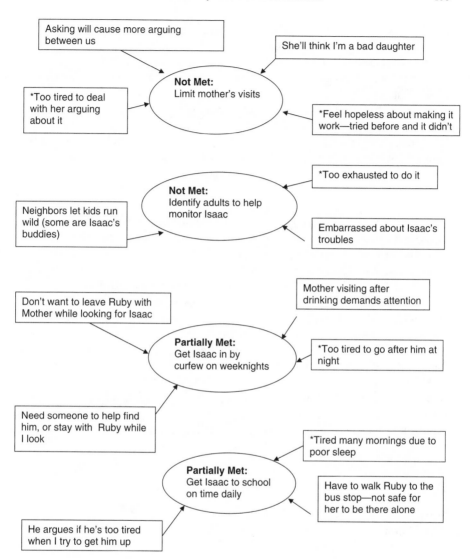

FIGURE 6.2. Fit circles for goals not met and partly met: Ellie's depression clues. Asterisks indicate drivers common across fit circles that signal Ellie's possible depression.

ing Ellie was feeling depressed. Tanya asked Ellie to rate her depression on a scale from 1 to 10. Ellie rated it as a 5. Tanya asked about two vegetative signs of depression—interrupted sleep and weight loss—and Ellie reported having trouble sleeping. After the family session the next day, Tanya asked Ellie in private for a depression rating again, and Ellie reported a 6. Tanya asked Ellie if she had ever sought help for depression, and Ellie said no, she didn't want people to think she was crazy. Tanya asked Ellie if they could meet the next day while the kids were in school to talk about how she might help Ellie with "that pesky 6." Ellie said she wasn't sure she needed any help, but that meeting the next day would be OK.

When Tanya returned, she suggested developing one fit circle on Ellie's feelings of hopelessness and another for feelings of exhaustion. The fit circles showed that visits from Ellie's mother persistently triggered both these negative feelings. The exhaustion occurred when Ellie couldn't get to sleep at night because she ruminated about what her mother had said during the arguments. Ellie also explained she would tell herself not to argue when she knew her mother had been drinking, but always ended up feeling the need to defend herself, and argued anyway. This sequence of interaction also made Ellie feel hopeless about ever being able to change anything—including Isaac. Ellie and Tanya, therefore, identified the grandmother's visits as a powerful proximal driver of Ellie's depressed feelings. Tanya asked for 30 minutes to talk with Ellie about her depression, as Ellie didn't think she could spare any more time and wanted Tanya to handle new complaints from Isaac's school and probation officer. The following brief excerpt illustrates first steps in showing how thoughts link to feelings, and how to examine evidence for and against a thought or belief that triggers bad feelings.

LINKING THOUGHTS TO FEELINGS AND BEHAVIORS:
EXAMINING THE EVIDENCE

TANYA: What kinds of events seem to trigger the bad feelings?

ELLIE: Mama comes over and tells me I don't help her enough.

TANYA: What kinds of thoughts does that comment trigger for you?

ELLIE: I just feel terrible.

TANYA: Terrible is the feeling or emotion you have in response to underlying thoughts. Try completing this sentence: "I feel terrible because I think.... "

ELLIE: She thinks I'm a bad daughter.

TANYA: Is that something she says to you?

ELLIE: Not really.

TANYA: So, it sounds like you are mind reading, thinking you know what your mother thinks even though she hasn't said the words.

ELLIE: Yeah.

TANYA: For a couple of minutes, right now, let's stick with what she actually says, and the thoughts and feelings you have in response to the things she says. What is something she said yesterday that triggered your bad feelings?

ELLIE: She said I don't make time to talk when she comes over.

TANYA: And if that was true, what would it mean?

ELLIE: That I'm a bad daughter.

TANYA: So, let's examine the evidence you are using when you think to yourself you are a bad daughter. On this piece of paper, I'm going to write down that thought. Then, I'm going to draw a line down the middle of the paper. On the left, we'll put all evidence that supports the idea that you are a bad daughter. On the right, we'll put all the evidence that contradicts that idea.

(Tanya and Ellie complete the Evidence Examination Chart shown in Figure 6.3.)

TANYA: Now, let's find out how much this evidence convinces you one way or the other about how true your belief is. We are going to weigh the evidence about this belief. Does it seem to you like the "against" came out ahead of "for"?

ELLIE: Yeah, but not by much.

TANYA: That's OK. So, with this evidence, if someone asked, "What kind of daughter are you," what would you say?

ELLIE: I'd say I'm an OK daughter, even pretty good sometimes.

TANYA: That sounds pretty accurate, given this evidence chart. We will also try to do this with other thoughts that connect to your feelings of sad-

Evidence for ...	Evidence against ...
I leave the room when she talks a lot.	She comes over almost every day.
I don't like having her over when she drinks.	I do her grocery shopping.
	I help clean her house.

Evidence arithmetic: 3/5 against (60%); 2/5 for (40%)

FIGURE 6.3. Testing Ellie's belief "I'm a bad daughter."

ness or hopelessness. You will notice that there is usually some evidence to support any belief—otherwise you wouldn't have it. We are going to learn together how to help you examine evidence on both sides of the question, though, so that you can weigh the evidence and then practice changing your belief. I will help you practice. First, we have one more thing to do right now. When you say, "I'm an OK daughter, even pretty good sometimes," what kinds of feelings do you have?

ELLIE: Well, not terrible.

TANYA: OK, that's a start. Why don't you say the sentence, and then see if you can name another feeling that comes with the sentence?

ELLIE: Ummmm. (*Repeats sentence.*) I guess I feel kind of calm.

TANYA: Calm. OK. I'm going to get another piece of paper to show how we can track the links between what you think and what you feel. We will also add a column that helps us see how what you feel connects with what you do. This kind of chart will also show us how your feelings, and what you do as a result of your feelings, can change when you change a thought or belief.

Next, Tanya introduced the Daily Tracking Chart (see Figure 6.4), and together they identified the thoughts and feelings associated with two other events. By using several different events to complete the Baseline Daily Tracking Chart, Tanya was helping Ellie to see that her negative thoughts come to mind automatically, and that there are connections between these automatic thoughts, bad feelings, and behaviors that often end up creating additional problems for her and her family. Tanya did not ask Ellie to do any homework connected to either evidence examination or the Daily Tracking Chart (see Figure 6.5), as she determined more in-session coaching was needed to ensure Ellie could generate evidence for both sides of a belief and

Event	Thought	Feeling	Behavior	Consequence
1. Mama comes in and says I didn't answer the phone when she called.	Here we go again. I'm a bad daughter. I can't take this anymore.	Sinking feeling. Exhausted. Hopeless.	Leave room. Check on Ruby to get away from Mama.	Mama talks and follows me. Ruby complains I interrupted her.
2. Isaac stays out past curfew.	This is a disaster. He'll go to prison for good.	Mad. Sad.	Avoid probation officer calls. Stay awake worrying.	Probation officer comes over. Exhausted in morning.

FIGURE 6.4. Baseline Daily Tracking Chart for Ellie Sanders.

Event	Thought	Feeling	Behavior	Consequence
1. Mama comes in and says I didn't answer the phone when she called.	I don't know if this is true. I don't know if this is a problem.	Frustrated. Confused.	Find out when she called. Find out what she needed when she called.	She doesn't remember what time she called or what she needed.
2. Isaac stays out past curfew.	This is a serious problem.	Worried. Mad.	Call Tanya to get help. Call neighbors for help.	Tanya will come watch the kids if I call by 10:00 P.M. Neighbors say they will call if they see him.

FIGURE 6.5. Intervention Daily Tracking Chart for Ellie Sanders.

was concerned that Ellie might feel worse if she could generate evidence for only one side.

During their individual meeting 2 days later, Tanya introduced Ellie to the idea of changing an automatic thought that follows a specific event, and finding out what kinds of feelings and behaviors might occur in response to a new thought. To facilitate this process, Tanya asked Ellie to help her complete another version of the Daily Tracking Chart, one that reflects what happens if you intervene in the sequence of thoughts, feelings, and behaviors that follows a negative event. Figure 6.5 shows the first few entries on the Intervention Daily Tracking Chart Tanya and Ellie developed during that session.

IMPROVING PROBLEM-SOLVING SKILLS

After the caregiver is able to replace automatic thoughts across several clearly identified problem situations for several days in a row, the therapist and caregiver work together to increase the caregiver's repertoire of problem-solving skills. This process involves several steps, identified below, along with examples from the Pesky 6 case.

1. *Identify* (a) the problem, (b) the desired outcomes, and (c) possible strategies to attain the outcomes. In the Pesky 6 case, (a) Ellie identified one problem as: Mama comes over without notice and usually has been drinking before she comes; (b) Ellie's desired outcome was: Mama asks before coming over and does not drink before coming; (c) at first, when brainstorming strategies, Ellie offered these: "Don't answer the door when she comes over. Leave the house with the kids when I see the cab drop her off. Call her during the day and tell her not to come." Tanya asked if she could add other

options to the list, and Ellie agreed. Tanya added: "Schedule days for Mama to come."

2. *Evaluate the costs and benefits of each strategy.* For the option of calling her mother to ask her not to come that evening, Ellie identified as a "cost" that getting into an argument over the phone was likely, and as a "benefit" that her mother would probably not come that night. Tanya and Ellie made a ledger that listed each solution (e.g., leave the house, call, and schedule in advance) on the left, benefits in the middle column, and costs on the right.

3. *Select a strategy.* Tanya suggested using the kind of arithmetic she and Ellie had used to weigh the evidence for and against Ellie's belief she was a bad daughter as one way to select which strategy to try first. Ellie identified more costs to scheduling visits in advance than she had for making the phone call: She couldn't just hang up if her mother became angry, she thought she would be a bad daughter if she asked her mother to schedule visits, and so on. So, Tanya took a detour from weighing the costs and benefits of the options to go back to examining the evidence for and against the "bad daughter" thought Ellie anticipated experiencing as a cost.

4. *Practice the strategy with the therapist and then in real-life settings.* There are several steps to practicing, and caregivers should be informed about these steps before starting to practice. Specifically, the therapist might need to model the new behavior before asking the caregiver to try it. The therapist also should provide feedback about the behaviors as the caregiver practices, first in role plays, and then in real-life situations. The therapist, therefore, needs to let the caregiver know, before practice begins, that therapist feedback will be both positive, as in "Ellie, your request was very clear and simple, and that kind of request might work pretty well with your mama in this situation, given what I know about her," and corrective, "Ellie, you didn't look at me when you made your request, and that made me think you didn't really mean it, so I tried to talk you out of it. Let's try it again, with the same clear and simple request, but this time try to look at me when you say it."

The therapist should ensure that the caregiver practices using the new strategies, first with the therapist in role plays and then in real-life settings. When first attempting the new strategies in real-life situations, it would be most helpful if the therapist is available to either observe or to provide immediate feedback and support as needed. The role-playing strategy can be tried again or in a different way if the attempted behavioral strategy does not go well.

REGULATING EMOTIONS: ANGER

In some cases, caregivers who have a hard time solving interpersonal problems effectively also have a hard time regulating their emotions, and those difficulties can interfere with the execution of strategies like the one illustrated above, in which Ellie tried to be assertive in making a request without going down the predictable path of having an argument with her mother. Ellie did not have this kind of problem regulating emotions, so for her, executing the skill of stating assertively her request of her mother required mostly practicing and getting feedback from Tanya, and tracking the connections between her thoughts, feelings, and actions when she became discouraged about trying. But, some caregivers do have such difficulties regulating their emotions, as evidenced, for example, by "flying off the handle" or becoming agitated and yelling in response to what seem to be relatively minor personal slights. If the emotion regulation problem occurs in the context of depression or anxiety, then proceeding with cognitive-behavioral strategies and medication, if needed, is likely to attenuate the problem.

Individuals without psychiatric diagnoses can also have problems with emotion regulation that interfere with treatment progress. For such individuals, problems regulating emotions might become a barrier to some aspect of treatment such as reducing parent–child or interparental conflict or meeting with school personnel after their son has been suspended. If emotion regulation is a barrier to change, the therapist can use the therapist–caregiver interactions to identify and address this problem. That is, the therapist can identify the emergence of the caregiver emotion that arises in ongoing therapist–caregiver interactions, tease out what aspects of the therapist's behavior prompt the caregiver to feel angry or hurt, validate the caregiver's feeling, and ask for permission to craft strategies together that allow the caregiver to express concerns before the emotional experience becomes too intense. In addition, therapists can use the relaxation and breathing exercises and systematic desensitization described and illustrated in the upcoming "Exposure-Based Treatment" section of this chapter to help caregivers regulate emotional responses to specific situations and interactions.

ACTIVITY SCHEDULING

Activity scheduling identifies particular days and times someone will do a particular activity. In the context of treating individuals with depression or anxiety, activities that have one or more of the following characteristics can be a helpful part of treatment.

1. *The activity solves a problem.* For example, a meeting between Ellie and her mother that focuses on scheduling her mother's visits would be an activity that helps solve one problem contributing to Ellie's depression.
2. *The activity is enjoyable to the person.* Taking a walk in a park near Ruby's school (a safer location than her own neighborhood) was one enjoyable activity for Ellie.

3. *The activity involves someone liked.* Ellie had one neighbor a block away she used to see occasionally when their children went to the same school. Ellie thought having coffee with that neighbor could be pleasurable.
4. *The activity keeps the person busy.* The value of being busy—when the activity is either solving a problem, enjoyable, or involves someone liked—lies in the fact that it's hard to have depressive or anxious cognitions when busy.
5. *The activity helps someone else.* Helping others makes many people feel good. As illustrated with Ellie, repeated sequences of certain kinds of helping interactions can also have negative consequences, as occurred with Ellie and her mother. So, if activity that helps someone else is going to be part of a treatment plan, the MST therapist should ensure that the helping behavior will be experienced positively by the client. In Ellie's case, activities that help someone else weren't added to the list until later in treatment, and then they occurred in the context of figuring out the kinds of "quid pro quo" needed to get help from neighbors.

Caregiver Anxiety

The CBT techniques used to help adults with depression are also effective for treating anxiety (Leahy, 2003). To recap, these techniques aim to help the individual:

- See the connections between thoughts, anxious feelings, and behavior.
- Evaluate the evidence for and against thoughts that trigger anxious feelings.
- Develop alternative thoughts, attend to the changes in feelings, and identify alternative behaviors connected to the new thoughts and feelings and
- Increase the array of problem-solving skills available in situations that can trigger the anxiety.

In addition, exposure-based treatment and relaxation techniques are other CBT strategies that can help individuals with anxiety disorders such as PTSD to think and react differently to people, places, and situations that trigger symptoms.

Exposure-Based Treatment

In exposure-based strategies, the therapist coaches the client to imagine the details of the specific situation that triggers anxiety and tolerate the intensity of the anxious feeling until it begins to subside. In a particular type of exposure, called systematic desensitization, the therapist also teaches the individual to use deep muscle relaxation skills. The rationale for pairing relaxation with imagining anxiety-provoking situations first developed when researchers found evidence that relaxation and fear were two incompatible responses, and fear could be dispelled in the face of relaxation (Meichenbaum, 1977; Wolpe & Lazarus, 1966). Parts of the brain activated by fear and stress stimulate bodily experiences, such as muscle tension, pounding heart, shortness of breath, sweating, and dizziness, that people with anxiety disorders often experience; and relaxation techniques can reduce these unpleasant effects (Cohen, Mannarino, & Deblinger, 2006). The goal of systematic desensitization, therefore, is to enable the individual, in a safe and well-coached setting, to tolerate the fear or anxiety associated with a particular person, place, or situation, and to experience that the fear or anxiety can be decreased to a manageable level.

ESTABLISHING A HIERARCHY AND IDENTIFYING LEVELS OF DISTRESS

In systematic desensitization, the therapist first helps the individual create a graduated hierarchy of anxiety-provoking scenes, with each scene somewhat more anxiety provoking than the one before. The therapist helps the individual rate the distress experienced on a scale from 0 to 100, usually in 10-unit increments. This rating is called a subjective unit of distress, or SUD, rating (Gambrill, 1977; Wolpe & Lazarus, 1966). After teaching the client how to use deep muscle relaxation, described briefly in the next paragraph, the therapist asks him or her to think about the least stressful item on the SUD scale (i.e., the item rated 10), indicate feelings of anxiety, and then relax until the anxiety disappears. This procedure is repeated until the previously stressful thought no longer evokes anxiety. Then, the client moves on to the next item on the scale and so forth. At later stages in the progression (e.g., when learning to relax during a scene with a SUD rating of 90 or 100), the aim is to reduce feelings of anxiety to more acceptable levels (e.g., equivalent to items previously rated at 10–30).

BREATHING CONTROL AND PROGRESSIVE MUSCLE RELAXATION

Breathing control and progressive muscle relaxation are two strategies used during the systematic desensitization process to reduce anxiety. These strategies can also be used to help caregivers manage other kinds of distressing feelings, such as intense anger that might be experienced during conflict with others, or the shame or guilt that might be experienced when asking for help. Breathing control teaches diaphragmatic breathing—individuals learn to take slow, measured breaths when they become aware of feeling angry (or anxious or sad) or when entering a potentially stressful situation. In a quiet, private place, the therapist teaches the individual to breathe slowly and regularly and to count internally when exhaling, saying "relax" (e.g., "1 relax, 2 relax, …, 10 relax") (Tompkins, 2004). As the person inhales, the therapist instructs him or her to push the stomach out, which results in distention of the diaphragm. At first, the therapist should be present when the caregiver tries to pair the controlled breathing with the experience of having the distressing emotion (anxiety, anger, sadness, guilt, shame). The therapist asks the caregiver to rate the degree of concentration, ease of breathing, and intensity of the emotion. Forms therapists and individuals can use to rate these experiences can be found in a book by Tompkins (2004), which is listed in the "Resources for Therapists" section of this chapter. After several practice sessions indicate the caregiver can use this strategy, the therapist and caregiver together determine how often (at least once daily is recommended) and where the caregiver can practice alone, using the rating forms, and bringing the forms back to individual sessions to review progress and barriers to implementing the strategy.

Progressive muscle relaxation is similar to breathing control exercises, but focuses on progressively relaxing difference muscle groups to reduce anxiety. The sample script below taken from Smith (1990, p. 123) illustrates the progressive muscle relaxation process.

> "Make a tight fist with your right hand.
> Hold the tension.
> Attend to the sensations of tension.
> And let go.
> Let the tension flow.
> Attend to the feelings of relaxation."

Similar to the previous breathing control exercises, the therapist and caregiver should identify specific times and quiet places to practice, tensing each muscle group for 10 seconds and relaxing for 10 seconds. Therapists can find examples of the sequencing of muscles to emphasize in relaxation training (e.g., arms, hands, fingers, etc.) as well as scripts, words (e.g., *calm, peace*), and images that might help clients to relax in Chapter 6 of McKay, Davis, and Fanning (2007). The following case example outlines some of the basic steps entailed in such procedures.

Case Example: Avoiding a Train Wreck by Treating Anxiety

"I know I should, but I just can't bring myself to do it, and I feel like a train wreck is coming!" Crystal Smith said to Angie, the MST therapist. Angie had been working for 3 weeks with the Smith family: Crystal; her sons, Sam, 16 years of age, and Max, 14 years old; and her husband of 4 years, Jack. Jack worked construction, and Crystal was not employed when Sam was referred to MST. Angie and Crystal were reviewing progress and barriers related to the intermediary treatment goals of getting Sam enrolled in a vocational training institute and applying for part-time jobs. These goals were priorities for the family, Sam's probation officer, and the judge. High family conflict and the fact that Sam left home for 24 hours after Angie helped his mother established a curfew and monitoring plan were among initial barriers to meeting the goals. Additional barriers included Jack's work schedule, which prevented him from assisting his wife and Sam with the process of searching for jobs and enrolling in vocational training. On the day that Crystal lamented being a "wreck," the monthly probation visit was only a week away, Jack would not be able to attend, and Crystal said she was so nervous about the visit that she was afraid she would get into an accident driving to the building.

Angie had noticed previously that Crystal seemed anxious whenever she talked about going to school to meet with her sons' teachers, searching for a job for herself, or reasons she had either quit or lost previous jobs. Crystal said things like "I canceled the meeting twice before I went," or "I called just before the interview to say I couldn't make it; something else had come up." Now, with two indicators of treatment progress for Sam unmet and a pending probation visit, Crystal was becoming distressed about not doing what she had told the probation officer she would do. Angie hypothesized that Crystal was experiencing social anxiety, generalized anxiety, or both. Accordingly, she asked Crystal if it would be all right to spend a few minutes to try to figure out what seemed so hard about taking Sam for an interview at the vocational training institute, and then about the upcoming probation meeting. Crystal agreed. Excerpts from the first part of that conversation follow.

ANGIE: What do you think will happen when you take Sam to the vocational school?

CRYSTAL: They will ask me all kinds of questions about why he was expelled, and I won't know what to say. I'll sound dumb, and Sam will say something "smart," and they'll think we're a bad family and they won't let Sam in.

ANGIE: Wow, that's a lot to worry about. We'll come back to this in a minute. First, I want to understand if this kind of experience is new to you, or if you've worried in this kind of way about other situations in your life. Is it OK to do that for a couple of minutes before we come back to solving this problem of getting to the vocational school?

CRYSTAL: OK.

ANGIE: A week ago, you said you needed to look for a job again to help make ends meet, and that you wished you could just get the job by filling out an application, instead of having to go in for an interview. What kinds of thoughts and feelings come up as you think about job interviews?

CRYSTAL: I just can't even stand thinking about it. I get so nervous, I can barely think.

ANGIE: I can see you are starting to look nervous now. You are tapping your foot, and looking around the room. I'd like to spend a few more minutes learning about the kinds of people, places, and situations that trigger anxious feelings in you. I'll write these down so we can both see them. Then, we can take a couple of the examples and learn more about what you think and feel and do in response. We can also talk about what happens in situations where you don't feel so anxious, and even feel comfortable. I'd like to do this with you because I think we will get some good clues about why it's so hard for you to go to the vocational school and probation meeting with Sam, and maybe even why it's so hard for you to interview for your own jobs.

Within about half an hour, Angie had evidence suggesting Crystal was socially anxious, and possibly also experienced some generalized anxiety. Crystal agreed to schedule some individual sessions with Angie to try to "get a grip" before the probation meeting. Angie planned to begin a Baseline Daily Tracking Chart (Figure 6.4) with Crystal, introduce and practice a couple of new thoughts to replace her anxious thoughts, and start to evaluate evidence for and against Crystal's anxiety-provoking thoughts. With only a week before the meeting, there was not enough time for Crystal to get adequate practice using these new strategies. And, Angie hadn't begun to assess and address the range of problem solving skills Crystal brought to potentially stressful situations, although she had some evidence from Crystal's comments that mostly Crystal tried to avoid the situations. Angie talked with the MST supervisor about the situation, and they determined that if Angie and Crystal could meet alone for several days the next week, systematic desensitization focusing on the probation meeting might be worth a try.

During the initial session, Angie worked with Crystal to develop a SUDs hierarchy associated with the probation meeting.

SUDs	Scene
10	Telling Sam it's time to go
20	Getting my coat on
30	Getting the keys to the car
40	Getting into the car
50	Driving
60	Seeing the gas station near the probation building
70	Parking the car in the probation building parking lot
80	Checking in at the front desk
90	Sitting in the probation officer's cubicle

100   The probation officer asking about vocational school
             and jobs

Next, Angie took 20 minutes getting Crystal to relax her body, using muscle relaxation techniques. Angie coached Crystal to close her eyes, breathe deeply, let worrisome thoughts go for a few minutes, and begin to become aware of her hands and arms. Angie wanted to get Crystal's baseline SUD rating down to about 20 before ending the first relaxation training session and moving on to pairing the scenes from the hierarchy with relaxation. This is because both Angie and Crystal needed evidence that Crystal could, in fact, relax enough to feel low or little distress before increasing distress levels by visualizing the anxiety-provoking scenes. They were trying to ensure that Crystal could relax when prompted.

During the week before the probation visit, Angie and Crystal had four individual relaxation sessions. At the end of these sessions, Angie continued to introduce the CBT strategies of daily tracking and evaluating evidence (Figures 6.3 and 6.4). These individual sessions occurred in addition to a family session focused on reducing conflict and recalibrating the monitoring plan for Sam following his going AWOL. By the end of the week, Crystal got her SUD rating down to 20 through the fifth step—driving. That was substantial progress for someone who had avoided many situations due to anxiety until the previous week. There was insufficient time, however, to go further into the hierarchy before the scheduled meeting. Consequently, Crystal was not entirely convinced she could get herself and Sam to the meeting safely, and thought she might still be tempted to skip the meeting entirely. In light of the urgency of the pending meeting (and the key MST aims of reducing rearrest and out-of-home placement) Angie decided it would be best if she drove Crystal and Sam to the probation meeting and later met alone with Crystal to address anxiety-related barriers to empowering the caregivers to be more effective with Sam.

Medication for Adults

Some caregivers prefer to try medication as a first step in treating depression or anxiety. Others have no particular opinion about medication and would rather try the behavioral strategies proposed by the MST therapist. And, some are very reluctant to try medication, even after implementation of CBT has produced only limited relief from symptoms. If the hallmark symptoms of depression or anxiety (summarized in the second paragraph of this chapter) continue under such circumstances, the MST therapist can help educate the caregiver about medication options and suggest contacting a psychiatrist.

Several Internet websites provide excellent information on the evidence-based use of medication in treating depression and anxiety. Moreover, this information is updated periodically as research findings are integrated. Specifically, the websites for the Texas Implementation of Medication Algorithms (TIMA), National Alliance on Mental Illness (NAMI), and National Institute of Mental Health (NIMH) provide easy to read information on the symptoms of depression and anxiety, effective medications, dosages required, length of time it takes to experience relief, what to do if the first medication doesn't seem to work, and medication side effects. The contact information for these websites appears in the resource section at the end of this chapter. Steps therapists can take to help caregivers become knowledgeable and effective collaborators with the physicians providing medication management services are described near the end of this chapter, in the context of helping empower caregivers and youth to be effective collaborators with physicians.

Individual Interventions with Youth

In addition to known peer, family, school, and neighborhood risk factors for antisocial behavior, several kinds of cognitive processes have also been identified as contributors to problem aggression in youth (McMahon & Forehand, 2003). Youth with problem aggression are more likely than others to:

- Pay attention to aggressive cues in the environment.
- Attribute the behavior of others to hostile intentions even when that behavior is neutral (cognitive distortions).
- Come up with fewer verbally assertive (cognitive deficits) and more physically aggressive solutions to social problems.
- Label arousal as anger rather than as fear or sadness.

Inspired by the interpersonal problem-solving approach pioneered in the late 1970s by Spivack and colleagues (Spivack, Platt, & Shure, 1976), several interventions for cognitive-behavioral and social problem-solving skill deficits have been designed to correct the cognitive distortions common among such youth and to increase the repertoire of behaviors they use in problematic situations. The most promising of these approaches are two cognitive-behavioral treatments typically conducted with small groups of youth, the Anger Coping Program, developed by Lochman and colleagues (Lochman, Nelson, & Sims, 1981) for children ages 9–12 years, and the Anger Control Training with Stress Inoculation program developed by Feindler and colleagues (Feindler, Marriott, & Iwata, 1984; Feindler & Guttman, 1994) for youth ages 12–18 years. A combined caregiver management and youth social skills training program developed by Kazdin and colleagues (Kazdin, Siegel, & Bass, 1992) has also been promising. More details about these approaches, case examples illustrating their use, and research about their effectiveness are provided in Weisz's (2004) *Psychotherapy for Children and Adolescents: Evidence-Based Treatments and Case Examples.*

For present purposes, what is noteworthy about these intervention programs is that they can be smoothly integrated into ongoing MST family-, peer-, and school-related interventions. Moreover, and importantly, these CBT-based approaches and MST both propose that reducing problem anger and aggression requires understanding the sequences of interaction that trigger these problems. In the context of MST, evidence often reveals that repeated sequences of caregiver–child, interparental, or familywide interactions (Principle 5) sustain aggressive behavior. Hence, family and behavioral parenting interventions are typically used in MST to reduce angry outbursts and aggressive behavior in youth. Interventions targeting family interactions provide opportunities to prevent aggressive outbursts rather than relying solely on helping the youth and family members manage the aggressive behavior after it occurs. Sometimes, however, aggressive behavior persists despite the implementation of family interventions and other strategies to address school- and peer-related treatment difficulties. When aggressive behavior persists, MST therapists can use CBT strategies to identify and help change the youth's faulty thinking patterns (distortions) and deficiencies in problem solving that might be sustaining the problem behavior even when ecological interventions are in place.

Several kinds of intervention techniques are usually involved in the use of CBT strategies for youth aggression:

1. Modeling the new behavior, for example, by demonstrating how to stop and think before pushing a classmate.
2. Role-playing exercises that allow the youth to practice new behaviors in situations that re-create the circumstances in which the problem behaviors occur.
3. Developing behavioral contingencies, which, in the case of MST, are generally established in conjunction with caregivers and provided by the caregivers.
4. Teaching self-monitoring and self-instruction, specifically helping the adolescent notice what he or she thinks and says internally when an event occurs, and learning to say different things to get through a situation in a way that does not involve aggression.
5. Problem-solving training, described earlier when individual interventions with adults were discussed, teaches youth how to engage in a sequential and deliberate process of solving problems that arise in social interactions.

Adult Support for Individual Youth Interventions

Although the MST therapist implements CBT strategies during individual sessions with youth, the therapist actively engages caregivers and teachers in anticipating and reinforcing (using behavioral contingencies and verbal praise) the changes initiated during these sessions. The therapist helps cultivate caregiver support and participation in the individual intervention with youth in at least five ways. The therapist:

1. Identifies the specific behavior targeted for change and alternative behaviors the youth is being coached to use instead. For example, Jim will go to his room rather than hitting his brother when they argue.
2. Helps caregivers notice and praise the adolescent's attempts to use new behaviors. The therapist might suggest, for example, that Jim's parents tell him they noticed he went to his room instead of hitting his brother and were glad he used that strategy.
3. Helps caregivers incorporate the problem behavior into rules, consequences, and rewards. For example, what consequence will occur if Jim hits his brother during an argument? What reward could be provided when Jim refrains from hitting his brother? And, how many times does he have to refrain to get the reward?
4. Helps caregivers model effective problem-solving strategies themselves when they participate in difficult interpersonal interactions. The therapist might suggest that Jim's parents demonstrate how to compromise when they disagree with each other about who will get Jim from the gym and make sure his brother still gets to his part-time job across the city on time.
5. When the problem behavior also occurs in school, the therapist works with caregivers and pertinent school personnel (teachers, assistant principal) to establish open lines of communication about the nature of the behavior and the kinds of actions the school and caregivers will take when the behavior occurs, and when it doesn't (see Chapter 5 on school–family linkages).

To help caregivers in this effort, therapists often make a chart that identifies the target behaviors being addressed during the individual sessions with the youth (e.g., describing a problem in terms of situational details; connecting the events, thoughts, and feelings the youth had in the situation; and identifying all possible strategies to solve a problem) and the types of behaviors that demonstrate the youth is trying to develop improved skills.

Problem-Solving and Social Skills Training for Youth: The Case of Tim Clayton

When aggressive or impulsive behavior is associated with a failure to think before acting, problem-solving training can be an effective means of helping teens think for themselves and act in a nonimpulsive manner on the basis of that thinking. In the context of MST, therapists most often use problem-solving skills training strategies with youth whose long history of socializing with deviant peers has provided little practice with the skills needed to succeed with prosocial peers and activities. For example, the youth might need to learn how to join a basketball game without the use of verbal or physical jousting, resolve differences about what to do with peers (e.g., "do we go to the movies or to the arcade?"), and interpret the meaning of behavior (e.g., "What did you hit me for, all I did was say you're a knucklehead?").

The essential steps of problem-solving approaches for adolescents are the same as those described earlier for adults. Sometimes, however, youth are less specific than adults about the details needed to re-create the problem situations and, thus, to effectively generate alternative solutions to the problem. The use of problem-solving steps with teenagers is illustrated in the example of Tim Clayton.

Tim was referred to MST after being expelled from school for assaulting a classmate and threatening bodily harm to the teacher who tried to intervene. The school pressed charges, and Tim was arrested. He and his older brother, Corey, lived with their father, Mike Clayton, who was a single parent. Mike's mother and the boys' grandmother, Mrs. Emma Clayton, acted as primary caregivers most of the week because the father worked alternating shifts at a factory. Mrs. Clayton described Tim as having "anger problems" in elementary school, and as becoming increasingly aggressive at the alternative middle school he attended. Mrs. Clayton said Tim could be a "good boy" at home, but she worried that Tim might hurt her if she "put her foot down," that he had "no use for his father," and that he "hangs with the wrong crowd." Diagnosed with high blood pressure and type 2 diabetes, Mrs. Clayton said, "I'll have a heart attack if Tim keeps this up," and that she would no longer be able to take care of the boys after school if Tim continued to behave badly.

Trevor, the MST therapist assigned to the case, initially worked to engage Mrs. Clayton and persuade her to work with him to decrease Tim's aggressive behavior at home and school. Some engagement efforts took place while Trevor drove Mrs. Clayton to her doctor's appointments (she would otherwise have had to take the bus) and to get her prescriptions filled. Next, having identified inconsistent parenting styles (Mr. Clayton had an authoritarian style, the grandmother a permissive one) and lack of monitoring (the father was often at work, and the grandmother went to bed by 8:30 P.M.

most evenings) as contributing to Tim's behavior problems, Trevor focused initially on establishing rules, rewards, and consequences that both caregivers could support. Mrs. Clayton, however, was afraid to implement the plan because she feared Tim would hurt her. Mrs. Clayton also reported that Tim seemed to leave home for the alternative school a few minutes later each morning, "loaded for bear," and that "his fuse is getting shorter." Similarly, Corey (Tim's brother) reported that Tim often boasted that he would "take on anyone who gets in my face" at school.

Thus, although the Clayton caregivers had agreed to make parenting changes and craft a behavior plan for Tim, the grandmother's concern about her physical safety and Mr. Clayton's frequent absences were barriers to implementing the plan. At the same time, increasing evidence indicated that Tim was getting into verbal and physical altercations at school. Trevor suggested to Mr. Clayton and his mother that, in addition to continuing his meetings with them and with the school, he meet individually with Tim to try to address the short-fuse problem, and they concurred. After meeting with the Claytons, Trevor suggested to Tim that they meet alone the next day so Trevor could better understand what bothered Tim about the scene at school. Knowing Tim liked a television show that involved forensic investigations, Trevor started the meeting by suggesting they consider this first conversation to be like the investigations on the show.

Introducing Problem Solving to Youth

After a minute or two of small talk, Trevor began, "Tim, I'd like to work together with you to try to crack the case of what goes wrong at school that triggers you to make threats or even go after someone physically. When you do those things, your dad, grandma, and the folks at school get alarmed that you'll hurt someone else or yourself, and end up in jail. Your grandma thinks maybe your fuse is getting shorter, and worries you could hurt her."

TIM: I would never do that, though.

TREVOR: That's a great relief to hear, but there's something about the way you are acting at home these days that makes her, and even your dad, worry that you might. So, let's leave aside the topic of Grandma for a minute and focus on this school thing.

TIM: That place is the pits, everyone there is a loser, and the teachers think they are military. Geez, the principal is even called "sergeant!"

TREVOR: I see you're pretty frustrated with the place, and you even seem to be getting kind of mad just talking about it.

TIM: You got that right.

TREVOR: So, here's what I'm thinking. Once we have cracked the case of what goes wrong at school, we can figure out how to make it better for you there. There are some tools we can use to crack the case and make things better. It will probably take a few meetings and some practice in between meetings for us to get used to the tools. Can we at least give it a good try, starting right now?

TIM: I suppose so.

TREVOR: The first tool we need is to identify the problem. Yesterday you said you were ready to go after anyone who got in your face at school. Let's think about a specific situation that's happened in the last week or two when someone did that.

1. *Identify the problem, including some detail about real-world situations in which the problem occurs.* The objective here is for the therapist and youth to describe the problem in terms of the ABCs discussed in Chapter 5: <u>A</u>ntecedents, or what happened prior to the situation; <u>B</u>ehaviors of concern, or what happened during the situation; and <u>C</u>onsequences, or what happened immediately and longer term following the problem situation. The therapist helps the teen identify the interrelationships between thoughts, feelings, and behaviors as they arise over time in the problem situation so that the youth can become more aware of his or her own impact on problem situations.

   a. First, Trevor asked *who* was involved. Tim began with a vague description.

     TIM: A bunch of tough guys try to get in my face.

     TREVOR: How many guys?

     TIM: Three of four usually, last week, four.

     TREVOR: What do you know about them that matters in this situation where they are in your face?

     TIM: Jimmy's a gang wanna-be, Bo just goes wherever Jimmy goes, and I don't really know the other two guys.

   b. Next, Trevor asked *where* the situation occurs.

     TIM: At school, mostly.

     TREVOR: Where at school?

     TIM: In the yard, mostly.

     TREVOR: When are you in the yard?

     TIM: Before the morning bell rings, after lunch, and when school gets out.

   c. Now, on to *what* happened. Who did or said whatever seemed to get the problem going? Tim's first response, "We just get into it," was too vague; Trevor wanted to get at who did or said what first, next, and so forth.

     Tim: I don't even remember how it started, but Jimmy yelled something nasty about my friend Reggie's girlfriend outside the cafeteria after lunch.

     Trevor: That's an important detail you remembered. What happened next?

In addition to details about the concrete events of the situation, Trevor asked about Tim's thoughts and feelings. "So, when the nasty thing was yelled, what did you think?" Following Tim's response of "I figured, here we go, we're not gonna take that," Trevor asked how Tim felt at that moment. "Pretty mad." Trevor asked, "What did you do?" and Tim responded that he yelled back, and "started getting myself ready for a fight." "What does getting ready look and feel like?" asked Trevor. After getting additional details about this situation, Trevor asked about another that had occurred at school. Tim defined the problem as: "Taking on the tough guys."

2. *Determine the youth's goals in the problem situation.* Next, the therapist helps the youth determine, given a problem situation, the outcome to be achieved. Criteria for goals are that they should be *assertive* (i.e., reflecting the feelings or opinions of the youth without being aggressive or passive) and should involve both *improving* something and *decreasing* something. For Tim, agreed-upon goals were to increase contact with the more positive student peers in the school (some of whom were in the gym rather than the schoolyard before school and after lunch) and decrease contact—including verbal and physical fights—with the tough guys.

3. *Generate alternative solutions.* Trevor introduced the next tool, "brainstorming," to Tim. The goal of brainstorming is to have the youth, with or without help, generate a list that includes solutions that might actually work and options that would probably lead to negative consequences. Criteria for brainstorming include:

   a. No idea is evaluated until the list is complete.
   b. The list should include realistic, unrealistic, and funny options.
   c. Aggressive, assertive, and passive options are required.

The therapist should emphasize having fun. And, it can be helpful for the teen to ask others—especially those who are socially desirable—for help generating options.

Tim first identified the following solutions: drop out of the school, skip the classes Jimmy and his buddies are in, and get more guys to take on Jimmy and his buddies. With some encouragement from Trevor to consider additional solutions, Tim added: walk away when Jimmy or his pals start to come near, go to the gym (supervised by an adult) instead of schoolyard, and get the sergeant on Jimmy's case.

4. *Evaluate these solutions.* For each option, the therapist and youth identify and discuss possible consequences, both immediate and long term, for others as well as the youth. After noting the consequences for each solution, the youth and therapist consider their relative merits. Using the same kind of ledger introduced in the caregiver intervention section, Trevor listed the solutions on the left, and put a "pro" column in the middle and a "con" column on the right. The negative consequences to Tim for skipping classes (falling further behind, violating probation) and taking Jimmy on (getting kicked out of the school, violating probation) outweighed the benefits (having fun instead of going to class, having the satisfaction of putting Jimmy and his pals in their place). Going to the gym came out even, because although the benefits column listed "like basketball," "have fun," and "avoid fights," the costs column included "look weak," "playing with new people," and "might look bad—don't play as well as those guys." Getting the sergeant on Jimmy's case wasn't viable, as Tim's behavior seemed at this point to be as big a problem as Jimmy's to the school authorities. But together, Tim and Trevor crafted another alternative—"See if sergeant could call a truce"—and evaluated the pros (fights could end) and cons (the sergeant blames me for the problem, the sergeant makes fun of me for asking for help, I look weak if anyone finds out it was my idea).

5. *Choose, practice, and implement a plan for the solution.* During this step, the therapist reviews the relative strengths and weaknesses of the solutions with the youth and helps him or her design a plan. All positive options should be considered. Either one or a combination of positive options can be used for the plan, which should be described in behaviorally specific terms (e.g., who does what, when, and where). If talking with another person is necessary, the goals of the conversation should be identified (e.g., What do you want to say to the sergeant, given you want him to help create and enforce a truce?). Developing and practicing sample scripts can be helpful. Even without a script, plenty of role-played practice with praise about specific words and behaviors and specific corrective feedback should precede *in vivo* implementation of the plan.

Tim and Trevor determined that going to the sergeant to broker a truce had low odds of working given the firm tactics the sergeant had used to deal with student problems in the past, and might also result in Tim being singled out for ridicule among other students. So, Tim and Trevor began with the "go to the gym" solution. For Tim, executing this solution would involve several steps: not going with his buddy Reggie to the schoolyard; possibly inviting Reggie to come to the gym instead; getting to the gym without responding to negative comments Jimmy and others were likely to make when they realized where Tim was going; signing in to the gym; introducing himself to the guys in the gym, some of them known to be good athletes; and joining an activity—basketball—he liked but thought he did not play as well as the others. For each of these steps, Trevor and Tim role-played how things might go. First, Tim provided details regarding, for example, what Reggie would say about going to the gym ("Are you crazy, we don't belong in there!") and what the guys in the gym might do when Tim came in (turn around and gawk). In addition, with assent from Tim and the Claytons and permission from the sergeant, Trevor went to the school to observe the students in the schoolyard, gym, and between classes. Obtaining such firsthand assessment information increased the probability that effective solutions could be generated.

6. *Implement the plan, evaluate, and redesign as needed.* During this final stage of problem solving the therapist helps the teen implement the plan, and all details surrounding the implementation are discussed. In some instances, the therapist might go with the youth and provide support, though, in the long run, adolescents need to learn how to use these skills on their own (Principle 9). Tim and Trevor agreed that Trevor would not accompany Tim when he tried his new solution, given likely negative reactions from other students and possibly school personnel. Trevor was concerned, however, that if the first try went badly, Tim might skip school for the rest of the afternoon, or head to the schoolyard and get into trouble after school. Tim and Trevor described the "go to the gym" plan to Mr. Clayton and his mother so that they could encourage use of the plan and be supportive after Tim's first attempt. In addition, Trevor arranged to pick Tim up right after school on that day.

If the plan does not work acceptably the first time, which is often the case, the therapist helps the youth reevaluate and redesign the plan. Doing so requires the teenager to develop the skills needed to objectively evaluate his or her performance. To facilitate this process, the therapist should model and encourage the use of self-monitoring statements that are specific and objective (e.g., "I didn't check out if it would be okay before I tried to get into the game") rather than global and distorted (e.g., "I was a total screw-up"). If the plan is successful, the therapist encourages the youth to describe the bases for the success and emphasizes internal attributions for positive outcomes (e.g., "I figured out that the game was ending soon and that it would make the most sense to ask if I could play in the next game.").

Social Skills Training

The part of Tim's solution that required interacting with the relatively unfamiliar, but possibly positive, peers in the gym illustrates a situation that comes up often when MST therapists are working with families to decrease a teen's contact with deviant peers and increase contact with more positive peers. Teens who have socialized with deviant peers for some time often need to brush up on the kinds of social skills required to successfully enter into contact with and be reasonably well accepted among more prosocial peers. Some teens already have most of these skills and can use them in certain situations, such as during class, in church, or when trying to attract the attention of a potential romantic interest. In Tim's case, for example, Mrs. Clayton noted that "good boy" behavior included Tim's "decent" manners at the table, when answering the telephone or door, and in public places like fast food restaurants. Moreover, Tim had gotten along with most students in his classes until seventh or eighth grade, and he reported having had fun during lunch through his middle school years. Thus, Tim possessed a reasonable range of positive social skills—the therapeutic task was to generalize his use of these skills to a broader range of situations.

When therapists have evidence that interventions designed to decrease association with deviant peers and increase association with more positive peers are failing because the youth is lacking social skills, then individual sessions to improve those skills might be warranted (see also Chapter 4). Several types of skills might be needed, including:

1. Making initial contact with an individual or group.
2. Reciprocating invitations.
3. Negotiating differences of opinion and compromising when others have different preferences about what to do or talk about.

The skills required for negotiation and compromise can be addressed within the problem-solving strategies identified previously. Helping the youth who has become most comfortable with deviant peers to hone skills to meet and join activities with more positive peers, however, typically requires special attention.

Making new social contacts requires skills such as maintaining eye contact, saying one's name, asking the name of the other person, and showing interest by asking questions that are not too personal. Tim was reasonably skilled on this front, as evidenced by his behavior when he met Trevor and any new friends his brother brought home. What Tim lacked was practice with group entry when the group was any other than his own buddies. Skills that are often useful to ease group entry include:

1. *Watch the group.* The youth should watch peers interacting with one another long enough to notice *what* they are doing (e.g., playing basketball, skateboarding, listening to songs on one another's iPods, just talking), and *how* they are doing it (is the talk fast or loud, does everyone talk at once, do some people tend to talk more than others, do people ask for the iPod or

just take it when they want to hear a song?). In Tim's case, the gym had four baskets. At two hoops, it looked like the guys were playing three-on-three games, but the players were mostly just calling for the ball. At the third basket, it looked like the guys were challenging each other to shoot from a specific position, as might be done in a game of "horse." Here, more casual conversation was taking place—not about basketball. At the last basket, it wasn't clear to Tim what was happening, but it didn't seem to have anything to do with basketball. Tim chose to watch the three-on-three games.

2. *Mirror to some extent, without appearing to be a mimic, the "what" and the "how" when trying to enter a group in conversation or other activity.* Here is where Tim's experience with deviant peers could have caused a false step in his first attempt to engage more prosocial peers. While not a very skilled basketball player, Tim did like to "mess around" with the ball with his buddies. They didn't play very often, but when they did it was a fairly physical version of street ball, and they often made up their own rules. In addition, even with other guys Tim considered to be "acquaintances" rather than friends, sarcasm and trash talk were fairly common practice even in opening greetings yelled across a street or hall. Tim and his buddies were as likely to signal an interest in an ongoing basketball game by grabbing the ball as by asking to join. Trevor and Tim therefore role-played different ways to approach the three-on-three players, as well as the group playing the game he didn't recognize, and the guys at the last basket, who seemed to be talking more than playing.

3. *Introduce yourself.* Introductions can be as simple as saying one's first name. In many situations, it is also important to convey how you come to be there. Because Tim had not been in the gym previously during lunch, for example, Trevor suggested he let the guys know he was interested in starting to play basketball again.

4. *Ask to join in.* As simple as this seems, finding appropriate words and actions that express a desire to become part of a conversation or activity with unfamiliar people can be difficult for anyone. Trevor suggested brainstorming phrases to try, again emphasizing having fun, but noting that some options might work and some might not. Trevor and Tim evaluated the approaches and picked the few that seemed to sound like Tim instead of like an adult, but did not include sarcasm or insult. These included, "Looks like you've already got a game going, any room for me?" and "Could I get into the game next round?"

As with the steps in problem solving outlined previously, the therapist should make sure the teen has practiced the skills in role plays that reflect the real-life situations in which they are needed, and provide specific praise and corrective feedback. The therapist and youth can determine whether it would be helpful for someone (the therapist, another peer, an older sibling) to be present during the first attempts in the real situation, and who, besides the therapist, should be available to debrief afterwards. As noted earlier, the therapist and youth also should let the caregivers know which skills are being practiced as well as the situations and days in which the youth will try to use the skills. Caregiver encouragement and support are also extremely valuable in facilitating the teenager's learning process.

Interventions for Specific Disorders Common among Youth Receiving MST

Evidence-based individual interventions are also relevant to two problems that are common among youth receiving MST and that have biological and psychosocial bases: ADHD and trauma-related symptoms.

Attention-Deficit/Hyperactivity Disorder

ADHD affects between 3% and 5% of school-age children in the United States (American Psychiatric Association, 2000; Barkley, 2006), and the diagnosis is three times as common in boys as in girls. The problems of hyperactivity and impulsivity tend to appear early in life, around 3–4 years of age, with attention problems becoming apparent during the early elementary school years. Attention problems tend to continue into adolescence, while hyperactivity and impulsivity problems tend to fade during adolescence. By late adolescence or young adulthood, 25% to 50% of youth previously diagnosed with ADHD lose the diagnosis or learn to cope well with the problem (Weisz, 2004). Because of these developmental changes, most psychosocial and medication approaches to the treatment of ADHD have been tested with children up to about 12 years of age. As discussed next, behavioral interventions and psychostimulant medications can be effective at reducing the symptoms of ADHD.

Behavioral Interventions

Reviews of evidence-based psychosocial treatments for youth (Daly, Xanthopoulos, Stephan, Cooper, & Brown, 2007; Weisz, 2004) have concluded that behavioral parent training interventions can improve parenting skills, child behavior in the home, and ADHD symptoms. In addition, behavioral classroom interventions (e.g., contingency management, daily report cards targeting symptoms and functional problems) have improved youth compliance with teacher demands and classroom rules as well as the quality of the children's social interactions with classmates. Because MST therapists operate in the home and school and at the interface of home–school interactions, they are well positioned to facilitate the effective implementation of family- and school-based interventions for ADHD.

Three well-conceived approaches to behavioral parent training have been developed for school-age youth with disruptive behavior problems and ADHD.

1. Parent training and family treatment (Patterson, 1976)
2. Help for the noncompliant child (McMahon & Forehand, 2003)
3. Defiant children program (Barkley, 2006)

These approaches are compatible with the behavioral parenting interventions incorporated into family interventions in MST and described in Chapter 3, even for youth without ADHD.

The positive effects of behavioral parent management treatments for youth with ADHD appear to fade over time, however. And, importantly, their effects have not been as promising for teens with ADHD (Weisz, 2004). Leading experts in the treatment of ADHD, therefore, have come to agree that an important aspect of treatment is to help parents and youth understand that managing the problematic symptoms of ADHD is likely to be a long-term process, similar to managing symptoms of, for example, a chronic illness such as diabetes. Possible explanations for the limited effects of parent management strategies on teen behavior include the influences of peers on adolescents (Weisz, 2004) and the increased cognitive sophistication of adolescents in comparison with children. MST is particularly well suited to address such possible influences, and to help caregivers and youth cultivate the resources and support needed to adjust management strategies as the youth matures (Principles 6 and 9).

Medications

Medications that stimulate the central nervous system are often prescribed for youth with ADHD (Daly et al., 2007), and common psychostimulants include methylphenidates (Ritalin, Concerta, Metadate, Focalin), mixed salts of a single-entity amphetamine product (Adderall, Adderall XR), and dextroamphetamine (Dexedrine, Dextrostat). Overall, research on the effectiveness and side effects of these medications has reached the following conclusions:

- The medications are safe and effective in managing core cognitive and behavioral symptoms associated with ADHD, such as inattention, impulsivity, and overactivity at home and in classrooms and social settings.
- Common side effects include decreased appetite, headaches, stomachaches, nausea, problems falling asleep, feeling fatigued, increased irritability, motor tics, social withdrawal, and stunted growth.

- Evidence is not consistent that these medications improve functional problems such as academic performance and social behavior.
- Little is known about the long-term behavioral effects of these medications.

In light of the fact that both behavioral and medication approaches are effective, how do they compare with each other and what happens when they are used together to treat ADHD? These questions were addressed by a large-scale multimodal treatment algorithm study (MTA Cooperative Group, 1999). Results showed that the effects of stimulant medication alone and behavior therapy alone on the core symptoms of ADHD were comparable, and that combining them seemed to produce stronger effects for the disruptive behavior problems associated with ADHD. In addition, parents and teachers found the combined behavioral and pharmacological approach to be more acceptable.

Implications for MST: Empowering Caregivers to Collaborate Effectively with Physicians

Some youth referred to MST were diagnosed with ADHD during their elementary school years and have previously been prescribed stimulant medications by a physician. Sometimes, a caregiver reports that a teacher, doctor, or counselor had suggested the youth might have ADHD, but a formal diagnosis was never obtained, and medications might or might not have been tried. When evidence indicates that symptoms of ADHD are contributing to referral problems or presenting barriers to treatment progress, and the youth has not been previously diagnosed and is not taking medication, MST therapists generally begin with family, behavioral, and school interventions. If the interventions are well implemented at home and school over a period of a few weeks but have little or no impact on the core symptoms of ADHD, the therapist can suggest the possibility of consulting with a child psychiatrist or pediatrician to determine whether the youth meets criteria for a diagnosis of ADHD, and, if so, what type and dose of medication might be appropriate.

To increase the odds of success for initial meetings and ongoing collaboration with physicians prescribing medications for youth, MST therapists generally take the following five steps.

1. *Obtain information about the psychiatric and pediatric resources in the community.* Who are the child psychiatrists and pediatricians who treat adolescents? Where do they work? What do other mental health professionals know about them? What do other families know about them? Are families generally satisfied with the services they receive? Are the physicians willing to provide medication management services only, with other mental health

professionals, such as the MST therapist, providing psychosocial aspects of treatment? What is the referral process like? How are services paid for? Because many communities have very few child psychiatrists, pediatricians and family practice physicians are the primary sources of medication for ADHD nationwide. Many MST programs have compiled community resource folders for therapists that contain information pertinent to answering questions about psychiatric and other mental health resources (as well as health, education, and recreation resources).

2. *Educate caregivers and youth.* When it comes to effective collaboration with service providers, knowledge increases power. Thanks in part to mental health–oriented consumer advocacy organizations such as NAMI, Children and Adults with Attention Deficit/Hyperactivity Disorder (CHADD), and even research funding organizations such as the NIMH, information about ADHD and medications for ADHD is available in simple, straightforward pamphlets and on websites. To help caregivers and youth prepare for meetings with physicians, the therapist can visit and download information from the websites identified in the resource section of this chapter. And, if the family also has access to a computer, the therapist and family can review the websites online together.

3. *Help schedule the meeting.* If caregivers are reluctant to call for an appointment, therapists might need to assist by being at the home when the call is made.

4. *Prepare for the meeting.* The therapist should help the caregiver and adolescent identify specific questions about what will happen during the initial appointment, the problems that bring the caregiver and youth to the physician, possible diagnoses, and possible treatments, including medications. Some people are very comfortable raising questions with physicians and asking for clarification if they don't understand the answers. If the caregiver is unsure about what to do or say, then the therapist should role-play scenarios that might arise during the doctor appointment.

5. *If asked, attend the meeting.* Some caregivers prefer that the MST therapist accompany them to the initial meeting with the physician or to a subsequent meeting if an earlier one did not go well. As long as attendance is acceptable to the caregiver, youth (assuming the youth is also attending), and physician, MST therapists often agree to this kind of request. In such circumstances, the therapist and caregiver clarify in advance the role the therapist will take in the meeting. Will the therapist primarily observe, and respond only if invited by the caregiver? Or, does the caregiver prefer to have the physician, caregiver, and therapist contribute relatively equally to the discussion about the nature of the problem, what is already being done in MST to address it, and how medication management by the physician fits into the overall treatment plan? Therapists and caregivers consider these kinds of questions before the first meeting with the physician, and then revisit the questions based on the outcomes of that meeting.

Finally, some communities have active chapters of advocacy organizations such as NAMI and CHADD. Caregivers might find it helpful to talk with others whose children have ADHD, and who might or might not also be on medication. The websites for these organizations have links to local chapters that might be of interest to such caregivers.

Trauma-Related Symptoms in Youth

Youth referred for MST, like many children, experience stressful events as they grow up—divorce, death of a family member, witnessing violence in the neighborhood, deprivations associated with poverty, and so on. These kinds of experiences can be painful, frightening, and confusing. They are generally not, however, traumatic. Traumatic events have distinct characteristics—they are sudden or unexpected; shocking; involve death or threat to life or bodily integrity; and/or invoke subjective feelings of intense terror, horror, or helplessness (American Psychiatric Association, 2000, p. 463). For children, examples of experiences that can be traumatic include physical or sexual abuse, witnessing or experiencing domestic violence, severe auto accidents, having a life-threatening illness, natural and man-made disasters, war, terrorism, and refugee conditions (Cohen et al., 2006).

Diagnosis of PTSD

To have a formal diagnosis of PTSD, youth must have a specified number of symptoms in the three clusters identified below(Cohen et al., 2006).

- Reexperiencing symptoms (e.g., intrusive or upsetting thoughts, physical or psychological distress when reminded of the events).
- Avoidance symptoms (e.g., avoiding people, places, or situations reminiscent of the traumatic events, emotional detachment or flatness).
- Hyper-arousal and mood symptoms (e.g., increased startle responses, hypervigilence, disturbed sleep, irritability, or angry outbursts).

Effects of Trauma

The effects of traumatic events on children can vary greatly (Cohen et al., 2006; Weisz, 2004):

- No substantive effects
- Depression
- Anxiety
- Anger and aggression
- Avoidance of certain situations

Importantly, however, the effects of trauma on children are influenced by:

- The nature and frequency of the traumatic events.
- Age and developmental status of the child.
- Relationship of the child to a perpetrator if physical or sexual abuse or neglect are the sources of trauma.
- Reaction to the trauma by the adults in the child's life.
- Family and other support.
- Other risk and resilience factors.

Some children who experience trauma develop trauma-related symptoms in the short term; many others do not. Similarly, short-term symptoms can linger and contribute to long-term mental health difficulties in some instances, but not in others.

When Is Trauma a Pertinent Fit Factor?

When youth referred to MST programs experience trauma-related symptoms that maintain referral problems or interfere with treatment progress, these symptoms seem most often related to youth physical or sexual abuse. In contrast, relatively few youth treated in standard MST programs have experienced traumatic events like surviving or witnessing life-threatening violence such as terrorist attacks, school shootings, or natural disasters. Thus, the focus of this section is on helping youth and families manage abuse-related symptoms in youth with serious antisocial behavior.

Assessing and treating symptoms of abuse can be challenging because child abuse cannot be substantiated by the presence or absence of any particular behavior in a child. In addition, unlike youth referred to treatment specifically for trauma-related symptoms, referral to MST typically means a variety of serious antisocial behaviors are clear treatment priorities of the family and referral sources. Thus, in exploring the possibility that youth symptoms interfering with treatment progress are abuse related, the following reminders are useful.

1. Therapists cannot assume a priori that victims of abuse require mental health treatment.
2. When abuse victims present mental health problems, these problems might or might not be the result of abuse (i.e., the problems might be linked with difficulties that preceded the abuse or have no relation to the abuse).
3. Assessment should consider the context and characteristics of the abusive incidents when evaluating the impact of abuse on the victim.

STANDARD MST EVIDENCE GATHERING

MST therapists faced with barriers to treatment progress that might be related to trauma engage in standard MST evidence gathering and hypothesis testing about trauma as a possible fit factor for specific problems. For example, some behaviors, such as irritability and angry outbursts, are identified in one of the three clusters of PTSD symptoms in children—hyperarousal and mood symptoms—but are also common in juvenile offenders who have not experienced trauma. On the other hand, symptoms such as intrusive or upsetting thoughts and physical or psychological distress when reminded of a particular event are not typical among offenders. Thus, MST therapists assessing the possibility that trauma symptoms are fit factors for irritability or anger would consider other fit factors (e.g., angry outbursts pay off in that caregivers drop demands, caregiver models similar behavior, youth has poor interpersonal problem-solving skills) as well as the traumatic incidents before incorporating specific, trauma-focused strategies in treatment for the youth.

UNDERSTANDING THE TRAUMATIC EVENTS

To adequately assess the role of traumas in youth symptoms, the therapist also needs evidence that traumatic events occurred. Although MST is generally present focused in assessing the fit of problems with the broader systemic context, to determine whether the problems experienced by a youth relate to abuse (or any other trauma), the therapist needs to obtain information about when and how often trauma occurred, and what kind of trauma it was—and evidence that the youth experienced the events as traumatic. If the therapist remains unclear about the nature and impact of abusive or other traumatic events after having interviewed the youth and caregivers, and reviewed other pertinent sources of information (e.g., child protective service reports), it might be helpful to ask the youth to complete a PTSD self-report instrument validated for clinical use. Copies of such instruments are now available online from the National Child Traumatic Stress Network website identified in the resource section of this chapter.

Interventions

Current treatments for youth experiencing trauma-related symptoms emphasize the correction of distortions in thinking, behavioral techniques including hierarchy-based exposure, social skills training, and in some cases medications (March, 2002). The cognitive-behavioral treatments for sexually abused children validated by Cohen and Mannarino and by Deblinger and colleagues in the early 1990s have been integrated into a treatment approach, trauma-focused cognitive-behavioral treatment (TF-CBT; Cohen et al., 2006), that can be used with a variety of abuse-related and other types of trauma. TF-CBT involves eight components that together create the acronym PRACTICE, identified subsequently. The strategies resembling those most often used in standard MST programs to address trauma-related symptoms in youth are identified with an asterisk.

> Psychoeducation and parenting skills*
> Relaxation*
> Affective modulation*
> Cognitive coping and processing*
> Trauma narrative
> In vivo mastery of trauma reminders
> Conjoint child–parent sessions*
> Enhancing future safety and development*

In the context of MST, a variety of interventions targeting family, peer, school, and individual factors sustaining referral problems are usually being implemented already, and some of these reflect one or more of the PRACTICE components. For example, the kinds of parenting skills used in TF-CBT to respond to the angry outbursts and aggression of a child include the behavior management strategies used in MST and described in Chapter 3 (e.g., praising specific behaviors, applying contingencies). Likewise, the relaxation techniques used for children in TF-CBT emanate from the same theoretical and research backgrounds as those described for use with adults earlier in this chapter, though adapted to the developmental level of young children. Similarly, strategies to address affective modulation in TF-CBT include the classic problem solving steps described in the case examples for adult and youth problem solving, including practicing in vivo strategies aimed at replacing maladaptive behaviors. On the other hand, therapists in MST programs do not typically go through the process of creating a trauma narrative with the youth and sharing that narrative with the youth's caregivers, as few have the training and expertise required to implement this strategy, and often youth symptoms have abated as the other strategies have been put in place.

Case Example: Jenny Simms

An illustration of the approach MST therapists might take to trauma-related symptoms that contribute to referral problems or become barriers to treatment progress is provided by the case of Jenny Simms. Like some other teenage girls referred to MST for serious antisocial behavior, Jenny was sexually promiscuous. Jenny frequently hooked up for casual sex with adult men near local bars, and had few friends of either gender in her own age range. Jenny's promiscuity was a source of parent–youth conflict, and had contributed to a violation of probation on more than one occasion.

In Jenny's case, prior sexual abuse was one possible fit factor for the promiscuity and other behavior that posed a health risk. Other fit factors included low parental monitoring, high parent–youth conflict, and Jenny's close affective bond with a similarly promiscuous older girl, a bond that occurred in the context of few other peer relationships. Ann, the MST therapist, worked with Jenny's mother, Mrs. Simms, to develop comprehensive intervention strategies that focused on increasing parental monitoring, decreasing mother–daughter conflict, establishing behavioral plans, and developing and monitoring a safety plan for Jenny.

In addition, Ann met with Jenny to assess whether cognitive distortions related to past sexual abuse played a role in her current sexual activity. When Ann asked Jenny what kinds of thoughts and feelings she had before heading out for a "hook-up," Jenny identified the following three thoughts: I'm damaged goods anyway; guys my age would never date me; and at least these guys are nice to me, which is more than I can say about Joe (stepfather who had sexually abused her). Ann asked Jenny to identify the feelings associated with each of these thoughts, following the CBT strategy of helping individuals link thoughts, feelings, and behaviors, described in earlier sections of this chapter. Jenny identified shame as the primary feeling associated with the thought that she was damaged goods, and both anger and sadness in response to thoughts about dating others her own age and the abuse perpetrated by her stepfather.

Next, Ann and Jenny identified behaviors associated with each thought and feeling. Isolating herself from peers her own age was one behavior associated with all three thoughts. Seeking out the attention of older men came up in response to the thought that boys her age would not date her and the feelings of anger and sadness that accompanied these feelings. In response to Ann's queries about people, places, or events that reminded Jenny of the abuse, Jenny said, "I really don't think about it much. We moved after he left, and I don't have to go anywhere near that apartment where we lived, so I'm okay." Ann tried to get a handle on physical reactions Jenny might have in response to memories of the abuse, and to possible reminders in everyday life such as the apartment building. Jenny reported feeling repulsed by the apartment building on the rare occasions she had seen it since moving away and by pictures of her stepfather, but not anxious or fearful. There was no evidence from Ann's assessment of the natural ecology that Jenny avoided school, neighbors, home, or other places in the community.

Thus, as a starting place for individual sessions, Ann and Jenny focused on the cognitions, feelings, and behaviors associated with the abuse that were part of the "fit" of Jenny's promiscuity. In addition and with Jenny's permission, Ann met with Jenny's mother, Mrs. Simms, to explain that she would like to meet alone with Jenny to address the aspects of the promiscuous behavior that seemed to be related to the past abuse. Ann described to Mrs. Simms the kinds of thoughts, feelings, and behaviors youth can have in response to sexual abuse, and the importance of trying to help Jenny understand the abuse in a new way, one that did not involve being down on herself and acting in ways that put her at risk for pregnancy, HIV and other sexually transmitted diseases, and other physical and emotional problems. Ann also explained that some meetings would involve both Mrs. Simms and Jenny, and that these meetings would focus on how Mrs. Simms could help Jenny understand that the abuse was not her own fault and did not make her "damaged goods."

As often occurs, Mrs. Simms still had a hard time making sense of the abuse and knowing how best to respond to Jenny when the subject came up—typically in the heat of confrontations about where Jenny had been well into the night. Although both Jenny and Mrs. Simms had been referred for counseling after the abuse was first revealed 3 years previously, neither felt the counseling was helpful, and both quit going after two sessions. As Ann inquired about what happened during those sessions, she developed the hypothesis that Mrs. Simms and Jenny had not learned about the possible effects of abuse on the youth, the nonoffending caregiver (Mrs. Simms), and on relationships with others in the social ecology. The TF-CBT process includes helping caregivers manage the confusion and conflicting feelings they often experience when their child has been abused, and preparing the caregiver and youth for conjoint sessions in which the caregiver acknowledges awareness and accountability for breaches of the child's safety and well-being. These interventions also occur in MST, sometimes in the form of a formal clarification session (Kolko & Swenson, 2002).

When Trauma-Related Anxiety Interferes with Functioning

Sometimes, in contrast with Jenny, an adolescent in MST does avoid certain people or places associated with abuse or other traumatic events due to fear and the physiological arousal and discomfort associated with such fear. When such avoidance interferes with the youth's functioning at home or school or in the community or presents barriers to attaining treatment goals, the therapist takes several steps. First, he or she helps the family to put an appropriate safety plan into place. In addition, the therapist might use the CBT components outlined in the problem-solving section of this chapter to help the youth manage emotional responses and anxiety that arise in the presence of people, places, or situations, and of intrusive thoughts or memories about such stimuli. The therapist might teach the youth deep breathing and muscle relaxation skills (Deblinger & Heflin, 1996) to manage anxiety and fearful reactions. In addition, when it is clear the youth is protected from further victimization and the caregivers are supportive of the youth's acknowledgment of the abuse, the therapist can introduce graduated exposure. In this strategy, the youth recapitulates the abusive incidents by beginning with situations that evoke lower levels of anxiety, followed by slightly more anxiety-provoking situations. For example, for Kenny, whose father was physically abusive of his mother after he had been drinking, an exposure hierarchy might begin with a scene in which Ken hears the father's staggering steps on the apartment stairs and continue through the following successively anxiety-arousing scenes.

> Father opens the apartment door.
> He calls out for a beer.
> Kenny brings the beer.
> Father asks where Kenny's mother is.
> Kenny says, "How should I know?"
> Father pounds the table and pushes back his chair.
> Kenny yells, "sit down!"
> Father slaps Kenny.
> Father goes to the bedroom to find Kenny's mother.
> Kenny hears arguing.
> Kenny hears his mother's body hit the wall.

The therapist, caregiver, and youth should determine together whether the adolescent would experience the caregiver's presence during exposure as supportive or intrusive, and whether the caregiver can participate effectively. In Kenny's case, for example, the mother who had been abused could not participate because the scenarios triggered her own fear and anxiety.

In summary, we have rarely found that adolescents in standard MST programs require referral for individual, outpatient based, trauma-focused treatment. If there is little change in the trauma-related problems of a youth after the therapist has incorporated the strategies described in this chapter, the therapist should take several steps. The first of these is to consider obtaining a psychiatric consultation, as medication can help reduce fear- and anxiety-related symptoms associated with PTSD (March, 2002). In addition, the therapist and family can find out whether any therapists in the community have been trained in TF-CBT and have received model-specific ongoing consultation, as both training and consultation appear to be important (North et al., 2008). Dissemination of TF-CBT is in its early stages, so finding such practitioners might be challenging. Finally, an alternative that might be helpful is to collaborate with a CBT-trained therapist who has worked with youth to address trauma-related symptoms.

Conclusion

In MST, therapists leverage the individual strengths of caregivers, youth, and others in the natural ecology to make therapeutic change. Persistent problems of individual caregivers or youth, such as depression, anxiety, anger, ADHD, or trauma-focused symptoms can present barriers to initial engagement or to treatment progress. This chapter has described strategies commonly used in MST to address such problems.

Resources for Therapists

Caregiver Interventions

Leahy, R. L. (2003). *Cognitive therapy techniques.* New York: Guilford Press.
National Institute of Mental Health (NIMH). Website: *www.nimh.nih.gov.*
Tompkins, M. A. (2004). *Using homework in psychotherapy: Strategies, guidelines, and forms.* New York: Guilford Press.

Youth Interventions

Barkley, R. A. (2006). *Attention Deficit Hyperactivity Disorder: A handbook for diagnosis and treatment* (3rd ed.). New York: Guilford Press. *The ADHD Report,* ADHD fact sheets, and other Russell Barkley products are available at his website: *www.russellbarkley.org.*
Children and Adults with Attention Deficit/Hyperactivity Disorder (CHADD). Website: *www.chadd.org.*
Children's Medication Algorithm Project (CMAP), Texas Department of State Health Services. Website: *www.dshs.state.tx.us/mhprograms/CMAP.shtm.*
Cohen, J. A., Mannarino, A. P., & Deblinger, E. (2006). *Treating trauma and traumatic grief in children and adolescents.* New York: Guilford Press.
National Child Traumatic Stress Network, Substance Abuse and Mental Health Services Administration. Website: *www.nctsnet.org.*

CHAPTER 7

Building Social Supports
for Families

An extensive body of research has shown that social capital (i.e., helpful resources available to individuals because of their social connections) provides significant protections against the ups and downs of life (Putnam, 2000). For example, adolescents who live in communities where people trust one another, join community organizations, volunteer, vote, and socialize (i.e., high in social capital) are less likely to drop out of school, become pregnant, get involved in violent crime, or die prematurely as a result of suicide or homicide. Increasing a child and family's social capital can have favorable immediate and long-term benefits.

The purpose of this chapter is to describe strategies therapists use to increase the social capital of adolescents and their families served by MST programs. Parents of youth with serious antisocial behavior need both practical and emotional support to manage the day-to-day struggles often associated with raising such children (e.g., monitoring peer associations and activities, setting and enforcing limits, negotiating school conflicts). In light of the scant resources (e.g., social supports, money, time; Marcenko

& Meyers, 1991; Oswald & Singh, 1996), systemic problems (i.e., marital problems, family transitions), concrete needs (i.e., subsistence wages, inadequate transportation), and personal difficulties (i.e., depression, anxiety, drug abuse) often experienced by caregivers of youth with serious antisocial behavior, it is no wonder that such caregivers can feel demoralized, hopeless, stigmatized, and socially isolated. Working alone to save one's child is extremely difficult. Fortunately, the "ties that bind" can help invigorate caregivers and provide some of the tools and resources they need to function effectively as parents.

This chapter begins with a brief description of factors that commonly contribute to low social support in families participating in MST programs. Then, strategies and tools are described that assess the types of social support a family needs, and the types of social support resources available to the family. Approaches therapists use to engage caregivers in the process of cultivating more social support are described next, with particular attention devoted to situations in which the caregiver is reluctant to approach others for help. Once engaged, therapists often need to help caregivers hone their interpersonal skills to successfully elicit support from others. Then, to help ensure that support from the natural ecology will be sustained as needed over time, therapists assist caregivers in identifying supports and developing a mutually satisfactory reciprocity in their relationship.

Factors That Can Limit Caregiver Social Supports

All parents need help to raise their children. Unfortunately, the caregivers in MST programs often do not have sufficient support. Youth presenting serious antisocial behavior usually need supervision throughout the day or during high-risk times when they are likely to get into trouble. With two-parent families, involvement of both caregivers is crucial, but enough resources still might not be available. In single-parent families, the caregiver might find it difficult to ensure supervision and monitoring alone. Many single parents work long hours at jobs that barely pay minimum wage, a reality that also increases the likelihood of social isolation and decreases opportunities to develop supportive relations.

As with any problem in MST, the first step toward intervening is to conduct a fit analysis of why a particular caregiver does not have social supports in the first place. Figure 7.1 shows some of the commonly observed individual and contextual factors that can limit social supports for caregivers in MST programs. Individual factors that can affect social supports include:

- Personality characteristics (e.g., emotional stability, sociability, temperament, trust, limited or ineffective interpersonal skills).
- Cognitive skills (e.g., attributional biases).

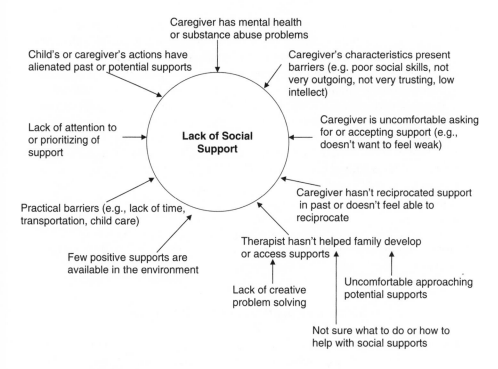

Caregiver has mental health
or substance abuse problems

Child's or caregiver's actions have
alienated past or potential supports

Caregiver's characteristics present
barriers (e.g. poor social skills, not
very outgoing, not very trusting, low
intellect)

Lack of attention to
or prioritizing of
support

**Lack of Social
Support**

Caregiver is uncomfortable asking
for or accepting support (e.g.,
doesn't want to feel weak)

Practical barriers (e.g., lack of time,
transportation, child care)

Caregiver hasn't reciprocated support
in past or doesn't feel able to
reciprocate

Few positive supports are
available in the environment

Therapist hasn't helped family develop
or access supports

Lack of creative
problem solving

Uncomfortable approaching
potential supports

Not sure what to do or how to
help with social supports

FIGURE 7.1. Factors often associated with lack of social support.

- Resources (e.g., time and energy).
- Mental health problems or substance abuse.

Contextual factors affecting the caregiver's informal and formal supports can include:

- Social or cultural mores regarding social contact and interactions (e.g., walk with your head down and avoid making eye contact in drug infested neighborhoods).
- Neighborhood stability (e.g., living in a community with transient populations).
- Poor transportation and child care.

Each of these drivers for lack of social support requires specific interventions.

In our experience, caregivers with low social support often struggle to deal effectively with people in a variety of interpersonal situations. That is, of the individual-level characteristics identified above, therapists often identify the *limited or ineffective interpersonal skills* of caregivers as barriers to the development of supportive relationships. To engage other people as sources of social support, caregivers need to have adequate social skills and interpersonal competencies. Once established, social relationships require reciprocity (i.e., giving and receiving of tangible and emotional resources) and equity (i.e., explicit or implicit rules regarding what is a fair exchange) to be sustained. Consequently, after identifying the types of social support needed by a family and possible sources of such support (described in the next section), the first steps a therapist takes on the road toward increasing social support often focus on helping caregivers develop and maintain interpersonal relationships that involve give-and-take and are satisfying in some way to all people involved. When the limited or ineffective interpersonal skills of caregivers present barriers to the development of social supports, we recommend that therapists refer to appropriate sections in Chapters 6 and 8 pertaining to development of problem-solving skills, reductions in anxiety, reductions in depression, reductions in substance use, and improving emotion regulation.

Steps in Building Social Supports

Families with multiple needs facing multiple stressors are likely to require social support to implement one or more desired changes during treatment and to sustain treatment-related changes after treatment has ended. Because it can take weeks to develop sustainable sources of social support, therapists should begin to scan the family's social ecology for evidence of the need and availability of such support as soon as treatment starts. The therapeutic activities required to build social support include getting buy-in from the caregiver, assessing all potential sources of support, matching the caregiver's needs to specific sources of support, developing concrete plans for engaging potential social supports, using skill acquisition procedures to teach caregivers the skills and competencies needed to take advantage of identified supports, and monitoring and adjusting implementation of the plan. Some of these activities logically occur before others. For example, a therapist usually gets buy-in from the caregiver to shore up social support before asking the caregiver to identify individuals who could provide such support. Other steps and strategies can occur simultaneously.

Getting Buy-In from the Caregiver to Pursue Social Supports

As with all MST interventions, the first step to intervention success is engaging the caregiver in the process of intervening in a particular domain (e.g., school, youth behavior at home, youth peer relations). In this case, the domain is the social world of the caregiver and family. Caregivers often have significant reservations or concerns about asking for help or involving others in their personal affairs. The therapist must address any concern a caregiver raises about pursuing social supports. In general, getting buy-in from the caregiver starts with providing a good rationale, using basic psychotherapy engagement and alignment processes described in Chapter 2, and anticipating and addressing caregiver concerns.

Rationale for Pursuing Social Support

Describing a problem in a way that resonates with the caregiver (e.g., using fit circles) is critical to motivating action to change the problem. For many caregivers, however, it is one thing to make changes on behalf of a son or daughter, and quite another to change something that seems to relate mostly to one's self. Thus, as happens when therapists approach a caregiver about trying individual treatment sessions to deal with depression or anxiety (see Chapter 6), therapists need to broach the subject of social support by providing a compelling rationale in a way that does not evoke a sense of inadequacy or blame in the caregiver. If the therapist is concerned about establishing a compelling rationale for the pursuit of social supports with a particular caregiver because experience suggests the caregiver might be particularly wary, reluctant, or even insulted by the prospect, then scripting out a rationale prior to a session can be helpful. Whether using a script or not, therapists should keep the following points in mind when approaching caregivers with the prospect of pursuing social support.

1. *Use language that is nonjudgmental and nonpejorative (i.e., maintain a strength focus).* For example, whenever possible, focus on the child's behavior and not the parent's need. "One thing that has probably been the most frustrating for you is that your son and the trouble he gets into have been consuming your life. You have to deal with teachers calling and complaining about his classroom behavior, his probation officer asking for one meeting after another, your friends and neighbors complaining about what they see him do in the neighborhood—and the days and nights when he is not home you worry about what he is doing and if he is okay. He needs an army of folks to keep him on the right track. I would like to talk with you about finding soldiers for that army."

2. *Therapist language should use the caregiver's words, phrases, and reoccurring themes* that have been observed during sessions and are consistent with his or her perspective. For example, a caregiver whose session narratives highlight strength and independence requires a rationale that frames social support as indicative of strength and independence. For such a caregiver the rational might begin with:

"A successful general needs competent soldiers to carry out the important day-to-day operations that lead to military success. As the general of your family, you have great ideas but not enough good soldiers lined up to carry out the missions you have planned to save your son. You can't be at all places at all times. I would like for us to begin thinking about recruiting more soldiers."

3. *The rationale should align with the caregiver's desired outcomes and treatment goals.* For example, if a major goal of the caregiver is for the child to be successful in school, then the rationale for pursuing social supports should directly reference school success.

4. *A good rationale builds on the fit assessment of the referral behavior,* or of barriers to achieving intermediary treatment goals the caregiver sees as important. Using the fit assessment for 15-year-old Steven Jackson's drug use depicted in Figure 7.2 as an example, increased social support might be helpful in addressing his lack of adult supervision after school, which is one

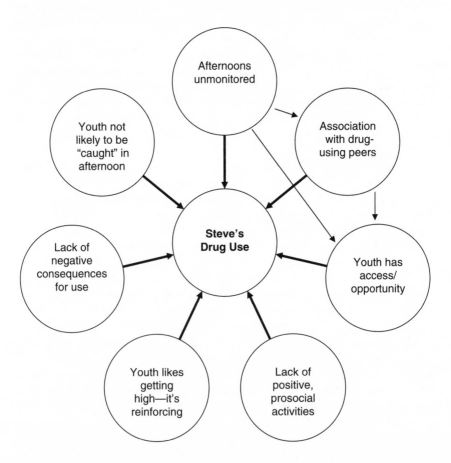

FIGURE 7.2. Fit of Steven Jackson's drug use.

of the key drivers linked to Steve's drug use, both directly and indirectly (by providing opportunity to associate with and access drugs). When establishing the session agenda in this case the therapist might say to Steve's mother, Mrs. Jackson:

"During our last session we agreed that the major drivers for Steve's drug use are that he hangs out with drug-using kids, he really likes using drugs, he does not have any real aversive consequences when he uses drugs, and he has few opportunities for participating in prosocial activities with kids who do not use drugs. It seems that Steve usually takes advantage of the time you are at work to hang out with those kids. Even though you call and check in on him he still manages to get out. Is that your understanding? Great!!! If it is OK I want to share with you an idea that I think will be helpful. As we've discussed before, you have been fighting a heroic battle to save your son, often alone, with little or no help. You work long and hard hours to make sure your family has a better life then you. Unfortunately, the more energy you put into making ends meet, the more opportunities Steve has to get into trouble. No parent should have to fight this battle alone. He needs to have more eyes and ears trained on him. We have to rally the village. I have some ideas about rallying your village that I would like to run by you. Are you interested?"

5. *Elicit questions or concerns with this new direction in treatment.* If the caregiver is not clear about any part of the rationale (in the example above, the caregiver might ask, "what village?"), the therapist must make things clear before moving on. If the caregiver has concerns ("How can I possibly talk to these people given how much I work?"), then the therapist addresses these concerns ("We will figure that out together, step by step").

6. *Provide an overview of the process that will be followed to identify and build social supports.* This plan includes, for example, an examination of the fit of the caregiver's lack of support, development of a plan to address those fit factors, and implementation of a plan for engaging the identified social supports.

Finally, the therapist's rationale for pursuing social supports should convey a sense of optimism or positive expectations. For example, the therapist should have excitement in his or her voice and body language when saying, "I have an idea that I think will make a world of difference. If we can get you some support, our plans to hold your son accountable, provide consequences, and get him involved in prosocial activities can work out, and he will stop using drugs." The caregiver should leave the session feeling reasonably confident that the recommended social support will make a difference.

When Caregiver Buy-In Is Not Achieved

Sometimes a caregiver absolutely refuses to pursue social supports. As with any other intervention, the therapist should not push a strategy the caregiver does not want to pursue, because that kind of pushing can damage the caregiver's engagement in other aspects of ongoing treatment. Indeed, anytime the therapist continues to advocate a strategy in the face of mounting caregiver skepticism, the therapist should step back and reconsider his or her options. For example, the therapist might accept the caregiver's "no," but leave the door open to revisit the topic in the future. "It really is your decision. How about we table it for now and think about it between now and the next time we meet?" or "It really is your decision. How about we see how it goes without getting additional help, but if we are still having problems with your son hanging out with those kids after school when you are at work, let's talk about it then."

Resource Needs

After caregiver buy-in is attained, the caregiver and therapist identify the exact nature of the support that is needed. Social support is a multidimensional construct that encompasses four main types of support (Quick, Nelson, Matuszek, Whittington, & Quick, 1996; Unger & Wandersman, 1985).

- *Instrumental* (e.g., financial assistance, help with housework and child care, borrowing a neighbor's car).
- *Emotional* (e.g., expressions of empathy, concern, love, trust, and caring).
- *Appraisal* (e.g., affirmation or feedback).
- *Informational* (e.g., parenting advice and suggestions for local resources).

A parent might need only one type of support or all types. Similarly, one person or multiple people might provide the support needed. The starting point, however, is determining the exact need the therapist is trying to fill within the MST treatment plan.

Needs during Treatment

Returning to Figure 7.2, a primary driver of Steve's drug use was his lack of monitoring after school. Although each driver on the fit circle contributing to his drug use will be tackled during treatment, the lack of adult monitoring and supervision after school clearly requires help from others—social supports. For the Jackson family, then, key support-related questions are (1) who can help monitor and supervise Steve after school, before his mother gets home from work? (2) what exactly and concretely does this person need to do? and (3) how will the family return the favor (i.e., reciprocity)?

In Steve's case, the family needed instrumental support primarily. In another case, however, the caregiver might need primarily emotional and appraisal support. For example, as a caregiver attempts to provide consistent limits in the face of youth resistance, he or she might benefit from having a friend or neighbor call each evening "to see how you are doing with your son" and say "I think holding him accountable for what he does is what he needs. You are tough enough to handle this."

Social Support Needed to Sustain Outcomes
after Treatment Is Completed

To support the sustainability of positive outcomes for teenagers (Principle 9), therapists and caregivers together typically complete fit circles for each successful outcome. During this process, it is important to identify the social support resources that contributed to the successful outcome, and to determine which of these are required to maintain the successes as treatment progresses and ends. For example, a caregiver might have been able to complete relevant tasks and follow through on therapeutic recommendations when the therapist was available to provide the encouragement or problem solving needed during critical moments of treatment implementation. However, because a mother dreads the reactions of her daughter when she follows through with disciplinary consequences (i.e., the daughter yells and screams and calls her names), the therapist is concerned that the mother will go back to withdrawing consequences after treatment ends. To prevent the reemergence of these problems, the therapist and mother must recruit a viable source of emotional and problem-solving support before treatment ends to help keep the consequences in place when she is under duress. Importantly, the identified support person must receive some type of positive payoff (e.g., thanks, meal, yard work) to sustain this support in the long term, as discussed subsequently.

Assuming the caregiver has agreed to begin to develop increased social support and the exact needs have been articulated, the next focus of treatment should be on identifying who is available in the caregiver's ecology that might be able to provide the support.

Assessment of Social Support

As described in Chapter 2, the initial and ongoing assessment of the social ecology of the adolescent and family is essential to understanding the fit of youth referral problems, identifying strengths in the ecology that can be used to address those problems, and anticipating barriers to making treatment progress. The identification of potential social support resources is part of this initial and ongoing process. Determining who is available to provide social support for a caregiver or family begins the moment the therapist meets the family—especially while constructing the family's genogram and completing their Strengths and Needs Assessment. Consistent with MST Principle 9 (maintenance and generalization) the assessment of social support should start on the informal end (e.g., friends, neighbors, extended family) of the social support continuum and move to the more formal end (e.g., social service agencies).

The Family Genogram as a Useful Starting Point

As described in Chapter 2, the genogram is one tool MST therapists use to understand who is in the family, how the family is configured, and key relationships among family members. This genogram, completed during the therapist's initial meetings with a family and updated as needed during treatment, can be a rich source of information about potential supports available to the caregiver and family. As the therapist is completing the family genogram, he or she can use the MST Assessment of Social Support Form (MASS; see Figure 7.3) to characterize the types of support provided (or not) by individuals identified. This form contains questions that elicit the type of information therapists and caregivers use to determine what kind of social support is available (i.e., instrumental, emotional, appraisal, information), who can provide it, and some information about the relationship between the caregiver and potential source of support. So, for example, when a caregiver is providing names of extended family members to the therapist for purposes of filling in the genogram, the therapist can ask where the person lives (a person's residence can suggest financial resources or proximity to the caregiver) and about any special competencies or resources that might be useful later in treatment. For example, Mrs. Jackson noted that her neighbor, Mrs. Johnson, stayed home all day due to her disability (see Figure 7.3). Also, Mrs. Johnson seemed lonely and eager for social contact, which might be beneficial in engaging her as instrumental support. On the other hand, Mrs. Johnson was somewhat ill tempered, which made Mrs. Jackson leery of asking her for help.

If the caregiver and other family members have difficulty completing the genogram, the therapist might need to obtain necessary information on the family through other professionals working with the family (e.g., social workers or probation officers). Therapists contact professionals with family permission and after ensuring all parties are clear about the nature and limits of confidentiality related to the information exchange. In addition, with the permission of the caregivers, the therapist typically meets with members of the extended family who live in the family's geographical area to learn more about them, obtain their perspectives on the referred youth and family, and ascertain how they might be helpful. The therapist adds the information learned from these multiple perspectives to the family's

Type of support	Question to ask caregiver	Person identified
Instrumental	1. If you needed a ride or car, whom would you ask?	
	2. If you needed to borrow money, whom would you ask?	
	3. If you needed someone to watch the kids, whom would you ask?	My neighbor, Mrs. Johnson
	4. If you needed food or clothing, whom would you call?	
Emotional	1. If you needed someone to listen, whom would you ask?	My cousin Sharon
	2. Whom would you call in an emergency with the kids?	My cousin Sharon
	3. Whom would you go to for a shoulder to cry on?	
	4. Whom do you share good news with?	
Appraisal	1. If you needed a second opinion about parenting, whom could you ask?	My cousin Sharon
	2. Whose opinion do you value?	
	3. Who has given you good advice?	My pastor
Informational	1. If you needed information about something at school or in the neighborhood, whom would you ask?	
	2. Where can you find out about kids' activities?	
	3. Who can tell you where to go for financial help?	

Support person	Special competencies	Limitations
Mrs. Johnson	Stays home all day (disabled)	Can't get around well, ill tempered
Sharon	Good parent, has two children in college and none in serious trouble; listens to me when I'm upset	Very busy
Pastor	Very supportive and kind	Very busy, afraid he'll tell others my business

FIGURE 7.3. MST Assessment of Social Support Form (MASS).

Strengths and Needs Assessment and the MASS. Over the course of treatment, the therapist updates the genogram and MASS periodically to identify potentially helpful family members and their strengths and limitations relative to therapeutic tasks at hand.

Potential Problem Using the Genogram

In some cases, caregivers might say, "I don't have any family" or "I don't have any family that I can count on," and the therapist discovers later in treatment that there are, indeed, relatives living nearby. When this happens, it is often the case that the relatives and family have distanced themselves from one another for a variety of reasons. Some reasons might pertain to challenging behavior of the referred youth, caregiver (depressed or using substances), or relative (in and out of jail), or to a history of interaction checkered by interpersonal conflict. As the therapist and caregiver put together the family genogram, the caregiver might convey angry, hurt, or otherwise negative feelings about some family members. Sometimes a caregiver will dismiss an extended family member entirely due to real or perceived slights that occurred years earlier. The therapist should respond to the negative affect with empathy and reflective listening (e.g., "It is hard for you to imagine that Aunt Ida would be helpful given how she mistreated and criticized you in the past."), but continue to query the caregiver about extended family members and where each lives. Families in MST programs often have extensive histories of failed relationships (one reason for needing social support interventions), including family relationships. Since social support interventions often include interpersonal problem solving to repair these family relationships, therapists should not allow a caregiver's negative assessment of relationships to derail efforts to identify all possible sources of support. At this point in the assessment process, developing a comprehensive list of all the "potential sources of support" is most important. Determining who will provide support comes later.

Using Brainstorming to Identify Extrafamilial Sources of Social Support

Brainstorming is a useful way to help caregivers identify other sources of support in their social network. A social network is a set of people such as friends, coworkers, neighbors, and parishioners. After identifying needs specific to a particular clinical problem, the therapist and caregiver can brainstorm who in the caregiver's social network might be "potentially" available to help address that need (e.g., monitor or supervise the youth during after school hours when the caregiver is working).

As discussed in Chapter 6, brainstorming is a component of social problem solving (see Nezu, Nezu, & D'Zurilla, 2007) that includes several steps. When introducing brainstorming strategies to the caregiver, the therapist identifies in advance the characteristics of the brainstorming process before using the process. The therapist notes that, as applied to the realm of social support, brainstorming involves the following:

- Generating as many ideas as possible about who can help with each identified need.
- Recording the name of each person identified on a piece of paper.
- Rejecting no one prematurely.
- Considering a wide variety of people (e.g., friends, neighbors, coworkers, parishioners) as potential resources.

The therapist might introduce the brainstorming process along the following lines.

"We have tried finding someone in your family who can help monitor and supervise your son after school when you are at work. Unfortunately, we haven't been able to identify anyone in your family who can help. I have been thinking that we need to expand our search and look outside of your family. I want to use a technique called brainstorming to help us generate a list of as many people as possible that might be available to help us. As we create this list, don't worry about whether or not the person will actually help or not—we'll deal with that later. I also want us to defer judging our ideas as we go, because later on we will evaluate each person on our list. Anytime we brainstorm ways of dealing with a problem it is important to remember that the more people we can list the better possible choices we will have later. I want us to stay as creative as possible and let our imaginations run wild. So, whoever comes to mind, I want you to write down that person's name."

To facilitate generalization and maintenance of problem solving skills, the therapist should reinforce the caregiver for implementing the process. For example, as the caregiver mentions various options, the therapist might say, "You are doing a great job being creative," or "I really like how you are deferring judgment." Once the list of potential supports has been created, the therapist and caregiver together review the list to assure a variety of options have been identified (e.g., friends, neighbors, coworkers, parishioners).

When No One Is Available to Provide Social Support

Occasionally, the therapist, caregiver, and other members of the youth's immediate family have explored all options and identified no viable resources. For example, no extended family live in the area, the neighbors are involved in criminal activities (e.g., one parent caught a neighbor climbing out of her living room window with a package of chicken she had just bought), and the caregiver does not have any friends or coworkers. In such cases, assuming that the development of social support is essential to achieving treatment goals, several options are available.

PROGRAMMING FOR SUCCESS

The first option is programming for success by increasing the possibility of the caregiver meeting others, particularly prosocial adults. This option is akin to the activity-scheduling interventions described in Chapter 6 as one of several strategies used to address depression and anxiety in caregivers. The therapist creates opportunities for the caregiver to make connections with community residents—the more opportunities created, the more likely the caregiver will meet someone that can help. The key question, of course, is where might the caregiver meet and engage with prosocial adults? As Willie Sutton, the famous Depression-era bank robber, replied when asked why he robbed banks, "that's where the money is." Where can you meet prosocial supportive people? Where there are high numbers of volunteers! Volunteer organizations, political action groups, and community service and religious organizations can all provide potential opportunities for caregivers to interact with prosocial adults who might become social support resources.

To capitalize on this strategy, the MST program should create and regularly update a library of volunteer organizations in the local community. One useful starting point is to select volunteer organizations engaged in activities that are consistent with a caregiver's strengths. For example, if a caregiver loves to cook, volunteering at a local homeless shelter might be a good option. If the caregiver loves to sing, a reasonable option might be to join a local church choir. Likewise, if the caregiver's youth is athletic, the caregiver might volunteer as the "team mother" (or father). Each of these choices provides an initial step in building the support network—meeting viable adults.

OTHER PARENTS

A second option is to determine whether any of the parents of the youth's friends are reasonably effective, as described in Chapter 4 on peer interventions. Concerned parents acting together can provide a degree of mutual support and oversight that can counter a youth's most antisocial inclinations. Indeed, on many occasions MST therapists have found that parents of their youth's friends are equally exasperated with their own youth's behavior and are very willing to act collaboratively with other caregivers.

THERAPIST SUPPORT

A third option is for the therapist and members of the MST team to provide the needed support until other resources can be found or this treatment goal becomes irrelevant (e.g., the caregiver has become efficient and effective in managing problems and raising children, independently). As the MST motto says, the therapist is responsible for "Whatever It Takes" to meet the clinical needs of families, even if that occasionally requires becoming a key social support, which is often the case earlier in treatment before other sources of support are cultivated. Given the focus of MST interventions on generalization and sustainability of treatment gains (Principle 9), therapists should continue to do "Whatever It Takes" to help caregivers and families develop indigenous supports.

REHABILITATION

The fourth option is rehabilitation, which means finding a way to use someone in the natural ecology—even someone with considerable troubles of his or her own, or with whom the caregiver's past interactions have been rocky—to provide the kind of help needed. Even individuals with an extensive history of criminal behavior can behave in prosocial ways and serve the best interests of children. In one case, for example, a group of prostitutes became a resource for monitoring and reporting the whereabouts of a daughter to her mother, confronting the daughter and calling the mother whenever they saw her hanging around a drug-infested park that bordered the red-light district. After the daughter ran away, the mother and therapist went to that park and the surrounding area to put up posters soliciting information about the daughter's whereabouts and seeking help with her return. The mother and therapist approached a group of prostitutes, showed them the daughter's picture, and asked them to call if they saw her. In showing them the daughter's picture the mother said, "I am trying hard to help my daughter have a better life than mine. But it seems that the harder I try, the more the streets call her. I don't know what else to do, but to continue to fight because she is worth saving. Please let me know if you see her, I'd really appreciate your help." With encouragement from the therapist, whenever the mother walked through this area she made it a point to engage these women in friendly conversation. In this case, then, the therapist and mother used available resources, despite their foibles, to serve a needed support function.

SHADOW

A final option available to the therapist who has not been able to identify available support is to shadow the caregiver as he or she goes about daily activities. The therapist might identify a potential source of support that the caregiver overlooked. For example, when walking through the neighborhood, are there people who speak to the caregiver (e.g., say hello)? Are neighbors sitting on the front stoop or looking out windows? Are signs posted indicating the presence of a neighborhood watch association or upcoming community activities? Sitting on the porch, forming a neighbor-hood watch, and planning community activities are signals of social inter-est and social capital that could, with cultivation, become resources for social support.

A Word about Formal Supports

Social supports range on a continuum from informal, proximal relation-ships (e.g., extended family, friends, neighbors, coworkers) to more formal and distal relationships with community organizations (e.g., YMCA, Meals on Wheels, My Sister's Place), to formal and even legally mandated relation-ships, as occurs when probation officers or social service case workers are assigned by departments of juvenile justice or child welfare to work with a family referred for MST. Thus far, our discussion has focused on finding potential social supports on the informal end of the continuum. This is intentional, as an expectation of MST (Principle 9) is that therapists must first utilize resources that are more likely to be sustainable once treatment ends.

Nevertheless, the needs of some youth with serious clinical problems and their families can exceed the capacity of informal social supports. For example, a grandmother with limited physical mobility due to a stroke who is prohibited from driving might need a rehabilitation center van to take her to medical appointments. Or, the psychiatric illness and physical vio-lence of a stepfather might pose such significant threats to the safety of a youth and his mother that formal respite care must be arranged, because no members of the extended family live in the community and the youth needs to continue to go to the community school. Over the past decade, the availability of community-based mental health services varying in levels of intensity commensurate with the needs of youth with serious emotional disturbances has increased in the United States (see Stroul & Friedman, 1994). However, research demonstrates that increased access to and satis-faction with such services does not translate into increased service effec-tiveness (Bickman, Summerfelt, & Noser, 1997; Bickman, Warren, Andrade, & Penaloza, 2000). Thus, if formal resources are the only ones available to meet a specified need of the youth and family, therapists should help fami-lies become educated consumers of these services, using the kinds of strate-gies to interview the resources as were described for interviewing medical professionals in Chapter 6. Thus, therapists must be knowledgeable about the full range of potential formal resources available in the community. As noted in Chapter 6, MST programs should develop a directory of profes-sionals that therapists have found to be helpful and effective in providing services to families. A similar kind of directory of formal social support resources can be helpful when a therapist and caregiver cannot cultivate informal supports.

Evaluating the Pros and Cons of Possible Supports

After social support resources and needs have been identified, the therapist assists the caregiver to select the person who can best help meet a particular need. Selecting the best possible person is essentially a cost–benefit analysis. Possible costs to the caregiver when he or she asks someone for help can include time and effort, psychological well-being (e.g., positive status in the family; embarrassment; being viewed as a weak, needy, or bad parent). To help assess the relative costs, the therapist can suggest the caregiver rate the difficulty of using each person on a scale from 1 (easy) to 10 (very difficult). Working through the Cost–Benefit Analysis Grid (Figure 7.4) for each specific need (first column) will help the caregiver select optimal supports and consider barriers and potential solutions for each potential support person.

Putting All the Pieces Together

Next, the caregiver and therapist must select the most appropriate source of social support and develop strategies to engage that person.

Selecting the Right Person

As discussed previously, the genogram and MASS form are tools therapists and caregivers use to identify the individuals who are currently providing various types of social support or who are potential sources of support. The Cost–Benefit Analysis Grid is used to evaluate the viability of possible candidates for a specific identified need. The grid can be used to help the caregiver select a person who has relatively low costs and is rated on the low

Specific need	Possible matching person	Pros of using this person	Cons of using this person	Costs and/ or reciprocal help for this person assisting with the task	Rating difficulty of using this person
Monitor Steve after school	Mrs. Johnson	Stays at home all day, lives across the street	Can't get around well, somewhat ill tempered	She likes social interaction and is lonely—bring dinner over and eat with her	5
	Cousin Sharon	Very good parent—has children in college	Very busy, lives 5 miles away	Can't think of what she needs from me	8

FIGURE 7.4. Cost–Benefit Analysis Grid for specific needs.

end of the difficulty rating scale (4 or less) for the desired need. Optimal choices have relatively low costs (i.e., minimal time, energy), but high benefits (i.e., will be successful). Suboptimal choices have high costs (i.e., time and effort, lowered self-esteem) and low benefits (i.e., not likely to provide what's needed). However, if the caregiver has limited social support options, the best available choice will need to be targeted.

In the case of the Jackson family, the neighbor, Mrs. Johnson, clearly provided the most viable option for obtaining the needed instrumental support. Importantly, the Jacksons could also provide a valuable resource to Mrs. Johnson as well—affording opportunities for much desired social interaction. Although, as noted earlier in Figure 7.3, cousin Sharon had considerable strengths pertaining to emotional and appraisal support, she was not a good fit for the specific instrumental need identified here.

Selecting the Right Time to Approach the Identified Person

The therapist and caregiver should consider the best time to approach the identified person. In deciding on an optimal time, the therapist and caregiver might ask, "Is the person in the right mood to listen and consider the request?" If the person seems angry or sad, it is probably not the best time to ask for help. Similarly, contacting someone at the end of a long work day when he or she is busy preparing dinner or early in the morning when preparing for work might not be the best times either. Conversely, asking during times people are more likely to be relaxed (e.g., weekends) and in good moods (e.g., after church) might increase the odds the caregiver will get a positive response.

Scripting the Dialogue

When a caregiver has limited social support and practice obtaining such support, it can be helpful for the therapist and caregiver together to create a specific script—using language that is most comfortable to the caregiver. For example, with Mrs. Johnson the script might read:

> "I would really appreciate if you would help check on my son after school. I'm particularly concerned about the time between when he gets home from school at 3:00 and when I get home at 6:00—especially if he is hanging out with any of his friends. Do you think that we could work out a way to do this?"

The therapist will also need to help script the caregiver's response to anticipated problems. In the example of the Jackson family, where the neighbor, Mrs. Johnson, was recruited to provide instrumental support, Mrs. Jackson was concerned with being criticized if she asked her for help. What if Mrs. Johnson did criticize her? How should Mrs. Jackson respond? Here, the therapist should brainstorm with the caregiver possible ways of responding to each concern raised. For example, the therapist might script and role-play the following approach (with the therapist playing the caregiver, and the Mrs. Jackson playing the neighbor):

NEIGHBOR: You are a bad parent if you need my help.

MOTHER: You think I am a bad parent. In what ways am I a bad parent?

NEIGHBOR: You know exactly what I am talking about.

MOTHER: Lord knows I have made some mistakes in raising my son, but I am trying to do better, and that is why I am asking for your help. If you told me specifically how I am a bad parent, I can start doing better.

NEIGHBOR: Well, for one thing you baby him too much. You let him get away with stuff.

MOTHER: Isn't that the truth! I do baby him too much. How would you suggest I not baby him? What should I do differently?

The caregiver should be free to modify the language of each script to make it more relevant to his or her social context. When a caregiver objects to the therapist's choice of words or phrases ask him or her How would you say this?

Practice

Once a script that makes sense to the caregiver and therapist has been created, they practice. As with the practice component of any interpersonal problem-solving intervention (see Chapter 6), the therapist first takes the role of the caregiver to provide a solid model for the caregiver. Then, a role play should be set up that reflects the realities of the expected situation. The therapist should feel free to interject some of the negative self-talk and worry that the caregiver has shared earlier, and model ways of responding to such cognitions in ways that will not undermine performance, but lead to success. Then, the therapist and caregiver switch roles, and the caregiver acts as herself while the therapist takes the role of the targeted social support person. The feedback component of interpersonal problem-solving interventions is implemented, as well. The therapist provides feedback about specific words and behaviors the caregiver used when pointing out what went well, and what needs improvement before trying again. The therapist also identifies problems in the role play and coaches ways to correct the problems in subsequent role plays until the therapist and caregiver concur that the role play was well executed and ready to implement with the identified person. The therapist and caregiver should agree on a time and date that the strategy will be used. Until then, the therapist should periodically check in with the caregiver to allay any performance related concerns.

Evaluating the Plan

The outcome of the plan should be assessed during the first meeting with the caregiver following plan implementation.

- What worked?
- What did not work?
- How difficult was it to carry out (rate difficulty)?

The therapist should remember to reinforce effort as well as examine factors that might have inhibited performance (e.g., negative emotions, worry). If unanticipated factors derailed performance, the therapist should take responsibility for not anticipating these (e.g., "I failed to prepare you to deal with ... My mistake!") and develop a plan to address such factors in subsequent efforts. Essentially, the plan is evaluated in the same way (e.g., using the do-loop) that all MST evaluations are evaluated.

Preparing the Identified Person to Help

In some cases, the therapist and/or caregiver will need to provide guidance to the targeted support person to make sure the support can be provided as envisioned. This guidance should not require much time (think minutes, not hours) or energy. It is usually a good idea for the therapist to be present when the caregiver provides explicit instructions to the identified person about the support that is needed. This will allow the therapist to observe and be certain that the support person has a clear understanding of what to do (e.g., "please be sure to watch ... "), address any questions or concerns that the caregiver failed to address, and gather information to later give the caregiver feedback on his or her performance.

Building In Reciprocity

Identifying social supports and asking for help is one thing, maintaining help is another. To build strong relations with informal and formal supports, caregivers use the same kinds of engagement skills that therapists use with families (e.g., emphasizing strengths and common goals). To sustain social support, caregivers must know how to reciprocate the help they receive.

Reciprocation is a two-step process. The first step is to determine what would be an equitable exchange based on community norms and personal choice. With respect to a fair exchange, the therapist might need to ask competent others from the caregiver's community (e.g., neighborhood caretakers) what kinds of things would be expected as a fair exchange for, say, monitoring or supervising a teenager during a certain time period. With respect to choice, the caregiver and/or therapist simply ask the person what he or she would want in exchange for the help. For example, a caregiver may ask the neighbor:

> "Thanks for agreeing to monitor my son after school when I'm at work. To better thank you for your help, I would like repay your kindness is some way. Is there something that I could do to help you in return, to show my appreciation for helping me?"

Some people may decline any offer and just want to do a favor. Regardless, the family should show appreciation for the help they receive and do so repeatedly. Sending a thank-you note, home-baked cookies, or a fruit basket can be a good start. One mother who made delicious pies periodically showed her appreciation by making pies for her neighbor. A father made it a point to send a letter to the school principal, copied to the teacher, detailing the support he received from this teacher at his daughter's school. Another caregiver sent a letter to a church, which was read in front of the congregation, specifically naming the church member who had helped the family. Particularly valuable from our perspective, are efforts by the youth to reciprocate efforts to support his or her family (e.g., washing the car, cutting grass, cleaning up the yard, running errands). The point is that there are any number of ways that caregivers can reciprocate the support they receive, and that such reciprocation clearly helps to sustain the support.

Conclusion

Working to increase social support can be daunting, especially when serving multistressed and multineed families trying to effectively raise an adolescent who engages in antisocial behavior. Increasing a family's utilization of social support takes time and effort. The "ties that bind," however, are critical to our health and welfare. Helping caregivers surround themselves with supportive family, friends, neighbors, coworkers, and others is critical to attenuating the stresses and strains of raising children with behavioral problems. None of us can make it alone. This chapter has sought to provide some basic strategies that we have found useful in helping families develop the skills and competencies needed to create strong social support networks.

CHAPTER 8

Treating Substance Abuse

Adolescent substance abuse is a common comorbid problem in populations of youth exhibiting significant behavioral disturbance. In a study of almost 2,000 youth between the ages of 10 and 18 years in an urban detention center, Teplin and colleagues (Teplin, Abram, McClelland, Dulcan, & Mericle, 2002) found that approximately half met diagnostic criteria for a substance use disorder within the past 6 months. Similarly, the caregivers of delinquent and substance abusing youth are at increased risk of having substance use disorders (Fleming, Brewer, Gainey, Haggerty, & Catalano, 1997; Jennison & Johnson, 1998). Thus, MST therapists frequently need to address substance abuse issues either directly in the youth they treat or in the caregivers of these youth where symptoms often present barriers to developing effective parenting skills (McGue, 1999).

As indicated in Chapter 1, research reveals substantial overlap between the factors contributing to juvenile criminal behavior and those promoting substance abuse. For instance, similar peer influences and family factors play important roles in exacerbating or attenuating risk for both adolescent substance abuse and conduct disorder (Elliott, 1994b; Farrell & Danish, 1993). Consistent with the best scientific evidence (National Institute on Drug Abuse, 1999), the key treatment implication of these findings is that adolescent substance abuse is a behavior that, like criminal offending, is best conceptualized as complex, multidetermined, and supported by the interplay of numerous risk factors (Dishion & Kavanagh, 2003). Not surprisingly then, several treatments that focus on the known risk factors for substance abuse have shown promising results (Waldron & Turner, 2008).

MST Substance-Related Research and Outcomes

MST has been identified as a promising or effective treatment of adolescent substance abuse by federal entities (e.g., National Institute on Drug Abue, 1999) and reviewers (e.g., Waldron & Turner, 2008). MST substance-related research and outcomes are outlined in Chapter 9 (see Table 9.1) and discussed in greater detail elsewhere (Saldana & Henggeler, 2008; Sheidow & Henggeler, 2008). For present purposes, a brief review of substance-related MST research with juvenile offenders and caregivers in MST programs is most pertinent.

Adolescents

Serious Juvenile Offenders

In early trials with serious juvenile offenders, MST demonstrated significantly decreased substance use and substance related problems in contrast with counterparts in comparison conditions (Henggeler et al., 1991). For example, in a 14-year follow-up, Schaeffer and Borduin (2005) showed that serious juvenile offenders who had received MST had fewer than half as many substance-related arrests as counterparts who had received individual therapy.

Substance-Abusing Juvenile Offenders

The promising nature of early findings with serious juvenile offenders who did not necessarily have substance use disorders led to new clinical trials targeting substance abusing and dependent adolescents in the juvenile justice system. Results from the first of these (Henggeler, Pickrel, et al., 1999) showed that youth who received MST, in comparison with counterparts who received usual community-based treatment, had reduced substance use posttreatment and demonstrated considerable reduction in days incarcerated and days spent in other out-of-home placements at 6-month follow-up (Schoenwald, Ward, Henggeler, Pickrel, & Patel, 1996). Importantly, 4-year follow-up of these youth revealed significantly higher rates of marijuana abstinence and less violent crime for the MST participants (Henggeler, Clingempeel, Brondino, & Pickrel, 2002).

Substance-Abusing Juvenile Offenders in Juvenile Drug Court

A second clinical trial with substance-abusing juvenile offenders was conducted in the context of juvenile drug court (Henggeler, Halliday-Boykins, et al., 2006). Findings showed that MST was more effective than comparison conditions at decreasing youth substance use and self-reported criminal offending. Importantly, findings also showed that the integration of contingency management (CM; Higgins, Silverman, & Heil, 2008) into MST accelerated decreases in youth substance use. The integration of CM into MST for treating adolescent substance abuse had been piloted successfully in the earlier Neighborhood Solutions Project (Swenson, Henggeler, Taylor, & Addison, 2005). As described next, even earlier research with substance abusing caregivers had set the stage for this integration.

Contingency Management with Substance-Abusing Caregivers

CM was first used within MST during a study (Henggeler, Rowland, et al., 1999) that examined the effectiveness of MST as an alternative to the emergency hospitalization of youth in psychiatric crisis (e.g., suicidal). In this study with youth presenting serious emotional disturbance, MST therapists were having difficulty sustaining stable youth home placements in approximately 26% of the cases due to parental substance abuse or dependence (Rowland, Halliday-Boykins, & Demidovich, 2003). To address this challenge, the investigators reviewed the extant adult substance abuse treatment literature and concluded that the community reinforcement approach (CRA, a variation of CM; Budney & Higgins, 1998) showed considerable promise, and importantly, was compatible with the conceptual and clinical emphases of MST. Both interventions:

- Use variations of functional analyses (i.e., fit circles for MST) to identify needs.
- Are goal oriented.
- Are action oriented in achieving those goals.
- Use behavioral and cognitive-behavioral interventions.
- Consider the broader systemic context in which clients are embedded.
- Have significant commitments to empirical validation.

Thus, this variation of CM was integrated into MST.

Although the effects of CRA with the substance-abusing caregivers in the study of alternatives to hospitalization were not evaluated formally, the subjective experiences of investigators and therapists regarding this treatment were very favorable. This positive experience led to the aforementioned integration of CM in the Neighborhood Solutions Project as well as to studies evaluating the ability of MST therapists to implement CM with caregivers to decrease their substance use and improve their parenting ability (Schaeffer, Saldana, Rowland, Henggeler, & Swenson, 2008) and to enhance treatment gains for substance-abusing youth in MST community-based programs (Henggeler, Sheidow, Cunningham, Donohue, & Ford, 2008). In addition, another variation of CM (i.e., reinforcement-based therapy; Jones, Wong, Tuten, & Stitzer, 2005) has been integrated into an adaptation of MST for treating child abuse and neglect (Schaeffer et al., 2008), with promising preliminary results.

Thus, based on 15 years of anecdotal experience, our own research, and an extensive body of literature supporting the effectiveness of CM with a wide array of substance abusing populations (Higgins et al., 2008), we believe that CM can provide a valuable enhancement to MST when treating substance abuse. Thus, we have concluded that:

1. *Standard MST, as specified in this volume, can be very effective in treating adolescent substance abuse.*
2. *The integration of CM into MST, as described in this chapter, can accelerate and enhance substance-related outcomes.*

As discussed later in this chapter, however, the effective integration and implementation of CM within MST programs (MST/CM) requires significant CM-specific training and ongoing quality assurance.

Determining the Need for Substance Use Treatment

One of the first steps in assessing whether a youth has a substance use problem that warrants intervention (either MST or MST/CM) is to better understand where that youth falls on the continuum of drug use.

A Continuum of Drug Use: From Abstinence to Dependence

Winters and his colleagues (Winters, Latimer, & Stinchfield, 2001) provide an excellent framework for conceptualizing the continuum from substance abstinence to dependence and for understanding the factors that must be considered in placing a particular youth along this continuum. Drawing from a report by the Center for Substance Abuse Treatment (1999), the 5-point continuum includes:

1. Abstinence—no substance use.
2. Experimental use—typically minimal use in the context of recreational activities.
3. Early abuse—more established use, greater frequency of use, often more than one drug used, and negative consequences of use beginning to emerge.
4. Abuse—history of frequent use and negative consequences have emerged.
5. Dependence—continued regular use in spite of negative consequences, and considerable activity devoted to seeking and using drugs.

As noted in community-based epidemiological studies, the majority of adolescents have used substances. Hence substance use by itself is rarely a criterion for intervention. Rather, treatment should be reserved for youth at the early abuse, abuse, and dependence points on the continuum. Importantly, Winters and colleagues noted that several additional factors should be considered in deciding whether interventions are warranted.

1. Use of some drugs (e.g., heroin) is sufficiently dangerous as to merit intervention even if negative consequences have not emerged.
2. Age should be considered. For example, a 12-year-old experimenting with marijuana might present a very different profile than a 17-year-old with similar use.
3. Acute ingestion of large quantities of a substance at any age is sufficiently risky to call for interventions.
4. Use of substances in inappropriate settings (e.g., school, while driving) might justify interventions.

Thus, the general rule for deciding whether interventions for substance use are needed is based on an observed link between substance use and negative life outcomes or high risk for such outcomes. For example, youth whose substance use puts them at risk for arrest, violation of probation, poor school performance, or family difficulties would be candidates for intervention.

Therapist Tasks: Assessing Youth Substance Use and the Need for Treatment

The primary tasks of MST therapists in this regard are to:

1. Determine if the adolescent is using substances.
2. Find out the quantity and impact of the youth's substance use.

3. Clarify the need for treatment of drug use.
4. Engage caregivers and teen in the treatment process.

Several tools, noted subsequently in this chapter, are available in the CM manuals to help therapists determine the need for treatment. For example, the Therapist Checklist (see Figure 8.1), taken from one of those manuals (Family Services Research Center, 2008), is designed to help therapists navigate these decisions.

Treating Substance Abuse with Standard MST

As described earlier, standard MST has been shown to be effective in reducing youth substance use and abuse. Substance abuse or dependence problems are approached by MST therapists in the same manner that other concerning behaviors are addressed. That is, therapists first gain consensus among stakeholders that the teen's substance use qualifies as a presenting problem. Then, therapists attempt to better understand the "fit" of this behavior across the different contexts in which the youth and family are embedded. Next, following the MST analytic process (see Figure 2.1), the therapist develops and implements interventions targeting the prioritized drivers of substance use. Importantly, MST therapists closely track the effectiveness of all interventions, often collecting and teaching family members to collect urine screens to monitor drug use.

The case example described in Chapter 2 highlights the standard MST approach to treating youth substance abuse (see Figures 2.2–2.5). Note that in this case, Rick was referred for marijuana use, so the therapist obtained information at intake concerning the frequency, intensity, and duration of his use (Figure 2.2). Next, an overarching treatment goal was developed, with the family targeting Rick's marijuana use (see Figure 2.4, overarching goal number 2), and a fit circle of his drug use was obtained (see Figure 2.5, first fit circle, prioritized drivers are in bold font). The therapist prioritized hanging with drug using peers, poor parental monitoring, and family conflict as the drivers needing immediate therapeutic attention to diminish Rick's drug use. As described more completely in Chapter 2, the therapist developed and implemented interventions targeting these and other drivers on this fit circle throughout the course of Rick's treatment. Importantly, the therapist obtained random urine drug screens routinely during treatment and taught Rick's father to do this as well. Thus, by the close of treatment, overarching treatment goal number 2 was met (Figure 2.4) in that Rick demonstrated clean urine screens for 10 consecutive weeks, and importantly, Rick's father was able to administer urine screens and effectively reward clean screens and punish dirty

EVALUATING DRUG USE AND THE NEED FOR TREATMENT

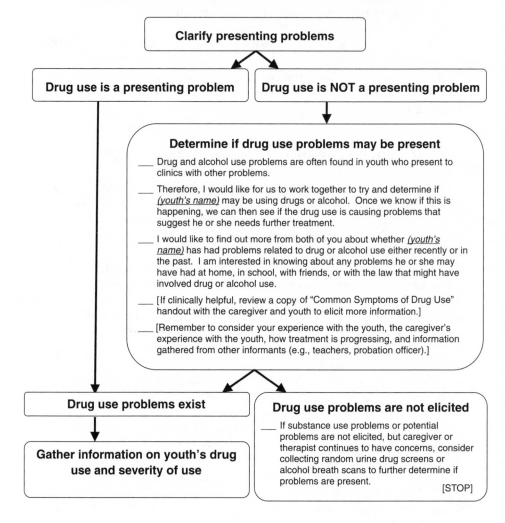

(continued)

FIGURE 8.1. Therapist Checklist. Regardless of which steps are implemented, therapists should always consult with their supervisor for guidance in making treatment plans and decisions.

Drug use problems exist

↓

Gather information on youth's drug use and impact of use

___ The next step is for us to better understand what drugs *(youth's name)* is using, how they are being used, and how they may be causing him or her problems.

___ I have some handouts that can help us with this process [dispense copies of the Commonly Abused Drugs Chart and the Substance Use Chart to both youth and caregiver].

___ Now, I'd like to fill in the Substance Use Chart with information that *(youth's name)* tells us. It may also help if we look at the Commonly Abused Drugs Chart so that we can see what some of the common names are for these drugs and what some of the consequences of their use can be. [Complete Substance Use Chart with youth and caregiver present.]

___ Now that we have a better sense of the drugs *(youth's name)* is using, I would like to step back a minute and talk with both of you about how you see *(youth's name)*'s drug use impacting his life. [Use "Domains of Functioning" handout to elicit information from both youth and caregiver about concerns they may have about the impact of drug use on youth and family functioning]

___ [To gather more information on the youth's substance use, administer the Client Substance Index— Short Form or CSI-SF to the youth.]

___ [To gather more information on the youth's substance use, administer the Modified CAGE Questionnaire to caregivers concerning their child. This measure may also be administered to youth.]

___ [Remember to consider the youth's age and drug of choice, whether incidents of acute ingestion of large quantities of the drug have occurred, and if drug use takes place in inappropriate settings (e.g., school, while driving).]

Substance use problems linked to youth functional impairment

Caregiver and youth willing to engage in treatment	**Caregiver or youth NOT willing to engage in treatment**
___ Go to Checklist Task #1: Overview of Contingency Management	___ Go to "Tips for Engaging Families"

Substance use problems NOT linked to youth functional impairment based on therapist and family opinion

___ Substance use interventions are not indicated at this time. Consider continuing to assess or collect information (i.e., random drug screens) about potential use and its impact on functioning.

[STOP]

FIGURE 8.1. *(continued)*

screens, thereby increasing the chances that abstinence would continue after MST treatment ended.

CM as Used within MST

This clinical overview of CM is based on the CM treatment manuals developed at the Family Services Research Center (Cunningham et al., 2004; Family Services Research Center, 2008).

What is CM?

CM is a set of psychological and behavioral strategies designed to:

1. Identify the combination of people, places, and things (including feelings and thoughts) that lead a person to use a drug and to want to continue using it.
2. Identify people, places, and things that are more satisfying or rewarding to the individual than drug use.
3. Detect the individual's drug use in an objective and measurable way.
4. Deliver positive consequences when the person has not used drugs and negative consequences when drug use is detected.
5. Develop effective self-management plans and drug refusal skills to facilitate abstinence.

Introducing CM to Families

Therapists introduce CM as an effective intervention, describe the four components of CM discussed subsequently, note that caregivers, the youth, and other family members will be involved in treatment, and provide information concerning the length of treatment. CM is described as a type of treatment that has been proven to help both adults and adolescents stop using alcohol and drugs (e.g., marijuana, cocaine, opium, and heroin) even when substance-related problems have been long lasting. The length of CM treatment will vary depending on the youth's and family's response and involvement, but the interventions can be completed during the usual duration of MST.

ABC Assessment of Drug Use

In the first component of CM, as with other functional analyses discussed in Chapters 5 and 6, therapists teach the youth and caregiver to conduct an ABC assessment of the youth's drug use. An ABC assessment is used to identify events in the environment that occur before, during, and after drug use. In conducting this assessment, the therapist, youth, and caregiver focus on three phases of behavior—The ABCs:

1. Antecedents (i.e., triggers or cues for drug use)
2. Behavior (i.e., actions leading to use, drug use itself)
3. Consequences (i.e., reinforcement, punishment) of the behavior

The basic rationale of the ABC assessment (Budney & Higgins, 1998) is that drug use is triggered by certain events, situations, and feelings, and maintained by immediate and long-term consequences.

The information obtained during the initial and subsequent ABC assessments serves as the foundation for designing treatment interventions (e.g., self-management plans) to help the youth avoid future drug use. MST therapists find that this aspect of treatment is often fairly easy to teach to families as the structure and process of obtaining ABC assessments resemble that of developing MST fit circles and serve similar functions.

Point-and-Level System

The purpose of the CM point-and-level system is to provide incentives for clean drug urine screens and alcohol breath scans and disincentives for dirty screens and scans. The point-and-level system is presented in the form of a contract that is signed by the youth, caregiver, and therapist. When a teenager has not used drugs and tests clean, he or she is rewarded with points that can be exchanged for various rewards or for access to important privileges provided by caregivers. Conversely, drug use is punished by the loss of points and valued privileges.

To implement the point-and-level system, the therapist:

1. Completes with the youth and caregiver a contract that lays out a system, including three levels, for earning, losing, and spending points.
2. Completes with the youth and caregiver a reward menu that identifies positive items and social activities or privileges that the youth wants to earn for having clean urine drug screens and alcohol breath scans.
3. Sets up and monitors a checkbook tracking system for points earned, spent, or lost.
4. Implements the contingency management point-and-level system.
5. Develops plans to sustain the point-and-level incentive system after treatment completion.

Self-Management Planning and Drug Refusal Skill Training

The therapist's objectives in this aspect of CM are to:

1. Help the adolescent develop strategies and skills to manage drug use triggers and contexts.
2. Teach caregivers to help the youth manage drug use triggers and contexts and reinforce the youth's successful management of these.
3. Generate as many alternative strategies as possible for managing drug use triggers and situations.
4. Develop drug refusal skills for those drug use situations that are unavoidable.

These particular interventions belong to the family of cognitive-behavioral strategies discussed throughout this volume, and especially in Chapter 6.

Self-Management Planning

The therapist introduces self-management planning after it is clear that the caregiver and adolescent are able to conduct an ABC assessment. Self-management planning is a collection of strategies and skills designed to better manage each identified drug use trigger and situation. As occurs with an ABC assessment, the self-management plan also is revised continuously during treatment. The therapist helps the youth and caregiver review and modify the self-management strategies each session, paying special attention to times when the youth relapses or when new triggers for drug use or non–drug use are identified.

Budney and Higgins (1998) identified three basic ways of handling drug use triggers and situations, and these strategies are used in CM.

1. *Avoid triggers and situations*—for example, taking a different route home from school to avoid the home of a peer where drug use occurs.
2. *Rearrange the environment*—for example, getting rid of items associated with triggers, such as pipes, bongs, rolling papers, and cigarette lighters.
3. *Make a new plan*—for example, developing different skills to cope with triggers and unavoidable contexts, and seeking social support from non-drug-using peers.

An example of a completed self-management plan is provided in Figure 8.2.

Name: *Joe S.*

Date: 7/1

Drug of choice: Marijuana

TRIGGER: *Seeing friend Mark in the halls at school—asks me to skip class and go smoke.*

Use this form to help create ways to manage the triggers of your drug use. This will help reduce the chances that triggers will lead to drug use. *Fill out one form for each trigger.*

Plan	Cost–Benefit Analysis		Difficulty (1–10 scale; 10 = most difficult)
	Benefits	*Costs*	
1. Talk to Mark ahead of time and let him know I am in this program where I get consequences for using pot. Also let him know that my P.O. could get me in serious trouble if he catches me skipping school and/or smoking pot.	Mark might stop trying to get me to smoke with him; then I wouldn't have to struggle to say no.	Mark might think I'm a loser for not smoking.	5
2. Figure out the times I usually run into Mark in the hallway and find a different route during those times. If there are situations when I just can't avoid it and happen to run into him, then I will use my drug refusal skills to avoid skipping class and using pot.	Reduce the chances of running into Mark so I don't experience the trigger at all.	I might still run into him at times if I can't avoid traveling that particular route and it may be difficult to refuse. I need to remember to use my drug refusal skills in this case!	3

FIGURE 8.2. Self-Management Planning Form (example).

Drug Refusal Skills Training

Drug refusal skills are a special subset of self-management strategies developed to assist the youth when encountering unavoidable social situations that would increase the risk of drug use. While drug refusal skills are particularly beneficial to access in unexpected situations, they also can be components of the self-management plan. Most drug relapses in youth occur when they are with peers (Brown, Myers, Mott, & Vik, 1994). Although many negative peers can be avoided, predicting and planning for all future situations is impossible. Therefore, developing effective skills for refusing drugs is crucial for long-term abstinence.

During this aspect of treatment the therapist:

1. Helps the teen develop drug refusal skills to use during unavoidable social situations that increase the risk of drug use.
2. Helps the youth develop a drug refusal style that is likely to be effective in his or her social context.
3. Provides opportunities (through role plays) for the adolescent to practice using drug refusal skills to manage drug offers in unavoidable social situations.
4. Teaches the caregiver to assist the youth in this process.

Drug-Testing Protocol

Behavioral contingencies are most effective when administered consistently and precisely and based on objective evidence (Budney & Higgins, 1998). Random urine drug screens are the preferred methods for providing this objective evidence. There are three very important reasons for using objective measures. First, even with the best of intentions to stop using illicit drugs, adolescents who abuse drugs often do not tell the truth about their substance use. Consequently, an adolescent's verbal report, while seemingly genuine and heartfelt, might not accurately reflect current drug use. Second, because the purpose of CM is to increase incentives for abstinence, providing rewards without adequate verification will undermine the program's integrity, and more importantly, will be insufficient to compete with existing drug use contingencies. Finally, objective monitoring coupled with negative (i.e., clean) results will set the stage for the youth to begin rebuilding trust with his or her caregivers. A positive parent–adolescent affective bond (e.g., what my parents think about me) is often reported as a major reason that teens keep from using drugs. Thus, therapists teach caregivers to obtain and interpret the results of random urine drug screens and alcohol breath scans that serve as the criteria for implementing the aforementioned components of CM.

Modifying CM for Caregivers

While CM interventions for youth and the training materials and methods required for therapists to implement CM have been well specified (Family Services Research Center, 2008), the methodology for implementing CM with caregivers is still a work in progress. In a recently completed project, CRA to Support Caregivers (Schaeffer et al., 2008), Rowland trained an MST therapist team to implement CRA (Cunningham et al., 2005) for caregiver substance abuse or dependence if this problem was negatively impacting desired clinical outcomes for the youth. Although much was the same (e.g., ABC assessments, self-management planning), experience gained during this trial revealed clinically relevant distinctions between treating the substance abuse of youth in MST programs and the substance abuse of their caregivers.

Engagement and Assessment

Therapists found that caregivers of MST youth most frequently abused alcohol and prescription drugs (i.e., benzodiazepines) rather than marijuana; thus treatment required clinical protocols for assessing adults for potentially dangerous withdrawal symptoms and linking them with detoxification facilities and physicians when indicated. Therapists also benefited from training that integrated certain motivational interviewing (Miller & Rollnick, 2002) techniques to help caregivers better appreciate the link between their own substance use problems and their teenager's presenting difficulties. In particular, therapists highlighted the importance of parental substance use as a driver for youth referral behaviors on the fit circles in ways that sustained caregiver engagement in treatment.

Social Supports

When therapists implement CM with youth, caregiver involvement in all aspects of CM is central to the treatment. If caregivers receive CRA, the MST therapist strongly encourages them to involve a supportive adult in treatment. As many substance dependent adults have few or very tenuous ties with non-drug-using family and friends, a substantive focus of treatment is to link caregivers with peers or family members who are willing to participate and support their CRA interventions (e.g., ABC assessments, self-management planning, provision of rewards through point-and-level system). To facilitate the inclusion of social supports, caregivers are awarded an additional 50 points, worth $50 in vouchers, when a social support person is successfully recruited and participates frequently in their treatment.

In summary, providing effective treatment for substance abusing caregivers of youth on MST teams has the potential to improve adolescent outcomes by increasing caregiver effectiveness. Our current work in this regard shows promise, but much remains to be accomplished before these interventions are ready for widespread dissemination.

Requirements for Integrating CM with MST

While standard MST, as described throughout this volume, is often effective in reducing adolescent substance use and has many similarities with the protocols that integrate CM with MST (i.e., MST/CM), these models include several meaningful differences. As summarized in Table 8.1, these differences pertain primarily to the emphasis and intensity of focus. For example, in contrast to MST programs, MST/CM *requires*:

- Frequent random drug testing.
- Funding for vouchers to use as incentives for clean drug screens.
- Development of self-management plans for all drug use triggers.
- Use of the point-and-level system.

The additional requirements for implementing MST/CM necessitate added training and ongoing quality assurance to support therapist implementation fidelity of the CM aspects of MST/CM. Thus, over and above the extensive MST quality assurance/improvement requirements for all MST programs, MST/CM requires:

- Additional training of program therapists and supervisors in each of the CM components.
- Additional training of the MST consultant if he or she is not CM proficient.
- Monthly review of audiotaped therapy sessions, supervisory sessions, and consultation.
- Monthly caregiver report on the validated CM adherence measure (Chapman, Sheidow, Henggeler, Halliday-Boykins, & Cunningham, 2008).

This training and quality assurance for CM is provided by experts in CM and MST.

Considering the supplementary requirements and added quality assurance, MST/CM is probably best suited for adoption in MST programs that have a clear and unambiguous focus on treating youth with substance abuse disorders (e.g., those referred by a juvenile drug court). Standard MST interventions are often entirely sufficient for programs in which only a subset of adolescents have substance abuse problems.

Conclusion

Standard MST is effective in treating adolescent substance abuse. Also, based on clinical experience, research, and an extensive body of literature supporting the effectiveness of CM, we believe that CM can provide a valuable enhancement to MST by accelerating favorable substance use outcomes. The clinical procedures for implementing CM with adolescents and the MST/CM

TABLE 8.1. Qualities That Differentiate MST/CM from Standard MST

Quality	MST/CM	Standard MST
Functional analysis	A formal functional analysis of drug use (ABC assessment) is done for each instance of drug use.	A functional analysis of drug-using behavior is sometimes used to supplement fit circles.
Self-management plans	A specific self-management plan is developed for all prioritized drug use triggers.	MST interventions are developed to address the prioritized drivers of drug use.
Drug refusal skills	Drug refusal skills are taught to all youth, using a specific structure and format, and involve extensive role play of drug refusal strategies.	Drug refusal skills are taught to some drug-using youth if the need is identified.
Point-and-level system with contract and vouchers	A well-specified contract is developed with each youth and caregiver, and a formalized plan is put into place that includes financial vouchers to obtain prosocial rewards provided by the treatment team as well as family-based incentives.	Family-based incentives are often provided to reinforce clean drug screens.
Drug testing	Required random urine drug screens and alcohol breath scans are done with each youth frequently enough to detect the youth's drug of choice.	Urine drug screens are often collected to assess drug use and to monitor the outcome of interventions.
Resource requirements	• Program funding for vouchers is required (approximately $100 to $150 per youth) • Urine drug-testing cups and alcohol breath scans are required for testing each youth 1–3 times a week.	• Vouchers not required • Urine drug cups and alcohol breath scans are requested for some youth, but not required for all.
Consultation resources	CM consultation is combined with weekly MST consultation. The MST consultant is required to have additional training and coaching in implementing CM within the context of MST.	Routine MST consultation is provided.
Training	Additional training is provided for each of the CM components.	Routine MST training is provided.
Additional QA procedures	• In addition to the routine tapes required as part of the MST QA/QI protocol, the team is required to submit monthly audiotapes to the MST/CM consultant of individual therapist sessions; group supervision; and consultation. • Caregiver reports of CM adherence are required monthly.	Routine MST tape reviews may include tapes of therapists implementing interventions targeting substance abuse.

quality assurance system that helps ensure fidelity to this process have been well explicated and are available for adoption. On the other hand, the procedures for implementing CM for caregivers of youth receiving MST are still being validated. While clinical experience supports the use of this approach with caregivers, the research has not yet been completed in this area. Hence, clinical guidelines and protocols for these procedures are not available for transport at this time.

MST Outcomes

This chapter provides a consumer-friendly overview of the favorable outcomes obtained in published MST clinical trials and briefly describes progress in adapting the basic MST model to serve youth with other serious
clinical problems and their families. First, however, the conclusions of leading government entities, consumer groups, and reviewers are highlighted to
provide independent perspectives on the body of MST outcome research.

Independent Reviews

Numerous groups of independent reviewers have supported the promise
and/or effectiveness of MST in treating serious antisocial behavior in adolescents. Before noting some of these groups and reviews, it is important
to remember that the development of MST has been based on the work of

giants (e.g., Bronfenbrenner, Elliott, Loeber, Thornberry, Haley, Minuchin), that hundreds of talented professionals have contributed and are contributing to its evolution, and that we can learn at least as much from failure (discussed later in the chapter) as success. That said, we remain proud that MST has been viewed favorably by leading researchers and entities charged with evaluating research. These entities include:

- President's New Freedom Commission on Mental Health (2003)
- Office of Juvenile Justice and Delinquency Prevention (2007)
- Center for Substance Abuse Prevention (2001)
- Center for Substance Abuse Treatment (1998)
- U.S. Surgeon General (U.S. Department of Health and Human Services, 1999; U.S. Public Health Service, 2001)
- National Institutes of Health (2006)
- National Institute on Drug Abuse (1999)
- National Alliance on Mental Illness (2003, 2008)
- National Mental Health Association (2004)
- Substance Abuse and Mental Health Administration's National Registry of Evidence-Based Programs and Practices (2007)
- Blueprints for Violence Prevention (Elliott, 1998)
- Institute for Public Policy Research (Margo, 2008)
- Washington State Institute for Public Policy (Aos, Miller, & Drake, 2006)
- Office of Justice Programs (2005)

Leading reviewers include:

- Burns, Hoagwood, and Mrazek (1999)
- Eyberg, Nelson, and Boggs (2008)
- Farrington and Welsh (1999)
- Hoge, Guerra, and Boxer (2008)
- Kazdin and Weisz (1998)
- Stanton and Shadish (1997)
- Waldron and Turner (2008)
- Weithorn (2005)

Findings from MST Clinical Trials

The Early Days: Efficacy Trials

MST was first developed in the context of a clinical research program led by Henggeler within the Psychology Department at Memphis State University (now University of Memphis) in the late 1970s. Findings from this early outcome research with families of inner-city delinquents were published nearly

10 years after the program started (Henggeler et al., 1986), and a second MST clinical trial with maltreating families was published shortly thereafter (Brunk, Henggeler, & Whelan, 1987). Following graduate school at Memphis State University, Borduin moved to the Department of Psychology at the University of Missouri–Columbia, where he developed an ongoing MST research program focusing on serious juvenile offenders. There, Borduin published a seminal randomized trial with serious juvenile offenders (Borduin et al., 1995; Schaeffer & Borduin, 2005) and the first randomized trials with juvenile sexual offenders (Borduin, Henggeler, Blaske, & Stein, 1990; Borduin & Schaeffer, 2001; Borduin, Schaeffer, & Heiblum, in press) conducted in the field. Together, the favorable outcomes (e.g., reduced rearrest and incarceration, improved family functioning; see Table 9.1) achieved in this work set the stage for sponsored research, funded by the National Institutes of Health, other federal entities, foundations, and state and county governments, that has expanded the domain of MST well beyond graduate schools in clinical psychology.

These early MST clinical trials, as is typical in treatment development research, were conducted in ways that maximized the chances that the treatment would show positive effects, if, indeed, it was an effective treatment. Thus, Henggeler and Borduin provided close clinical supervision and oversight to highly motivated graduate students who served as therapists. Moreover, the MST programs were largely sheltered from the many challenges of real-world program implementation by being housed in the research-friendly and financially stable confines of academic university departments. Clinical trials in which the conditions are arranged to optimize the emergence of positive outcomes are known as *efficacy* studies (Weisz, Donenberg, Han, & Weiss, 1995). Although efficacy studies often also restrict participation to clients with less serious and more highly circumscribed clinical problems, MST studies have never had such restrictions in the inclusion of participants. Thus, from the outset, MST has focused on the multiple and interrelated problems that juvenile offenders and their families often present to service providers.

Effectiveness Trials

With clear evidence that MST could be effective in improving family functioning and decreasing the antisocial behavior of delinquents, the next phase of research evaluated outcomes when MST was implemented in real world clinical settings with considerably less direct oversight from expert supervisors than had occurred in the efficacy studies. Two such randomized clinical trials were conducted in South Carolina. Both of these *effectiveness* studies (which more closely replicated real-world clinical conditions) focused on violent and chronic juvenile offenders at imminent risk of incarceration, and were conducted in community mental health centers with public-sector, master's-level practitioners as therapists. With Henggeler serving the role of distal MST consultant, the first study (Henggeler, Melton, & Smith, 1992; Henggeler, Melton, Smith, Schoenwald, & Hanley, 1993) demonstrated substantive long-term reductions in rearrest and incarceration (see Table 9.1). In the second study (Henggeler et al., 1997), ongoing consultant support from Henggeler was withdrawn, and the extent of favorable outcomes decreased considerably. Importantly, this latter study was the first to measure therapist fidelity to the MST protocols, and results showed clear links between high treatment fidelity and better youth outcomes. The fidelity–outcome link has become an important theme in MST research as well as in the broader transport of evidence-based practices to community settings.

Details of all published MST clinical trials (including those with non-offender samples) are provided in Table 9.1 Overall, the results of those trials with serious juvenile offenders show that MST has relatively consistently:

- Reduced short- and long-term (up to 14 years) rates of criminal offending.
- Reduced rates of out-of-home placements.
- Decreased substance use.
- Decreased behavior and mental health problems.
- Improved family functioning.
- Provided cost savings in comparison with usual mental health and juvenile justice services.

Efficacy–Effectiveness Hybrid Trials for Substance Abuse

In light of favorable reductions in substance use achieved in early trials of MST with juvenile offenders (Henggeler et al., 1991), two subsequent trials were subsequently conducted with juvenile offenders meeting diagnostic criteria for substance abuse or dependence. These trials were part efficacy (e.g., conducted under the rubric of the Medical University of South Carolina) and part effectiveness (e.g., using real-world practitioners, minimal or no clinical oversight from Henggeler, minimal participant exclusion criteria). In the first study (see Table 9.1), MST demonstrated favorable short-term (Henggeler, Pickrel, et al., 1999) and long-term (Henggeler, Clingempeel, et al., 2002) reductions in substance use as well as improved school attendance (Brown, Henggeler, Schoenwald, Brondino, & Pickrel, 1999) and cost efficiency (Schoenwald et al., 1996). The second study was conducted in the context of a juvenile drug court (Henggeler, Halliday-Boykins, et al., 2006; Rowland, Chapman, & Henggeler, 2008). Here, the integration of MST into drug court was shown to enhance substance-related outcomes for the youth and their nearest-age sibling. In addition to this research focusing on

(text continues on page 275)

TABLE 9.1. Published MST Outcome Studies

Study	Population	Comparison	Follow-up	MST outcomes
Henggeler et al. (1986) N = 57[a]	Delinquents	Diversion services	Posttreatment	• Improved family relations • Decreased behavior problems • Decreased association with deviant peers
Brunk, Henggeler, & Whelan (1987) N = 33	Maltreating families	Behavioral parent training	Posttreatment	• Improved parent–child interactions
Borduin, Henggeler, Blaske, & Stein (1990) N = 16	Adolescent sexual offenders	Individual counseling	3 years	• Reduced sexual offending • Reduced other criminal offending
Henggeler et al. (1991)[b]	Serious juvenile offenders	• Individual counseling • Usual community services	3 years	• Reduced alcohol and marijuana use • Decreased drug-related arrests
Henggeler, Melton, & Smith (1992) N = 84	Violent and chronic juvenile offenders	Usual community services—high rates of incarceration	59 weeks	• Improved family relations • Improved peer relations • Decreased recidivism (43%) • Decreased out-of-home placement (64%)
Henggeler et al. (1993)	Same sample		2.4 years	• Decreased recidivism (doubled survival rate)
Borduin et al. (1995) N = 176	Violent and chronic juvenile offenders	Individual counseling	4 years	• Improved family relations • Decreased psychiatric symptomatology • Decreased recidivism (69%)
Schaeffer & Borduin (2005)	Same sample		13.7 years	• Decreased rearrests (54%) • Decreased days incarcerated (57%)
Henggeler et al. (1997) N = 155	Violent and chronic juvenile offenders	Juvenile probation services—high rates of incarceration	1.7 years	• Decreased psychiatric symptomatology • Decreased days in out-of-home placement (50%) • Decreased recidivism (26%, nonsignificant) • Treatment adherence linked with long-term outcomes

(continued)

TABLE 9.1. *(continued)*

Study	Population	Comparison	Follow-up	MST outcomes
Henggeler, Rowland, et al. (1999) N = 116 (final sample = 156)	Youth presenting psychiatric emergencies	Psychiatric hospitalization	4 months postrecruitment	• Decreased externalizing problems (CBCL) • Improved family relations • Increased school attendance • Higher consumer satisfaction
Schoenwald, Ward, et al. (2000)	Same sample		4 months postrecruitment	• 75% reduction in days hospitalized • 50% reduction in days in other out-of-home placements
Huey et al. (2004)	Same sample		16 months postrecruitment	• Decreased rates of attempted suicide
Henggeler et al. (2003)	Same sample		16 months postrecruitment	• Favorable 4-month outcomes, noted above, dissipated
Sheidow et al. (2004)	Same sample		16 months postrecruitment	• MST cost benefits at 4 months, but equivalent costs at 16 months
Henggeler, Pickrel, & Brondino (1999) N = 118	Substance-abusing and substance-dependent delinquents	Usual community services	1 year	• Decreased drug use at posttreatment • Decreased days in out-of-home placement (50%) • Decreased recidivism (26%, nonsignificant) • Treatment adherence linked with decreased drug use
Henggeler, Pickrel, Brondino, & Crouch (1996)	Same sample			• 98% rate of treatment completion
Schoenwald et al. (1996)	Same sample		1 year	• Incremental cost of MST nearly offset by between-groups differences in out-of-home placement
Brown et al. (1999)	Same sample		6 months	• Increased attendance in regular school settings
Henggeler, Clingempeel, et al. (2002)	Same sample		4 years	• Decreased violent crime • Increased marijuana abstinence

(continued)

272

TABLE 9.1. *(continued)*

Study	Population	Comparison	Follow-up	MST outcomes
Borduin & Schaeffer (2001)— preliminary report N = 48	Juvenile sexual offenders	Usual community services	9 years	• Decreased behavior problems and symptoms • Improved family relations, peer relations, and academic performance
Borduin, Schaeffer, & Heiblum (in press)—full report				• Decreased caregiver distress • Decreased recidivism for sexual crimes (83%) • Decreased recidivism for other crimes (50%) • Decreased days incarcerated (80%)
Ogden & Halliday-Boykins (2004) N = 100	Norwegian youth with serious antisocial behavior	Usual child welfare services	6 months postrecruitment	• Decreased externalizing and internalizing symptoms • Decreased out-of-home placements • Increased social competence • Increased consumer satisfaction
Ogden & Hagen (2006a)	Same sample		24 months postrecruitment	• Decreased externalizing and internalizing symptoms • Decreased out-of-home placements
Ellis, Frey, et al. (2005a) N = 127	Inner-city adolescents with chronically poorly controlled type 1 diabetes	Standard diabetes care	7 months postrecruitment	• Increased blood glucose testing • Decreased inpatient admissions • Improved metabolic control
Ellis, Naar-King, et al. (2005)	Same sample		7 months postrecruitment	• Decreased medical charges and direct care costs
Ellis, Frey, et al. (2005b)	Same sample		7 months postrecruitment	• Decreased diabetes stress
Ellis et al. (2007)	Same sample		13 months postrecruitment	• Decreased inpatient admissions sustained • Favorable metabolic control outcomes dissipated

(continued)

TABLE 9.1. *(continued)*

Study	Population	Comparison	Follow-up	MST outcomes
Rowland et al. (2005) *N* = 31	Youth with serious emotional disturbance	Hawaii's intensive Continuum of Care	6 months postrecruitment	• Decreased symptoms • Decreased minor crimes • Decreased days in out-of-home placement (68%)
Timmons-Mitchell et al. (2006) *N* = 93	Juvenile offenders (felons) at imminent risk of placement	Usual community services	18-month follow-up	• Improved youth functioning • Decreased substance use problems • Decreased rearrests (37%)
Henggeler, Halliday-Boykins, et al. (2006) *N* = 161	Substance-abusing and substance-dependent juvenile offenders in drug court	Four treatment conditions, including family court with usual services and drug court with usual services	12 months postrecruitment	• MST enhanced substance use outcomes • Drug court was more effective than family court at decreasing self-reported substance use and criminal activity
Rowland et al. (2008) *N* = 70	Nearest-age siblings		18 months postrecruitment	• Evidence-based treatment decreased sibling substance use
Stambaugh et al. (2007)[a] *N* = 267	Youth with serious emotional disturbance at risk for out-of-home placement	Wraparound	18-month follow-up	• Decreased symptoms • Decreased out-of-home placements (54%)
Sundell et al. (2008) *N* = 156	Youth met diagnostic criteria for conduct disorder	Usual child welfare services in Sweden	7 months postrecruitment	• No outcomes favoring either treatment condition • Low treatment fidelity
Letourneau et al. (in press) *N* = 127	Juvenile sexual offenders	Usual sex-offender-specific treatment	12 months postrecruitment	• Decreased sexual behavior problems • Decreased delinquency, substance use, and externalizing symptoms • Reduced out-of-home placements

[a]Quasi-experimental design (groups matched on demographic characteristics); all other studies are randomized.

[b]Based on participants in Henggeler et al. (1992) and Borduin et al. (1995).

substance-abusing juvenile offenders, Schaeffer and Borduin have demonstrated 14-year reductions in substance-related arrests for youth participating in the Borduin et al. (1995) efficacy trial, and Timmons-Mitchell, Bender, Kishna, and Mitchell (2006) showed favorable substance-related outcomes in their independent transportability trial discussed subsequently. Sheidow and Henggeler (2008) provide a more detailed overview of substance-related MST outcome research.

Transportability Trials

During the past decade the emergence of MST Services (*mstservices.com*), which supports the transport of MST to community settings, has enabled several groups of independent investigators to examine the effectiveness of such transport to distal real-world clinical settings. Independent of the first and second generations of MST experts, MST Services has helped communities develop MST programs, train practitioners in the model, and sustain these programs.

Replicating Favorable Outcomes from Efficacy and Effectiveness Studies

As presented in Table 9.1, two independent groups of investigators have recently evaluated the effectiveness of MST with juvenile offenders. In a four-site study conducted in Norway, Ogden and colleagues (Ogden & Hagen, 2006a; Ogden & Halliday-Boykins, 2004) provided the first fully independent replication of the favorable outcomes that MST achieved in the aforementioned efficacy and effectiveness research (e.g., decreased youth symptoms and out-of-home placement, high consumer satisfaction). Similarly, Timmons-Mitchell and colleagues (Timmons-Mitchell et al., 2006) provided the first such replication with serious juvenile offenders in the United States, showing that MST improved youth functioning, decreased recidivism, and decreased substance use problems. Together, these studies clearly demonstrate the transportability of MST and its potential to play a substantive role in reducing criminal offending and youth incarceration on a large scale. If standard MST programs for serious juvenile offenders can achieve outcomes similar to those obtained in these real-world community trials, the public good will be well served.

   In addition to conducting rigorous clinical trials, independent investigators have conducted quasi-experimental and benchmarking studies. Using a quasi-experimental design in a mental health services systems of care site (Stroul & Friedman, 1994), Stambaugh and colleagues (2007) compared the effectiveness of MST versus wraparound, a widely disseminated family-based intervention for youth with serious emotional disturbance whose primary aim is to prevent out-of-home placements. Participants were youth with serious emotional disturbance who were at risk for out-of-home placement. Many were also involved in the juvenile justice system. Results at an 18-month follow-up showed that MST was significantly more effective than wraparound at decreasing youth symptoms; and relative to wraparound, MST decreased out-of-home placements by 54%.

In benchmarking studies, the strength of treatment effects in a community-based implementation of an evidence-based treatment is usually compared with the strength of the effects achieved in previous clinical trials of that treatment. Two MST benchmarking studies have recently been conducted. Ogden, Hagen, and Anderson (2007) found that MST clinical outcomes (i.e., reducing antisocial behavior and out-of-home placement) in the second year of program operation matched or surpassed those achieved during the first year, when the aforementioned Norwegian clinical trial was conducted. Importantly, this study empirically demonstrated program maturation effects (i.e., that MST programs become more effective as they mature), which have long been suspected. Similarly, Curtis and colleagues (Curtis, Ronan, Heiblum, & Crellin, in press) compared pre–post findings from MST programs in New Zealand with results from clinical trials conducted in the United States. The investigators reported extraordinarily high rates of treatment completion (98%), and clinical outcomes were consistent with those achieved across previous MST studies. Such findings provide further support for the viability of MST in both real world and international contexts.

Failures to Replicate

On the other hand, as can occur with individual clinical cases in treatment, transportability trials of MST have not always proven effective. Though not published or submitted for peer review, Leschied and Cunningham (2002) reported on a large four site randomized trial comparing MST with usual services in Ontario, Canada, during the late 1990s, when MST was first being disseminated. Although short-term family- and youth-level outcomes were favorable for MST, the MST programs averaged a 10% reduction in convictions, which is considerably below the findings observed in the published trials of MST. Although the quantity and quality of the adherence data collected at each site are largely unknown, overall adherence was clearly lowest in the site with the worst outcomes, a finding that was essentially replicated in Ogden's multisite trial in Norway and accentuates the importance of treatment fidelity in achieving youth outcomes (see also Chapter 10).

Likewise, a more recent multisite study conducted in Sweden (Sundell et al., 2008) failed to find outcomes favoring the MST condition. Again, treatment fidelity was very low across sites, and there was some, but not entirely consistent, indication that therapist adherence was linked with more favorable youth outcomes (e.g., higher adherence was associated with lower recidivism). Interestingly, with regard to reduced symptomatology, youth in the MST condition in Sweden fared at least as well as counterparts in the successful Norwegian and U.S. trials, suggesting that the failure to attain MST effects might have been due to the relative strength of usual services (i.e., the comparison condition) in Sweden.

Finally, it should be noted that not all reviewers have viewed MST outcomes favorably. Disagreeing with those cited at the beginning of this chapter, Littell and colleagues (Littell, Popa, & Forsythe, 2005) concluded in their meta-analysis that MST was not significantly more effective than alternative services in reducing youth crime and out-of-home placement. This review relied heavily on the unpublished Canadian study in drawing its conclusions and included many methodological anomalies (see critiques by Henggeler, Schoenwald, Borduin, & Swenson, 2006; Ogden & Hagen, 2006b). Moreover, the conclusions of the Littell review have not been replicated in other meta-analyses of MST (Aos et al., 2006; Curtis, Ronan, & Borduin, 2004).

Program Evaluations in Real-World Settings

In addition to the more rigorous published evaluations of MST discussed previously, independent program evaluations have been conducted in attempts to learn more about the parameters of MST effectiveness. These evaluations have generally been conducted in states where widespread transport of MST programs has occurred. Pertinent examples of these evaluations include:

Florida's Redirection Project

In 2004, the Florida legislature funded the Redirection Program to address the growing number of juvenile offenders committed to residential facilities for nonlaw violations of probation. Using MST and functional family therapy, this program has served more than 2,000 youth and families, reduced felony recidivism by 31%, and saved millions of dollars in avoided residential placement (Office of Program Policy Analysis and Government Accountability, 2007).

MST Programs in Pennsylvania

The Prevention Research Center at Pennsylvania State University (Chilenski, Bumbarger, Kyler, & Greenberg, 2007) evaluated outcomes for several MST programs in the state that had served more than 400 youth and families. Across programs, findings showed substantial reductions in substance use, delinquency, academic failure, truancy, and out-of-home placements.

Connecticut's MST Progress Report

Service systems in Connecticut first adopted MST in 1999, and approximately 30 MST teams are operating at the present time. The Connecticut Center for Effective Practices conducted an extensive qualitative and quantitative evaluation of the MST network of programs (Franks, Schroeder, Connell, & Tebes, 2008) and concluded that MST is "working to reduce recidivism and help some of Connecticut's most high-risk children and youth remain in their homes and communities" (p. 23), and that results appear to be sustained over time. Importantly, this evaluation also identified implementation challenges. For example, workforce issues were very difficult to resolve in light of the rapid expansion of MST statewide, and some stakeholders believed that the efficacy of MST might have been oversold.

Adaptations to the Basic MST Model

Several groups of researchers have recognized that interventions for clinical problems other than serious antisocial behavior can be developed using the fundamental components of the MST model (e.g., focus on serious clinical problems with multidetermined causation, intervention design guided by treatment principles, home-based model of service delivery, strong quality assurance system, integration of evidence-based treatment techniques, and view that caregivers are the key to long-term outcomes). Hence, without varying the fundamental components of MST, investigators have adapted the model to meet the needs of youth with other types of serious clinical problems. In some cases (e.g., substance abuse, sexual offending) the adaptations have been relatively circumscribed, while in other cases (e.g., child abuse and neglect, serious emotional disturbance, chronic health conditions) the adaptations have been more extensive.

Adaptation Pilot to Dissemination

The evolution of MST adaptations has followed a general treatment development framework (see Figure 9.1).

1. A pilot study is conducted to specify and determine the feasibility and preliminary effects of the adaptation.
2. If preliminary results are promising, a controlled efficacy trial is conducted to determine whether the adaptation can achieve desired clinical outcomes under relatively favorable intervention conditions.
3. If these results are promising, controlled effectiveness trials are conducted to examine the effectiveness of the adaptation in community practice settings and to identify barriers to success.

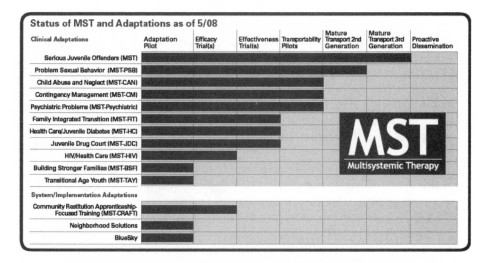

FIGURE 9.1. Status of MST and adaptations. Copyright by MST Institute. Reprinted by permission.

4. Assuming more favorable results, the adaptation is implemented in several community-based MST programs, under close oversight by adaptation developers, to further refine the real-world viability of the adaptation.
5. Then, the adaptation is ready for broader dissemination.

Adaptations Being Transported on at Least a Limited Basis

Figure 9.1 lists the status of MST adaptations as of May 2008. Note that several of these adaptations are currently being disseminated on limited (i.e., transportability pilots) or more extensive bases. Findings from two efficacy trials (Borduin et al., 1990, in press) and one effectiveness trial (Letourneau et al., in press) with juvenile sexual offenders are presented in Table 9.1, and the MST adaptation for juvenile sexual offenders is being actively transported. Results from efficacy and effectiveness trials for the MST adaptation for youth with psychiatric problems are also presented in Table 9.1 (Henggeler, Rowland, et al., 1999; Rowland et al., 2005; Stambaugh et al., 2007). More extensive clinical specification has been published (Henggeler, Schoenwald, et al., 2002), and the MST-Psychiatric adaptation is being further tested in other community practice settings. Also being transported is an adaptation that integrates contingency management into MST for treating adolescent substance abuse (Henggeler, Halliday-Boykins, et al., 2006; see Table 9.1 and Chapter 8) and an adaptation for child abuse and neglect (Swenson et al., 2005).

Adaptations for Chronic Pediatric Health Care Conditions

Perhaps the most extensive adaptations to the basic MST model are being conducted by Ellis, Naar-King, and their colleagues at Wayne State University. They have taken the lead in adapting and evaluating the use of MST for improving the health outcomes of youth with challenging and costly health care problems (MST-Health Care [MST-HC]). MST was selected as the platform for this work because of its capacity to overcome barriers to service access and to address the multidetermined nature of difficulties in following complex medical adherence regimens. In a randomized clinical trial, these investigators evaluated the capacity of MST-HC to improve the health status of adolescents with type 1 diabetes who had chronically poor metabolic control, and significant findings favoring the MST-HC condition emerged for several key outcomes (Ellis, Frey, et al., 2005a, 2005b; Ellis, Naar-King, et al., 2005). In light of these promising outcomes, this research group has also successfully pilot-tested adaptations of the MST model for other challenging health problems such as HIV (Cunningham, Naar-King, Ellis, Pejuan, & Secord, 2006; Ellis, Naar-King, Cunningham, & Secord, 2006), and Letourneau (Family Services Research Center, Medical University of South Carolina) is currently conducting a hybrid efficacy/effectiveness trial for HIV-infected youth.

New Adaptation Pilots

Other adaptations are in their pilot stages. The Building Stronger Families project, for example, integrates the MST adaptation for child maltreatment (Swenson et al., 2005) with reinforcement-based therapy (Gruber, Chutuape, & Stitzer, 2000; Jones et al., 2005), a promising intervention for drug-abusing adults, to reduce child maltreatment and foster care placement that has been driven by caregiver substance abuse. Similarly, the BlueSky Project has integrated MST, functional family therapy, and multidimensional treatment foster care into a continuum of care to serve as an alternative to residential placement for juvenile offenders in New York City. Trupin and colleagues (Trupin, Kerns, Walker, & Lee, in press) at the University of Washington have integrated MST with other evidence-based treatments to address the current and postrelease needs of incarcerated juvenile offenders with co-occurring disorders. As a final example, Davis (University of Massachusetts) and Sheidow (Family Services Research Center, Medical University of South Carolina) are currently conducting a pilot that adapts MST to serve transition age youth (i.e., 18–22 years of age) with mental health and behavioral needs.

Conclusion

From the beginning, the development, validation, and refinement of MST has been based on rigorous scientific research. Through the early development of treatment protocols, efficacy studies, effectiveness research, and transportability trials, much has been learned about the clinical emphases and structures that facilitate therapists' work with youth and families. Moreover, creative investigators have adapted the fundamental MST model to fit the needs of youth with other types of serious clinical problems, and tested these adaptations—often with excellent results. Importantly, with new research—successes and failures—we continue to learn lessons that inform MST practices in the field. In particular, as described in the final chapter, in the attempt to understand the conditions that best support the effective implementation of MST in community settings, MST investigators are making substantive contributions to the emerging field of implementation science (Fixsen, Naoom, Blasé, Friedman, & Wallace, 2005).

CHAPTER 10

Quality Assurance
and Improvement
Fundamental to MST Programs Worldwide

> **IN THIS CHAPTER**
>
> ■ The MST quality assurance
> and improvement system (MST QA/QI system).
> ■ MST program development and support.
> ■ Research supporting QA/QI linkages
> with youth outcomes.
> ■ Beyond early adopters: A network approach
> to QA/QI replication.

The promise of MST for juvenile offenders—reducing criminal activity and substance use; preventing out-of-home placement; improving family, peer, and school functioning; and cost savings—has attracted service systems, payers, practitioners, and families in 32 states and nine nations to establish MST programs. Delivering on that promise, one family at a time, no matter how new or how seasoned the MST therapist or program, is the function of the quality assurance and improvement system. This chapter describes the quality assurance and improvement system designed to support the implementation of MST at multiple levels of the practice context—therapist, clinical supervisor, expert consultant, program management, and service provider organization hosting the program. The system was designed to replicate, for therapists working in diverse community contexts, the specialized clinical training, supervision, and expert consultation provided to therapists in the successful randomized trials with juvenile offenders and their families discussed in Chapter 9. *Optimizing youth outcomes is the unswerving focus of this system.*

The MST quality assurance/quality improvement (QA/QI) system is illustrated in Figure 10.1. Core components are:

- Manuals for therapists, supervisors, consultants, and organizations.
- Training and quarterly booster training for therapists and supervisors.
- On-site clinical supervision for therapists.
- Expert consultation for therapists and supervisors.
- Program development and support for the organization operating the MST program.
- Validated measures of implementation adherence for therapists, supervisors, and consultants.
- A Web-based implementation tracking and feedback system provided through the MST Institute (*www.mstinstitute.org*).

As illustrated in Figure 10.1, these are not stand-alone components, but instead are integrated into a feedback loop. Consistent with a continuous quality improvement philosophy, the system engages all individuals involved in the MST program to continually enhance "the processes associated with providing a good or service that meets or exceeds customer expectations"

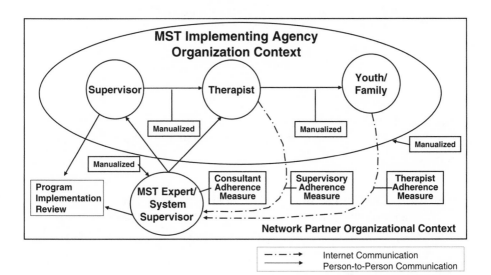

FIGURE 10.1. The MST QA/QI system. Adapted from Henggeler, Schoenwald, Rowland, and Cunningham (2002). Copyright 2002 by The Guilford Press. Adapted by permission.

(Shortell, Bennett, & Byck, 1998, p. 594). The feedback loop integrates data and qualitative feedback about MST implementation at the level of the family, therapist, supervisor, expert consultant, and organization operating the MST program. The QA/QI system aims to increase the odds that problems with implementation fidelity and youth outcomes will be detected and addressed at all levels of the clinical context on an ongoing basis.

Across the entire QA/QI system, the hypothesis-testing process articulated in the do-loop (see Chapter 2) is used to identify factors and interaction patterns that support or compromise the implementation of MST to achieve positive youth outcomes. So, for example, if an MST program was receiving inappropriate referrals (e.g., youth referred primarily for abuse or neglect), such referrals would be conceptualized as a problem subject to the MST analytic process. Evidence regarding possible drivers of that problem would be considered. Sometimes, a single, powerful driver is at issue, as occurs when a judge orders all youth in court to an MST program, instead of juvenile offenders meeting eligibility criteria. Other times, a combination of organizational and service system factors contributes to the problem. A provider organization contracted by juvenile justice to provide MST to juvenile offenders and by child welfare to provide family preservation services to families with abused children might have a wait-list for the family preservation program, but not for the MST program and thus the organization might be referring overflow abuse cases to MST.

The next section of this chapter describes each of the major MST QA/QI components, and concluding sections present empirical support for the QA/QI system and strategies to support large-scale adoption and implementation of MST.

Components of the MST QA/QI System

The three broad components of the QA/QI system are training, organizational support, and implementation measurement and reporting.

Training

Professionals are trained in the MST model through four venues: an initial 5-day orientation training, quarterly 1.5-day booster training sessions on site, weekly clinical supervision on site, and weekly expert consultation.

Initial 5-Day Orientation Training

MST therapists, on-site supervisors, and other clinicians within the provider organization who are likely to participate in some aspect of treatment for youth in the program (e.g., a staff psychiatrist who might evaluate and prescribe medication for an adolescent or caregiver) participate in 5 days of initial orientation training. The first morning of the orientation week is designed to bring together the MST team, the management and leadership of the organization operating the MST program, and key community stakeholders (e.g., representatives of referral and funding agencies, probation officers, judges) to launch the new MST program. Several of these stakeholders likely played roles in bringing the MST program to the community (MST program development is discussed later in the chapter).

The remainder of the orientation week focuses on the therapists and MST supervisor. The trainers, one of whom is the expert consultant who will be providing ongoing training and consultation to the team, use (1) didactic approaches to lay out the rationale for MST assessment and intervention strategies and (2) experiential approaches to enable participants to observe and practice using such strategies in role-play situations. The sequencing of topics covered during this week largely mirrors the organization of this book. Therapists are asked to read the treatment manual prior to training so that less time is spent explaining terms (e.g., structural or strategic family therapy, cognitive-behavioral therapy) and more time can be devoted to helping therapists conceptualize cases and role-play interventions from an MST perspective.

Quarterly Booster Training

As therapists gain field experience with MST, the expert consultant working with the team conducts quarterly 1.5-day booster training sessions on site. The booster sessions are designed to enhance the knowledge and skills of the team so they can more effectively address clinical challenges they are facing (e.g., marital interventions, treatment of caregiver depression). The consultant and team use audio or video review and enactment (via role play) of particularly difficult cases to identify and problem solve barriers to progress and practice implementing needed intervention strategies. Materials for conducting booster sessions are catalogued in a booster library available to MST consultants, and each booster is tailored to the specific strengths and needs of the team. Therapists evaluate each booster, and consultants use this feedback to improve future booster experiences. Between booster sessions, the consultant and clinical supervisor observe therapist implementation of the skills and strategies emphasized during the booster, and identify and address barriers to such implementation (e.g., booster provided insufficient practice opportunities, follow-up on use of strategies did not occur in supervision).

Supervision

The main objective of MST supervision is to help therapists learn and use the clinical skills—conceptual and behavioral—needed to effectively implement MST with each and every youth and family served. The clinical role of the supervisor is described in Chapter 2. The present chapter focuses on the specifications for supervision and the training of the supervisor.

SUPERVISION MANUAL

The MST supervisory manual (Henggeler & Schoenwald, 1998) is structured to orient supervisors to processes that are important to the success of MST supervision, therapist adherence, and child and family outcomes. The first section of the manual describes the structure and process of MST supervision and its rationale. Briefly, supervision occurs in a small group format to optimize opportunities for learning and team collaboration. Practitioner and supervisor preparation before, during, and following supervision are viewed as crucial to the efficient functioning of supervision. Likewise, the length, frequency, and structure of supervision aim to make efficient use of professional time. The second section focuses on understanding the fit of identified problems within the family's systemic context and developing overarching goals for each youth and family. The third section concentrates on the development of intermediary goals (i.e., goals that represent steps toward achieving the overarching goals) and the specification of interventions based on the MST treatment principles to meet these goals. In addition, considerable attention is devoted to helping clinicians identify and overcome barriers to intervention success. The final section of the manual addresses the developmental objectives of supervision, specifically, the strategies that supervisors can use to detect and advance the clinical skills of MST therapists and teams. Each calendar quarter, the supervisor and each therapist on the team together craft an individualized clinician development plan that reflects the strengths and needs of the therapist with respect to the array of skills and competencies required to effectively implement MST and achieve positive youth outcomes. Strategies to further develop skills and competencies are devised and implemented (e.g., supervisor review of audio- or videotaped sessions with families). In addition, the manual includes sections aimed at resolving difficulties that arise during supervision and barriers that arise in the treatment of families. Thus, overall, the MST supervisory process is highly goal oriented and problem focused, with the clear mission of facilitating the attainment of desired youth and family outcomes.

SUPERVISOR TRAINING AND SUPPORT

The training and support of the on-site clinical supervisor involves several strategies. Specifically, the MST expert consultant:

- Provides the initial supervisor orientation training prior to or during the initial 5-day training.
- Reviews the supervisor's notes on the case summaries discussed during supervision and consultation weekly.

- Reviews and debriefs at least one audiotape of group supervision with the supervisor monthly.
- Collaborates with the supervisor in the creation of an individualized supervisor development plan and reviews that plan quarterly.
- Reviews the individualized clinician development plans created conjointly by the supervisor and therapists.
- Is available for individual consultation when the supervisor seeks assistance with supervision-related, case-specific, therapist-related, organizational, or external stakeholder issues affecting the performance of the MST team and youth outcomes.

In addition, booster sessions for MST supervisors are available and tailored to the opportunities and challenges awaiting supervisors with different levels of MST experience. For organizations operating large MST programs (i.e., multiple teams and supervisors), the consultant conducts the supervisor booster training on site. For organizations with few supervisors, supervisor boosters are provided at a central location, so that supervisors with similar levels of experience from different programs can come together for the booster.

Consultation

The MST expert consultant teaches clinicians and supervisors how to implement MST effectively and how to identify and address clinical, team-level, organizational, and systemic barriers to achieving positive outcomes for adolescents and families. Consultants are expected to be highly knowledgeable regarding the theoretical and empirical underpinnings of MST and about the evidence base on child and adolescent mental health treatments and services. Consultants are also expected to be effective trainers and coaches of individuals who are already practicing mental health professionals when they join an MST program. Thus, and in contrast with the clinical training tasks faced by instructors in most university-based graduate programs, MST consultants have the responsibility of augmenting and changing the existing clinical practices of experienced professionals. To succeed in this endeavor, the consultant has to cultivate sufficient engagement with the clinical team to be a credible and valued source of knowledge, skill, and clinical recommendations.

CONSULTATION MANUAL

The consultation manual (Schoenwald, 1998) specifies the knowledge base and skills individuals must master to effectively consult with the MST program. Whereas the provider organization's MST supervisor and therapists are responsible for day-to-day decision making regarding case particulars, the MST consultant is responsible for contributing to the rapid development of the clinicians' ability to bring MST-like thinking and interventions to the cases and to sustain that ability over time. Throughout the initial and booster training sessions, and during weekly telephone consultation, the consultant identifies and reinforces the knowledge, skills, strategies, and therapist and supervisor strengths that support the implementation of MST. The manual describes common barriers to treatment, supervision, and consultation success as well as strategies for overcoming these barriers. Thus, the consultant is responsible for helping to generate training and ongoing support strategies at each of these clinical levels.

PROCEDURES AND MATERIALS

The consultant devotes 1 hour of phone time per week to consultation for each team of three to four clinicians and their clinical supervisor. At least 24 hours prior to the consultation, teams fax or e-mail case summaries (described in Chapter 2) for each case to the consultant. When the case summaries and telephone discussion indicate barriers to treatment progress, the consultant recommends on the telephone specific strategies to overcome the barriers and checks to ensure therapists and supervisors understand and can follow the recommendations. When obstacles are related to organizational, service system, fiscal, or policy and political issues, the consultant collaborates with the supervisor to determine who should be involved in problem-solving discussions (e.g., clinical supervisor, administrator, leadership of provider organization, state official contracting with provider), who should signal the need for discussion (e.g., consultant, supervisor, program director, provider organization director), and what forum is best for initial discussions (e.g., individual phone call, conference call, on-site meeting during the next booster session).

CONSULTANT TRAINING AND SUPPORT

In the early years of MST transport, doctoral-level psychology professionals, most of whom had not previously served as MST therapists or supervisors, were trained by the authors of this book to provide, from South Carolina, ongoing training and consultation to MST teams in geographically dispersed communities. Today, many MST experts are individuals living in those communities who themselves were successful MST supervisors, as described in the final section of this chapter. The initial training process for expert consultants has been codified in on-the-job training manuals, and the rate at which individuals complete that process varies as a function of (1) prior experience and proficiency with MST, (2) demonstrated convergence with established performance standards across different training elements (e.g., 5-day orientation, telephone consultation, booster trainings, supervisor training, use of QA/QI system), and of course, (3) individual strengths and needs. In general, it takes about 9 months before a new consultant can serve a full complement of teams. A full-time consultant can provide effective telephone consultation and accommodate the travel associated with initial orientation and booster training sessions for about 10 teams at a time. As a consultant affects 30 to 40 therapists treating 360 to 480 families at a time, the ripple effect of consultant competency can be considerable!

To increase the likelihood that consultants will become and remain effective, ongoing training, support, and monitoring are provided. Consultants receive their initial training from an MST coach—a seasoned consultant with a track record of successful consultation across programs and time who is trained in the coaching process. Ongoing support and monitoring of consultation quality occurs through (1) a weekly meeting with the coach (by telephone or in person, depending upon location of consultant and coach); (2) digital recording of all consultations, a random selection of which undergoes independent review and feedback; (3) establishment and quarterly review of a consultant development plan; (4) booster sessions that bring together groups of expert consultants at least twice annually; and (5) individual or group peer supervision on specific topics as requested by the consultants.

Organizational Support for MST Programs

Organizations operating MST programs typically have many years of experience providing mental health services for children in their communities. Most of these organizations operate multiple intervention programs for children and adults, and some operate intervention programs in several cities, regions, and states. Within the United States, most of the organizations operating MST programs are private, but contracted by public agencies (e.g., juvenile justice, child welfare, mental health) to serve particular youth populations. Several strategies are used to support the implementation and outcomes of MST programs in these busy and diversified organizations, including an organizational manual for administrators; a pre-implementation program development process; and ongoing organizational support. Before we describe these strategies, the cogent reasons for emphasizing the importance of strong organizational support are explained.

Rationale for Providing Strong Organizational Support

Why, one might ask, do we devote considerable attention to the organizations operating, or that want to operate, an MST program? The answer comes in part from our experience collaborating with organizations and funding entities in the transport and implementation of MST over the past decade, and in part from research on the importance of organizations to the success and failure of new technologies. As an example from our experience, in locales with unionized clinicians, some organizations sought to provide 24-hour/7-day-per-week coverage for MST families by using an organization-wide on-call system that rotated coverage across all clinicians in the organization, rather than among MST therapists and supervisors. Such a practice decreases family access to MST and compromises the fidelity of the program. At the service system level, factors that can affect implementation of MST include: (1) legal mandates and the policies and regulations associated with them, (2) funding levels and mechanisms, and (3) the effectiveness of collaboration among the stakeholders that influence who can receive and deliver an intervention program and how it is delivered (Edwards, Schoenwald, Henggeler, & Strother, 2001). For example, reimbursement based on a predetermined quantity of services (i.e., number of sessions) or face-to-face contacts with the youth are inconsistent with MST implementation, which focuses on building the capacity of caregivers and others to addresses risk factors in the youth's social ecology. Thus, organizational-level factors such as these must be addressed proactively to support the fidelity of MST programs.

Likewise, research reveals that, across numerous industries, individuals and organizations often decide to adopt a new program and frequently fail to implement it successfully (Real & Poole, 2005). Of course, organizations vary with respect to their interest in adopting new technologies, whether evidence-based treatments or anything else. But, even in organizations open to change and eager to innovate, specific policies and procedures are needed to support the adequate implementation of new technologies (Klein & Knight, 2005). Indeed, leading advocates of evidence-based violence prevention programs for youth have noted that a common shortcoming in the effective transport of these programs to community settings has been a lack of attention to program implementation procedures (Dane & Schneider, 1998; Fixsen et al., 2005; Mihalic, 2004). The following organizational-level structures and procedures have been developed to address this shortcoming.

Organizational Manual

The MST organizational manual (Strother, Swenson, & Schoenwald, 1998) is a resource for administrators of organizations establishing MST programs. Most of the program practices specified in the manual (e.g., treatment duration, 24-hour/7-day availability of therapists, low caseloads, group supervision, and availability of expert consultation) are based on procedures used in randomized trials of MST. Other policies and practices emerged in response to the types of organizational and service system circumstances described in the previous section. Thus, the organizational manual provides an introduction to the theory and practice of MST and describes specific domains of MST program administration, such as quality control and evaluation, program financing, staff recruitment and retention, and youth referral and discharge criteria. Policies and procedures that support the clinical implementation of MST are also described. These include, for example, (1) negotiation of interagency agreements that allow the MST team to "take the clinical lead"; (2) establishment of an MST-specific on-call system; and (3) availability of technological and practical resources such as cellular phones for therapists and insurance for therapist or agency vehicles used in the line of service provision (e.g., home visits or transporting clients as needed for intervention purposes, such as to school meetings). Appendices, provided to facilitate development of an MST program, include cost-estimating forms, job descriptions, and recommendations for forming a community advisory board.

Program Development

MST program development is a process that begins with a community's initial expression of interest in MST and continues through the day that a new MST program first treats a youth and family. The process typically unfolds in seven stages. As much as a year, and sometimes longer, can be required to complete the program development process. Further information about the activities that typically occur during these stages and how to access materials used to facilitate those activities is available through the MST Services website at *www.mstservices.com*.

1. *Initial information collection.* This step occurs when someone representing an agency that funds services (e.g., juvenile justice, mental health, a behavioral health care system) contacts a purveyor of the MST QA/QI system, either MST Services or a Network Partner (the nature of Network Partners is described in the final section of this chapter), to express interest in starting an MST program. Discussing a few key questions (e.g., intended target population) typically helps the interested party either eliminate MST from further consideration or take the next step, which is assessing the feasibility of an MST program in a particular locale.

2. *MST needs assessment.* To help communities determine whether the needs that prompted stakeholder interest in starting an MST program are likely to be met by MST, and whether an MST program is viable in a specific practice context, the MST purveyor works together with key stakeholders to (1) identify the community need for MST (e.g., clearly defining the target population, defining geographic coverage area, and determining number of potential referrals in that area by referral source); (2) develop a financial plan and assess sufficiency of funding to sustain the program through start-up and as fully operational; (3) cultivate the commitment of pertinent agencies (i.e., service provider organization and the agencies providing referral and funding) to implementing MST with fidelity, using the quality assur-

ance and improvement protocols associated with the model; and (4) cultivate commitment from key community stakeholders.

After these first two steps have been successfully navigated, the organizations and MST purveyor together make a "Go" or "No Go" decision. "Go"
does not mean an MST program will definitely be established—rather, it
means that interested agencies and the MST purveyor will go through the
next steps of the process of program development to verify viability.

3. *MST critical issues sessions.* If a "Go" decision has been made, then
the MST purveyor and organizations planning to fund and implement MST
specify how critical program components will be developed. Nearly a dozen
issues (e.g., inclusion/exclusion criteria, discharge criteria, outcomes measurement) are discussed, and an individualized MST Goals and Guidelines
document is developed that lays out how these issues will be addressed in a
particular MST program serving a particular community.

4. *Site readiness review meeting.* Once funding sources and mechanisms and a service provider organization are solidified, a larger group that
includes individuals who will be responsible for the day-to-day operations
of the funding and service organizations, and of other entities that can affect
how and when youth and families can receive MST, join the conversation.
Middle management and front-line staff of such entities (e.g., departments
of probation, public defenders, officers of the court) are often more familiar
than directors with day-to-day procedures that can affect who is served by
MST and how. Thus, this larger group must review the final implementation plan and consider any adjustments that might be needed. Sometimes,
this meeting reveals differences of policy or opinion between two or more
agencies, or between agencies and the MST purveyor, that must be resolved
before moving forward. For example, the chief of probation might require
probation officers to sign off on all treatment plans for youth on probation,
when neither the provider organization nor the MST purveyor know of that
requirement and both would be concerned about its impact on the substance
and confidentiality of treatment.

5. *Follow-up.* Subsequent conference calls and face-to-face meetings,
as needed, are dedicated to working through the alignment of potentially
conflicting policies and procedures arising from the site readiness review
meeting that could affect MST implementation.

6. *Staff recruitment and orientation training.* The process of recruiting
and hiring MST therapists and clinical supervisors often begins before the
site readiness review meeting and continues until all members of the new
team are hired. Consultation from the MST purveyor is provided regarding
advertising, recruitment, and hiring of MST clinicians, given the workforce
and job market in the particular locale.

7. *Ongoing program implementation support.* The 5-day initial orientation training described previously is the last step before the MST program

opens its doors to youth and families. The week following this orientation marks the beginning of an ongoing program implementation process in which the QA/QI procedures (e.g., booster training, on-site supervision, expert consultation, use of fidelity measures) continue as long as youth and families are served by the MST program.

Ongoing Organizational Support

Several mechanisms are used to provide ongoing support to the organizations hosting MST programs.

PROGRAM IMPLEMENTATION REVIEW

This semiannual review is designed to enable the service provider organization implementing MST, the MST purveyor, and key stakeholders (referral and funding sources) to examine together (1) the extent to which the program goals regarding the target population, referral process, fidelity of MST implementation, and youth outcomes are being met; (2) barriers to meeting expectations in a particular domain (e.g., inadequate number of referrals, lower than expected therapist adherence); and (3) specific intervention strategies to overcome those barriers before the next semiannual review takes place. The domains assessed in this review are based on the checklist used to guide the development of the Goals and Guidelines document for the MST program.

ONGOING PROBLEM SOLVING OF ORGANIZATIONAL AND STAKEHOLDER BARRIERS TO IMPLEMENTATION

As noted in the section on consultation, when barriers to treatment progress in a particular case relate to attributes of the provider organization or service system, MST consultants work with the therapists, on-site supervisor, and other pertinent personnel in the organization (e.g., division directors, program managers, organization directors) to address those barriers. For example, a consultant might notice from the case summaries that, over a period of 2 weeks, all therapists on a team saw families three times per week, rather than at the varying rates expected due to diverse clinical need. Upon further inquiry, the consultant might then learn that the organization has placed a limit on therapist visits because the payer has limited payment for them. Such limitations are incompatible with MST and would be addressed by the consultant.

SUPPORT FOR PROGRAM DIRECTORS

In organizations operating a small number of teams, the on-site clinical supervisor of the team is the primary representative of the MST program in the provider organization and for community stakeholders. The supervisors are supported in that role primarily by the MST consultant. In organizations operating several MST teams, however, it is recommended that a program director position be established to (1) facilitate consistency of MST implementation by teams across the organization, (2) advocate collectively for MST teams within the organization and with external stakeholders, and (3) keep an eye on the sustainability of the program given the ever-changing financial and political contingencies affecting services for youth in the program. Typically, program directors are recruited from a pool of successful MST supervisors and are intimately familiar with the day-to-day clinical operations of MST. MST Services provides orientation materials and training for program directors and hosts a monthly voluntary peer networking conference call in which directors from different organizations can learn from one another about opportunities and challenges they face.

Implementation Measurement and Reporting

A Web-based platform to support the reporting, scoring, and interpretation of therapist adherence, supervisor adherence, and youth outcomes is available via the MST Institute (*www.mstinstitute.org*), with the consultant adherence measure slated to go online in 2009. The therapist adherence measure has been validated in randomized trials of MST and in the community-based implementation of MST as evaluated through the 45-site MST Transportability Study. The supervisor and consultant adherence measures were not used in randomized trials (in which there was only one clinical supervisor, and the consultant was an MST developer), but were developed and validated in community-based studies.

Therapist Adherence Measure

The 26-item, Likert-format Therapist Adherence Measure (TAM; Henggeler & Borduin, 1992) was developed by expert consensus to assess therapist adherence to the nine principles of MST. The TAM was shown in two randomized clinical trials of MST with juvenile offenders (Henggeler et al., 1997; Henggeler, Pickrel, et al., 1999) to predict long-term reductions in youth arrests, days incarcerated, substance use, aggression, and other antisocial behavior problems as well as improvements in family functioning (Huey et al., 2000; Schoenwald, Henggeler, Brondino, & Rowland, 2000). Although caregiver, therapist, and youth reports on the measure were obtained in these trials, caregiver reports were the best predictors of youth outcomes (Schoenwald, Henggeler, et al., 2000). Data from a large and diverse sample of caregivers and therapists in the MST Transportability Study allowed further examination of the psychometric properties of the original TAM and inclusion of 12 new items that indexed whether treatment sessions focused on important aspects of the youth's school, peer, and neighborhood/social support systems. Nine of these items were retained in further psychometric analyses of the TAM, resulting in a 28-item scale (19 original TAM items plus 9 new items) known as the TAM—Revised (TAM-R; Henggeler, Borduin, Schoenwald, Huey, & Chapman, 2006). The TAM-R provides a single summary score that taps overall adherence to the MST model.

Supervisor Adherence Measure

The 43-item, Likert-format Supervisor Adherence Measure (SAM; Schoenwald, Henggeler, & Edwards, 1998) was developed by expert consensus and is based on the rational constructs of supervision described in the MST Supervisory Manual (Henggeler & Schoenwald, 1998). Therapists rate their MST supervisor on the SAM at 2-month intervals. The initial SAM validation study (Henggeler, Schoenwald, Liao, Letourneau, & Edwards, 2002) revealed three SAM subscales, and scores on some of these scales correlated with TAM scores, although sometimes in unexpected directions. The much larger sample of families, therapists, and supervisors in the MST Transportability Study allowed further exploration of the psychometric properties of the SAM. Thirty-seven of the original 43 items of the SAM were retained, and these comprised four subscales (Schoenwald, Chapman, & Sheidow, 2006; Schoenwald, Sheidow, & Chapman, in press):

- Supervisor adheres to the structure and process of supervision.
- Supervisor promotes adherence to the MST treatment principles.
- Supervisor promotes use of the MST analytic process.
- Supervisor promotes clinician development of the competencies needed to implement MST.

Consultant Adherence Measure

The 44-item, Likert-format Consultant Adherence Measure (CAM; Schoenwald, 2001) was developed by expert consensus and is based on the rational constructs of consultation described in the MST consultation manual (Schoenwald, 1998). Therapists and supervisors rate their MST expert consultant on the CAM at 2-month intervals. Analyses of consultants across two study samples yielded a three-factor structure (Schoenwald, Sheidow, & Letourneau, 2004):

- Consultant competence (i.e., knowledge and skill in MST and in teaching MST)
- MST procedures (i.e., focus on MST assessment and intervention procedures)
- Alliance (i.e., attentiveness to and support of therapists)

Youth Outcome Measurement

The ultimate outcomes typically sought by communities establishing MST programs for juvenile offenders include reductions in rearrest, out-of-home placements, and costs as well as improved individual, family, and school functioning. The specific outcomes for which an MST program is held accountable are detailed in the MST Goals and Guidelines document described earlier. Therapist-reported information on these domains is reported via the MST Institute website after the youth is discharged from treatment.

Many programs, however, have difficulty obtaining data on posttreatment outcomes such as rearrests. Barriers to data collection include insufficient resources (e.g., staff time), inadequate understanding of data collection procedures, novelty of collecting posttreatment outcome data for any treatment program in the community, and a reduced sense of need or urgency to obtain hard data about outcomes based on a general level of satisfaction with the MST program. To address these barriers, the cost of administrative staff time required to obtain outcome data is now estimated for new providers and built into the quality assurance package provided by the MST purveyor. In addition, the site assessment process is being revised to encourage participants to describe the specifics of record keeping at relevant agencies, resolve issues of confidentiality that arise when data are requested, and establish acceptable methods and timing of data collection. Implementation of these outcome measurement procedures should further enhance the effectiveness of the MST QA/QI system.

Empirical Support for the MST QA/QI System

The overriding usefulness of a QA/QI system is determined by its capacity to enhance outcomes. Research examining the linkages among the components of the MST quality assurance system and pertinent outcomes demonstrates substantive progress toward this aim.

Links between Therapist Adherence and Youth Outcomes

As noted in the description of the TAM, the outcomes of MST have been shown in randomized trials to vary with therapist adherence, with higher adherence predicting better long-term criminal and out-of-home placement outcomes and improvements in youth behavior and family functioning. Importantly, the MST Transportability Study replicated this linkage in community-based implementation. Specifically, caregiver ratings on the TAM predicted reductions in youth behavior problems at the end of treatment and through a 1-year posttreatment follow-up (Schoenwald, Sheidow, Letourneau, & Liao, 2003; Schoenwald, Carter, Chapman, & Sheidow, 2008). Moreover, the link between adherence and youth outcomes has extended to criminal outcomes over the long term. For example, at the highest level of therapist adherence, the average annual rate of youth criminal charges at 4 years following treatment completion was 47% lower than that for the lowest level of adherence (Schoenwald, Chapman, Sheidow, & Carter, in press).

Supervisor Adherence, Therapist Adherence, and Youth Outcomes

Analyses of SAM and TAM data from the Transportability Study indicate that supervisor adherence predicted therapist adherence, reductions in youth behavior problems through 1 year following treatment (Schoenwald et al., 2006; Schoenwald, Sheidow et al., in press), and long-term criminal charges (Schoenwald et al., 2006). These findings support the proposition that adherence to the MST supervision protocol directly affects therapist fidelity and youth behavioral and criminal outcomes of MST in community settings.

Consultant Adherence, Therapist Adherence, and Youth Outcomes

The effects of consultant adherence on therapist adherence and youth outcomes was assessed in two samples of therapists, consultants, and families, one of which was drawn from the Transportability Study (Schoenwald et al., 2004). Across both samples, the consultant competence and alliance scales of the CAM predicted therapist MST adherence. As expected, the direction of the relationship was positive for the consultant competence scale. Alliance, however, was negatively related to therapist adherence especially when consultant competence was low. In other words, consultants with strong alliances with therapists, but low competence, had adverse effects on the therapists' adherence. With respect to youth outcomes, higher ratings on the CAM MST procedures scale was associated with improvements in youth behavior problems posttreatment, and higher ratings on the consultant competence scale predicted improved youth functioning. Consistent with the finding that high alliance predicted lower therapist adherence when the consultant competence was low, youth behavior problems also deteriorated when alliance was high in the presence of low consultant competence. Thus, although a supportive alliance between consultant and therapist might help keep therapists engaged in consultation, consultant competence and a focus on MST procedures are needed to improve youth outcomes.

Therapist and Client Predictors of Adherence and Youth Outcomes

Among the variables that could differentiate treatment as provided in research studies and community-based practice settings are the individuals providing treatment (e.g., therapists in research studies are often more highly trained). Thus, examination of therapist variables that might affect adherence and outcomes in usual care settings has been of interest in MST transport and evaluation efforts. So far, therapist professional training and experience, endorsement of the MST model, perceived difficulty and rewards of doing MST, and perceived similarity of MST to treatments the therapist used in the past have not been associated with therapist adherence ratings (Schoenwald et al., 2005). But, when therapists perceived the flexible hours required to implement MST as a problem, adherence ratings suffered. The good news in these findings is that the training, clinical supervision, expert consultation, and feedback system used to support therapist implementation of MST are likely sufficient to enable clinicians from diverse professional backgrounds to implement this complex and individualized treatment in usual care settings. The findings also demonstrate, however, that adherence can be negatively affected by concrete, practical aspects of the implementation of MST, such as the 24-hour-per-day, 7-day-per-week availability of therapists to client families. Easing the burden of such practicalities, consequently, should be addressed in supervision and consultation as needed.

In addition, although neither therapist nor caregiver demographics nor severity of youth problems affected adherence, ethnic and gender similarity in therapist–caregiver dyads did predict higher caregiver adherence ratings and greater reductions in youth behavior problems 6 months posttreatment (Halliday-Boykins, Schoenwald, & Letourneau, 2005). The relationship between caregiver–therapist similarity and outcomes did not hold, however, in predicting youth criminal behavior (Schoenwald & Chapman, 2008a). Given the mixed findings with respect to the impact of therapist–caregiver similarity on outcomes, the shortage of qualified professionals of all ethnic groups in the mental health workforce, and the fact that matching professionals and consumers on the basis of ethnicity is reminiscent of segregation, further research is needed on which aspects of treatment are affected by ethnic and gender matching in ways that affect youth outcomes.

Organizational Factors, Therapist Adherence, and Youth Outcomes

Organizations can affect the implementation and outcomes of new technologies. Staff turnover in organizations has been a challenge as MST goes to scale and is a problem in the mental health workforce in general. Although lower than national averages, the annualized therapist turnover rate in MST programs participating in the Transportability Study was 21% (Sheidow, Schoenwald, Wagner, Allred, & Burns, 2006). Turnover was predicted by a combination of low salaries and organizational climates characterized by emotional exhaustion. Importantly, turnover predicted less youth behavioral improvement 1 year after treatment and greater rates of criminal activity up to 2.4 years posttreatment (Schoenwald & Chapman, 2008b). The mechanisms by which turnover affects youth outcomes in MST are not yet known, but researchers plan to study this topic. Meanwhile, the existing findings support the proposition that provider organizations and service systems paying for MST would do well to establish salaries that adequately compensate therapists and supervisors for the intensive effort and irregular work schedule needed to implement MST effectively. The MST team, organization hosting the MST program, and expert consultant should also monitor the extent of emotional exhaustion in the workplace climate and address factors sustaining that difficulty.

In contrast, other key aspects of organizations (e.g., climate, structure) examined in the MST Transportability Study appear to have limited effects on child outcomes relative to therapist adherence (Schoenwald et al., 2003; Schoenwald, Carter, et al., 2008; Schoenwald, Chapman, et al., in press). Different types of organizational characteristics than those assessed in this study (e.g., culture, leadership, resources, readiness to change), however, might affect the implementation and outcomes of MST and other evidence-based treatments, and research is now examining these issues (see, e.g., Glisson et al., 2008; Henggeler et al., 2007; Henggeler, Chapman, et al., 2008; Palinkas et al., 2008). Alternatively, perhaps the breadth, intensity, and foci of the QA/QI system have enabled MST programs to overcome organization-related barriers to program effectiveness. At any rate, the findings presented in this section provide relatively strong and consistent support for the value and usefulness of the MST QA/QI system.

Network Partners: Going to Scale with QA/QI

Currently, the QA/QI system as implemented by MST Services and its 15 Network Partners (four of them international) reaches approximately 17,300 youth in 32 states and nine countries annually, with two additional countries slated to start up programs by the end of 2008. Network Partners were first established around 2000 to accommodate several needs articulated by providers and funders. Provider organizations were often asked by service systems to expand their MST capacity, and these organizations were eager to cultivate internally the expertise needed to train therapists and supervisors in MST and to pursue the development of MST programs in other locales in their area. Similarly government agencies supporting MST programs often wished to expand the number of programs within a state, region, or country. To meet continued demand for program development, MST Network Partners were established in organizations and sites that had strong track records in developing and implementing MST programs. The organizations that serve as Network Partners have developed the capacity to carry out the entire MST transport and implementation process described previously, from pre-implementation site assessment through training and ongoing consultation. Empirical examination of the effectiveness of this strategy for developing indigenous expertise in MST and its transport is a priority of our research.

At the same time, to capitalize on the expertise and learning opportunities among the clinicians, provider organizations, government agencies, and third-party payers responsible for populations served by the Network Partners and by MST Services, a Web-based portal for discussion and feedback has been established, as has a quarterly conference call and annual meeting. This national and international practice community shares strategies to navigate the challenges of implementation and program sustainability encountered in their respective communities and service systems. This information, in turn, is used to revise the materials and processes that support the still evolving protocol to cultivate indigenous expertise. The Network Partners are also critical to propelling forward new research that represents several steps in the cycle from effectiveness to dissemination (see, e.g., Schoenwald & Hoagwood, 2001). They are increasingly the venue for empirical testing via randomized effectiveness trials of MST internationally; for adaptations of MST for populations such as juvenile sex offenders, juvenile offenders involved in drug courts, and physically abused adolescents (see Chapter 9 for descriptions of these studies and their outcomes); and for generating discussion of lessons learned with model developers and purveyors of other evidence-based treatments. Such discussions are aimed at developing strategies that can support the larger-scale transport and implementation of evidence-based treatments and conducting research to examine the effectiveness of those strategies.

Conclusion

Implementing with fidelity a complex, evidence-based treatment tailored to the individual strengths and needs of delinquent youth and their families can be a daunting task even for seasoned professionals. The MST quality assurance and improvement system described in this chapter is designed to support therapists in accomplishing that task in collaboration with the families they serve. The system is designed to help interested communities develop and sustain effective MST programs, and provides training, ongoing clinical support, and qualitative and quantitative feedback on clinical and program implementation. It continues to evolve on the basis of research and lessons learned in collaboration with community and international partners.

References

Alexander, J. F., & Parsons, B. V. (1982). *Functional family therapy: Principles and procedures.* Carmel, CA: Brooks & Cole.

American Psychiatric Association. (2000). *Diagnostic and statistical manual of mental disorders* (4th ed., text rev.). Washington, DC: Author.

Aos, S., Miller, M., & Drake, E. (2006). *Evidence-based public policy options to reduce future prison construction, criminal justice costs, and crime rates.* Olympia: Washington State Institute for Public Policy.

Barkley, R. A. (2006). *Attention deficit hyperactivity disorder: A handbook for diagnosis and treatment* (3rd ed.). New York: Guilford Press.

Baumrind, D. (1989). Rearing competent children. In W. Damon (Ed.), *Child development today and tomorrow* (pp. 349–378). San Francisco: Jossey-Bass.

Baumrind, D. (1991). The influence of parenting style on adolescent competence and substance use. Special issue: The work of John P. Hill: I. Theoretical, instructional, and policy contributions. *Journal of Early Adolescence, 11,* 56–95.

Baumrind, D. (2005). Patterns of parental authority and adolescent autonomy. In J. Smetana (Ed.), *New directions for child development: Changes in parental authority during adolescence* (pp. 61–69). San Francisco: Jossey-Bass.

Becker, B. E., & Luthar, S. S. (2002). Social-emotional factors affecting achievement outcomes among disadvantaged students: Closing the achievement gap. *Educational Psychologist, 37,* 197–214.

Berndt, T. J. (2002). Friendship quality and social development. *Current Directions in Psychological Science, 11,* 7–10.

Bickman, L., Summerfelt, W. T., & Noser, K. (1997). Comparative outcomes of emotionally disturbed children and adolescents in a system of services and usual care. *Psychiatric Services, 48,* 1543–1548.

Bickman, L., Warren L. E., Andrade, A. R., & Penaloza, R. V. (2000). The Fort Bragg continuum of care for children and adolescents: Mental health outcomes over 5 years. *Journal of Consulting and Clinical Psychology, 68,* 710–716.

Biglan, A., Brennan, P. A., Foster, S. L., & Holder, H. D. (2004). *Helping adolescents at risk: Prevention of multiple problem behaviors.* New York: Guilford Press.

Borduin, C. M., Henggeler, S. W., Blaske, D. M., & Stein, R. (1990). Multisystemic treatment of adolescent sexual offenders. *International Journal of Offender Therapy and Comparative Criminology, 35,* 105–114.

Borduin, C. M., Mann, B. J., Cone, L. T., Henggeler, S. W., Fucci, B. R., Blaske, D. M., et al. (1995). Multisystemic treatment of serious juvenile offenders: Long-term prevention of criminality and violence. *Journal of Consulting and Clinical Psychology, 63,* 569–578.

Borduin, C. M., & Schaeffer, C. M. (2001). Multisystemic treatment of juvenile sexual offenders: A progress report. *Journal of Psychology and Human Sexuality, 13,* 25–42.

Borduin, C. M., Schaeffer, C. M., & Heiblum, N. (in press). A randomized clinical trial of multisystemic therapy with juvenile sexual offenders: Effects on youth social ecology and criminal activity. *Journal of Consulting and Clinical Psychology.*

Bornstein, M. H. (Ed.). (2002). *Handbook of parenting: Social conditions and applied parenting* (Vol. 4, 2nd ed.). Mahwah, NJ: Erlbaum.

Bridgeland, J. M., Diulio, J. J., & Morison, K. B. (2006). The silent epidemic: Perspectives of high school dropouts. A report by Civic Enterprises and Peter D. Hart Research Associates for the Bill and Melinda Gates Foundation. Available at *www.gatesfoundation.org/UnitedStates/Education/TransformingHighSchools/ RelatedInfo/SilentEpidemic.htm.*

Bronfenbrenner, U. (1979). *The ecology of human development: Experiments by design and nature.* Cambridge, MA: Harvard University Press.

Brown, S. A., Myers, M. G., Mott, M. A., & Vik, P. W. (1994). Correlates of success following treatment for adolescent substance abuse. *Applied and Preventive Psychology, 3,* 61–73.

Brown, T. L., Henggeler, S. W., Schoenwald, S. K., Brondino, M. J., & Pickrel, S. G. (1999). Multisystemic treatment of substance abusing and dependent juvenile delinquents: Effects on school attendance at posttreatment and 6-month follow-up. *Children's Services: Social Policy, Research, and Practice, 2,* 81–93.

Brunk, M., Henggeler, S. W., & Whelan, J. P. (1987). A comparison of multisystemic therapy and parent training in the brief treatment of child abuse and neglect. *Journal of Consulting and Clinical Psychology, 55,* 311–318.

Budney, A. J., & Higgins, S. T. (1998). *A community reinforcement plus vouchers approach: Treating cocaine addiction* (NIH Publication No. 98-4309). Rockville, MD: U.S. Department of Health and Human Services, National Institutes of Health, National Institute on Drug Abuse.

Bukowski, W. M., Newcomb, A. F., & Hartup, W. W. (1996). *The company they keep: Friendship in childhood and adolescence.* New York: Cambridge University Press.

Burns, B. J., Hoagwood, K., & Mrazek, P. J. (1999). Effective treatment for mental disorders in children and adolescents. *Clinical Child and Family Psychology Review, 2,* 199–254.

Center for Substance Abuse Prevention. (2001). *Strengthening America's families: Model family programs for substance abuse and delinquency prevention.* Salt Lake City, UT: Department of Health Promotion and Education, University of Utah.

Center for Substance Abuse Treatment, Denver Juvenile Justice Integrated Treatment Network. (1998). *Strategies for integrating substance abuse treatment and the juvenile justice system: A practice guide.* Denver: Denver Juvenile Justice Integrated Treatment Network.

Center for Substance Abuse Treatment. (1999). *Treatment of substance use disorders among adolescents* (Treatment Improvement Protocol [TIP] Series 3) (K. C. Winters, Ed.). Rockville, MD: Author.

Chamberlain, P. (2003). *Treating chronic juvenile offenders: Advances made through the Oregon Multidimensional Treatment Foster Care model.* Washington, DC: American Psychological Association.

Chapman, J. E., Sheidow, A. J., Henggeler, S. W., Halliday-Boykins, C., & Cunningham, P. B. (2008). Developing a measure of therapist adherence to contingency management: An application of the Many-Facet Rasch Model. *Journal of Child and Adolescent Substance Abuse, 17,* 47–68.

Chilenski, S. M., Bumbarger, B. K., Kyler, S., & Greenberg, M. T. (2007). *Reducing youth violence and delinquency in Pennsylvania: PCCD's research-based programs initative.* Prevention Research Center for the Promotion of Human Development, Pennsylvania State University.

Cohen, J. A., Mannarino, A. P., & Deblinger, E. (2006). *Treating trauma and traumatic grief in children and adolescents.* New York: Guilford Press.

Cummings, E. M., Davies, P. T., & Campbell, S. B. (2000). *Developmental psychopathology and family process: Theory, research, and clinical practice.* New York: Guilford Press.

Cunningham, P. B., Naar-King, S., Ellis, D. A., Pejuan, S., & Secord, E. (2006). Achieving adherence to antiretroviral medications for pediatric HIV disease using an empirically supported treatment: A case report. *Journal of Developmental and Behavioral Pediatrics, 27,* 44–50.

Cunningham, P. B., Rowland, M. D., Swenson, C. C., Henggeler, S. W., Schoenwald, S. K., Randall, J., et al. (2005). *Community reinforcement approach to support caregivers.* Charleston: Family Services Research Center, Department of Psychiatry and Behavioral Sciences, Medical University of South Carolina.

Cunningham, P. B., Schoenwald, S. K., Rowland, M. D., Swenson, C. C., Henggeler, S. W., Randall, J., et al. (2004). *Implementing contingency management for adolescent substance abuse in outpatient settings.* Charleston: Family Services Research Center, Department of Psychiatry and Behavioral Sciences, Medical University of South Carolina.

Curtis, N. M., Ronan, K. R., & Borduin, C. M. (2004). Multisystemic treatment: A meta-analysis of outcome studies. *Journal of Family Psychology, 18,* 411–419.

Curtis, N. M., Ronan, K. R., Heiblum, N., & Crellin, K. (in press). Dissemination and effectiveness of multisystemic treatment in New Zealand: A benchmarking study. *Journal of Family Psychology.*

Daly, B. P., Xanthopoulos, M. S., Stephan, S. H., Cooper, C. J., & Brown, R. T. (2007). Evidence-based interventions for childhood disorders: Summary of the report of the APA Working Group on Psychotropic Medications for Children and Adolescents. *Emotional and Behavioral Disorders in Youth, 7,* 31–32, 48–55.

Dane, A. V., & Schneider, B. H. (1998). Program integrity in primary and early secondary prevention: Are implementation effects out of control? *Clinical Psychology Review, 18,* 23–45.

Deblinger, E., & Heflin, A. H. (1996). *Treating sexually abused children and their nonoffending parents: A cognitive behavioral approach.* Thousand Oaks, CA: Sage.

Dishion, T. J., Dodge, K. A., & Lansford, J. E. (2006). Findings and recommendations: A blueprint to minimize deviant peer influences in youth interventions and programs. In K. A. Dodge, T. J. Dishion, & J. E. Lansford (Eds.), *Deviant peer influences in programs for youth: Problems and solutions* (pp. 366–394). New York: Guilford Press.

Dishion, T. J., & Kavanagh, K. (2003). *Intervening in adolescent problem behavior: A family-centered approach.* New York: Guilford Press.

Dodge, K. A., Dishion, T. J., & Lansford, J. E. (Eds.). (2006). *Deviant peer influences in programs for youth.* New York: Guilford Press.

Eddy, J. M., & Chamberlain, P. (2000). Family management and deviant peer association as mediators of the impact of treatment condition on youth antisocial behavior. *Journal of Consulting and Clinical Psychology, 68,* 857–863.

Edwards, D. L., Schoenwald, S. K., Henggeler, S. W., & Strother, K. B. (2001). A multi-level perspective on the implementation of Multisystemic Therapy (MST): Attempting dissemination with fidelity. In G. A. Bernfeld, D. P. Farrington, & A. W. Leschied (Eds.), *Offender rehabilitation in practice: Implementing and evaluating effective programs* (pp. 97–120). London: Wiley.

Elliott, D. S. (1994a). Serious violent offenders: Onset, developmental course, and termination. The American Society of Criminology 1993 presidential address. *Criminology, 32,* 1–21.

Elliott, D. S. (1994b). *Youth violence: An overview.* Boulder, CO: University of Colorado, Center for the Study and Prevention of Violence, Institute of Behavioral Science.

Elliott, D. S. (1998). *Blueprints for violence prevention* (Series Ed.). University of Colorado, Center for the Study and Prevention of Violence. Boulder, CO: Blueprints Publications.

Ellis, D. A., Frey, M. A., Naar-King, S., Templin, T., Cunningham, P. B., & Cakan, N. (2005a). Use of multisystemic therapy to improve regimen adherence among adolescents with type 1 diabetes in chronic poor metabolic control: A randomized controlled trial. *Diabetes Care, 28,* 1604–1610.

Ellis, D. A., Frey, M. A., Naar-King, S., Templin, T., Cunningham, P. B., & Cakan, N. (2005b). The effects of multisystemic therapy on diabetes stress in adolescents with chronically poorly controlled type 1 diabetes: Findings from a randomized controlled trial. *Pediatrics, 116,* e826–e832.

Ellis, D. A., Naar-King, S., Cunningham, P. B., & Secord, E. (2006). Use of multisystemic therapy to improve antiretroviral adherence and health outcomes in HIV-infected pediatric patients: Evaluation of a pilot program. *AIDS, Patient Care, and STD's, 20,* 112–121.

Ellis, D. A., Naar-King, S., Frey, M. A., Templin, T., Rowland, M., & Cakan, N. (2005). Multisystemic treatment of poorly controlled type 1 diabetes: Effects on medical resource utilization. *Journal of Pediatric Psychology, 30,* 656–666.

Ellis, D. A., Templin, T., Naar-King, S., Frey, M. A., Cunningham, P. B., Podolski, C., et al. (2007). Multisystemic therapy for adolescents with poorly controlled type I diabetes: Stability of treatment effects in a randomized controlled trial. *Journal of Consulting and Clinical Psychology, 75,* 168–174.

Emery, R. E. (1994). *Renegotiating family relationships: Divorce, child custody, and mediation.* New York: Guilford Press.

Emery, R. E. (1999). *Marriage, divorce, and children's adjustment* (2nd ed.). Thousand Oaks, CA: Sage.

Emery, R. E. (2004). *The truth about children and divorce: Dealing with the emotions so you and your children can thrive.* New York: Viking/Penguin.

Emery, R. E., & Sbarra, D. A. (2002). What couples therapists need to know about divorce. In A. S. Gurman & N. S. Jacobson (Eds.), *Clinical handbook of couple therapy* (3rd ed., pp. 508–532). New York: Guilford Press.

Eyberg, S. M., Nelson, M. M., & Boggs, S. R. (2008). Evidence-based psychosocial treatments for children and adolescents with disruptive behavior. *Journal of Clinical Child and Adolescent Psychology, 37,* 215–237.

Family Services Research Center. (2008). *Implementing contingency management for adolescent substance abuse in outpatient settings* (2nd ed.). Charleston: Family Services Research Center, Department of Psychiatry and Behavioral Sciences, Medical University of South Carolina.

Farrell, A. D., & Danish, S. J. (1993). Peer drug associations and emotional restraint: Causes or consequences of adolescents' drug use? *Journal of Consulting and Clinical Psychology, 61*(2), 327–334.

Farrington, D. P., & Welsh, B. C. (1999). Delinquency prevention using family-based interventions. *Children and Society, 13,* 287–303.

Feindler, E. L., & Guttman, J. (1994). Cognitive-behavioral anger control training for groups of adolescents: A treatment manual. In C. W. LeCroy (Ed.), *Handbook of child and adolescent treatment manuals.* New York: Lexington Books.

Feindler, E. L., Marriott, S. A., & Iwata, M. (1984). Group anger control training for junior high school delinquents. *Cognitive Therapy and Research, 8,* 299–311.

Fisch, R., Weakland, J. H., & Segal, L. (1982). *The tactics of change: Doing therapy briefly.* San Francisco: Jossey-Bass.

Fixsen, D. L., Naoom, S. F., Blasé, K. A., Friedman, R. M., & Wallace, F. (2005). *Implementation research: A synthesis of the literature.* Tampa: University of South Florida, Louis de la Parte Florida Mental Health Institute, National Implementation Research Network.

Fleming, C. B., Brewer, D. D., Gainey, R. R., Haggerty, K. P., & Catalano, R. F. (1997). Parent drug use and bonding to parents as predictors of substance use in children of substance abusers. *Journal of Child and Adolescent Substance Abuse, 6,* 75–86.

Franks, R. P., Schroeder, J. A., Connell, C. M., & Tebes, J. K. (2008). *Unlocking doors: Multisystemic therapy for Connecticut's high-risk children and youth: An effective home-based alternative treatment.* Connecticut Center for Effective Practice, Child Health and Development Institute of Connecticut.

Gambrill, E. D. (1977). *Behavior modification: Handbook of assessment, intervention, and evaluation.* San Francisco: Jossey-Bass.

Glisson, C., Schoenwald, S. K., Kelleher, K., Landsverk, J. Hoagwood, K. E., Mayberg, S., et al. (2008). Therapist turnover and new program sustainability in mental health clinics as a function of organizational culture, climate, and service structure. *Administration and Policy in Mental Health and Mental Health Services Research, 35,* 124–133.

Gruber, K., Chutuape, M. A., & Stitzer, M. L. (2000). Reinforcement-based intensive outpatient treatment for inner city opiate abusers: A short-term evaluation. *Drug and Alcohol Dependence, 57.*

Haley, J. (1987). *Problem-solving therapy* (2nd ed.). San Francisco: Jossey-Bass.

Haley, J. (1993). *Uncommon therapy: The psychiatric techniques of Milton H. Erickson, M.D.* New York: Norton.

Halliday-Boykins, C. A., Schoenwald, S. K., & Letourneau, E. J. (2005). Caregiver–therapist ethnic similarity predicts youth outcomes from an empirically based treatment. *Journal of Consulting and Clinical Psychology, 73,* 808–818.

Henggeler, S. W. (Ed.). (1982). *Delinquency and adolescent psychopathology: A family-ecological systems approach.* Littleton, MA: John Wright-PSG.

Henggeler, S. W., & Borduin, C. M. (1990). *Family therapy and beyond: A multi-systemic approach to treating the behavior problems of children and adolescents.* Pacific Grove, CA: Brooks/Cole.

Henggeler, S. W., & Borduin, C. M. (1992). *Multisystemic Therapy Adherence Scales.* Unpublished instrument. Charleston: Department of Psychiatry and Behavioral Sciences, Medical University of South Carolina.

Henggeler, S. W., & Schoenwald, S. K. (1998). *The MST supervisory manual: Promoting quality assurance at the clinical level.* Charleston, SC: MST Institute.

Henggeler, S. W., Borduin, C. M., Melton, G. B., Mann, B. J., Smith, L., Hall, J. A., et al. (1991). Effects of multisystemic therapy on drug use and abuse in serious juvenile offenders: A progress report from two outcome studies. *Family Dynamics of Addiction Quarterly, 1*(3), 40–51.

Henggeler, S. W., Borduin, C. M., Schoenwald, S. K., Huey, S. J., & Chapman, J. E. (2006). *Multisystemic Therapy Adherence Scale—Revised (TAM-R).* Unpublished instrument. Charleston: Department of Psychiatry and Behavioral Sciences, Medical University of South Carolina.

Henggeler, S. W., Chapman, J. E., Rowland, M. D., Halliday-Boykins, C. A., Randall, J., Shackleford, J., et al. (2007). If you build it, they will come: Statewide practitioner interest in contingency management for youths. *Journal of Substance Abuse Treatment, 32,* 121–131.

Henggeler, S. W., Chapman, J. E., Rowland, M. D., Halliday-Boykins, C. A., Randall, J., Shackleford, J., et al. (2008). Statewide adoption and initial implementation of contingency management for substance abusing adolescents. *Journal of Consulting and Clinical Psychology, 76,* 556–567.

Henggeler, S. W., Clingempeel, W. G., Brondino, M. J., & Pickrel, S. G. (2002). Four-year follow-up of multisystemic therapy with substance-abusing and substance-dependent juvenile offenders. *Journal of the American Academy of Child and Adolescent Psychiatry, 41,* 868–874.

Henggeler, S. W., Halliday-Boykins, C. A., Cunningham, P. B., Randall, J., Shapiro, S. B., & Chapman, J. E. (2006). Juvenile drug court: Enhancing outcomes by integrating evidence-based treatments. *Journal of Consulting and Clinical Psychology, 74,* 42–54.

Henggeler, S. W., Letourneau, E. J., Chapman, J. E., Borduin, C. M., Schewe, P. A., & McCart, M. R. (in press). Mediators of change for multisystemic therapy with juvenile sexual offenders. *Journal of Consulting and Clinical Psychology.*

Henggeler, S. W., Melton, G. B., Brondino, M. J., Scherer, D. G., & Hanley, J. H. (1997). Multisystemic therapy with violent and chronic juvenile offenders and their families: The role of treatment fidelity in successful dissemination. *Journal of Consulting and Clinical Psychology, 65,* 821–833.

Henggeler, S. W., Melton, G. B., & Smith, L. A. (1992). Family preservation using multisystemic therapy: An effective alternative to incarcerating serious juvenile offenders. *Journal of Consulting and Clinical Psychology, 60,* 953–961.

Henggeler, S. W., Melton, G. B., Smith, L. A., Schoenwald, S. K., & Hanley, J. H. (1993). Family preservation using multisystemic treatment: Long-term follow-up to a clinical trial with serious juvenile offenders. *Journal of Child and Family Studies, 2,* 283–293.

Henggeler, S. W., Pickrel, S. G., & Brondino, M. J. (1999). Multisystemic treatment of substance abusing and dependent delinquents: Outcomes, treatment fidelity, and transportability. *Mental Health Services Research, 1,* 171–184.

Henggeler, S. W., Pickrel, S. G., Brondino, M. J., & Crouch, J. L. (1996). Eliminating (almost) treatment dropout of substance abusing or dependent delinquents through home-based multisystemic therapy. *American Journal of Psychiatry, 153,* 427–428.

Henggeler, S. W., Rodick, J. D., Borduin, C. M., Hanson, C. L., Watson, S. M., & Urey, J. R. (1986). Multisystemic treatment of juvenile offenders: Effects on adolescent behavior and family interactions. *Developmental Psychology, 22,* 132–141.

Henggeler, S. W., Rowland, M. D., Halliday-Boykins, C., Sheidow, A. J., Ward, D. M., Randall, J., et al. (2003). One-year follow-up of multisystemic therapy as an alternative to the hospitalization of youths in psychiatric crisis. *Journal of the American Academy of Child and Adolescent Psychiatry, 42,* 543–551.

Henggeler, S. W., Rowland, M. D., Randall, J., Ward, D. M., Pickrel, S. G., Cunningham, P. B., et al. (1999). Home based multisystemic therapy as an alternative to the hospitalization of youths in psychiatric crisis: Clinical outcomes. *Journal of the American Academy of Child and Adolescent Psychiatry, 38,* 1331–1339.

Henggeler, S. W., Schoenwald, S. K., Borduin, C. M., Rowland, M. D., & Cunningham, P. B. (1998). *Multisystemic treatment of antisocial behavior in children and adolescents.* New York: Guilford Press.

Henggeler, S. W., Schoenwald, S. K., Borduin, C. M., & Swenson, C. C. (2006). Methodological critique and meta-analysis as Trojan horse. *Children and Youth Services Review, 28,* 447–457.

Henggeler, S. W., Schoenwald, S. K., Liao, J. G., Letourneau, E. J., & Edwards, D. L. (2002). Transporting efficacious treatments to field settings: The link between supervisory practices and therapist fidelity in MST programs. *Journal of Clinical Child and Adolescent Psychology, 31,* 155–167.

Henggeler, S. W., Schoenwald, S. K., Rowland, M. D., & Cunningham, P. B. (2002). *Serious emotional disturbance in children and adolescents: Multisystemic therapy.* New York: Guilford Press.

Henggeler, S. W., Sheidow, A. J., Cunningham, P. B., Donohue, B. C., & Ford, J. D. (2008). Promoting the implementation of an evidence-based intervention for adolescent marijuana abuse in community settings: Testing the use of intensive quality assurance. *Journal of Clinical Child and Adolescent Psychology, 37,* 682–689.

Higgins, S. T., Silverman, K., & Heil, S. H. (2008). *Contingency management in substance abuse treatment.* New York: Guilford Press.

Hoge, R. D., Guerra, N. G., & Boxer, P. (Eds.). (2008). *Treating the juvenile offender.* New York: Guilford Press.

Hollon, S. D., Jarrett, R. B., Nierenberg, A. A., Thase, M. E., Trivedi, M., & Rush, A. J. (2005). Psychotherapy and medication in the treatment of adult and geriatric depression: Which monotherapy or combined treatment? *Journal of Clinical Psychiatry, 66,* 455–468.

Howell, J. C. (2003). *Preventing and reducing juvenile delinquency: A comprehensive framework.* Thousand Oaks, CA: Sage.

Hoza, B., Molina, B. S. G., Bukowski, W. M., & Sippola, L. K. (1995). Peer variables as predictors of later childhood adjustment. Special issue: Developmental processes in peer relations and psychopathology. *Development and Psychopathology, 7,* 787–802.

Huey, S. J., Henggeler, S. W., Brondino, M. J., & Pickrel, S. G. (2000). Mechanisms of change in multisystemic therapy: Reducing delinquent behavior through therapist adherence and improved family and peer functioning. *Journal of Consulting and Clinical Psychology, 68,* 451–467.

Huey, S. J., Henggeler, S. W., Rowland, M. D., Halliday-Boykins, C. A., Cunningham, P. B., Pickrel, S. G., et al. (2004). Multisystemic therapy effects on attempted suicide by youth presenting psychiatric emergencies. *Journal of the American Academy of Child and Adolescent Psychiatry, 43,* 183–190.

Huey, S. J., & Polo, A. J. (2008). Evidence-based psychosocial treatments for ethnic minority youth: A review and meta-analysis. *Journal of Clinical Child and Adolescent Psychology, 37,* 262–301.

Individuals with Disabilities Education Act Amendments of 1997. H.R. 5, 105th Cong. (1997).

Jennison, K. M., & Johnson, K. A. (1998). Alcohol dependence in adult children of alcoholics: Longitudinal evidence of early risk. *Journal of Drug Education, 28,* 19–37.

Jones, H. E., Wong, C. J., Tuten, M., & Stitzer, M. L. (2005). Reinforcement-based therapy: 12-month evaluation of an outpatient drug-free treatment for heroin abusers. *Drug and Alcohol Dependence, 79,* 119–128.

Kazdin, A. E. (2003). Problem-solving skills training and parent management training for conduct disorder. In A. E. Kazdin & J. R. Weisz (Eds.), *Evidence-based psychotherapies for children and adolescents* (pp. 241–262). New York: Guilford Press.

Kazdin, A. E. (2007). Mediators and mechanisms of change in psychotherapy research. *Annual Review of Clinical Psychology, 3,* 1–27.

Kazdin, A. E., Siegel, T. C., & Bass, D. (1992). Cognitive problem-solving skills training and parent management training in the treatment of antisocial behavior in children. *Journal of Consulting and Clinical Psychology, 60,* 733–747.

Kazdin, A. E., & Weisz, J. R. (1998). Identifying and developing empirically supported child and adolescent treatments. *Journal of Consulting and Clinical Psychology, 66,* 19–36.

Kim, J. E., Hetherington, E. M., & Reiss, D. (1999). Associations among family relationships, antisocial peers, and adolescents' externalizing behaviors: Gender and family type differences. *Child Development, 70,* 1209–1230.

Klein, K. J., & Knight, A. P. (2005). Innovation implementation: Overcoming the challenge. *Current Directions in Psychological Science, 14*(5), 243–246.

Kolko, D. J., & Swenson, C. C. (2002). *Assessing and treating physically abused children and their families.* Thousand Oaks, CA: Sage.

Lahey, B. B., Moffitt, T. E., & Caspi, A. (Eds.). (2003). *Causes of conduct disorder and delinquency*. New York: Guilford Press.

Larson, R. W., & Verma, S. (1999). How children and adolescents spend time across the world: Work, play, and developmental opportunities. *Psychological Bulletin, 125*, 701–736.

Leahy, R. L. (2003). *Cognitive therapy techniques*. New York: Guilford Press.

Lebow, J. L. (Ed.). (2005). *Handbook of clinical family therapy*. Hoboken, NJ: Wiley.

Leschied, A., & Cunningham, A. (2002, February). *Seeking effective interventions for serious young offenders: Interim results of a four-year randomized study of multisystemic therapy in Ontario, Canada*. London: Centre for Children & Families in the Justice System.

Letourneau, E. J., Henggeler, S. W., Borduin, C. M., Schewe, P. A., McCart, M. R., Chapman, J. E., et al. (in press). Multisystemic therapy for juvenile sexual offenders: 1–year results from a randomized effectiveness trial. *Journal of Family Psychology*.

Linehan, M. M. (1993). *Cognitive-behavioral treatment of borderline personality disorder*. New York: Guilford Press.

Littell, J. H., Popa, M., & Forsythe, B. (2005). *Multisystemic therapy for social, emotional, and behavioral problems in youth aged 10–17*. Campbell Collaborative Library, Issue 4: Wiley.

Lochman, J. E., Nelson, W. M., & Sims, J. P. (1981). A cognitive-behavioral program for use with aggressive children. *Journal of Clinical Child Psychology, 10*, 146–148.

Lochman, J. E., & Wells, K. C. (2002). Contextual social-cognitive mediators and child outcome: A test of the theoretical model in the Coping Power program. *Development and Psychopathology, 14*, 945–967.

Loeber, R., & Farrington, D. P. (Eds.). (1998). *Serious and violent juvenile offenders: Risk factors and successful interventions*. Thousand Oaks, CA: Sage.

Loeber, R., Farrington, D. P., Stouthamer-Loeber, M., & Van Kammen, W. B. (1998). *Antisocial behavior and mental health problems: Explanatory factors in childhood and adolescence*. Mahwah, NJ: Erlbaum.

Maccoby, E. E., & Martin, J. A. (1983). Socialization in the context of the family: Parent–child interactions. In E. M. Hetherington (Ed.), P. H. Mussen (Series Ed.), *Handbook of child psychology, Vol. 4: Socialization, personality, and social development* (pp. 1–101). New York: Wiley.

Marcenko, M. O., & Meyers, J. C. (1991). Mothers of children with developmental disabilities: Who shares the burden? *Family Relations, 40*, 186–190.

March, J. S. (2002). *Diagnosis and treatment of the childhood-onset anxiety disorders*. Available at www2.mc.duke.edu/PCAAD/PCAAD March.htm.

Margo, J. (2008). *Make me a criminal: Preventing youth crime*. London: Institute for Public Policy Research.

Mash, E. J., & Barkley, R. A. (Eds.). (2006). *Treatment of childhood disorders* (3rd ed.). New York: Guilford Press.

McGue, M. (1999). Behavioral genetic models of alcoholism and drinking. In K. E. Leonard & H. T. Blane (Eds.), *Psychological theories of drinking and alcoholism* (2nd ed., pp. 372–421). New York: Guilford Press.

McKay, M., Davis, M., & Fanning, P. (2007). *Thoughts and feelings: Taking control of your moods and your life* (3rd ed.). Oakland, CA: New Harbinger.

McMahon, R. J., & Forehand, R. L. (2003). *Helping the noncompliant child* (2nd ed.). New York: Guilford Press.

Meichenbaum, D. (1977). *Cognitive-behavior modification: An integrative approach.* New York: Plenum Press.

Mihalic, S. (2004). The importance of implementation fidelity. *Emotional and Behavioral Disorders in Youth, 4,* 83–86, 99–105.

Miller, W. R., & Rollnick, S. (2002). *Motivational interviewing: Preparing people for change* (2nd ed.). New York: Guilford Press.

Minuchin, S. (1974). *Families and family therapy.* Cambridge, MA: Harvard University Press.

Minuchin, S., & Fishman, H. C. (1981). *Family therapy techniques.* Cambridge, MA: Harvard University Press.

Minuchin, S., Nichols, M. P., & Lee, W. Y. (2007). *Assessing families and couples.* Boston: Allyn & Bacon.

MTA Cooperative Group. (1999). A 14-month randomized clinical trial of treatment strategies for attention-deficit/hyperactivity disorder. *Archives of General Psychiatry, 56,* 1073–1086.

Munger, R. L. (1993). *Changing children's behavior quickly.* Lanham, MD: Madison Books.

Munger, R. L. (1999). *Rules for unruly children: The parent discipline bible.* Boys Town, NE: Boys Town Press. Available at *www.parenting.org/ebook/index.asp.*

National Alliance on Mental Illness. (2003, Fall). Multisystemic therapy: An evidence-based practice for serious clinical problems in adolescents. *NAMI Beginnings,* Issue 3, pp. 8–10.

National Alliance on Mental Illness. (2008, Winter). Medicaid coverage of multisystemic therapy. *NAMI Beginnings,* Issue 10, pp. 5–8.

National Institute on Drug Abuse. (1999). *Principles of drug addiction treatment: A research-based guide* (NIH Publication No. 99-4180). Rockville, MD: U.S. Department of Health and Human Services, National Institutes of Health.

National Institutes of Health. (2006). State-of-the-Science Conference statement: Preventing violence and related health-risking, social behaviors in adolescents. *Journal of Abnormal Child Psychology, 34,* 457–470.

National Mental Health Association. (2004). *Mental health treatment for youth in the juvenile justice system: A compendium of promising practices.* Alexandria, VA: Author.

National Youth Employment Coalition. (2005). PEPNet guide to quality standards for youth programs. Washington, DC: Author. Available at *www.nyec.org/page.cfm?pageID=123.*

Nezu, A. M., Nezu, C. M., & D'Zurilla, T. J. (2007). *Solving life's problems.* New York: Springer Publishing.

North, M. S., Gleacher, A. A., Radigan, M., Greene, L., Levitt, J. M., Chassman, J., et al. (2008). The Evidence-Based Treatment Dissemination Center (EBTDC): Bridging the research–practice gap in New York State. *Emotional and Behavioral Disorders in Youth, 8,* 9–17.

Office of Justice Programs. (2005). *The OJP what works repository: Working group of the federal collaboration on what works.* Washington, DC: Author.

Office of Juvenile Justice and Delinquency Prevention. (2007). *The Office of Juvenile*

Justice and Delinquency Prevention's Model Programs Guide (MPG). Available at *www.dsgonline.com/mpg2.5//TitleV_MPG_Table_Ind_Rec.asp?id=363*.

Office of Program Policy Analysis and Government Accountability. (2007, February). *Redirection pilots meet and exceed residential commitment outcomes: $5.8 million saved*. Tallahassee: Florida Legislature.

Ogden, T., & Hagen, K. A. (2006a). Multisystemic therapy of serious behaviour problems in youth: Sustainability of therapy effectiveness two years after intake. *Journal of Child and Adolescent Mental Health, 11*, 142–149.

Ogden, T., & Hagen, K. A. (2006b). Virker MST?: Kommentarer til en systematisk forskningsoversikt og meta-analyse av MST. *Nordisk Sosialt Arbeid, 26*, 222–233.

Ogden, T., Hagen, K. A., & Andersen, O. (2007). Sustainability of the effectiveness of a programme of multisystemic treatment (MST) across participant groups in the second year of operation. *Journal of Children's Services, 2*, 4–14.

Ogden, T., & Halliday-Boykins, C. A. (2004). Multisystemic treatment of antisocial adolescents in Norway: Replication of clinical outcomes outside of the U.S. *Child and Adolescent Mental Health, 9*(2), 77–83.

Oswald, D. P., & Singh, N. N. (1996). Emerging trends in child and adolescent mental health services. In T. H. Ollendick & R. J. Prinz (Eds.), *Advances in clinical child psychology* (pp. 331–365). New York: Plenum Press.

Palinkas, L. A., Schoenwald, S. K., Hoagwood, K., Landsverk, J., Chorpita, B. F., Weisz, J. R., et al. (2008). An ethnographic study of implementation of evidence-based practice in child mental health: First steps. *Psychiatric Services, 59*, 738–746.

Patterson, G. R. (1976). *Living with children: New methods for parents and teachers*. Champaign, IL: Research Press.

Patterson, G. R., Reid, J. B., & Dishion, T. J. (1992). *Antisocial boys*. Eugene, OR: Castalia Publishing.

Peake, T. H., Borduin, C. M., & Archer, R. P. (2000). *Brief psychotherapies*. Montvale, NJ: Jason Aronson.

Pierce, G. R., Sarason, B. R., & Sarason, I. (1995). *Handbook of social support and the family*. New York: Plenum Press.

President's New Freedom Commission on Mental Health. (2003). *Achieving the promise: Transforming mental health care in America*. Rockville, MD: DHHS.

Prinstein, M. J., & Dodge, K. A. (Eds.). (2008). *Understanding peer influence in children and adolescents*. New York: Guilford Press.

Pryor, J., & Emery, R. E. (2004). Divorce and children's well-being. In R. Unsworth (Ed.), *How American children lead their lives* (pp. 170–190). Piscataway, NJ: Rutgers University Press.

Putnam, R. D. (2000). *Bowling alone: The collapse and revival of American community*. New York: Simon & Schuster.

Quick, J. D., Nelson, D. L., Matuszek, P. A., Whittington, J. L., & Quick, J. C. (1996). Social support, secure attachments, and health. In C. L. Cooper (Ed.), *Handbook of stress, medicine, and health* (pp. 269–287). Boca Raton, FL: CRC Press.

Real, K., & Poole, M. S. (2005). Innovation implementation: Conceptualization and measurement in organizational research. *Research in Organizational Change and Development, 15*, 63–134.

Reid, J. B., Patterson, G. R., & Snyder, J. (Eds.). (2002). *Antisocial behavior in children and adolescents: A developmental analysis and model for intervention.* Washington, DC: American Psychological Association.

Robin, A. L., & Foster, S. (1989). *Negotiating parent–adolescent conflict: A behavioral family systems approach.* New York: Guilford Press.

Roid, G. H. (2003). *The Stanford-Binet Intelligence Scales—Fifth Edition.* Itasca, IL: Riverside Publishing.

Roseth, C. J., Johnson, D. W., & Johnson, R. T. (2008). Promoting early adolescents' achievement and peer relationships: The effects of cooperative, competitive, and individualistic goal structures. *Psychological Bulletin, 134,* 223–246.

Rowland, M. D., Chapman, J. E., & Henggeler, S. W. (2008). Sibling outcomes from a randomized trial of evidence-based treatments with substance abusing juvenile offenders. *Journal of Child and Adolescent Substance Abuse, 17,* 11–26.

Rowland, M. D., Halliday-Boykins, C. A., & Demidovich, M. (2003). *Caregiver substance use disorder: Impact on parenting.* Poster presentation, 50th annual meeting of the American Academy of Child and Adolescent Psychiatry, Miami, FL.

Rowland, M. D., Halliday-Boykins, C. A., Henggeler, S. W., Cunningham, P. B., Lee, T. G., Kruesi, M. J. P., et al. (2005). A randomized trial of multisystemic therapy with Hawaii's Felix Class youths. *Journal of Emotional and Behavioral Disorders, 13,* 13–23.

Saldana, L., & Henggeler, S. W. (2008). Improving outcomes and transporting evidence-based treatments for youth and families with serious clinical problems. *Journal of Child and Adolescent Substance Abuse, 17,* 1–10.

Sampson, R. J., & Laub, J. H. (2005). A life-course view of the development of crime. *Annals of the American Academy of Political and Social Science, 602,* 12–45.

Sanders, M. R. (1996). New directions in behavioral family intervention with children. In T. H. Ollendick & R. J. Prinz (Eds.), *Advances in clinical child psychology* (Vol. 18, pp. 283–330). New York: Plenum Press.

Schaeffer, C. M., & Borduin, C. M. (2005). Long-term follow-up to a randomized clinical trial of multisystemic therapy with serious and violent juvenile offenders. *Journal of Consulting and Clinical Psychology, 73*(3), 445–453.

Schaeffer, C. M., Saldana, L., Rowland, M. D., Henggeler, S. W., & Swenson, C. C. (2008). New initiatives in improving youth and family outcomes by importing evidence-based practices. *Journal of Child and Adolescent Substance Abuse, 17,* 27–45.

Schoenwald, S. K. (1998). *Multisystemic therapy consultation manual.* Charleston, SC: MST Institute.

Schoenwald, S. K. (2001). *The MST Consultant Adherence Measure.* Charleston: Family Services Research Center, Medical University of South Carolina.

Schoenwald, S. K., Carter, R. E., Chapman, J. E., & Sheidow, A. J. (2008). Therapist adherence and organizational effects on change in youth behavior problems one year after Multisystemic Therapy. *Administration and Policy in Mental Health and Mental Health Services Research, 35,* 379–394.

Schoenwald, S. K., & Chapman, J. E., (2008a). *Limits of caregiver–therapist ethnic similarity effects on youth outcomes of an empirically based treatment.* Manuscript in preparation.

Schoenwald, S. K., & Chapman, J. E. (2008b). *Therapist turnover affects youth outcomes of an empirically supported treatment.* Manuscript submitted for review.

Schoenwald, S. K., Chapman, J. E., & Sheidow, A. J. (2006, March). Implementation fidelity in MST. In S. K. Schoenwald & J. Reid (Co-Chairs), *Community-based model programs panel: Implementing with fidelity. Evidence-Based Programs: Research-to-Practice Conference (Blueprints for Violence Prevention).* Denver, CO.

Schoenwald, S. K., Chapman, J. E., Sheidow, A. J., & Carter, R. E. (in press). Long-term youth criminal outcomes in MST transport: The impact of therapist adherence and organizational climate and structure. *Journal of Clinical Child and Adolescent Psychology.*

Schoenwald, S. K., Heiblum, N., Saldana, L., & Henggeler, S. W. (2008). The international implementation of multisystemic therapy. *Evaluation and The Health Professions, Special Issue: International Translation of Health Behavior Research Innovations, Part I, 31,* 211–225.

Schoenwald, S. K., Henggeler, S. W., Brondino, M. J., & Rowland, M. D. (2000). Multisystemic therapy: Monitoring treatment fidelity. *Family Process, 39,* 83–103.

Schoenwald, S. K., Henggeler, S. W., & Edwards, D. (1998). *MST Supervisor Adherence Measure.* Charleston, SC: MST Institute.

Schoenwald, S. K., & Hoagwood, K. (2001). Effectiveness, transportability, and dissemination of interventions: What matters when? *Psychiatric Services, 52,* 1179–1189.

Schoenwald, S. K., Letourneau, E. J., & Halliday-Boykins, C. A. (2005). Predicting therapist adherence to a transported family-based treatment for youth. *Journal of Clinical Child and Adolescent Psychology, 34*(4), 658–670.

Schoenwald, S. K., Sheidow, A. J., & Chapman, J. E. (in press). Clinical supervision in treatment transport: Effects on adherence and outcomes. *Journal of Consulting and Clinical Psychology.*

Schoenwald, S. K., Sheidow, A. J., & Letourneau, E. J. (2004). Toward effective quality assurance in evidence-based practice: Links between expert consultation, therapist fidelity, and child outcomes. *Journal of Child and Adolescent Clinical Psychology, 33,* 94–104.

Schoenwald, S. K., Sheidow, A. J., Letourneau, E. J., & Liao, J. G. (2003). Transportability of multisystemic therapy: Evidence for multi-level influences. *Mental Health Services Research, 5,* 223–239.

Schoenwald, S. K., Ward, D. M., Henggeler, S. W., Pickrel, S. G., & Patel, H. (1996). MST treatment of substance abusing or dependent adolescent offenders: Costs of reducing incarceration, inpatient and residential placement. *Journal of Child and Family Studies, 5,* 431–444.

Schoenwald, S. K., Ward, D. M., Henggeler, S. W., & Rowland, M. D. (2000). MST vs. hospitalization for crisis stabilization of youth: Placement outcomes 4 months post-referral. *Mental Health Services Research, 2,* 3–12.

Seaburn, D., Landau-Stanton, J., & Horwitz, S. (1996). Core techniques in family therapy. In R. H. Mikesell, D. Lusterman, & S. H. McDaniel (Eds.), *Integrating family therapy: Handbook of family psychology and systems theory.* Washington, DC: American Psychological Association.

Sexton, T. S., Alexander, J. F., & Mease, A. L. (2004). Levels of evidence for the models and mechanisms of therapeutic change in family and couple therapy. In M. J. Lambert (Ed.), *Bergin and Garfield's handbook of psychotherapy and behavior change* (5th ed., pp. 590–646). New York: Wiley.

Sheidow, A. J., Bradford, W. D., Henggeler, S. W., Rowland, M. D., Halliday-Boykins, C., Schoenwald, S. K., et al. (2004). Treatment costs for youths in psychiatric crisis: Multisystemic therapy versus hospitalization. *Psychiatric Services, 55,* 548–554.

Sheidow, A. J., & Henggeler, S. W. (2008). Multisystemic therapy with substance using adolescents: A synthesis of research. In A. Stevens (Ed.), *Crossing frontiers: International developments in the treatment of drug dependence* (pp. 11–33). Brighton, UK: Pavilion.

Sheidow, A. J., Schoenwald, S. K., Wagner, H. R., Allred, C. A., & Burns, B. J. (2006). Predictors of workforce turnover in a transported treatment program. *Administration and Policy in Mental Health and Mental Health Services Research, 1,* 1–12.

Shortell, S. M., Bennett, C. L., & Byck, G. R (1998). Assessing the impact of continuous quality improvement on clinical practice: What it will take to accelerate progress. *Milbank Quarterly, 76,* 593–624.

Smith, J. C. (1990). *Cognitive Behavioral Relaxation Training: A new system of strategies for treatment and assessment.* New York: Springer.

Sparrow, S. S., Cicchetti, D. V., & Balla, D.A. (2005). *Vineland Adaptive Behavior Scales—Second edition.* Bloomington, MN: Pearson.

Spivack, G., Platt, J. J., & Shure, M. B. (1976). *The problem-solving approach to adjustment.* San Francisco: Jossey-Bass.

Stambaugh, L. F., Mustillo, S. A., Burns, B. J., Stephens, R. L., Baxter, B., Edwards, D., et al. (2007). Outcomes from wraparound and multisystemic therapy in a center for mental health services system-of-care demonstration site. *Journal of Emotional and Behavioral Disorders, 15,* 143–155.

Stanton, M. D., & Shadish, W. R. (1997). Outcome, attrition, and family-couples treatment for drug abuse: A meta-analysis and review of the controlled, comparative studies. *Psychological Bulletin, 122,* 170–191.

Steinberg, L., Lamborn, S. D., Darling, N., Mounts, N. S., & Dornbusch, S. M. (1994). Over-time changes in adjustment and competence among adolescents from authoritative, authoritarian, indulgent, and neglectful families. *Child Development, 65,* 754–770.

Strother, K. B., Swenson, M. E., & Schoenwald, S. K. (1998). *Multisystemic therapy organizational manual.* Charleston, SC: MST Institute.

Stroul, B. A., & Friedman, R. M. (1994). *A system of care for children and youth with severe emotional disturbances* (rev. ed.). Washington, DC: Georgetown University Child Development Center, National Technical Center for Children's Mental Health, Center for Child Health and Mental Health Policy.

Substance Abuse and Mental Health Services Administration. (2007). National registry of evidence-based programs and practices. Available at *www.nrepp.samhsa.gov/programfulldetails.asp?PROGRAM_ID=102.*

Sundell, K., Hansson, K., Löfholm, C. A., Olsson, T., Gustle, L. H., & Kadesjö, C. (2008). The transportability of multisystemic therapy to Sweden: Short-term results from a randomized trial of conduct disordered youth. *Journal of Family Psychology, 22,* 550–560.

Swenson, C. C., Henggeler, S. W., Taylor, I. S., & Addison, O. W. (2005). *Multisystemic therapy and neighborhood partnerships: Reducing adolescent violence and substance abuse.* New York: Guilford Press.

Swenson, C. C., Saldana, L., Joyner, C. D., Caldwell, E., Henggeler, S. W., & Rowland, M. D. (2005). *Multisystemic therapy for child abuse and neglect.* Charleston: Family Services Research Center, Department of Psychiatry and Behavioral Sciences, Medical University of South Carolina.

Teplin L. A., Abram K. M., McClelland G. M., Dulcan, M. K., & Mericle, A. A. (2002). Psychiatric disorders in youth in juvenile detention. *Archives of General Psychiatry 59*, 1133–1143.

Teplin, L. A., McClelland G. M., Abram K. M, & Mileusnic, D. (2005). Early violent death among delinquent youth: A prospective longitudinal study. *Pediatrics, 115*, 1586–1593.

Thornberry, T. P., & Krohn, M. D. (Eds.). (2003). *Taking stock of delinquency: An overview of findings from contemporary longitudinal studies.* New York: Kluwer/Plenum.

Timmons-Mitchell, J., Bender, M. B., Kishna, M. A., & Mitchell, C. C. (2006). An independent effectiveness trial of multisystemic therapy with juvenile justice youth. *Journal of Clinical Child and Adolescent Psychology, 35*, 227–236.

Tompkins, M. A. (2004). *Using homework in psychotherapy. Strategies, guidelines, and forms.* New York: Guilford Press.

Trupin, E., Kerns, S., Walker, S., & Lee, T. (in press). Family Integrated Transitions: A promising program for juvenile offenders with co-occurring disorders. *Psychiatric Services.*

Unger, D. G., & Wandersman, A. (1985). The importance of neighbors: The social, cognitive, and affective components of neighboring. *American Journal of Community Psychology, 13*, 139–169.

U.S. Department of Education. (1998). *Dropout rates in the United States: 1998.* Washington, DC: National Center for Education Statistics. Available at *www.ed.gov.*

U.S. Department of Health and Human Services. (1999). *Mental health: A report of the Surgeon General.* Rockville, MD: U.S. Department of Health and Human Services, National Institutes of Health, National Institute of Mental Health.

U.S. Public Health Service. (2001). *Youth violence: A report of the Surgeon General.* Washington, DC: Author.

Vitaro, F., Brendgen, M., & Tremblay, R. E. (2000). Influence of deviant friends on delinquency: Searching for moderator variables. *Journal of Abnormal Child Psychology, 28*, 313–325.

Waldron, H. B., & Turner, C. W. (2008). Evidence-based psychosocial treatments for adolescent substance abuse. *Journal of Clinical Child and Adolescent Psychology, 37*, 238–261.

Wechsler, D. (2001). *Wechsler Individual Achievement Test—Second Edition (WIAT-II).* Bloomington, MN: Pearson.

Wechsler, D. (2003). *Wechsler Intelligence Scale for Children—Fourth Edition (WISC-IV).* Bloomington, MN: Pearson.

Weisz, J. R. (2004). *Psychotherapy for children and adolescents: Evidence-based treatments and case examples.* New York: Cambridge University Press.

Weisz, J. R., Donenberg, G. R., Han, S. S., & Weiss, B. (1995). Bridging the gap between laboratory and clinic in child and adolescent psychotherapy. *Journal of Consulting and Clinical Psychology, 63*, 688–701.

Weithorn, L. A. (2005, Summer). Envisioning second-order change in America's responses to troubled and troublesome youth. *Hofstra Law Review, 33*(4).

Wierson, M., & Forehand, R. (1994). Parent behavioral training for child noncompliance: Rationale, concepts, and effectiveness. *Current Directions in Psychological Science, 3,* 146–150.

Wilcox, B. L., Turnbull, H. R., & Turnbull, A. P. (1999–2000). Behavioral issues and IDEA: PBS and the FBA in the disciplinary context. *Exceptionality, 8,* 173–187.

Wilkinson, G. S., & Robertson, G. J. (2006). *Wide Range Achievement Test—Fourth Edition (WRAT4).* Lutz, FL: Psychological Assessment Resources.

Winters, K. C., Latimer, W. W., & Stinchfield, R. (2001). Assessing adolescent substance use. In E. F. Wagner & H. B. Waldron (Eds.), *Innovations in adolescent substance abuse interventions* (pp. 1–29). New York: Pergamon Press.

Wolpe, J., & Lazarus, A. A. (1966). *Behavior therapy techniques: A guide to the treatment of neuroses.* London: Pergamon Press.

Woodcock, R. W., McGrew, K. S., & Mather, N. (2001a). *Woodcock–Johnson Tests of Cognitive Abilities—Third Edition (WJTCA-III).* Itasca, IL: Riverside.

Woodcock, R. W., McGrew, K. S., & Mather, N. (2001b). *Woodcock–Johnson Tests of Achievement—Third Edition (WJTA-III).* Itasca, IL: Riverside.

Index

"f" following a page number indicates a figure;
"t" following a page number indicates a table.